American Society of Plumbing Engineers
Data Book

A Plumbing Engineer's Guide to System Design and Specifications

Volume 3

Special Plumbing Systems

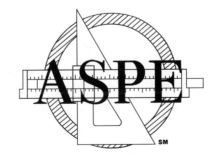

American Society of Plumbing Engineers
8614 W. Catalpa Ave., Suite 1007
Chicago, IL 60656

The ASPE Data Book is designed to provide accurate and authoritative information for the design and specification of plumbing systems. The publisher makes no guarantees or warranties, expressed or implied, regarding the data and information contained in this publication. All data and information are provided with the understanding that the publisher is not engaged in rendering legal, consulting, engineering, or other professional services. If legal, consulting, or engineering advice or other expert assistance is required, the services of a competent professional should be engaged.

American Society of Plumbing Engineers
8614 W. Catalpa Ave., Suite 1007
Chicago, IL 60656
(773) 693–2773 • Fax: (773) 695–9007
E-mail: aspehq@aspe.org • Internet: www.aspe.org

Copyright © 2001 by American Society of Plumbing Engineers

ISBN 1–891255–16–9
Printed in the United States of America

10 9 8 7 6 5 4 3 2 1

Data Book
Volume 3
Special Plumbing Systems

Data Book Chairperson: Anthony W. Stutes, P.E., CPD

ASPE Vice-President, Technical: David Chin, P.E., CPD / J. Joe Scott II, CPD

Editorial Review: ASPE Technical and Research Committee

Technical and Research
Committee Chairperson: Norman T. Heinig, CIPE

CONTRIBUTORS

Chapter 1
Patrick L. Whitworth, CPD
Anthony W. Stutes, P.E., CPD
Robert L. Love, P.E., CIPE

Chapter 2
Patrick L. Whitworth, CPD
Anthony W. Stutes, P.E., CPD
Forrest A. Flanagan, CPD
Chris Buckley, CPD

Chapter 3
Patrick L. Whitworth, CPD
Anthony W. Stutes, P.E., CPD

Chapter 5
Courtney R. Millburn, P.E., CIPE

Chapter 6
Patrick L. Whitworth, CPD
Anthony W. Stutes, P.E., CPD
Robert L. Love, P.E., CIPE
Marvin Trietsch

Chapter 7
Patrick L. Whitworth, CPD
Anthony W. Stutes, P.E., CPD
Michael Frankel, CPD

Chapter 9
Patrick L. Whitworth, CPD
Anthony W. Stutes, P.E., CPD
Michael Frankel, CPD

Chapter 10
Michael Frankel, CPD

About ASPE

The American Society of Plumbing Engineers (ASPE) is the international organization for professionals skilled in the design and specification of plumbing systems. ASPE is dedicated to the advancement of the science of plumbing engineering, to the professional growth and advancement of its members, and to the health, welfare, and safety of the public.

The Society disseminates technical data and information, sponsors activities that facilitate interaction with fellow professionals, and, through research and education programs, expands the base of knowledge of the plumbing engineering industry. ASPE members are leaders in innovative plumbing design, effective materials and energy use, and the application of advanced techniques from around the world.

WORLDWIDE MEMBERSHIP — ASPE was founded in 1964 and currently has 7,500 members. Spanning the globe, members are located in the United States, Canada, Asia, Mexico, South America, the South Pacific, Australia, and Europe. They represent an extensive network of experienced engineers, designers, contractors, educators, code officials, and manufacturers interested in furthering their careers, their profession, and the industry. ASPE is at the forefront of technology. In addition, ASPE represents members and promotes the profession among all segments of the construction industry.

ASPE MEMBERSHIP COMMUNICATION — All members belong to ASPE worldwide and have the opportunity to belong and participate in one of the 61 state, provincial or local chapters throughout the U.S. and Canada. ASPE chapters provide the major communication links and the first line of services and programs for the individual member. Communications with the membership is enhanced through the Society's bimonthly newsletter, the *ASPE Report,* and the monthly magazine, *Plumbing Engineer.*

TECHNICAL PUBLICATIONS — The Society maintains a comprehensive publishing program, spearheaded by the profession's basic reference text, the *ASPE Data Book.* The *Data Book,* encompassing forty-six chapters in four volumes, provides comprehensive details of the accepted practices and design criteria used in the field of plumbing engineering. New additions that will shortly join ASPE's published library of professional technical manuals and handbooks include: *High-Technology Pharmaceutical Facilities Design Manual, High-Technology Electronic Facilities Design Manual, Health Care Facilities and Hospitals Design Manual,* and *Water Reuse Design Manual.*

CONVENTION AND TECHNICAL SYMPOSIUM — The Society hosts biennial Conventions in even-numbered years and Technical Symposia in odd-numbered years to allow professional plumbing engineers and designers to improve their skills, learn original concepts, and make important networking contacts to help them stay abreast of current trends and technologies. In conjunction with each Convention there is an Engineered Plumbing Exposition, the greatest, largest gathering of plumbing engineering and design products, equipment, and services. Everything from pipes to pumps to fixtures, from compressors to computers to consulting services is on display, giving engineers and specifiers the opportunity to view the newest and most innovative materials and equipment available to them.

CERTIFIED IN PLUMBING DESIGN — ASPE sponsors a national certification program for engineers and designers of plumbing systems, which carries the designation "Certified in Plumbing Design" or CPD. The certification program provides the profession, the plumbing industry, and the general public with a single, comprehensive qualification of professional competence for engineers and designers of plumbing systems. The CPD, designed exclusively by and for plumbing engineers, tests hundreds of engineers and designers at centers throughout the United States biennially. Created to provide a single, uniform national credential in the field of engineered plumbing systems, the CPD program is not in any way connected to state-regulated Professional Engineer (P.E.) registration.

ASPE RESEARCH FOUNDATION — The ASPE Research Foundation, established in 1976, is the only independent, impartial organization involved in plumbing engineering and design research. The science of plumbing engineering affects everything . . . from the quality of our drinking water to the conservation of our water resources to the building codes for plumbing systems. Our lives are impacted daily by the advances made in plumbing engineering technology through the Foundation's research and development.

American Society of Plumbing Engineers
Data Book
(4 Volumes — 45 Chapters)

(The chapters and subjects listed for these volumes are subject to modification, adjustment and change.
The contents shown for each volume are proposed and may not represent the final contents of the volume.
A final listing of included chapters for each volume will appear in the actual publication.)

Table of Contents

ILLUSTRATIONS

TABLES

1

Fire-Protection Systems

INTRODUCTION

There are two distinct purposes of fire protection: life safety and property protection. Although providing for one generally results in some protection for the other, the two goals are not mutually inclusive. A program that provides early notification for an evacuation of the building's occupants meets the objective of life safety; however, it provides no protection for property. Conversely, it is possible that adequate property protection provisions might not suffice to protect life.

It is not usually practical to eliminate all combustible materials or all potential ignition sources. Absolute safety from fire is not attainable, but means must be provided to minimize the potential for fire and the damage done by fire. The requirements of the applicable building code and other pertinent regulations must be met when designing a fire-protection system. The recommendations of the National Fire Protection Association (NFPA) should be considered. Often, NFPA standards are incorporated into the local building code requirements. In addition, many owners require that their insurance carriers be consulted.

This chapter is intended to acquaint the engineer with the design principles of fire-protection systems for buildings and other structures. The selection of a site for a structure is very important in terms of fire protection and the engineer should be directly involved in this process. Obtaining optimum protection for life and property requires consultation with the owner's insurance carrier; the local fire department; the local authority having jurisdiction; and, in many cases, a specialist in all phases of fire prevention and protection.

Fire-protection system design has become a major responsibility of the plumbing engineer. It should be noted, however, that the design of fire-protection systems should be performed only by experienced fire-protection designers or engineers. Although this chapter provides the plumbing engineer with a basic, systematic approach to fire-protection systems design, it does not attempt to answer all the questions concerning the subject.

Prior to designing an automatic sprinkler system or one of the other types of fire-suppression system discussed in this chapter, the engineer should become as familiar as possible with the fundamentals, types, and effectiveness of automatic fire-protection systems.

AUTOMATIC FIRE-PROTECTION SYSTEMS

History and Objectives

Automatic sprinkler protection was first introduced as lengths of perforated pipe, which were predominantly installed in mill buildings in the era from 1850 to approximately 1880. With the introduction of the first true heat-actuated automatic sprinkler, known as the "Parmalee head," in 1878, the automatic sprinkler system as we know it today was born.

Since 1897, the NFPA has been compiling records on fires in sprinklered buildings. These records show that over 95% of all the fires in sprinklered buildings have been controlled or extinguished.

The NFPA statistics show that properly designed sprinkler systems rarely fail to control the spread of or extinguish a fire. The major cause of sprinkler-system failure is inadequate water supply due to under-designed systems or closed water-control valves.

The primary objective of residential sprinklers is to achieve life safety in dwelling units. Residential sprinklers are installed to provide tenable space for a period of time. In all systems except the deluge system, during a fire situation, only those sprinkler heads directly affected by the fire will open. This confines the concentration of the discharging water to the fire area. Under normal conditions, automatic sprinkler systems do not require a large quantity of water. In some cases, the water demand for such a system is less than the fire-hose demands established by NFPA and insurance underwriters for buildings without automatic fire-suppression systems.

A major concern of property owners is that of excessive water damage by sprinkler systems. As stated earlier, the water discharging from automatic sprinklers is concentrated over the fire area. If an adequate means of alerting the local fire department to an automatic water-flow condition is provided, the overall water damage suffered will be far less than it would be if the fire department were summoned after the fire had grown to major proportions.

System Design

(See also "Hydraulic Design of Sprinkler Systems" later in this chapter.)

Fire hazard evaluation The first step in the design of an automatic sprinkler system is the determination of the overall fire hazard. The key factors affecting the overall fire hazard are the following:

1. Type of building construction.

2. External building exposures.

3. The building occupancy.

4. Fire growth rate.

5. The combustible fuel loading of the contents.

Of the items listed above, numbers 4 and 5 are the most important factors affecting the selection of the type of automatic sprinkler system and its design parameters.

For example, a typical office building presents a significantly lower fire potential than does a building used for plastics manufacturing. Piled or racked storage poses significant hazards, particularly when it exceeds 8 ft in height. Early-suppression, fast-response (ESFR) and large-drop sprinklers are available for use in these situations, which provide more water to the fire from the ceiling system and, thereby, reduce the need for in-rack sprinklers. The type of materials stored and the packaging used also affect the design of the spinkler system. The engineer has many resources at his disposal to help determine the design parameters. Design criteria can be sought from the NFPA standards, specifically NFPA 13, 30, 231, 231C, 14, and 15. The major resources for determining the design are the authority having jurisdiction and the building owner's insurance company. Many insurance companies follow the recommendations developed by the NFPA; however, some have their own requirements, which surpass these recommendations. These insurance underwriters may require that the design be in accordance with Factory Mutal or ISO requirements.

NFPA standards refer to the authority having jurisdiction. By definition, the authorities having jurisdiction are the local building inspector, the insurance underwriter, local fire department, state fire marshal, and local officials. It is important that the requirements of all these agencies be investigated. Sometimes the state building codes are more stringent than the NFPA standards and the insurance underwriter's requirements.

Always, the more stringent requirements should be utilized.

Fire loads and resistance ratings The nature and potential magnitude of a fire in a building are directly related to the amount, composition, and physical arrangement of combustibles, either as contents of the building or as materials used in its construction. The total amount of combustibles is referred to as the "fire load" of a building and is expressed in pounds per square foot (lb/ft^2) (kilograms per square meter [kg/m^2]), with an assumed calorific value for ordinary cellulosic materials of 7000 to 8000 Btu/lb (16.3 to 18.6 MJ/kg). If this Btu (J) content is applied when organic materials are present in large proportions, the weights must be adjusted accordingly.

The temperatures used in standard fire tests of building components are indicated by the nationally recognized time-temperature curve, shown in Figure 1-1. The fire resistance of the construction of building assemblies, such as walls and floors/ceilings (determined by standard fire tests), is expressed in hours.

The fire load contributed by highly combustible materials, such as plastics and flammable liquids, can severely impact the effectiveness of a fire-protection system. Protection systems for these types of material require a complete evaluation and should be designed by an experienced fire-protection engineer.

Classes of fires A generally accepted method of classification separates combustible materials into four types, defined by the effectiveness of extinguishing media:

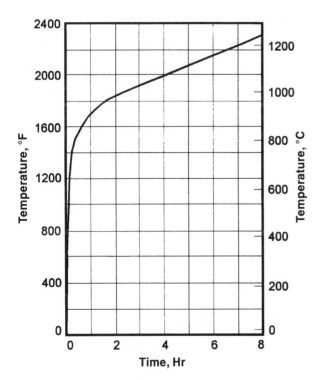

Figure 1-1 Time-Temperature Curve for Standard Fire Test

1. *Class A fires* Involve ordinary combustibles, such as wood and paper, and are readily extinguishable by water, cooling, or coating with a suitable dry chemical.

2. *Class B fires* Involve flammable liquids where smothering is effective and a cooling agent must be applied.

3. *Class C fires* Involve live electrical equipment where the extinguishing agent must be nonconductive.

4. *Class D fires* Involve metals that burn (magnesium, sodium, and powdered aluminum) and special powders are necessary to extinguish the fire.

The correct selection of an extinguishing agent is critical to the control and extinguishing of a fire.

Water supply determination Of primary concern is the availability of municipal water supplies of sufficient pressure and quantity to meet the design demands of the fire-protection sprinkler system. The points to be considered for the water supply include:

1. Quantity, static pressure at no flow and residual pressure at design flow, and the availability of water.

2. The overall fire demand, including duration of flow.

3. The reliability of the source.

4. The size, material of construction, and age of mains.

5. Water supply makeup.

The overall fire demand is established either by hydraulic calculations performed by the engineer, by code, or through the insurance rating organization. The following paragraphs focus on the other four items listed above.

Quantity and availability The amount of water available from a network of underground water mains—whether they be private yard mains or the public water supply—can be determined by the design engineer in several ways. (Refer to NFPA standard 291.) The simplest method is to seek the history of fire flow tests in the area through the local water and fire departments, the insurance loss control consultants, or, for private systems, plant personnel. If test results are not current or you suspect that there has been a change in the water supply since the latest hydrant flow test, a new hydrant flow test should be requested through the local authorities (i.e., water department, fire department, or plant management).

To conduct a fire flow test, the following equipment/information is necessary:

1. Hydrant butt cap, with dial-spring gauge.

2. Pitot tube and blade with an attached dial-spring pressure gauge.

3. Hydrant wrench.

4. Nozzle pressure flow tables.

5. Knowledge of the water main's sizing and piping layout.

Once all the necessary equipment is assembled, a minimum of two operable fire hydrants should be selected. It is recommended practice that the residual pressure hydrant (test hydrant) be as close as possible to the structure under design and downstream from the flow hydrant. After selecting the hydrants for the test, the engineer should now have the hydrant butt cap with its pressure gauge placed on the test hydrant. The engineer should have the water department or maintenance personnel operate the hydrants to limit the liability for damage. Special provisions may be required to accommodate the large volume of water that will discharge during a test.

Once the butt cap is in place, the hydrant should be opened slightly to allow the air in the hydrant barrel to bleed off past the open bleed cock on the hydrant butt. After the air is bled off, the hydrant can be opened fully and the bleed cock can be closed. The pressure that registers on the gauge at this time is the static pressure (pressure with no flow). The second hydrant can now be approached.

To start the test, one hydrant butt should be opened. The coefficient of discharge should be sought by determining the construction and roughness of the inside lip of the hydrant butt. In addition, the actual inside diameter of the butt should be measured to confirm its diameter. After this data has been recorded, the flow hydrant can now be opened fully. Some caution should be exercised when opening the hydrant. It should never be opened rapidly, and the path of discharge should be investigated to ensure that personnel will not be injured and that property will not be damaged by the stream or the residual standing water.

After the hydrant has been opened, it should be allowed to flow for 2 to 5 min to allow debris to clear the hydrant barrel and to stabilize the water flow before the pitot tube is inserted into the stream. When the pitot tube is inserted into the water stream, it should be placed in the centerline of the stream, at approximately ½ of the diameter of the butt opening. The reading on the pressure gauge attached to the pitot tube can then be read. Simultaneously, the residual pressure (flowing pressure) must be read on the test hydrant (see Figure 1-2).

The pitot reading and residual pressure should now be recorded. For best results, the pitot reading should not be less than 10 psi (68.9 kPa) nor greater than 30 psi (206.8 kPa); similarly, the static pressure should drop 25 to 50%

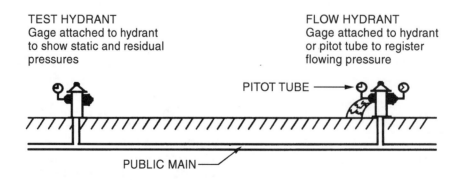

TEST HYDRANT
Gage attached to hydrant to show static and residual pressures

FLOW HYDRANT
Gage attached to hydrant or pitot tube to register flowing pressure

PITOT TUBE

PUBLIC MAIN

Figure 1-2 Method of Conducting Flow Tests

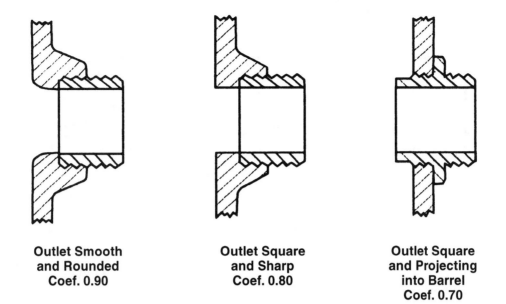

Outlet Smooth
and Rounded
Coef. 0.90

Outlet Square
and Sharp
Coef. 0.80

Outlet Square
and Projecting
into Barrel
Coef. 0.70

Figure 1-3   Three General Types of Hydrant Outlet and Their Coefficients of Discharge

Source: NFPA Standard 291.

under the test conditions. In addition, it is also a good idea to flow a quantity at least equal to the fire demand.

Now the data gathered during this test can be used to determine the quantity of water flowed and the amount of water available for fire-fighting operations. First, to determine the quantity of water flowed, the pitot pressure, the hydrant butt size, and the discharge coefficient are used. By finding the pitot pressure and hydrant butt size from a given table (supplied by the manufacturer), a theoretical flow can be found, using the following formula:

Equation 1-1

$$Q = 29.83cd^2\sqrt{P}$$

where

Q   =   Flow discharge, gpm (L/s)

c   =   Coefficient of discharge

d   =   Diameter of outlet, in. (mm)

P   =   Pitot (velocity) pressure, psi (kPa)

By multiplying this figure by the hydrant coefficient, the actual flow is established (see Figure 1-3).

The flow available at any pressure along the established flow curve can be found by using the following equation:

Equation 1-2

$$Q_R = \left(\frac{H_R}{H_F}\right)^{0.54} Q_F$$

where

Q_R =   Flow at desired residual pressure, gpm (L/s)

Q_F =   Flow from hydrant flow test, gpm (L/s)

H_R =   Head drop from static pressure to desired residual pressure, psi (kPa)

H_F =   Head loss (static) during hydrant test, psi (kPa)

The results of a hydrant flow test can be plotted on $N^{1.85}$ graph paper to develop the characteristic flow curve for the piping network (water supply) for the test location. A typical water-supply graph no. $N^{1.85}$ is shown in Figure 1-4. Either the formula method discussed above or the graph method can be used to determine water availability.

Example 1-1

Determine water demand at the desired residual pressure, given the following flow test conditions:

Static pressure: 70 psi (482.6 kPa)
Residual pressure: 50 psi (344.7 kPa)
Pitot reading: 24 psi (165.5 kPa)

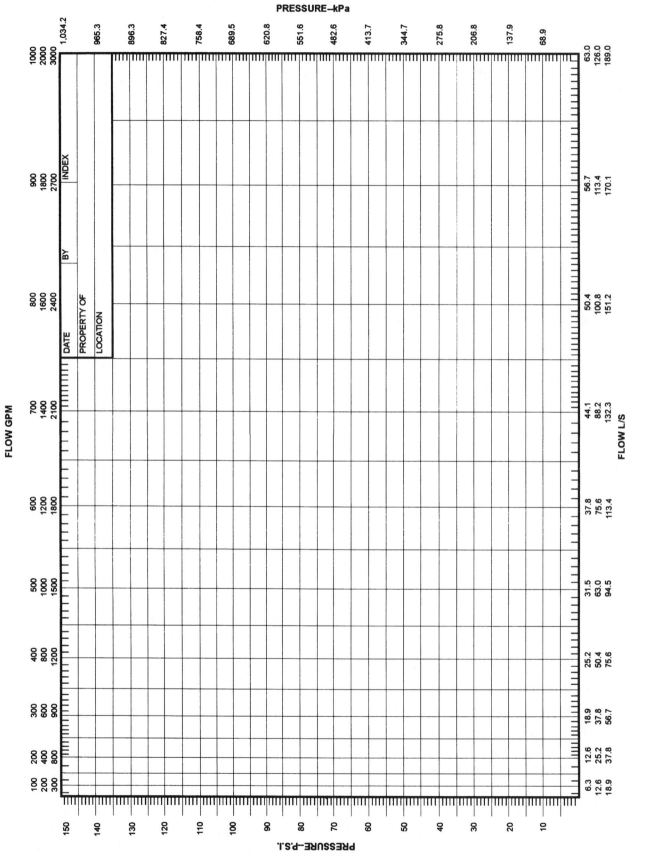

Figure 1-4   Water Supply Graph No. N$^{1.85}$

Table 1-1 GPM (L/s) Flow Table

Pitot Pressure, psi (kPa)	Nozzle Orifice Diameter, in. (mm)				
	1 (25.4)	1⅛ (28.6)	1¼ (31.8)	1½ (38.1)	1¾" (44.5)
6 (41.4)	73 (4.6)	93 (5.8)	114 (7.2)	164 (10.3)	224 (14.1)
8 (55.2)	84 (5 3)	107 (6.7)	132 (8.3)	190 (12.0)	259 (16.3)
10 (68.9)	94 (5.9)	119 (7.5)	148 (9.3)	212 (13.4)	289 (18.2)
12 (82.7)	103 (6.5)	131 (8.2)	162 (10.2)	233 (14.7)	317 (20.0)
14 (96.5)	112 (7.1)	141 (8.9)	175 (11.0)	251 (15.8)	342 (21.5)
16 (110.3)	120 (7.6)	151 (9.5)	187 (11.8)	269 (16.9)	366 (23.1)
18 (124.1)	127 (8.0)	160 (10.1)	198 (12.5)	285 (18.0)	388 (24.4)
20 (137.9)	134 (8.4)	169 (10.6)	209 (13.2)	300 (18.9)	409 (25.8)
22 (151.7)	140 (8.8)	177 (11.2)	219 (13.8)	315 (19.8)	429 (27.0)
24 (165.5)	146 (9.2)	185 (11.7)	229 (14.4)	329 (20.7)	448 (28.2)
26 (179.3)	152 (9.6)	193 (12.2)	238 (15.0)	343 (21.6)	466 (29.3)
28 (193.1)	158 (10.0)	200 (12.6)	247 (15.6)	356 (22.4)	484 (30.5)
30 (206.8)	164 (10.3)	207 (13.0)	256 (16.1)	368 (23.2)	501 (31.6)
35 (241.3)	177 (11.2)	223 (14.0)	276 (17.5)	398 (25.1)	541 (34.1)
40 (275.8)	189 (11.9)	239 (15.1)	295 (18.6)	425 (26.8)	578 (36.4)
45 (310.3)	201 (12.7)	254 (16.0)	314 (19.8)	450 (28.3)	613 (38.6)
50 (344.7)	211 (13.3)	267 (16.8)	330 (20.8)	475 (29.9)	646 (40.7)
60 (413.7)	231 (14.6)	293 (18.5)	362 (22.8)	520 (32.8)	708 (44.6)
70 (482.6)	250 (15.7)	316 (19.9)	391 (24.6)	562 (35.4)	765 (48.2)
80 (551.6)	267 (16.8)	338 (21.3)	418 (26.3)	601 (37.9)	818 (51.5)
90 (620.5)	283 (17.8)	358 (22.6)	443 (27.9)	637 (40.1)	867 (54.6)
100 (689.5)	299 (18.8)	378 (23.8)	467 (29.4)	672 (42.3)	914 (57.6)

Pitot Pressure, psi (kPa)	Hydrant Butt Orifice Diameter, in. (mm)				
	2⅜ (60.3)	2½ (63.5)	2⅝ (66.7)	4 (101.6)	4½" (114.3)
6 (41.4)	412 (25.9)	457 (28.8)	500 (31.5)	1170 (73.7)	1480 (93.2)
8 (55.2)	475 (29.8)	528 (33.3)	575 (36.2)	1351 (85.1)	1710 (107.7)
10 (68.9)	538 (33.9)	590 (37.2)	650 (40.9)	1510 (95.1)	1910 (120.3)
12 (82.7)	588 (37-0)	646 (40.7)	712 (44.9)	1655 (104.3)	2100 (132.3)
14 (96.5)	625 (39.4)	698 (44.0)	775 (48.8)	1787 (112.6)	2260 (142.4)
16 (110.3)	662 (41.7)	746 (47-0)	825 (52.0)	1910 (120.3)	2420 (152.5)
18 (124.1)	712 (44.9)	791 (49.8)	875 (55.1)	2026 (127.6)	2570 (161.9)
20 (137.9)	750 (47.3)	834 (52.5)	925 (58.3)	2136 (134.5)	2710 (170.7)
22 (151.7)	788 (49.6)	875 (55.1)	962 (60.6)	2240 (141.1)	2840 (178.9)
24 (165.5)	825 (52.0)	914 (57.6)	1012 (63.8)	2340 (147.4)	2970 (187.1)
26 (179.3)	850 (53.6)	951 (59.9)	1050 (66.1)	2435 (153.4)	3090 (194.7)
28 (193.1)	888 (55.9)	987 (62.2)	1088 (68.5)	2527 (159.2)	3210 (202.2)
30 (206.8)	925 (58.3)	1022 (64.4)	1125 (70.9)	2616 (164.8)	3320 (209.2)
32 (220.6)	950 (59.8)	1055 (66.5)	1062 (66.9)	2702 (170.2)	3430 (216.1)
34 (234.4)	975 (61.4)	1088 (68.5)	1200 (75.6)	2785 (175.4)	3540 (223.0)
36 (248.2)	1012 (63.8)	1119 (70.5)	1238 (78.0)	2866 (180.8)	3640 (229.3)
38 (262.0)	1038 (65.4)	1150 (72.4)	1262 (79.5)	2944 (185.8)	3740 (235.6)
40 (275.8)	1062 (66.9)	1180 (74.3)	1300 (81.9)	3021 (190.3)	3840 (241.9)
42 (289.6)	1088 (68.5)	1209 (76.2)	1338 (84.3)	3095 (195.0)	3935 (247.9)
44 (303.4)	1112 (70.1)	1237 (77.9)	1362 (85.8)	3168 (199.6)	4030 (253.9)
46 (317.2)	1137 (71.6)	1265 (79.7)	1400 (88.2)	3239 (204.1)	4120 (259.6)
48 (330.9)	1162 (73.2)	1293 (81.4)	1425 (89.8)	3309 (208.5)	4205 (264.9)
50 (344.7)	1188 (74.8)	1319 (83.1)	1450 (91.3)	3377 (212.7)	4290 (270.3)

Hydrant butt: 2½ in. (63.5 mm)
Coefficient: 0.9

From Table 1-1, the theoretical flow can be found to be 914 gpm (57.6 L/s). By multiplying by the coefficient of 0.9, the actual flow is found.

Q_F = 0.9 × 914 gpm
   = 822.6 gpm
   = 823 gpm

(Q_F = 0.9 × 57.6 L/s
   = 51.8 L/s)

By plotting this on the $N^{1.85}$ graph paper, the characteristic flow curve can be established.

Similarly, using Equation 1-2, we can find the flow available at 20 psi (137.9 kPa) residual pressure:

$$Q_R = \left(\frac{H_R}{H_F}\right)^{0.54} \times Q_F$$

H_R = 70 – 20 = 50 psi

H_F = 70 – 50 = 20 psi

Q_F = 823 gpm

Q_R = $\left(\frac{50}{20}\right)^{0.54}$ × 823 gpm

Q_R = $(2.5)^{0.54}$ × 823 gpm

Q_R = 1349.85 = 1350 gpm

[H_R = 482.6 – 137.9 = 344.7 kPa

H_F = 482.6 – 344.7 = 137.9 kPa

Q_F = 51.8 L/s

Q_R = $\left(\frac{344.7}{137.9}\right)^{0.54}$ × 51.8 L/s

Q_R = 85.0 L/s]

The flow of 1350 gpm (85 L/s) is the maximum water available at 20 psi (137.9 kPa) residual pressure for fire-protection purposes. Most water purveyors consider 20 psi (137.9 kPa) the lowest allowable under supply pressure to prevent backflows in the water-supply system.

Water-supply reliability A water supply's reliability can be determined by evaluating the method by which the pipe network is fed.

Municipal water supplies consist of three types:

1. Elevated reservoirs.

2. Direct pump.

3. Combined.

The elevated reservoir is reliable as it does not depend on electrical power to provide the water pressure. The same reasoning holds true for private supplies. With reliability in mind, a designer should make an attempt to design an automatic fire-protection system that can function properly without the introduction of a booster fire pump. If this cannot be accomplished, then a fire pump will need to be added to provide the water supply. (See the discussion under "Fire Pumps" later in this chapter.)

The size and age of mains The size of the fire mains plays an important part in the ability of the water supply to produce adequate fire flows for fire-protection systems. What may not be obvious to the casual observer, however, is how time and the corrosiveness of the water can affect the inside diameter of the supply mains. For example, a cast-iron pipe 30 years old, with moderately corrosive water, will have its friction factors increased by a factor of 3 over new cast-iron pipe. (For an in-depth discussion of this subject, refer to the NFPA *Fire Protection Handbook*.)

Water-supply piping system makeup A water-supply piping system that consists of one large supply line feeding a series of dead-ended branch mains is far less efficient than a system of pipes that are looped and gridded together. For example, an 8-in. (203.2-mm) main flowing 2000 gpm (126 L/s) that is fed from one direction will have 4.62 psi/1000 ft (31.8 kPa/304.8 m) of pipe friction loss. If that same main were fed from two directions, the flow could be balanced to 1000 gpm (63 L/s) from each side (assuming equivalent pipe characteristics and lengths). The friction loss would then be reduced to 1.128 psi/1000 ft (7.8 kPa/ 304.8 m), or reduced by a factor of 4.

This same principle holds true for sprinkler-system piping which is discussed in detail under "Selecting Pipe and Hangers for Sprinkler Systems" later in this chapter.

Automatic sprinkler-system selection Once evaluations have been made of the fire hazard and the water supply, the type of sprinkler system to be installed can be selected. There are five basic types of system:

- Wet-pipe system.
- Dry-pipe system.
- Pre-action system.
- Deluge system.
- Combined dry-pipe and pre-action system.

Wet-pipe system The wet-pipe system employs automatic (closed, fusible link or glass-bulb type) sprinklers attached to piping containing water under pressure at all times. When fire occurs, individual sprinklers are actuated by the heat, and water flows immediately. This system is generally used whenever there is no danger of the water in the pipes freezing and there are no special conditions requiring one of the other systems.

General description The wet-pipe sprinkler system has sealed sprinklers attached to piping that contains water under pressure at all times. When a sprinkler is opened by fire, which fuses the heat-sensitive link or bulb, water discharges immediately.

The flow of water raises the alarm valve clapper from its seat (see Figure 1-5) and thereby lifts the pilot valve disc from the nozzle. This permits water to enter the alarm line. A water motor gong is actuated by the flow. An optional pressure switch may be attached on the alarm line to provide an electric signal. This electric signal can also be sent to the building's main fire-alarm control panel.

The alarm valve (see Figure 1-5) is installed in either a vertical or a horizontal position in the main water supply to the wet-pipe sprinkler system. Figure 1-6 illustrates a typical wet-alarm valve riser diagram. Variable-pressure water supply where the supply pressure may fluctuate, which is the most common type of water supply encountered, requires the use of a retard chamber with the alarm valve to prevent false alarms. Where the water supply has constant pressure (as it does from a gravity tank, pressure tank, or reservoir), the alarm valve is used without the retard chamber. In cases where a local alarm is adequate, water is admitted directly to a water motor-driven gong (see Figure 1-7). If no water motor gong is required, a vane-type water-flow indicator (see Figure 1-8) can be inserted in the supply pipe to indicate, electrically, a water flow.

Operation Should a pressure surge occur, raising the clapper momentarily and lifting the pilot valve disc from the nozzle, a small amount of water will pass into the retard chamber. If only a relatively small amount of water enters the retard chamber, the water will drain off through the retard chamber drain. However, should water escape through a sprinkler or from damaged piping, sustained water flow through the alarm valve will result. The clapper will move from its seat and lift the pilot valve disc allowing a large volume of water to flow through the nozzle and into the retard chamber. The bleeding capacity through the retard chamber drain cannot keep up with the incoming volume. The retard chamber fills and water now flows through the alarm line to actuate the water motor gong and the optional alarm pressure switch, if used.

After a fire operation or test, the water in the alarm line will drain out through the retard chamber drain.

Dry-pipe system A dry-pipe system has automatic sprinklers attached to piping containing air under pressure.

When a sprinkler's sealed orifice is opened by heat from a fire, air pressure is reduced, the dry-pipe valve is then opened by water pressure, and water flows to any opened sprinklers. Dry-pipe systems operate more slowly than wet types and are more expensive to install and to maintain. For these reasons, they are normally installed only where necessary, generally where freezing is a problem.

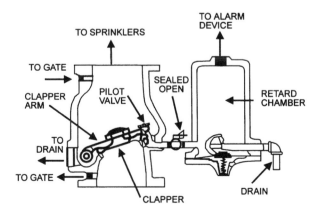

Figure 1-5 Alarm Check Valve

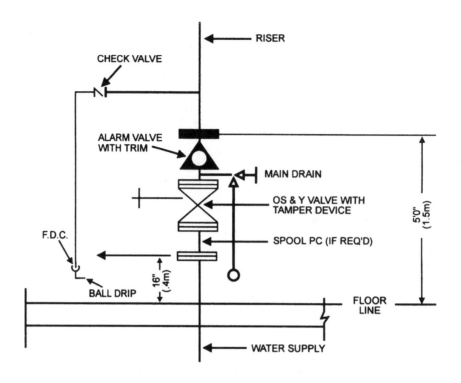

Figure 1-6   Typical Wet-Alarm Valve Riser

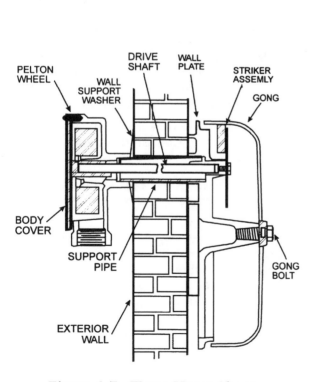

Figure 1-7   Water Motor Alarm

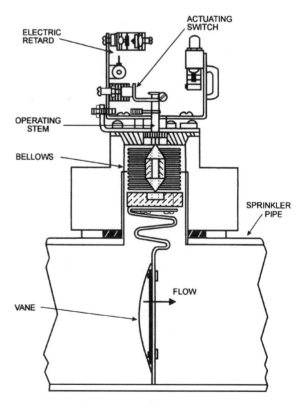

**Figure 1-8   Vane-Type
Water-Flow Indicator**

General description The dry-pipe sprinkler system is designed to provide sprinkler protection for buildings or areas subject to below freezing temperatures. The dry valve is installed in a heated area or in an insulated, heated valve enclosure protected against any occurrence of freezing temperatures.

Air under pressure, manually or automatically maintained in sprinkler piping, keeps the clapper or the dry valve closed (see Figure 1-9). Figure 1-10 illustrates a typical dry-pipe valve riser diagram. The fire-department connection is made between the dry-pipe valve and the riser check valve. Operation of the dry-pipe equipment occurs when fire temperature fuses a sprinkler, letting sprinkler piping air pressure escape. This destroys the pressure differential that normally keeps the dry valve closed and allows water to flow into the sprinkler piping. The air pressure required to keep the clapper in a closed position varies directly with water-supply pressure.

A hydraulically operated fire alarm is standard; however, many installations also have an electric fire alarm gong that sounds when water flow into the sprinkler-piping system actuates the alarm switch. This electric switch can also be used to signal the building's main fire-alarm control panel.

Large dry-pipe systems are installed with an accelerator, a device that accelerates dry valve operation. The accelerator is actuated by a drop in piping pressure. It then functions to apply remaining pressure from the sprinkler piping to the intermediate chamber of the dry valve. Added to the water pressure below the clapper, this more quickly eliminates the differential to open the clapper. Exhausters are also available to assist in the quick discharge of air prior to operation. The time of water flow on dry-pipe systems is based on system volume, generally not more than 750 gal (2838.75 L) for any 1 dry-pipe valve. This volume can be exceeded if water is delivered in 60 s or less.

Normal condition Under normal conditions, the dry-pipe sprinkler system has "sealed" automatic sprinklers retaining air pressure in the sprinkler piping. It is only after a sprinkler seal fuses and opens to release the air (under pressure) in the sprinkler piping that the dry-valve clapper opens and water from the water-supply main flows through it into the sprinkler piping. The dry valve has two functions:

1. To keep the clapper closed and withhold water from the sprinkler piping until fire fuses a sprinkler seal.

2. To trigger a fire alarm when the clapper opens.

When "set," the rubber-faced dry-valve clapper rests with the rubber facing in contact with two concentric seat rings. The annular chamber, or intermediate chamber, is connected to

Figure 1-9 Dry-Pipe Valve: (a) Air pressure maintains clapper closed; (b) Venting of air allows clapper to open and water to flow.

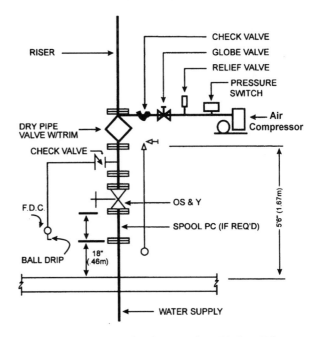

Figure 1-10 Typical Dry-Pipe Valve Riser

the alarm devices such as the water motor gong and alarm switch. The clapper area that the water exerts its force against is the diameter of the inner seat ring. The clapper area that the compressed air exerts its force against is the diameter of the outer seat ring, which is considerably larger than the inner diameter. This difference in area enables the lesser air pressure (over a greater area) above the clapper to overcome the clapper. Priming water is added to some dry valves to provide a positive system through the intermediate chamber and its alarm outlets.

Electric air compressor—automatic For dry-pipe systems the piping water capacity must be calculated to determine air capacity, which is used in the selection of the correct size air compressor.

NFPA standards require that air compressors be capable of restoring normal air pressure in a system in a period of 30 min. Factory Mutual Engineering Division standards require that compressors be capable of restoring normal air pressure plus 25% pressure in 30 min.

To calculate a system's capacity in gallons (liters), determine the total pipe footage (meters) for each size pipe then multiply by the corresponding factor from the Table 1-2.

Table 1-2 Factors for Determining Water Capacity per Foot of Pipe

Pipe Size, in. (mm)	Factor, gal/ft (L/m)
1 (25)	0.045 (0.52)
1¼ (32)	0.078 (0.90)
1½ (40)	0.106 (0.122)
2 (50)	0.174 (0.201)
2½ (65)	0.248 (0.286)
3 (80)	0.383 (0.442)
3½ (90)	0.513 (0.592)
4 (100)	0.660 (0.761)
5 (125)	1.04 (1.20)
6 (150)	1.50 (1.73)
8 (200)	2.66 (3.07)

Note: For Schedule 40 pipe 1–6 in. (25.4–152.4 mm) and Schedule 30 pipe 8 in. (203.2 mm).

When the total capacity in gallons (liters) is determined, multiply by 0.012 to obtain the free-air delivery in cubic feet per minute (cfm) (m³/min).

Note: Where one air compressor supplies more than one dry-pipe system, the largest capacity system shall determine the compressor size.

Accelerator An accelerator is an accessory device used on large dry-pipe systems to hasten dry-valve operation. NFPA Standard 13 requires that each standard dry valve controlling a system with a capacity of more than 500 gal (1892 L) must be provided with an accelerator, with the

Table 1-3 Pipe or Tube Materials and Dimensions

Materials and Dimensions	Standard
Ferrous Piping (Welded and Seamless)	
Spec. for black and hot-dipped zinc-coated (galvanized) welded and seamless steel pipe for fire-protection use[a]	ASTM A795
Spec. for welded and seamless steel pipe[a]	ANSI/ASTM A53
Wrought steel pipe	ANSI B36.10M
Spec. for elec.-resistance welded steel pipe	ASTM A135
Copper Tube (Drawn, Seamless)	
Spec. for seamless copper tube[a]	ASTM B75
Spec. for seamless copper water tube[a]	ASTM B88
Spec. for general requirements for wrought seamless copper and copper-alloy tube	ASTM B251
Fluxes for soldering applications of copper and copper alloy tube	ASTM B813
Brazing filler metal (Classification BCuP-3 or BCuP-4)	AWS A5.8
Solder metal, 95-5 (tin-antimony-Grade BETA)	ASTM B32
Nonmetallic piping specification for special listed chlorinated polyvinyl chloride (CPVC) pipe	ASTM F442
Specification for special listed polybutylene (PB) pipe	ASTM D3309

Source: NFPA 13, Tables 2-3.1 and 2-3.5.

[a]Denotes pipe or tubing suitable for bending according to ASTM standards.

following exceptions: the 60-s limit does not apply to dry systems with a capacity of 500 gal or less or 750 gal or less when equipped with a quick-opening device.

In a fire condition, the accelerator redirects air pressure from the system piping into the intermediate chamber of the dry-pipe valve. This air pressure assists the water-pressure differential and opens the dry-pipe valve more quickly.

Pre-action system A pre-action system is installed where there is a need to counteract the operational delay of a conventional dry-pipe system and to eliminate the danger of water discharge resulting from accidental damage to automatic sprinklers or piping. In a pre-action system, the water-supply valve (deluge valve) is actuated independently of the opening of sprinklers, i.e., the valve is opened by the operation of an automatic fire-detection system and not by the fusing of sprinklers.

General description The pre-action sprinkler system is installed in small, heated or unheated occupancies where a sensitive, advanced alarm is desirable for the evacuation of personnel and the notification of firefighting agencies. It is equipped with automatic sprinklers (sealed heads). The use of automatic sprinklers differentiates it from the deluge system.

In these sprinkler systems, the piping contains air at atmospheric pressure. Normally, except for systems in explosive vapor areas, these systems are actuated by electric heat detectors. Another, less common method is the utilization of heat-actuated devices (H.A.D.), which are located on air-filled piping. An abnormal rate-of-temperature rise, caused by fire, develops a pressure in the H.A.D.s more rapidly than it can escape through the compensating vent, causing the sounding of a fire alarm.

The pre-action valve allows the sprinkler piping to be filled with water and causes the sounding of a fire alarm. As in conventional systems, a sprinkler head must be fused to allow the flow of water from the piping system.

Pre-action systems operate faster and result in less fire and water damage compared to conventional dry pipe systems. They are limited to 1000 sprinklers. Pendent sprinklers must be of an approved, dry-pendent design only if in an area subject to freezing.

Deluge system The purpose of a deluge system is to deliver water to the entire area of a fire in the least amount of time possible. It accomplishes this by admitting water to sprinklers or spray nozzles that are open at all times. By using automatic fire-detection devices of the type used in pre-action systems or controls designed for individual hazards, it can apply water to fire more quickly than is possible with a system whose operation depends on the opening of sprinklers as the fire spreads. Deluge systems are suitable for extra-hazard occupancies in which flammable liquids are handled or stored, and where there is a possibility that fire may flash ahead of the operation of ordinary automatic sprinklers.

General description The deluge sprinkler system is equipped with open sprinklers and is installed in heated or unheated extra-hazard occupancies where an instantaneous discharge of water from all sprinkler heads is necessary. Where high values of discharge are involved or where spray nozzles, foam-water sprinklers, or other foam applicators are used, the system should be supervised.

In these sprinkler systems, the piping contains air at atmospheric pressure. As with pre-action systems, except in explosive vapor areas, these systems are normally actuated by electric heat detectors. Another, less common activation method is the utilization of heat-actuated devices (H.A.D.s), which are located on air-filled piping. An abnormal rate-of-temperature rise, caused by fire, develops a pressure in the H. A. D.s more rapidly than it can escape through the compensating vent, causing the deluge valve to trip. The tripping of the deluge valve permits water to enter the sprinkler piping for immediate discharge onto the fire and causes the sounding of a fire alarm.

Deluge systems are used for fast, total application of water in extra-hazardous areas and in "water-spray" systems. Deluge valves are essentially check valves with a clapper latched in the closed position, (see Figure 1-11). The actuating system unlatches the valve, allowing water to enter the piping system and flow out the heads. The more common design of the deluge valve employs a single differential diaphragm in which the water pressure bears on both sides, while the top side adjoins a closed chamber (see Figure 1-12). The actuating system opens the closed chamber, allowing the water to push the dia-

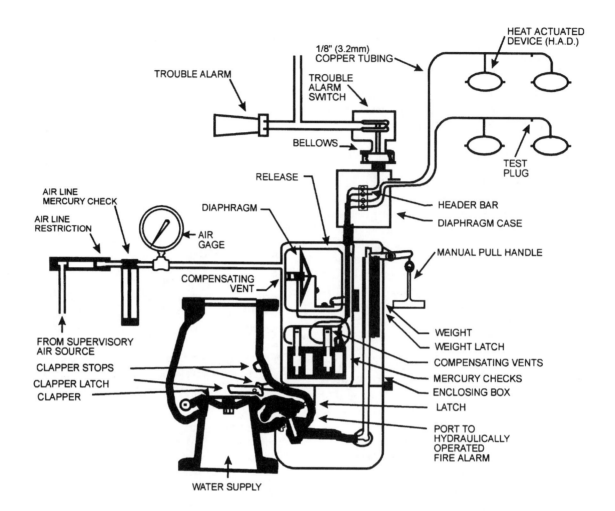

Figure 1-11   Automatic Deluge Valve

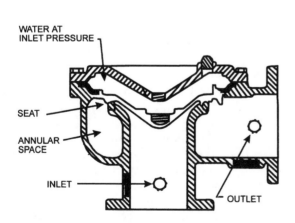

**Figure 1-12   Deluge Valve with Single
Differential Diaphragm**

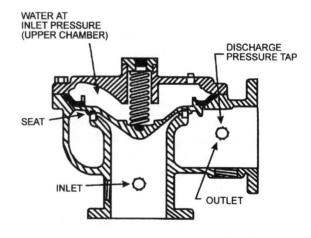

**Figure 1-13   Deluge Valve with Outlet
Pressure Regulator**

phragm up and off the water seat, releasing water to the system.

A modification of the valve uses a pressure regulator that maintains (on the outlet side) any predetermined pressure less than the available system pressure (see Figure 1-13). This allows the system to discharge at a constant rate.

Combined dry-pipe and pre-action system A combined dry-pipe and pre-action sprinkler system is one that employs automatic sprinklers attached to a piping system containing air under pressure and has a supplemental fire-detection system installed in the same areas as the sprinklers. Operation of the fire-detection system, as by a fire, actuates tripping devices that open dry-pipe valves simultaneously and without loss of air pressure in the system. Operation of the fire-detection system also opens approved air-exhaust valves at the end of the feed main, which facilitate the filling of the system with water, which usually precedes the opening of sprinklers. The fire-detection system also serves as an automatic, early-warning fire-alarm system.

Selecting pipe and hangers for sprinkler systems

Pipe NFPA 13 requires that pipe used in sprinkler systems shall have chemical properties, physical properties, and dimensions of material at least equivalent to the standards shown in Table 1-3.

Hangers

- Pipe hangers shall be Underwriters' Laboratories listed. Hangers shall be arranged to maintain the required pitch for free expansion and contraction.

- Each vertical line shall be supported at its base using a hanger placed in the horizontal line near the riser.

- Hangers shall be installed in accordance with the requirements of the National Fire Protection Association. Figure 1-14 illustrates common types of acceptable hangers.

- Hangers shall meet seismic requirements in areas prone to seismic movement.

Hydraulic design of sprinkler systems Sprinkler systems can be hydraulically calculated to ensure adequate protection where non-calculated systems might prove deficient and to save money by mathematically demonstrating

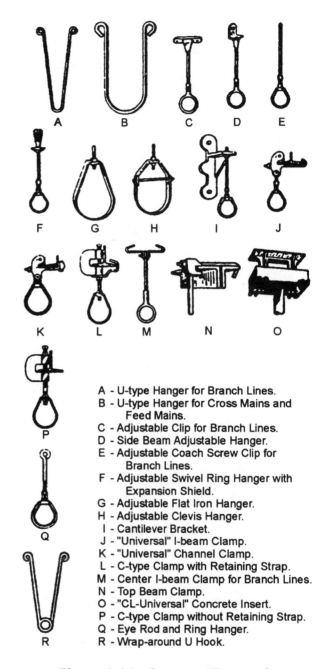

A - U-type Hanger for Branch Lines.
B - U-type Hanger for Cross Mains and Feed Mains.
C - Adjustable Clip for Branch Lines.
D - Side Beam Adjustable Hanger.
E - Adjustable Coach Screw Clip for Branch Lines.
F - Adjustable Swivel Ring Hanger with Expansion Shield.
G - Adjustable Flat Iron Hanger.
H - Adjustable Clevis Hanger.
I - Cantilever Bracket.
J - "Universal" I-beam Clamp.
K - "Universal" Channel Clamp.
L - C-type Clamp with Retaining Strap.
M - Center I-beam Clamp for Branch Lines.
N - Top Beam Clamp.
O - "CL-Universal" Concrete Insert.
P - C-type Clamp without Retaining Strap.
Q - Eye Rod and Ring Hanger.
R - Wrap-around U Hook.

Figure 1-14   Common Types of Acceptable Hangers

that the smaller pipe can do the job. The important premise in either case is that the amount of water needed to be discharged from sprinklers to achieve fire control is known. If the required discharge is known, then hydraulic calculation is possible. In fire-protection terminology, the required sprinkler discharge rate is known as the "design density" in gallons per minute per square foot (gpm/ft^2) (L/s/m^2).

Example 1-2

If an individual sprinkler is protecting 100 ft² (9.3 m²) and discharging at a rate of 25 gpm (1.58 L/s), determine the "design density" in gallons per minute per square foot (gpm/ft²) (L/s/m²).

Equation 1-3

$$\text{Design Density} = \frac{\text{gpm}}{\text{ft}^2} = \frac{25 \text{ gpm}}{100 \text{ ft}^2}$$

$$= 0.25 \text{ gpm/ft}^2$$

$$(\text{Design Density} = \frac{\text{L/s}}{\text{m}^2} = \frac{1.58 \text{ L/s}}{9.3 \text{m}^2}$$

$$= 0.17 \text{ L/s/m}^2)$$

If the required design density were 0.33 gpm/ft² (0.22 L/s/m²), the sprinkler described above would be required to produce at least 33 gpm (0.33 gpm/ft² × 100 ft²) (2.08 L/s [0.22 L/s/m² × 9.3 m²]). Hydraulic calculations would be used in this case to prove that 33 gpm (2.08 L/s) would be available.

The National Fire Protection Association, Factory Mutual, Industrial Risk Insurers, and other fire-protection organizations, through tests and studies, have established design densities that are appropriate for a wide range of occupancy classifications.

Another critical concept that must be understood in hydraulic calculations is that all the sprinklers in the sprinkler system being designed are not expected to discharge simultaneously. For design purposes, only a portion of the sprinklers should be considered to be operating. This is a realistic assumption since the history of wet-pipe sprinkler system performance indicates that in at least 85% of all fires in sprinkler buildings *not more than ten sprinklers operate*. It should be noted, however, that high hazard and flash fires from dust, combustible residues, vapors, etc. may require the operation of more than ten sprinkler heads. The area in the building in which all the sprinklers are considered to be discharging water is called the "area of sprinkler operation," or sometimes simply the "design area." The units of the design area are designated in square feet (square meters).

The required size of the design area varies. NFPA Standard no. 13 allows the designer some flexibility in the sizing of the design area, usually permitting an area between 1500 and 5000 ft² (139.3 and 464.5 m²) in size. Other authorities have different ranges. In many cases, the insurance industry or government authorities require a specific design area based on a specific hazard classification. Otherwise, the designer is free to choose any area within the acceptable range. It must be noted that the required minimum design density will vary with the hazard classification and the size of the design area.

The design area is to be located in the most hydraulically remote part of the fire area. In essence, the design area must be composed of the most demanding portion of the sprinkler system. If the calculations prove that the water supply available is adequate for the most demanding part of the system, then it logically follows that the water supply will be adequate for any part of the system. The most hydraulically remote area is not always easy to identify. In a non-looped and ungridded system (i.e., a conventional "tree system"), the hydraulically most remote area is usually the area most physically remote from the water-supply source. However, it is important to understand that physical remoteness is not a fail-safe criterion for hydraulic remoteness, particularly when the engineer is dealing with looped or gridded piping systems.

The essential difference between a hydraulically calculated sprinkler system and a pipe-schedule sprinkler system lies in the regulation of pipe sizing. For a sprinkler system designed in accordance with the NFPA Standard no. 13 pipe schedules, only a limited number of sprinklers may be supplied by a given pipe size. In a hydraulically calculated system, however, there is no limit to the number of sprinklers that can be supplied by any size pipe, the size is solely dictated by the rate of flow. However, the total square footage covered by a single fire riser is restricted, normally to 52,000 ft² (4831 m²), except 40,000 ft² (3716 m²) in storage occupancies. The calculations simply must prove that the pipe size and configuration will be adequate to deliver the required densities from the available water supply.

Information required for hydraulic calculation

1. Water-supply information.

   A. Static pressure, psi (kPa).

   B. Residual pressure, psi (kPa).

   C. Flow rate, gpm (L/s).

D. Location and elevation of test.

E. Total supply available.

2. Hazard classification (occupancy).

A. By insurance company or NFPA standards.

B. Density and area requirements.

C. Duration of flow requirements.

D. Hose stream allowance.

E. Pressure allowance.

3. Piping material (friction loss).

A. Lightwall pipe.

B. Schedule 40 pipe.

C. Copper.

D. Cement-lined pipe.

4. Sprinkler heads.

A. Obtain sprinkler head "K" factor from technical data sheets.

B. Temperature rating.

C. Special coating requirements.

Information needed for design   Prior to designing a fire-sprinkler system, the following information must be obtained:

1. *Estimate of the water demand for the sprinkler system*   This can be obtained by calculating the product of the density, design area, and overage factor. The density and design are normally specified by NFPA 13, or the fire insurance underwriter, and both relate to the type of hazard to be protected.

Example 1-3

Given the following conditions of a sprinkler system:

Design density = 0.2 gpm/ft^2 (0.135 L/s/m^2)
Design area   = 3000 ft^2 (278.7 m^2)
Overage factor = 1.20

Determine the system demand of the given sprinkler system.

Equation 1-4

$$\text{System demand} = \text{Density (gpm/ft}^2\text{)} \times \text{Design area} \times \text{Overage factor}$$

$$= 0.2 \times 3000 \times 1.20$$

$$= 720 \text{ gpm}$$

$$[\text{System demand} = \text{Density (L/s/m}^2\text{)} \times \text{Design area} \times \text{Overage factor}$$

$$= 0.135 \times 278.7 \times 1.20$$

$$= 45.4 \text{ L/s}]$$

2. *Estimate of the total demand for the sprinkler system and hose outlets*   This can be determined by adding the sprinkler-system demand to the hose demand. The hose demand is normally specified by NFPA 13 or an insurance underwriter.

Example 1-4

If the minimum hose demand shall be 250 gpm (15.7 L/s), determine the total demand for Example 1-3.

Equation 1-5

Total demand = System demand + Other demand

$$= 720 \text{ gpm (45.4 L/s)} + 250 \text{ gpm (15.7 L/s)}$$

$$= 910 \text{ gpm (61.1 L/s)}$$

3. *The pressure available*   The pressure available at the water supply with the total demand flowing can be determined from a graph of the water-supply characteristics (flow and pressure) at the water-supply point.

4. *End-head flows and pressures*   The end-head flow is that flow required to provide the minimum specified water density by the actual floor area tributary to a sprinkler head. The actual floor area per sprinkler is usually less than the specified maximum allowable area per sprinkler, due to the geometric constraints of the building.

The end-head sprinkler pressure at its required minimum flow can be determined from Equation 1-7 (see below) or from sprinkler-head characteristic tables; however, it should never be less than 7 psi (0.44 kPa).

Example 1-5

Given the following conditions:

Occupancy = Machine shop
Hazard   = Ordinary, Group 2 per NFPA 13, A-2-1.2.2
Maximum
spacing   = 130 ft^2 (12.1 m^2) per NFPA 13, Table 4-2.2

K Factor   = 5.6 (for a nominal ½ in.
                [12.7 mm] orifice size)
Density   = Ordinary, Group 2 is 0.20 gpm/ft^2
                (0.135 L/s/m^2)
Area   = 1500 ft^2 (139.3 m^2)
                (min. per NFPA 13)

Determine (1) the end-head sprinkler flow and (2) the head sprinkler pressure.

Step 1: The end-head sprinkler flow or gpm (L/s) head:

Equation 1-6

Q = Design area × Design density

Q = 130 ft^2 (12.1 m^2) × 0.20 gpm (0.135 L/s/m^2)

  = 26.08 gpm (0.145 L/s)

Step 2: The end-head pressure:

Equation 1-7

$$p = \left(\frac{Q}{K}\right)^2$$

$$= \left(\frac{26}{5.6}\right)^2$$

  = 21.56 psi

$$[p = \left(\frac{0.145}{5.6}\right)^2$$

  = 148.65 kPa]

This is the end-head starting pressure. The starting pressure may be reduced by using a large orifice head ("K" = 8.0).

$$p = \left(\frac{26}{8.0}\right)^2$$

  = 10.56 psi
    (min. = 7 psi)

$$[p = \left(\frac{0.145}{8.0}\right)^2$$

  = 72.8 kPa
    (min. = 48.26 kPa)]

5. *Average pressure loss per foot* The average pressure loss per foot is the unit pressure loss that may be expended in friction losses as the water travels through the sprinkler piping and sprinklers. It is determined by dividing the pressure available for the system by the system equivalent pipe length.

6. *Sizing of the sprinkler piping system* The hydraulic pipe schedule is a table of standard sprinkler system pipe sizes with associated flows that will produce the average friction loss per foot allowed in the system under consideration.

STANDPIPE SYSTEMS

Standpipe systems can be classified into three categories as defined by the National Fire Protection Association in Standard no. 14, *Standpipe and Hose Systems*. The purpose of installing a standpipe system is to provide a readily accessible water supply for fire-department personnel and/or trained occupant use during fire situations.

Classifications

- *Class I*   For use by fire departments and those trained in handling heavy fire streams, 2½-in. (65-mm) hose.
- *Class II*   For use primarily by the building occupants until the arrival of the fire department, 1½-in. (40-mm) hose.
- *Class III*   For use either by fire departments and those trained in handling heavy hose streams, 2½-in. (65-mm) hose, or by the building occupants, 1½-in (40-mm) hose.

Locating and Determining the Number of Standpipe Risers

The number of standpipe risers and hose valves can be determined by the guidelines established in NFPA 14. Though some state and local building codes may differ, as a rule of thumb, each room or segment of a building that requires standpipes must be within reach of a 100-ft (30.5-m) fire hose with a 30-ft (9.14-m) hose stream. In other words, each and every room must be accessible for entry with the 100 ft (30.5 m) of fire hose and each portion of that room must be reached by a 30-ft (9.14-m) hose stream.

After examining the architectural floor plans, the number of risers and hose valves can be determined using the distance guideline discussed above. Most building codes and the NFPA require that the risers and 2½-in. (65-mm) hose valves for Classes I and III standpipe systems be located inside fire-rated stairs or smoke-proof towers. This is to allow the fire department the opportunity to make their connection to the riser inside a protected area prior to entering the floor under the fire condition. It is extremely important for the designer to become totally familiar with the local building code requirements so that any deviation from the NFPA's recommended procedures can be properly justified.

Sizing

Sizing of standpipe risers and branch mains, if applicable to the installation, varies according to the system configuration, local and state building code requirements, the building hazard, and the size of the building. Since there are several factors involved in the standpipe system, it is recommended that the designer check with the local and state codes as well as the NFPA standards to ensure that the system will meet local requirements.

Water Supply

Based on the NFPA and most fire-protection agencies, the adequate water supply required for the proper performance of standpipe systems is as follows:

- *Classes I and III* A water-supply system must be capable of providing 500 gpm (31.5 L/s) at a pressure of 100 psi (689.5 kPa) at the uppermost outlet for the first riser and 250 gpm (15.75 L/s) for each additional riser with a maximum required water supply of 1250 gpm (78.75 L/s). The standard fire stream is 250 gpm (15.75 L/s). In order to provide this flow from a 2½ in. (65-mm) fire hose with the standard 1⅛-in. (28.6-mm) bore nozzle, a nozzle pressure of 50 psi (344.74 kPa) is needed. Since the friction loss through the 2½-in. (65-mm) fire hose flowing 250 gpm (15.75 L/s) is 15 psi (103.42 kPa), the outlet pressure at the riser valve must be 100 psi (689.5 kPa).

- *Class II* A water-supply system must be capable of providing 100 gpm (6.3 L/s) at 100 psi (689.5 kPa) at the uppermost outlet.

If the water supply to the standpipes cannot provide the required volume and pressure, the system must be upgraded to ensure an adequate supply or a fire pump must be added to the system.

SPECIAL EXTINGUISHING SYSTEMS

Dry-Chemical Extinguishing System

The total flooding system consists of a supply of dry chemical permanently connected to fixed discharge piping, with fixed nozzles discharging into an enclosed space or enclosure around a hazard. The system may be:

1. *Engineered* These systems are based on known factors of chemical flow, pressure, friction losses, and pressure drops. Detection and activation are by automatic operation using either electric, electronic, or mechanical detection and discharge. Many authorities require a full discharge test after installation for verification of the effectiveness of such a system or require a room air-pressure test.

2. *Pre-engineered* These systems have been fire-tested for a listing with a recognized laboratory. The manufacturer's instructions are specific regarding installation, pipe size, nozzle pressures, and types and quantities of chemicals to be used. Most pre-engineered systems are designed for automatic operation, using electric, electronic, or mechanical detection and discharge. A manual pull station is required to be installed at an exit.

A dry chemical was originally used to extinguish Class B fires. It consisted of a sodium bicarbonate base with additives to prevent caking and to improve the fluid flow characteristics. Later, multipurpose dry chemicals, effective on Class A, B, and C fires, were developed.

Dry chemicals are effective on surface fires, especially on flammable liquids. When used in Class A fires, they do not penetrate the burning material to suppress deep-seated fires. Water is used as a backup when a fire involves porous or loosely packed material. The major effect of dry chemicals is that they break the chain reaction of combustion; a minor effect, in Class A fires, is that they smother fires. Fires that are likely to rekindle are not effectively controlled by dry chemicals.

Dry chemicals can be discharged in local applications, where the hazard is not enclosed or the enclosure does not form an effective fire boundary, by hand-held extinguishers, wheeled portable equipment, nozzles on fixed piping or hose lines. Chemical application may be tank-side, overhead, or a combination of both.

Hand hose-line systems consist of a hose and nozzle connected to a dry chemical supply by direct connection to the storage container or by fixed piping. One or more hose reels can be supplied by the same chemical supply.

Twin-agent units using dry chemicals for early flame knockdown, followed by a foam application to prevent re-flash, are becoming a more common means of fire suppression. The type and size of the chemical used is determined by the type and size of the hazard and units can vary in size from a few pounds (kilograms) to several tons (metric tons) of dry chemical. These chemicals can also be used for extinguishing fires by total flooding when they are distributed through a piped system with special discharge nozzles. The expellant gas is usually dry nitrogen. Refer to NFPA Standard 17.

Dry-Powder Extinguishing System

Dry-powder extinguishing agents are different from dry-chemical extinguishing agents and are effectively used to put out combustible-metal fires. No extinguisher can be used universally on all fires involving combustible metals, and such fires should not be fought by untrained personnel.

Several proprietary dry powders are currently available; however, none should be used without first consulting the manufacturer. The applicable NFPA standards for combustible metals are nos. 480 and 651 (magnesium), 481 (titanium), 482 (zirconium), and 65 and 651 (aluminum).

Carbon-Dioxide Extinguishing System

The minimum requirements for design, installation, maintenance, and testing of carbon-dioxide extinguishing systems can be found in NFPA Standard 12.

The operating principle of a carbon-dioxide extinguishing system is its ability to reduce the oxygen content surrounding a hazard to a point at which combustion cannot continue. Also, carbon dioxide cools fire areas. It should also be noted that it will fail to support life as well; thus, care should be exercised in its application.

Carbon dioxide is an odorless, colorless gas at ordinary temperatures. When used for fire protection, it is stored under pressure in either high-pressure cylinders or a refrigerated, low-pressure tank. Under normal conditions, the gas is compressed into a liquid. The colder the storage temperature, the denser the liquid.

When a carbon-dioxide system is discharged, the pressure in the storage container acts as the propellant, forcing the stored liquid through pipelines to discharge nozzles. Each pound of carbon dioxide will expand to approximately 8 ft^3 (0.224 m^3) vapor at atmospheric pressure. Most of the liquid expands to a gas, but a portion forms particles of dry ice or snow-like appearance. The "snow" increases the mass of the discharge allowing it to be projected for some distance. It absorbs heat and reduces temperature.

A minimum concentration of 34% by volume will handle most common materials, others may require an inerting atmosphere up to 100%. Some burning materials, such as stacked paper, furs, electrical insulation, and baled cotton contain so much oxygen in pores or other internal spaces that they must be "soaked" in a smothering atmosphere for periods ranging from several minutes to several hours.

Carbon dioxide may be applied by either total flood or local application method. Total flooding is used where the hazard is contained in a room, compartment, or other enclosure that will allow the carbon-dioxide atmosphere to remain in contact with the burning materials for a long enough period to extinguish a fire and prevent its reignition.

Local application is used where a hazard cannot be readily enclosed. Rate and duration of discharge, length of piping, and the usable capacity of storage containers are critical factors, as the discharge of carbon dioxide is soon dissipated and has no continuing effect. System design for this type of application is considerably more complex than it is for flooding an enclosure. The type of nozzles to be used and their locations and discharge rates must be determined within accurate limits.

Local application is commonly used for the largest and most valuable industrial processes, such as for oil quench tanks, flow-coating paint machines, steel and aluminum mills, printing presses, and power-generating equipment.

Carbon dioxide as used for fire-protection systems is available in high-pressure or low-pressure equipment. High-pressure systems (850 psi/70°F [5.86 kPa/21.1°C]) use gas compressed in standard cylinders. Low-pressure systems use carbon dioxide stored at 300 psi/0°F (2.07 kPa/ –17.8°C) in refrigerated, insulated tanks. Low-pressure systems are capable of multiple discharges since the duration of discharge is limited; several hazards may be simultaneously protected through the use of multi-directional valves.

Foam Extinguishing System

Foam, mostly a mass of air- or gas-filled bubbles formed by chemical or mechanical means, is most useful in controlling fires involving flammable liquids with a low flash point and specific gravity that are lighter than water. The mass of bubbles forms a cohesive blanket that extinguishes the fire by excluding air and cooling the surface and by separating the fuel from the fire.

Foam is not suitable for use on fires involving compressed gases or on live electrical equipment. Because of the water content, 94–97%, foam cannot be used on fires involving burning metals and is not effective on oxygen-containing materials. For fires involving water-soluble liquids, such as polar solvents, a special alcohol-resistant AFFF foam concentrate must be used. Foam can be applied to the fire surface or to the subsurface, such as in petrochemical tanks. Polar solvents must be surface applied. Systems can be fixed or semi-fixed.

There are distinct types of foam available that are suitable for fire control. (Refer to NFPA Standards 11, 11A, 13, 16, 16A, and 30.)

1. *Mechanical foam* This type of foam is made by the mechanical mixing of water and synthetics. Examples include Aqueous Film-Forming Foam (AFFF) and alcohol-resistant foams; a fluoroprotein-mixed chemical concentrate; and a protein-mixed chemical concentrate. Protein and fluoroprotein foams are the least expensive, have excellent burn-back resistance, but do not "knock down" the fire as quickly as AFFF, which drains quickly but is not as heat resistant or as stable. Alcohol-resistant foams are somewhere between the two, but cost twice as much as protein. The volume of foam generated is dependent on the expansion ratio of the foam selected. Low-expansion foams expand at a ratio of 8–10:1. Medium-expansion foams expand at a ratio of 20–100:1. Mechanical foam can be conducted through pipe lines and discharged through a fixed chamber mounted in a bulk-fuel storage tank or it can be conducted through hoses and discharged manually through special nozzles. This foam can also be distributed through a specially designed sprinkler system. NFPA Standard no.11 details the use of this foam and no. 16 describes foam-water sprinkler systems.

2. *High-expansion foam* This foam can be generated in volumes that are 100–1000 times that of the water used. The foam is formed by the passage of air through a screen constantly wetted by a solution of chemical concentrate, which usually has a detergent base. The foam can be conducted by ducts, either fixed or portable, and can be manually applied by portable generators. High-expansion foam is useful for extinguishing fires by totally flooding indoor confined spaces, such as mine tunnels, or by local application. It extinguishes by displacing air from the fire and by the heat-absorbing effect of converting the foam water into steam. The foam forms an insulating barrier for exposed equipment or building components. However, high-expansion foam is generally not reliable when used outdoors, where it is subject to wind currents, and, although it is nontoxic, it has an effect of disorienting people. NFPA Standard no. 11A covers high-expansion foams.

The type of discharge device that should be used with a specific type of foam is based upon the listings from the manufacturer. Conventional open-head sprinklers may be used with AFFF or alcohol-resistant foams. However, foam-water sprinkler heads should be used for protein or fluoroprotein foams. Aspirating or non-aspirating nozzles can affect the knockdown time and the foam's blanket-forming ability. Foam can also be supplied using oscillating-type monitors.

Foam can be supplied from a diaphragm (bladder) tank using water pressure for making foam and distribution, or from an in-line pressure proportioning system that utilizes an atmospheric tank with a supply-pressure pump.

Foam disposal after discharge can cause problems. Although most foams are biodegradable, because their biological oxygen demand (BOD) is high, they cannot be directly discharged to the sewer or storm-water systems. A holding tank with a treatment system may, therefore, be required.

Gaseous Fire-Suppression Systems

Introduction For many years, halogenated agent (Halon 1211 and Halon 1301) fire-suppression systems were utilized to protect high-value equipment, materials, and buildings. Halon 1301 was a particularly good extinguishing agent as it interfered with the chain reaction of fire, left no residues, and was nontoxic. Halons contain compounds that consist of chlorine, bromine, fluorine, and carbon, which are commonly known as "chlorofluorocarbons" (CFCs). CFCs are extremely stable compounds that do not break down chemically until reaching the earth's upper atmosphere. In September 1987, 24 nations of the United Nations signed an agreement to phase out production of refrigerants and Halons that are detrimental to the earth's ozone layer. This agreement is commonly referred to as the "Montreal Protocol." Both Halon 1211 and Halon 1301 were phased out of production in 1994, except for essential uses, and CFCs were phased out in 1996. Some Halons still exist in manufacturer's inventories.

The current replacement fire-suppression gases for Halon 1301 are inert gases, hydrochlorofluorocarbons (HCFCs), HCFC blends, heptafluorocarbons (HFCs) and perflourocarbons (PFCs), each a clean extinguishing agent. Due to the characteristics of these substitute agents, all or part of existing Halon storage and distribution systems may need replacement for use with the new agents. Replacement agents for Halon 1301 include: inert gases; HFC-227EA, an HCFC; R-595, an HCFC blend; heptafluoropropane, an HFC and perfluorobutane, a PFC. Currently, the only known replacement gas for Halon 1211 being produced is perfluorohexane, a PFC. All of these agents are accepted for use for Class A, B, and C fires and are colorless, odorless, and electrically nonconductive. The agents are stored in pressure vessels, pressurized to 360 psi (2,482 kPa) with dry nitrogen, that can be manifolded together for large system applications.

These agents, other than the inert gases, are chemical inhibitors that react with the transient products of combustion, terminating the combustion chain reaction, thereby stopping the flame propagation. The inert gases are a mixture of argon, nitrogen, and carbon dioxide that reduces the oxygen content below a point necessary to maintain combustion. (Inert gases are also used for explosion prevention.) Although inert gases have a low level of toxicity, the decomposition products generated by their breaking down in the presence of very high amounts of heat may be dangerous. They may be used in occupied areas if the design concentration does not exceed the "no observed adverse effect level" (NOAEL) of 43%. Heptafluoropropane may be used in occupied areas if the design concentration does not exceed the NOAEL of 9%. This agent contains fluorine and may decompose into hydrogen fluoride, which may be noxious and/or irritating. Halon may be used in occupied areas if the design concentration does not exceed the NOAEL of 5%. This agent contains materials that may decompose into irritating byproducts and, at high temperatures, may form toxic fluorides and bromides. Perfluorobutane may be used in occupied areas if the design concentration does not exceed the NOAEL of 40%. It is recommended, however, that egress from the protected areas be done during the countdown period between the verification of a fire and the release of any of these agents.

Descriptions and design requirements of all these replacement agents are given in detail in NFPA Standard no. 2001, *Clean Extinguishing Agent.* Halon information may be found in NFPA Standard 12A. Although this chapter discusses Halon 1301 because it is still available, the other remaining replacement systems are also discussed.

Design procedure Modern concepts of fire protection for buildings of various occupancies include consideration of a clean-agent extinguishing system as either an alternative or an addition to a traditional fire-protection sprinkler system for rooms or areas considered special in nature from a fire-protection point of view or of high value because of the equipment and/or materials housed in those areas. Specific applications must be reviewed with the local fire authorities having jurisdiction and the owner's insurance underwriter, but the following steps could be considered as a basis for further, detailed design.

1. First, determine if the authority having jurisdiction and the owner's insurance underwriter allow one or more of these agents in addition to sprinklers. Some authorities have determined that these systems are not acceptable alternatives to sprinklers if the

release of the agent does not extinguish the fire, as may occur in the case of a "deep-seated" fire. In this case, there is no fire-extinguishing backup after the system has been discharged, unless an automatic reserve system is installed. Even with the use of reserve systems, the agent quantity may not be sufficient to completely extinguish a deep-seated fire. If a clean-agent system is installed in addition to a fire-protection sprinkler system to protect the same floor area, then the sprinklers should release after the clean-agent system has been exhausted when the ceiling temperature equals the fusible link temperature rating of the sprinkler head. In this situation, the equipment in the fire area could possibly be damaged due to water discharge, but the building and most of the equipment and records will be saved from total loss by the sprinkler system.

2. The next step is to determine the quantity of agent necessary, which depends on the following:

    A. Square footage (square meters) and the volume or cubic footage (cubic meters) of the space to be protected, including any under-floor (raised-floor) areas that are commonly utilized in electronic spaces. According to the specific application, the under-floor area may be on a separate zone(s) than the room space(s).

    B. Minimum agent concentration required for the hazard classification, as established by NFPA Standard 2001 or 12A, or by the authority having jurisdiction.

    C. Minimum length of time that the agent concentration is to be maintained to ensure extinguishment of the fire.

    D. The rate of extended discharge should be sufficient to maintain the desired concentration for the duration of application.

    E. Flooding factors used to determine the quantity of agent required should provide an extra allowance of agent for natural leakage of the agent from the space under protection due to gaps in doors, windows, and penetrations through walls and floors for electrical cables and ductwork in all ceilings, walls, and under-floor areas. Note that ducts that recirculate air between the room and subfloor space need not be considered for leakage because the agent will not leak

outside the structural enclosure, all of which is one agent discharge zone. This, of course, assumes the above and under-floor systems are in one zone.

    F. The "connected standby" is an integral part of the system. Connected standby (reserve) is sometimes required by the jurisdictional authority or owner in important systems or continually operated areas, such as telephone exchanges, data processing rooms, or mainframe computer rooms. The reserve system is arranged to discharge on a delayed basis after the primary bank of cylinders has released or failed to release. Normally, the requirement for 100% connected reserve is established by the owner or insurance underwriter for the building or equipment as an extra precaution against building loss, but it is not a requirement of the NFPA standards.

3. Now that the quantity of agent has been established based on the foregoing criteria, the next step is to decide if the agent cylinders will be located within the space to be protected or in a separate room outside the space being protected but adjacent to the space to reduce pipe lengths between the cylinders and protected areas. Locating multiple cylinders or spheres, either exposed or concealed, at ceiling height or under the raised floor in the protected space may be more economical than storing cylinders outside the area because then long piping systems are not required.

It is important to confirm approximate diameters, lengths, and widths of cylinders so that, if a separate storage room is to be used, ceiling heights, raised floor heights, and floor areas can be finalized with the architect and owner. The agent-equipment supplier should be consulted at this point regarding standard cylinder sizes, required clearances between cylinders and walls, access for cylinder replacement from an outside supply truck, weight of the equipment (for structural engineering design), and anchoring and support methods for attaching cylinders or spheres to walls or hanging from or above ceilings. If multiple spheres are used at ceiling height within the protected space, agent piping is often not required because discharge is achieved directly from the nozzle mounted on the sphere(s).

4. It is now time to locate the pipe runs from the cylinders to the discharge nozzles to ensure uniform discharge and design concentration of the agent throughout the protected space, generally within 10–60 s. If a separate agent storage room is to be used, it is particularly important that the length of piping between the storage room and the point of discharge is properly sized to ensure complete flooding of the room to the design concentration and within a maximum of 10–60 s. The longer the pipe run, the longer is the time before the agent reaches the most remote nozzle on the system. Generally, pipe runs are located at or above the ceiling to work in conjunction with architectural requirements regarding aesthetics.

5. Pipe sizing is usually established by a fire-protection engineer or the extinguishing-agent equipment supplier based on computerized programs for pipe size determination, with proper data input related to room size and volume, air infiltration, the hazard being protected, and the specifics about the agent used. Any such program must be listed or approved by a third-party agency, such as Underwriters Laboratories (UL) or Factory Mutual Engineering (FM).

6. Special precaution in design is necessary to ensure proper support and anchoring of the piping, as the force of the agent under pressure moving through the pipe systems can cause pipe movement, ruptured joints, or other dangerous conditions. Ceiling clips are recommended to hold down lay-in ceiling tiles during high-pressure agent discharge.

7. The method of initiating or triggering the system must be considered, along with various alternatives. Products of combustion (ionization and/or photoelectric) type smoke detectors located at ceiling height, or under raised floors when applicable, within the protected space are normally used at approximately 250–400 ft^2 (23.2–37.2 m^2) per detector as the first signal that there is a fire. However, the maximum area per detector is based on the airflow through the protected space, in accordance with NFPA Standard 72. From the detector, the signal is sent to an agent control panel normally located near the exit door from the protected space.

The most common sequence of events for the control panel is as follows:

A. First smoke detector activates: bell rings in the protected area, signal is sent to the building fire-alarm control panel.

B. Second smoke detector activates: alarm horn or bell sounds, countdown timer delay (30 s) starts, air-handling equipment shuts down, signal is sent to the building fire-alarm control panel.

C. Time delay expires: agent discharges immediately, electrical equipment shuts down, strobe light and local discharge horns are activated, signal is sent to the building fire-alarm control panel.

There are alternatives to the above-described initiation sequence, such as "counter-zoning," which requires at least one detector to alarm from two different detector zones in the protected space before system discharge. This requires the establishment of multiple detection zones in the protected space.

The control panel is commonly equipped with a light indicating that the agent is discharging, a 30-s time delay relay, an alarm relay, a shutdown relay, a "dead-man" abort station, and a manual-release station. In the event that the fire can be brought under control by other means, or until the fire is confirmed, the abort station may be used to prevent the release of the agent. Most authorities having jurisdiction have strict limitations or prohibitions against the use of manual stop or abort stations.

Building fire-alarm systems should be equipped with the ability to receive a signal from the clean-extinguishing agent system control panel and indicate to fire-department personnel where the fire is within the building. If the building fire-alarm control panel does not have this capability, a separate graphic annunciator should be provided with the extinguishing-agent control equipment.

Testing procedure on site Actual discharge testing of Halon systems is no longer permitted, due to environmental considerations. It is common, however, for a complete functional test of the system after installation to be required to ensure proper operation of all mechanical and electrical equipment, detection system, discharge control, abort, power shutdown, air-handling unit shutdown, fire damper, and door closure circuits. A fan pressurization test of the space integrity and an acceptance test may also be required. Refer to Chapter 4 of NFPA Standard 2001 for complete inspection, testing, and training requirements for clean-extinguishing agent systems. Refer to NFPA Standard 12A for Halon system requirements.

Elevator Shaft Protection Systems

Most model and state building codes require protection of all shafts that penetrate the floors of a building. This normally entails rating the walls and protecting all penetrations. In noncombustible and nonaccessible shafts, protection inside the shaft is not normally required. However, elevator shafts require sprinkler protection at least at the top and bottom of the shaft.

All sprinkler piping must be located outside the shaft, except for the short horizontal branch that feeds the sprinkler head(s). An accessible, and monitored, isolation valve must be provided on the main line feeding the shaft sprinklers, outside the shaft.

ASME A17.1, *Safety Code for Elevators and Escalators*, states that the main-line power supply to the elevator must be automatically disconnected prior to the application of water. This is required because the electrical components and brakes on an elevator do not perform predictably when wet.

Therefore, a pre-action type sprinkler system should be employed when protecting elevator shafts; this will prevent accidental water discharge onto the elevator. It is recommended that a smoke detector be placed at the top of the shaft, which will alarm the system control panel and initiate elevator recall upon actuation. For the next step, there are two options available, as follows:

1. The first option requires a sprinkler head to fuse to allow water into the piping system. When water flow is detected, a signal is sent that disconnects power to the elevator without time delay.

2. The second option requires a heat detector at the top of the shaft that, with a time delay, allows the elevator to complete recall and then disconnects power to the elevator and allows water to fill the piping. The sprinkler head fusible link, which is at a higher temperature than the heat detector setting, must fuse before water flows.

FIRE PUMPS

The performance requirements and accessories for pumps, whether motor or engine-driven, are basically the same. The related components of the specific drivers, however, vary in installation, operation, and maintenance.

To the owner, a fire pump represents a reduction in the insurance rate; to the insurance company, it is a substantial reduction in risk. To all concerned, a fire pump has characteristics suited for firefighting and is built to rigid specifications, which sets it apart from ordinary water pumps. The fire pump is the first line of defense against fire damage. The applicable NFPA standard is no. 20.

Fire pumps are used to supply water for automatic sprinkler systems, standpipes, and fire hydrants. NFPA Standard no. 20 classifies horizontal split-case fire pumps for positive suction pressure. Vertical turbine pumps are used when suction lift is required. Labeled fire pumps are made in specific sizes—500, 750, 1000, 1500, 2000, and 2500 gpm (31.5, 47.3, 63, 94.5, 126 and 157.5 L/s). Pressure selections range from 40 to 100 psi (275.8 to 689.5 kPa) for low-pressure fire pumps (sometimes referred to as booster fire pumps) and from 100 to 340 psi (689.5 to 2344.2 kPa) or more for standard fire pumps.

The fire pump must meet the following requirements:

1. Each pump must be capable of withstanding a hydrostatic pressure of twice the maximum pressure.

2. Pumps must furnish not less than 150% of the rated head at 65% of rated pressure (shut-off not to exceed 120% of the rated pressure).

3. The maximum pump brake horsepower must not exceed the rating of the particular driver.

In addition, each pump must have listed pressure gauges and be fitted with a suitable air-relief valve. With certain exceptions, a ¾-in. (19.1-mm) casing relief valve is required to prevent overheating of the pump when it operates against a closed valve. When there is a possibility that the pump pressure will exceed the safe working pressure of the system, and always when a diesel driver or variable-speed driver is used, a listed main relief valve must be furnished.

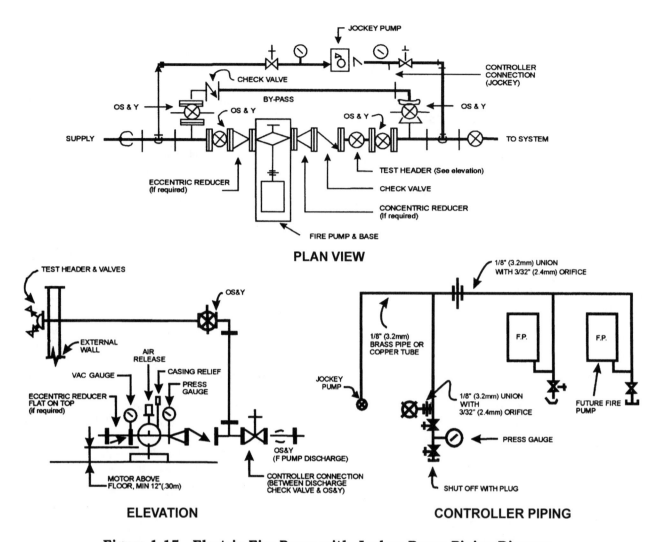

Figure 1-15   Electric Fire Pump with Jockey Pump Piping Diagram

Fire pumps are driven by either electric motors or diesel engines. All fire-pump motor drivers are required to be rated for continuous duty and must not be used at voltages in excess of 110% of the rated voltage. At rated voltage and frequency, the full load ampere rating must not be exceeded under any pumping conditions.

If the fire pump is electric, power must be uninterruptible with properly protected power cabling and emergency power. Alarms should sound if normal power is interrupted. If the fire pump is diesel, provisions must be made for a day tank for fuel storage, engine cooling, exhaust pipe discharge location and sufficient airflow for cooling, combustion, and ventilation.

The motor-control equipment must be factory assembled, wired, and tested, as well as specifically approved for fire service. Drivers are automatically started by signal from a pressure or deluge valve.

The jockey pump is normally required in all pressured systems. This automatic electric pump has a capacity of 10–15 gpm (4.72–7.08 L/s) or less. The intent is to maintain pressure when it is lost to minor leaks, not to keep up with sprinkler discharge. Its controller is set to start at about 10 psi (69 kPa) above the start signal for the fire pump and to stop at full pressure. Figure 1-15 illustrates a typical electric fire pump with jockey-pump piping diagram.

FIRE EXTINGUISHERS

Most fires start small and could easily be extinguished if the proper quantity and type of extinguishing agent were used in a timely manner. Portable fire extinguishers are the first line of defense. However, they must be properly located and of the proper type for the hazard protected, and they must be used while the fire is small enough for them to be effective. Fire extinguishers should be installed regardless of other fire prevention/protection measures taken.

Fire extinguishers are available to extinguish all A, B, C, or D classification fires, and are available with these extinguishing agents: carbon dioxide, dry chemical, water, halogenated agent, foam, and special compounds for use with combustible metals. Some extinguishers will extinguish only one class of fire, and some may be suitable for two or three classes of fire, but none are suitable for all classes. Rating numerals are used to provide a rating of the effectiveness of an extinguisher, e.g., a 4-A extinguisher will discharge twice as much extinguishing agent as a 2-A unit. The numerical rating for Class B extinguishers is based on the quantity of burning flammable liquid to be extinguished. Class C and D extinguishers do not have numerical ratings.

In selecting, consideration should be given to the type of hazard and the potential size of fire involvement. For the proper type and fire-extinguisher rating, and proper locations, the designer should refer to NFPA Standard 10.

A light hazard exists where there are few combustibles and small fires are expected, such as in offices and schools. Ordinary hazards are those with moderate amounts of combustibles and medium size fires are considered, such as in auto showrooms, light manufacturing facilities, and parking garages. An extra hazard exists where a severe fire may occur, such as in a woodworking shop or a high-piled warehouse. Class A rated extinguishers are often used for general building protection (paper, wood, cloth) and use water, AFFF, multi-purpose dry chemical, and halogenated extinguishing agents. Class B extinguishers include carbon dioxide, dry chemicals, AFFF and halogenated types for use on flammable liquid fires (gasoline, grease, oil, paint), and may be located in kitchens, laboratories, and generator rooms. Class C rated agents include carbon dioxide, dry chemical, and halogenated types for use on electrical equipment fires. Class D extinguishing agents are special dry-powder agents for use on combustible metals. It should be noted that multi-purpose dry chemicals leave a residue when used. Delicate electrical or electronic equipment could be damaged if A-B-C dry chemical extinguishing agents are used. The use of other extinguishing agents, such as other dry chemical type or halogenated units, may be required. Also, the designer should ensure that the agent used will not have an adverse reaction with any burning materials.

Extinguishers should be mounted with the top no more than 5 ft (1.5 m) above the floor, but with the bottom a minimum of 18 in. (.46m) above the floor. For larger units, in excess of 40 lb (18 kg), the top should be 3.5 ft (1.1 m) above the floor. Extinguishers shall be easily visible and accessible. The actual travel distance to extinguishers, including walking around partitions and equipment, becomes a critical factor for quick fire control. The maximum distance should not exceed 75 ft (22.8 m) for Class A and D fires and should not exceed 50 ft (15.25 m) for Class B and C fires. It is beneficial to locate extinguishers in normal paths of travel, near exits and entrances, where uniform distribution is possible and where the units will be readily available. It should be noted that up to one-half of the required extinguishers for Class A fires may be replaced by small hose stations. Wheeled extinguishers are usually intended for outdoor placement and use by trained personnel. These units are also used to provide additional protection, and should not be located more than 50 ft (15.25 m) from the hazard. Tables 1-4 and 1-5 should be used for size and placement (NFPA 10).

EFFECT OF FIRE-PROTECTION SYSTEMS DESIGN AND EQUIPMENT ON OTHER TRADES

Fire-protection design extends beyond the installation of the sprinkler system. The total building team becomes a part of the design effort. The architect and the heating, plumbing, air-conditioning, and electrical engineers are an integral part of the fire-protection system design process. The following is a partial list of items that should be reviewed by the fire-protection team prior to final drawings and specifications being issued for construction:

- State building code.
- Fire-wall locations.

Table 1-4

	Light (Low) Hazard Occupancy	Ordinary (Moderate) Hazard Occupancy	Extra (High) Hazard Occupancy
Minimum rates, single extinguisher	2-A[a]	2-A[a]	4-A[b]
Maximum floor area per unit of A type extinguisher	3000 ft^2 (278.7 m^2)	1500 ft^2 (139.4 m^2)	1000 ft^2 (92.9 m^2)
Maximum floor area for extinguisher	11,250 ft^2 [c] (1045 m^2)	11,250 ft^2 [c] (1045 m^2)	11,250 ft^2 [c] (1045 m^2)
Maximum travel distance to extinguisher	75 ft (22.8 m)	75 ft (22.8 m)	75 ft (22.8 m)

Source: NFPA 10.

[a] Up to two water-type extinguishers, each with 1-A rating, can be used to fulfill the requirements of one 2-A rated extinguisher for light (low) hazard occupancies.

[b] Two 2½-gal (9.48 L) water-type extinguishers can be used to fulfill the requirements of one 4-A rated extinguisher.

[c] See NFPA 10, Appendix E-3-3.

- Smoke-door locations.
- Smoke-exhaust locations.
- Manual fire-alarm locations.
- Sprinkler-flow switch locations.
- Standpipe and hose locations.
- Municipal and fire-department connections.
- Tank locations.
- Local codes and ordinances.
- Fire-door locations.
- Smoke-detector locations.
- Smoke-damper locations.
- Fire-alarm signaling-device locations.
- Valve supervisory-switch locations.
- Fire-pump locations.
- Standby power.

Table 1-5

Type of Hazard	Basic Minimum Extinguisher Rating	Maximum Travel Distance to Extinguishers, ft (m)
Light (low)	5-B	30 (9.15)
	10-B	50 (15.25)
Ordinary (moderate)	10-B	30 (9.15)
	20-B	50 (19.25)
Extra (high)	40-B	30 (9.15)
	80-B	50 (15.25)

Source: NFPA 10.

Notes: (1) The specified ratings do not imply that fires of the magnitudes indicated by these ratings will occur, but are, rather, to give the operators more time and agent to handle difficult spill fires that may occur. (2) For fires involving water-soluble flammable liquids, see NFPA 10, 2-3.4. (3) For specific hazard applications, see NFPA 10, Section 2-3.

The fire-protection engineer and the electrical engineer should coordinate the zones of fire detection and protection. The architect and the fire-protection engineer should coordinate the building fire zones with the fire-protection system with respect to fire walls, fire and smoke doors, and space for the fire-protection equipment. The HVAC engineer should coordinate the building fire zones and the smoke-exhaust system with the fire-protection engineer. The plumbing engineer should coordinate the water supply with the fire-protection engineer. The electrical, plumbing, fire-protection, and HVAC engineers should coordinate the fire pump and standby generator locations and requirements.

As a result of the size and complexity of today's structures, the entire fire-protection team is required to supply a system of fire detection, smoke control and fire supression with the ultimate goal of safety to the occupants of the structure and protection of the owner's investment.

REFERENCES

National Fire Protection Association (NFPA). 1986. *Fire protection handbook.* 16th ed.

——. 1976. *Automatic sprinkler and standpipe systems,* by John L. Bryan.

——. n.d. *Standard for portable fire extinguishers,* Standard no. 10.

——. n.d. *Low-expansion foam,* Standard no. 11.

——. n.d. *Medium and high-expansion foam systems,* Standard no. 11A.

——. n.d. *Carbon dioxide extinguishing systems,* Standard no. 12.

——. n.d. *Halon 1301 fire extinguishing systems,* Standard no. 12A.

——. n.d. *Installation of sprinkler systems,* Standard no. 13.

——. n.d. *Installation of standpipe and hose systems,* Standard no. 14.

——. n.d. *Water spray fixed systems for fire protection,* Standard no. 15.

——. n.d. *Deluge foam-water sprinkler systems and foam-water spray systems,* Standard no. 16.

——. n.d. *Installation of closed-head foam-water sprinkler systems,* Standard no. 16A.

——. n.d. *Dry chemical extinguishing systems,* Standard no. 17.

——. n.d. *Installation of centrifugal fire pumps,* Standard no. 20.

——. n.d. *Installation of private fire service mains and their appurterances,* Standard no. 24.

——. n.d. *Flammable and combustible liquids code,* Standard no. 30.

——. n.d. *National fire alarm code,* Standard no. 72.

——. n.d. *General storage,* Standard no. 231.

——. n.d. *Rack storage of materials,* Standard no. 231C.

——. n.d. *Clean agent extinguishing systems,* Standard no. 2001.

APPENDIX 1-A

The following factors were used to convert inch-pound measurement units to metric units.

1 inch = 25.4 mm

1 foot = 0.348 m

1 gallon = 3.785 L

1 square foot (ft^2) = 0.0929 m^2

1 gallon per minute (gpm) = 0.063 L/s

1 psi = 6.8948 kPa

1 gpm/ft^2 = 0.6781 L/s/m^2

1 foot per minute (ft/min) = 5.08 mm/s

1 cubic foot (ft^3) = 0.028 m^3

1 cubic foot per minute (cfm) = 28.32 L/min

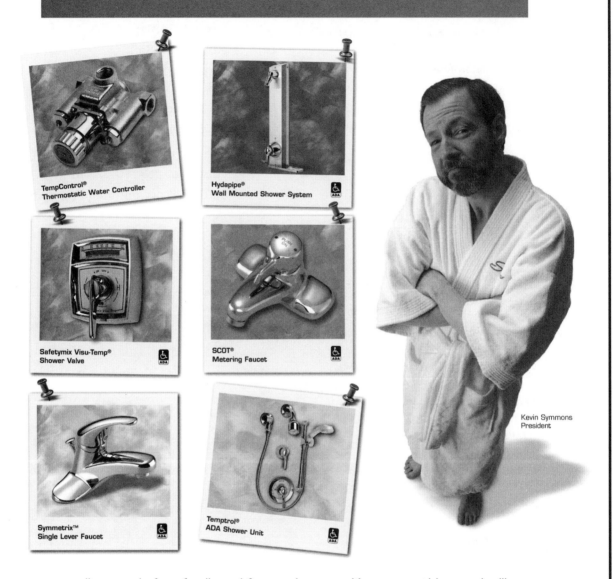

Plumbing Design for Health-Care Facilities

INTRODUCTION

Health-care facilities, nursing homes, medical schools, and medical laboratories require plumbing systems that are more complex than those for most other types of building. The plumbing designer should work closely with the architect and facility staff and be involved in meetings and discussions in order to fully understand the plumbing requirements for any new or special medical equipment. The plumbing design must be coordinated with the civil, architectural, structural, mechanical, and electrical designs to ensure that adequate provisions have been made for utility capacities, for the necessary clearances and space requirements of the piping systems and related plumbing equipment, and for compliance with applicable codes. Health-care facilities may have different requirements or be exempt from some codes and standards, such as water and energy conservation codes and regulations regarding the physically challenged. The plumbing engineer should consult with the administrative authority in order to ensure conformance with local ordinances.

This chapter discusses the provisions that may be encountered by the plumbing professional in the design of a health-care facility, including the following: plumbing fixtures and related equipment, the sanitary drainage system, the water-supply system, laboratory waste and vent systems, pure-water systems, and medical-gas systems.

PLUMBING FIXTURES AND RELATED EQUIPMENT

Selection Process

Meetings of the plumbing engineer with the architect and the facility staff to discuss the general and specific requirements regarding the plumbing fixtures and related equipment are usually held after the architect has prepared the preliminary drawings. At these meetings, the plumbing designer should assist in the selection of plumbing fixtures. Following these sessions, the plumbing designer can prepare the preliminary drawings and coordinate with the architect and facility staff the required piping systems and the plumbing fixture space requirements. In detailing the piping system spaces and plumbing fixture locations, the plumbing engineer should refer to the framing drawings. It is common for the architect to locate the piping shafts and the spaces in direct conflict with the framing; it is the plumbing designer's responsibility to give the architect directions regarding the space requirements, fixture arrangement, and pipe-shaft size and locations.

Following the meetings held with the architect and hospital staff, and with the preliminary drawings available, the plumbing designer should prepare an outline specification for the plumbing fixtures and related equipment. A guide to the required plumbing fixtures and equipment for health-care facilities is provided in Table 2-1 and is discussed later in this section.

A review of applicable code requirements regarding the quality and types of plumbing fixtures

Table 2-1   Recommended Plumbing Fixtures and Related Equipment

Medical-Care Areas

Area	Elongated Water Closet, FlushValve	Urinal	Handwashing Lavatory	Shower	Drinking Fountain / Water Cooler	Mop Service Basin	Counter Sink, Single Compartment	Counter Sink, Double Compartment	Clinic Sink, Flushing Rim	Scrub-up Sink	Utility Sink	Sink, Triple Compartment	Plaster Sink, Plaster Trap	Cup Sink	Floor Drain	Floor Drain, Flushing Rim	Emergency Shower	Emergency Eyewash	Bathtub / Shower	Sitz Bath	Bedpan Washer	Waste Grinder	Ice Maker	Arm / Leg Bath	Immersion Bath	Glass Washer	Infant Bathtub
Public/Staff Restrooms	●	●	●	●	●	●									●												
Staff Lounge	●	●	●		●		●																●				
Patient Rooms	●		●	●																	●						
Isolation Rooms	●		●	●																	●						
Nurse Stations							●																				
Nursery			●																								●
Formula Room			●				●																			●	
Intensive-Care Room	●		●							●																	
Outpatient-Services Area	●		●		●										●												
Emergency Rooms	●		●		●				●		●																
Exam/Treatment Room	●		●				●																				
Labor Room	●		●	●																							
Janitor's Closet			●			●									●												
Clean Linen Holding							●																				
Soiled Linen Holding								●	●																		
Nourishment Station			●				●																●				
Patient Bathing Area	●		●	●											●				●								
Critical-Care Area	●		●			●									●					●							
Pharmacy							●																				
Surgical Scrub-up										●																	
Anesthesia Workroom							●																				
Surgical Supply Services								●																			
Surgical Cleanup Room									●																		
Doctors' Locker Room	●	●	●	●																							
Nurses' Locker Room	●		●	●																							
Recovery Room			●						●												●						
Fracture Room			●										●														
Cleanup/Utility Room			●				●		●												●						
Sub-Sterilizing Room							●																				
Medical Laboratory	●	●	●		●	●	●							●	●		●	●								●	
Physical Therapy Room	●		●				●								●					●				●	●		
Cystoscopic Room	●		●	●					●							●					●						
Autopsy Room	●		●	●		●	●		●							●					●						
Dietary Services	●	●	●			●	●	●				●			●							●	●				
Laundry Facility	●		●								●				●												
Family Waiting Room	●		●		●																						

is always required. In addition to the local codes, it is necessary for the plumbing engineer to refer to the special hospital code requirements published by the local hospital authorities, the state hospital or health-department authorities, the Joint Commission for the Accreditation of Hospitals Organization (JCAHO), and the US Department of Health and Human Services. The architect may investigate these special requirements; however, the plumbing designer must be familiar with them since they contain many other applicable requirements (in addition to the table indicating the plumbing fixtures necessary for a particular installation).

General Requirements

Plumbing fixtures in health-care facilities should be of dense, impervious materials having smooth surfaces. Plumbing fixtures of vitreous china, enameled cast iron, and stainless steel are commonly used. Fixture brass—including faucets, traps, strainers, escutcheons, stops, and supplies—should be chromium plated in a manner approved by the administrative authority. Die-cast metals should not be used. Faucets should have a laminar flow device (no alternative) of brass, Monel metal, or stainless-steel trim. Each plumbing fixture in health-care facilities should be provided with individual stop valves. Each water-service main, branch main, and riser shall have valves. Access shall be provided at all valves. All submerged inlets, faucets with hose adapters, and flush valves must be equipped with approved vacuum breakers. Backflow-prevention devices shall be installed on hose bibbs, supply nozzles used for the connection of hoses or tubing, and at other locations where the potable water supply must be protected from contamination.

All plumbing fixtures, faucets, piping, solder, and fluxes used in potential drinking-water areas should comply with the latest maximum lead content regulations. Facilities for the physically challenged shall be in compliance with the Americans with Disabilities Act (ADA) accessibility guidelines.

Fixtures for Specific Health-Care Areas

General-use staff and public areas

Water closets Vitreous china, siphon-jet water closet with elongated bowl design with open-front seat, less cover, should be specified. Wall-hung water closets are preferred for easy cleaning; however, floor-set models are also acceptable by most local jurisdictions. All water closets should be operated by water-saver flush valves.

Lavatories and sinks Vitreous china, enameled cast iron or stainless-steel lavatories and sinks should be specified. The most commonly specified size is 20 × 18 × 7½ in. deep (508 × 457.2 × 190.5 mm deep). Hands-free controls (foot or knee controls) are generally employed for staff use and for scrub-up sinks. In public areas, codes should be checked for the requirement of self-closing valves and/or metered valves. Stops should be provided for all supply lines. Aerators are not permitted; use laminar flow devices. Insulated and/or offset p-traps should be used for handicapped fixtures.

Faucets Valves should be operable without hands, i.e., with wrist blades or foot controls or electronically. If wrist blades are used, blade handles used by the medical and nursing staff, patients, and food handlers shall not exceed 4½ in. (11.43 cm) in length. Handles on scrub sinks and clinical sinks shall be at least 6 in. (15.24 cm) long. Water spigots used in lavatories and sinks shall have clearances adequate to avoid contaminating utensils and the contents of carafes, etc.

Urinals Vitreous china wall-hung urinals with flush valves. Flush valves should be equipped with stops and may be of the exposed or concealed design.

Showers The shower enclosures and floor specified by the plumbing engineer may be constructed of masonry and tile or of prefabricated fiberglass. Showers and tubs shall have nonslip walking surfaces. The shower valve should automatically compensate for variations in the water-supply pressure and temperature to deliver the discharge water at a set temperature that will prevent scaldings.

Drinking fountains and water coolers Drinking fountains are available in vitreous china, steel and stainless steel. Units for exterior installations are available in suitable materials. Refrigerated water coolers are available in steel or stainless steel. All of these materials are acceptable by most local administrative authorities. These units may be of the surface-mounted, semi-recessed or fully-recessed design.

Chilled water for drinking purposes should be provided between 45 and 50°F (7.2 and 10.0°C) and obtained by chilling water with a refrigeration compressor. The compressor may be enclosed in a cabinet with the dispenser (water cooler), installed in a wall cavity behind a grill adjacent to the dispenser, or remotely located for single or multiple dispensers. A remotely installed unit for multiple dispensers (central system) should have a recirculation system.

Mop-service basins Floor-mounted mop-service basins can be obtained in precast or (terazzo) molded-stone units of various sizes. The plumbing engineer should specify the most suitable model. Rim guards are normally provided to protect the rims from damage and wall guards are provided to protect walls from splashing and chemical stains. The water-supply fixture is usually a two-handle mixing faucet mounted on the wall with a wall brace, vacuum breaker, and hose adapter.

Floor drains Floor drains in toilet rooms are optional in most cases; however, there are many instances where the floor drains are required by the applicable codes. The plumbing designer should give consideration to maintaining a trap seal in the floor drain through the use of deep-seal p-traps and/or trap primers. Floor drains shall not be installed in operating and delivery rooms.

Patient rooms These rooms (private or semi-private) usually are provided with a toilet room containing a water closet, a lavatory, and a shower or bathtub. (Some hospitals use common shower and bath facilities for a group of patient rooms.) The plumbing fixtures should conform with the following recommendations:

The water closet should be vitreous china, wall-hung or floor-mounted design, with an elongated bowl. All water closets should be operated by a flush valve. Water closets should have open-front seats, less cover. Bedpan lugs and bedpan washers are often required by the local codes. Bedpan-flushing devices shall be provided in each inpatient toilet room; however, installation is optional in psychiatric and alcohol-abuse units, where patients are ambulatory.

The lavatory should be a minimum of 20 × 18 × 7½ in. (508 × 457.2 × 190.5 mm) deep. Lavatories should be installed at least 34 in. (863.6 mm) above the floor. Mixing faucets should be of the

gooseneck-spout design and provided with wrist-blade handles, electronic, or hands-free controls.

The shower is usually constructed of masonry and tile, acrylics, or fiberglass. The shower bases should be nonslip surfaces. The shower valve should automatically compensate for variations in the water-supply pressure and temperature to deliver the discharge water at a set temperature that will prevent scalding. Grab bars, located within the shower enclosure, are usually required by the local codes. The plumbing engineer should always check with the local administrative authority regarding approved designs.

Bathtubs can be constructed of cast iron, fiberglass, acrylics, or steel. Faucets should be as they are for showers. Shower heads may be of the stationary design, but in many locations hand-held showers are required.

A lavatory intended for use by doctors, nurses, and other hospital staff is sometimes required by the local ordinances. This particular lavatory is usually located on the wall near the door with a gooseneck spout and hands-free controls.

A water closet and lavatory, with a fixed or fold-away water closet made of stainless steel, may be considered. This concept, as well as the construction of the unit, must be accepted by the administrative authority.

Ward rooms Ward rooms are infrequently found in health-care facilities, particularly in the private hospital field. These rooms require at least 1 lavatory. This lavatory should be a minimum 20 × 18 in. (508 × 457.2 mm) and made of vitreous china or stainless steel. The faucet should be of the gooseneck-spout design and provided with wrist-blade handles or hands-free controls.

Nurseries The hospital's nursery is usually provided with a minimum size 20 × 18 in. (508 × 457.2 mm) lavatory with hands-free controls and a high gooseneck spout. An infant's bathtub, wall- or counter-mounted with an integral large drainboard and rinsing basin, is provided. Water-supply fittings are filler spouts over the basins with separate hand-valve controls. The spout and the spray are usually supplied and controlled through a thermostatic mixing valve. The ultimate in maintaining a safe water temperature is a separate supply tank.

Intensive-care rooms These rooms usually have utility sinks with hands-free controls with high gooseneck spouts. A water-supply fitting equipped with a gooseneck spout and provision for bedpan washing (either at an immediately adjacent water closet or at a separate bedpan washing station within an enclosure in the room) should be provided. Newer designs have included combination lavatory/water closets for patient use, especially in cardiac-care units.

Emergency (triage) rooms The plumbing fixtures provided in emergency rooms include a utility sink with an integral tray and a water-supply fitting with a gooseneck spout and wrist-blade handles. A vitreous china clinic sink (or a flushing-rim sink), for the disposal of solids, with the water-supply fitting consisting of a flush valve and a separate combination faucet with vacuum breaker mounted on the wall above the plumbing fixture, should also be provided.

Examination and treatment rooms These rooms are usually provided with vitreous china or stainless-steel lavatories. The water-supply fitting should be a hands-free valve equipped with a high, rigid, gooseneck spout. For a particular examination room or a group of patient rooms, an adjacent toilet room is provided containing a specimen-type water closet for inserting a specimen-collecting bedpan. The toilet room also requires a lavatory and a water supply with wrist-blade handles or hands-free controls and with a gooseneck spout.

Physical-therapy treatment rooms The plumbing fixtures and related equipment for these rooms usually include hydrotherapy immersion baths and leg, hip, and arm baths. These units are generally furnished with electric-motor-driven whirlpool equipment. The water is introduced into the stainless-steel tank enclosure by means of a thermostatic control valve to prevent scalding, usually wall mounted adjacent to the bath for operation by a hospital attendant. The water supply should be sized to minimize tub fill time. The immersion baths are usually provided with overhead hoists and canvas slings for facilitating the lifting in and out of the bath of a completely immobile patient. A hydrotherapy shower is sometimes required. These showers usually consist of multiple shower heads, sometimes as many as 12 to 16, vertically mounted in order to direct the streams of water at a standing patient by means of a sophisticated

control console operated by a hospital attendant.

Cystoscopic rooms Among the various plumbing fixtures required in cystoscopic rooms are the following: wall-mounted clinic sinks equipped with flush valves and bedpan washer and combination faucets; lavatories provided with water-supply fittings and gooseneck spouts; and, in a separate adjacent room, specimen water closet and a lavatory. If a floor drain is installed in cystoscopy, it shall contain a nonsplash, horizontal-flow flushing bowl beneath the drain plate.

Autopsy room The autopsy room table is usually provided with cold and hot-water supplies, with a vacuum breaker or backflow preventer, and a waste line. It is necessary that the plumbing designer consult with the table manufacturer and the administrative authority regarding the requirements of the autopsy room table. Drain systems for autopsy tables shall be designed to positively avoid splatter or overflow onto floors or back siphonage and for easy cleaning and trap flushing. The autopsy room is also usually equipped with a stainless steel or vitreous china sink with hands-free fittings, a clinic sink and a "blood" type floor drain. Adjacent to the autopsy room a water closet and a shower room are usually provided. Many autopsy rooms are equipped with waste-disposal units integral with the sink.

Nourishment stations These stations are usually provided on each patient room floor near the nurse station for serving nourishment between regularly scheduled meals. A sink, equipped for hand washing with hands-free controls, an icemaker, and a hot-water dispenser (optional) to provide for the patient's service and treatment should be provided.

Pharmacy and drug rooms The plumbing fixtures for these rooms include medicine and solution sinks. These units can be counter-type or made of stainless steel or vitreous china with a mixing faucet and a swing spout. A solids interceptor should be considered for compounding areas.

Operating-room areas No plumbing fixtures or floor drains are required in the hospital's operating room. However, the scrubbing station located adjacent to the operating room should have at least two scrub sinks, usually made of vitreous china or stainless steel, furnished with hands-free water-supply fittings, and equipped with gooseneck spouts. These sinks should be large and deep enough to allow scrubbing of hands and arms to the elbow. A soiled workroom, designed for the exclusive use of the hospital's surgical staff, should be located near the operating room area. This workroom should contain a vitreous china, flushing-rim clinical sink, for the disposal of solids, with the water-supply fittings consisting of a flush-valve bedpan washer and a separate faucet mounted on the wall above the fixture and hand-washing facilities consisting of a vitreous china or stainless-steel lavatory with a gooseneck spout and equipped with wrist-blade handles. Substerile rooms should be equipped with an instrument sterilizer and general-purpose sink. The plumbing designer should consult with the instrument sterilizer manufacturer for any special requirements for the equipment. The general-purpose sink can be countertop-mounted and equipped with a hands-free water-supply fitting with a gooseneck spout.

Recovery rooms The rooms for the post-anesthesia recovery of surgical patients should include a hand-washing facility, such as a vitreous china or stainless-steel lavatory equipped with a gooseneck spout and wrist-blade handles; and a vitreous china, flushing-rim, clinical sink for the disposal of solids, with the water-supply fitting consisting of a flush valve and a separate faucet mounted on the wall above the fixture with a vacuum breaker. A bedpan washer should also be installed next to the clinical sink. The type of bedpan washer will depend upon the hospital's method of washing and sterilizing bedpans.

Birthing rooms Each birthing room should include a vitreous china lavatory provided with a gooseneck spout and wrist-blade handles or hands-free controls. Each labor room should have access to a water closet and a lavatory. A shower should be provided for the labor-room patients. The shower controls, including pressure/thermostatic mixing valve, should be located outside the wet area for use by the hospital's nursing staff. A water closet should be accessible to the shower facility.

Anesthesia workrooms This area is designed for the cleaning, testing, and storing of the anesthesia equipment and should contain a work counter-mounted sink. The sink is usually made of stainless steel. The faucet should be of the gooseneck spout design with wrist-blade handles and/or hands-free controls.

Fracture rooms A large-size, vitreous china plaster, work sink equipped with a combination water-supply fitting and wrist-blade handles, gooseneck spout, and plaster trap on the waste line (located for convenient access) should be provided.

Kitchens and Laundries

The plumbing designer should consult with the architect and the food-service consultant for kitchen equipment utility requirements. Typically, one of these people should provide location and rough-in drawings for all kitchen equipment. Normally required are toilet fixtures for kitchen staff, food preparation sinks, hand-wash sinks, pot and pan-wash sinks, dishwashers, glassware washers, floor drains, hose bibbs, mixing stations, and grease interceptors. Kitchen grease traps shall be located and arranged to permit easy access without the necessity of entering food preparation or storage areas. Grease traps shall be of the capacity required and shall be accessible from outside the building without the necessity of interrupting any services. In dietary areas, floor drains and/or floor sinks shall be of a type that can be easily cleaned by the removal of a cover. Provide floor drains or floor sinks at all "wet" equipment (such as ice machines) and as required for the wet cleaning of floors. The location of floor drains and floor sinks shall be coordinated to avoid conditions where the location of equipment makes the removal of covers for cleaning difficult. Also, the kitchen equipment may require other utility services, such as fuel gas, steam, and condensate.

When considering laundry facilities, the plumbing designer should consult with the architect and the laundry consultant for equipment utility requirements. These facilities require large-capacity washers/extractors and dryers, presses, and folding machines. Waste-water drainage may require lint intercepters. These facilities are prime candidates for heat and water-recovery systems. Also, the laundry equipment may require other utility services, such as fuel gas, steam, and condensate.

The hot-water temperatures required for these areas (100, 140, and 180°F [38, 60, and 82°C]) are discussed in *Data Book*, Volume 2, Chapter 6, "Domestic Water-Heating Systems."

Unique Fixtures

Fixture-unit values for the unique fixtures found in health-care facilities can be found in Table 2-2.

Laboratory Rooms

Laboratory sinks Most of the time architects provide the countertops and sinks, usually made of epoxy or other acid-resistant materials, in their specifications. However, occasionally the plumbing designer is responsible for selecting the laboratory sinks. Laboratory sinks should be acid resistant and can be of stainless steel, stone, or plastic. Laboratory and cup sinks are currently available in epoxy resin, composition stone, natural stone, ceramic or vitreous china, polyester fiberglass, plastic, stainless steel, and lead. The lead type is not recommended where mercury, nitric, hydrochloric or acetic acids are used.

Often these laboratory sinks are furnished with the laboratory equipment as rectangular sinks or cup sinks mounted in, or as part of, counter tops and as cup sinks in fume hoods. Rules of thumb that can be used when the sink sizes are not recommended by the laboratory staff are as follows:

1. Sinks with a compartment size of 12 × 16 × 7.5 in. (304.8 × 406.4 × 190.5 mm) for general laboratory work areas.

2. Sinks with a compartment size of 18 × 24 × 10 in. (457.2 × 609.6 × 254 mm) for classroom work and tests.

3. Sinks with a compartment size of 24 × 36 × 12 in. (609 × 914.4 × 304.8 mm) for washing large equipment.

The sink itself and sink outlet should be chemically resistant, a minimum of 316 stainless steel, and so designed that a stopper or an overflow can be inserted and removed easily. The outlet should be removable and have a strainer to intercept any materials that might cause a stoppage in the line. Unless an industrial water system is employed that isolates the laboratory water systems from the potable water system, via a central backflow-prevention device, all faucets should be provided with vacuum breakers. Supply fittings for distilled or deionized water are usually either virgin plastic or tin lined and, where central systems are used, should be able to withstand higher pressures. Many fitting types, especially PVC, can handle pressures up to but not exceeding 50 psig (344.74 kPa). In these cases, pressure regulation is required.

Cup sinks These are small, 3 × 6 in., 3 × 9 in., or 3 × 11 in. (76.2 × 152.4 mm, 76.2 × 228.6 mm, or 76.6 × 279.4 mm) oval sinks for receiving chemicals, normally from a condensate or a supply line. They are designed to fit into the center section between the table tops; against a wall; or on raised, back ledges. These sinks are also common in fume hoods.

Laboratory glass washers are usually included, either furnished by the laboratory equipment supplier or selected by the plumbing designer. Automatic washers are available. In addition to waste or indirect waste services, these units require hot water (usually 140°F [60°C] boosted to 180°F [82°C]) internal to the unit, distilled or deionized water, and compressed air. Manual-type glass bottle and tube washers may also be required in these rooms. Tube washers may have manifold-type supply fittings using cold water only. The manifolds can be fitted with a number of individually serrated tip outlets provided with separate controls and vacuum breakers.

Emergency showers should be included throughout and located in the adjacent corridors or at the door exits. The showers must be accessible, require no more than 10 s to reach, and be within a travel distance of no greater than 100 ft (30.5 m) from the hazard rooms. The shower head is a deluge-type shower with a 1-in. (25.4 mm) nominal cold water, stay-open design, supply valve operated by a hanging pull rod, or a chain and pull ring, or a pull chain secured to the wall. A floor drain may be provided, if required. If floor drains are provided, trap primers should be incorporated.

Eye and face-wash fountains are also required. These are wall or counter-mounted units with a foot-pedal or wrist-blade-handle-operated, water-supply fixture; double side-mounted, full face-wash outlets; or deck-mounted, hand-held (with hose) face and body-spray units. The latest edition of the ANSI standard for emergency eyewash and shower equipment and local codes should be consulted. A tempered water supply should be considered.

Laboratory service outlets for gas, air, nitrogen, vacuum, and other required gas services may be furnished as part of the related equipment under another contract or may be included

Table 2-2 Hospital Plumbing Fixtures

Fixture	Fixture Units			GPM (L/S)		GPH (L/H)
	Total Water	Cold Water	Hot Water	Cold Water	Hot Water	Hot Water
Aspirator, fluid suction	2	2	—	3 (.19)	—	—
Aspirator, laboratory	2	2	—	3 (.19)	—	—
Autopsy table, complete	4	3	2	8 (.50)	4½ (.28)	20 (75.7)
Autopsy table, aspirator	2	2	—	3 (.19)	—	—
Autopsy table, flushing hose	2	2	—	3 (.19)	—	—
Autopsy table, flushing rim	3	3	—	4½ (.28)	—	—
Autopsy table, sink and faucet	3	2½	2½	4½ (.28)	4½ (.28)	20 (75.7)
Autopsy table, waste disposal	1½	1½	—	4 (.25)	—	—
Bath, arm	4	2	3	3 (.19)	7 (.44)	35 (132.5)
Bath, emergency	4	2	3	3 (.19)	7 (.44)	15 (56.8)
Bath, immersion	20	7	15	15 (.95)	35 (2.21)	450 (1,703.3)
Bath, leg	10	4	7	8 (.50)	16 (1.01)	100 (378.5)
Bath, sitz	4	2	3	3 (.19)	7 (.44)	30 (113.6)
Bed pan, washer, steam	10	10	—	25 (1.58)	—	—
Cleaner, sonic	3	2½	2½	4½ (.28)	4½ (.28)	20 (75.7)
Cuspidor, dental and surgical	1	1	—	2 (.13)	—	—
Cuspidor, dental chair	1	1	—	2 (.13)	—	—
Drinking fountain	1	1	—	2 (.13)	—	—
Floor drain, flushing type	10	10	—	25 (1.58)	—	—
Hose, bed pan general	2	1½	1½	3 (.19)	3 (.19)	5 (18.9)
Hose, bed pan private	1	1	1	3 (.19)	3 (.19)	8 (30.3)
Laundry tub	3	2½	2½	4½ (.28)	4½ (.28)	30 (113.6)
Lavatory, barber	2	1½	1½	3 (.19)	3 (.19)	15 (56.8)
Lavatory, dental	1	1	1	3 (.19)	3 (.19)	8 (30.3)
Lavatory, general	2	1½	1½	3 (.19)	3 (.19)	8 (30.3)
Lavatory, private	1	1	1	3 (.19)	3 (.19)	4 (15.1)
Lavatory, nursery	2	1½	1½	3 (.19)	3 (.19)	8 (30.3)
Lavatory, scrub-up	2	1½	1½	3 (.19)	3 (.19)	10 (37.9)
Lavatory, treatment	1	1	1	3 (.19)	3 (.19)	4 (15.1)
Microscope, electron	1	1	—	0.2 (.01)	—	—
Sanistan	10	10	—	25 (1.58)	—	—
Sanitizer, boiling, instrument	2	—	2	—	3 (.19)	10 (37.9)
Sanitizer, boiling, utensil	2	—	2	—	3 (.19)	10 (37.9)
Shower, general	4	2	3	1½ (.09)	3½ (.22)	50 (189.3)
Shower, private	2	1	2	1½ (.09)	3½ (.22)	20 (75.7)
Shower, obstetrical	4	2	3	1½ (.09)	3½ (.22)	50 (189.3)
Shower, therapeutic	15	6	11	15 (.95)	35 (2.21)	400 (1,514)
Sink, barium	3	2½	2½	4½ (.28)	4½ (.28)	15 (56.8)
Sink, clean-up room	3	2½	2½	4½ (.28)	4½ (.28)	15 (56.8)
Sink, central supply	3	2½	2½	4½ (.28)	4½ (.28)	15 (56.8)
Sink, clinical	10	10	3	25 (1.58)	3 (.19)	10 (37.9)
Sink, clinical, bed pan hose	10	10	4	25 (1.58)	4½ (.28)	15 (56.8)
Sink, floor kitchen	4	3	3	4½ (.28)	4½ (.28)	20 (75.7)
Sink, formula room	4	3	3	4½ (.28)	4½ (.28)	20 (75.7)
Sink, cup	1	1	—	3 (.19)	—	—
Sink, laboratory	2	1½	1½	3 (.19)	3 (.19)	5 (18.9)
Sink, laboratory and trough	3	2½	1½	5 (.32)	3 (.19)	5 (18.9)
Sink, pharmacy	2	1½	1½	3 (.19)	3 (.19)	5 (18.9)
Sink, plaster	4	3	3	4½ (.28)	4½ (.28)	15 (56.8)

in the plumbing work. In either case, the plumbing designer should be knowledgeable about the various types of service outlet currently available, the materials (or construction), and the usage (diversity). It is desirable to have bodies of cast red brass, brass forgings, or brass bar stock that are specially designed for laboratory use and, where possible, made by one manufacturer. Handles should be made of forged brass and provided with screw-in-type, color-coded index discs. All outlets should be properly labeled. Serrated tips should be machined from solid stock or forgings. The service fittings should be chrome plated over nickel plating or copper plating. The outlets in fume hoods should have an acid and solvent-resistant, plastic coating over the chrome-plated surface or be made of acid-resistant materials. Nonmetallic fittings are also available.

Special Equipment

Dialysis machines Dialysis machines require a funnel drain or floor sink and cold-water hose bibb with vacuum breaker.

Heart-and-lung machines Heart-and-lung machines also require a funnel-type drain. If the apparatus is located in the operating room, an indirect waste is required.

Electron microscopes Electron microscopes require filtered, backflow-protected, cold water or circulated chilled water.

Stills Stills for producing distilled water require cold water with a vacuum breaker and floor sinks or funnel drains.

Sterilizers Sterilizers require an acid-resistant floor sink or funnel drains, a backflow-protected water supply and sometimes steam and condensate connections.

Film-processing equipment Film-processing (x-ray) areas require an acid-resistant floor sink or funnel drains for indirect waste; and a hot, cold and/or tempered water supply operating between 40 and 90°F (4.4 and 32.2°C). Drain piping for any photo-developing equipment should not be brass or copper. Polypropylene, high-silica, cast-iron, corrosion-resistant piping and drains should be used. Silver recovery and neutralization may be required; consult with the local authority.

Dental equipment Dental areas should include console services (water, air, medical gas, nitrous oxide and waste); and for oral surgery a separate surgical vacuum system should be provided.

The plumbing engineer should always consult with the equipment manufacturer's authorized representative and the local administrative authority, in order to determine the equipment requirements and the acceptability under the jurisdiction's applicable codes, during the preliminary design.

DRAINAGE SYSTEMS FOR LABORATORIES

In addition to the conventional sanitary drainage systems (those found in most buildings), special sanitary drainage systems may be required in health-care facilities.

Insofar as possible, drainage piping shall not be installed within the ceiling or exposed in operating or delivery rooms, nurseries, food-preparation centers, food-serving facilities, food-storage areas, central services, electronic data-processing areas, electric closets, and other sensitive areas. Where exposed, overhead drain piping in these areas is unavoidable, special provisions shall be made to protect the space below from leakage, condensation, or dust particles.

Acid-Waste Drainage Systems

Acid-waste drainage systems require special design criteria because the corrosive solutions demand special handling from the actual work area to an approved point at which such acid waste (and fumes) can be safely neutralized and discharged. The plumbing engineer must exercise extreme care in this regard.

Acid-resistant waste and vent systems are necessary where acids with a pH lower than 6.5 or alkalis with a pH greater than 8.5 are present. These special conditions are commonly encountered in hospitals, research facilities, and laboratories. Since acid fumes are often more corrosive than the liquid acids themselves, proper drainage and venting is imperative.

Nationally recognized standards for sanitary systems that handle acid wastes and other reagents are set forth in model plumbing codes; such systems are often further regulated by local building and safety or health department requirements. For these reasons, the plumbing engineer should check for all special design conditions that may affect the project.

Strong acids and caustics may enter the sanitary-waste system in large quantities and at elevated temperatures. These substances can mix to form highly corrosive and even dangerous compounds. Common laboratory procedures encourage neutralization or flushing with copious amounts of water in order to dilute and cool these chemicals to more acceptable levels. However, the plumbing engineer must protect the acid-waste system by designing for the maximum hazard conditions that might be brought about by any human error, poor housekeeping, or accidental spillage.

Corrosive-Waste Systems Materials

Borosilicate glass pipe Sizes range from 1½ to 6-in. (40 to 150-mm) pipe. Mechanical joint, flame resistance, and clear pipe allow for easy visual inspection and high corrosion resistance.

High-silicon cast iron Sizes range from 1½ to 4-in. (40 to 100-mm) pipe. Mechanical joint, flame resistance, high corrosion resistance, fire stop at floor penetration equal to cast iron. More fragile and heavier than standard-weight cast iron and easier to break in the field. Excellent application for moderate to high-budget project.

Polypropylene Sizes range from 1½ to 6-in. (40 to 150-mm) pipe. Mechanical or heat-fusion joints. Mechanical joints are not recommended for straight runs or sizes over 2 in. (50 mm); they should be used to access p-traps or other maintenance areas. Flame resistant and acceptable within most jurisdictions (meets 25/50 flame/smoke criteria), newer UL listed methods are close to glass in cost. Consult local authority for approval. Light weight and easy to install. Good application for moderate acids at low temperatures. Must be installed by qualified technicians. Inexpensive compared to borosilicate glass or high-silicone cast iron.

Double-containment waste piping With ever-increasing pressure to protect our environment, double-containment (pipe within a pipe) systems have become a consideration. Usually made of polypropylene inside and PVC or fiberglass outside. Systems should be pitched toward a containment vault for collection of leaking fluid.

Alarm systems can be employed to detect leaks at the collection basin or, if the budget and the nature of the liquid allow, sensors can be installed between the pipe walls that can pinpoint the original leak location. The latter could reduce the amount of excavation or exploration required to find the leak.

Discharge to Sewers

Many local jurisdictions require that the building's sanitary-sewer discharge be at an acceptable pH level before it can be admitted into a sanitary-sewage system. In such cases, it is recommended that a clarifying (or neutralizing) tank be added to the sanitary system. Small ceramic or polypropylene clarifiers with limestone can be located under casework for low flow rates; however, sufficient space must be allowed above the unit for servicing. Unless properly maintained and monitored, this type of system can be rendered ineffective. Large clarifiers and neutralizers may be regulated by the requirements of a local industrial-waste department.

Acidic-Waste Neutralization

The lower the pH number, the higher the concentration of acid. Discharging high concentrations of acid into a public sewer may cause considerable corrosion to piping systems and eventual failure. Most local authorities do not allow acid wastes to be discharged to a public sewer without some form of treatment.

The neutralization of acidic wastes is generally and most economically dealt with through an acid-neutralization tank. An acid-neutralization tank may be constructed of polyethylene, molded stone, stainless steel, or another acid-resistant material. Tanks are sized to provide a dwell time of 2 to 3 h (refer to Table 2-3). Limestone or marble chips fill the interior of the tank, helping to neutralize incoming acid wastes. Chips may be 1 to 3 in. (25.4 to 76.2 mm) in diameter and should have a calcium carbonate content in excess of 90%. A discharge pH sensor and routine maintenance schedule must be provided to ensure that the system operates properly. An example of a neutralization tank is depicted in Figure 2-1.

Acid-Waste Solids Interceptor

As with many sewer systems, it is impossible to control all materials discarded to the drain system. Unless building effluent is controlled, many unwanted items, such as glass fragments and needles, will find their way to the neutralization tank, thereby clogging the limestone or marble chips.

When this happens, replacement of the chips is required. One way to prolong chip life is to install an acid-waste solids interceptor immediately upstream of the neutralization tank, as shown in Figure 2-2, although maintenance of

the interceptor may have to be done quite frequently.

Acid-Waste Metering Detail

Many local authorities require some means of sampling effluent from industrial, institutional, and laboratory buildings. An example of a device used for this purpose is a sampling manhole, depicted in Figure 2-3. This unit is installed as the last component before neutralized acidic wastes or treated industrial wastes are discharged to a public sewer. There are as many types of sampling point requirements as there are municipal

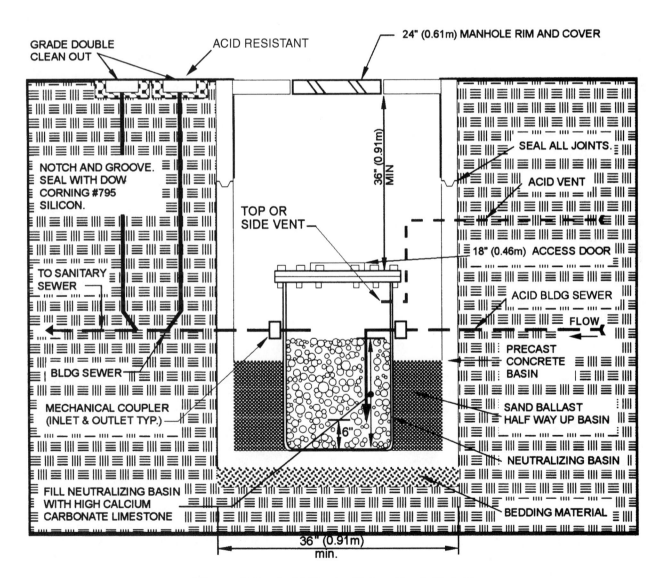

Figure 2-1 Acid-Neutralizing Tank Detail

Table 2-3　Acidic-Waste Neutralization Tank Sizing Table

Number of Lab Sinks	Tank Size, gal (L)	
2	5	(18.9)
4	15	(56.8)
8	30	(113.6)
16	55	(208.2)
22	75	(283.9)
27	90	(340.7)
30	108	(408.8)
40	150	(567.8)
50	175	(662.4)
60	200	(757.0)
75	275	(1 040.9)
110	360	(1 362.6)
150	500	(1 898.5)
175	550	(2 081.8)
200	650	(2 460.3)
300	1200	(4 542)
500	2000	(7 570)
600	3000	(11 355)

Note: For commercial and industrial laboratories, the number of lab sinks should be multiplied by a 0.5 use factor.

sewer authorities. Consult local code authorities for individual requirements.

Traps for Laboratory Sinks

The trap is recognized by most plumbing engineers as the weakest link in the acid-waste system. The trap must be acid resistant. If strong acids and solvents collect in an ordinary trap, failure of the system will occur. Three types of acid-waste traps are currently in common use: p-traps, drum traps, and centrifugal drum traps. (Running and s-traps are not allowed by many local plumbing codes because of the potential for trap siphoning.)

1. *P-traps* maintain a water seal to keep the acid fumes from reentering the work area.

2. *Drum traps* provide a greater water seal and are frequently used to separate either precious metals or other matter before they enter the drainage system to become lost or cause a stoppage in the sink. Drum traps with removable bottoms should be installed high

enough above the floor for servicing. P-traps, including some of the simple drum traps, can easily be back-siphoned if the head pressures are extreme.

3. *Centrifugal drum traps* are designed to prevent back-siphonage conditions.

Laboratory Waste and Vent Piping

Sizing for under-table waste and vent piping, as determined by the local plumbing codes, should be suitable for the installation and allow for future expansion. Approved corrosion-resistant piping should be used for vent piping as well, since acid fumes are also highly corrosive. Space is often limited under tables and in vent areas. The space-saving features of mechanical joint piping have proven to be useful in many installations.

Note: When fusion-joint, plastic piping systems are used, mechanical joints should be installed at traps and trap arms for maintenance reasons.

Special island (or loop) venting is frequently used when cabinets or work tables are located in the center of the laboratory area.

The transportating of acid waste, above and below the ground, must be done in approved, corrosion-resistant piping (acceptable to the local administrative authority) and continued to a suitable point where neutralization can occur or where sufficient water or chemicals can be introduced to bring the pH level of the solution to an acceptable level. Acids below a pH of 6.5 normally may not be admitted into the sanitary-sewage system or emitted into surrounding soil, polluting (or degenerating) local ground water. High-silicon cast iron with hub-and-spigot joints may be caulked with teflon, or neoprene gaskets may be used for sealing. This type of joint will allow flexibility and, when properly supported, is particularly recommended on the horizontal runs where the expansion and contraction of pipe from heated chemicals can cause leaking. Plumbing codes require proper bed preparation and careful backfilling on all below-ground piping, particularly plastic piping.

The plumbing engineer should check the manufacturer's recommendations in order to evaluate the severity of the chemicals to be used. A listing of the common chemicals and how these substances react with the various materials must be considered by the designer.

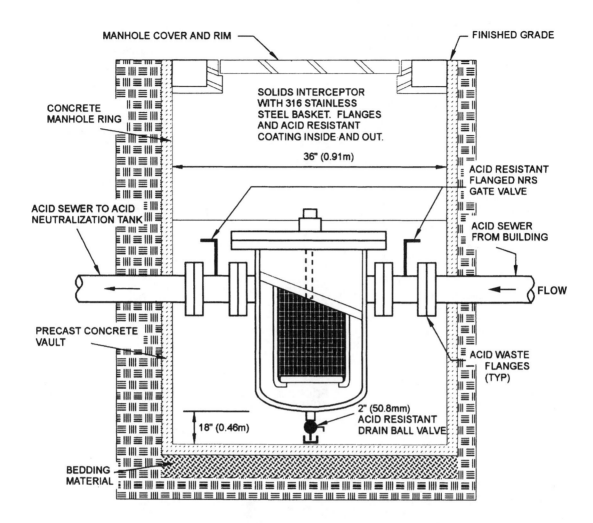

Figure 2-2   Acid-Waste Solids Interceptor Detail

WATER-SUPPLY SYSTEMS

A domestic-water supply of adequate flow volume and pressure must be provided for all the plumbing fixtures and related equipment. Systems typically encountered in these types of facility are as follows:

1. Potable-water systems.

   A. Cold water.

   B. Hot water (at various temperatures).

   C. Chilled water.

   D. Controlled-temperature (tempered) water.

   E. Hot water recirculation.

2. Non-potable water systems.

3. Pure-water systems.

   A. Distilled water.

   B. Deionized (or demineralized) water.

   C. Reverse osmosis.

Health-care facilities should have dual domestic-water services installed to ensure provision of an uninterrupted supply of water. The design should consider water-conservation provisions. Many local jurisdictions have strict water-conservation laws in effect. Water recycling may be a consideration for use in landscaping,

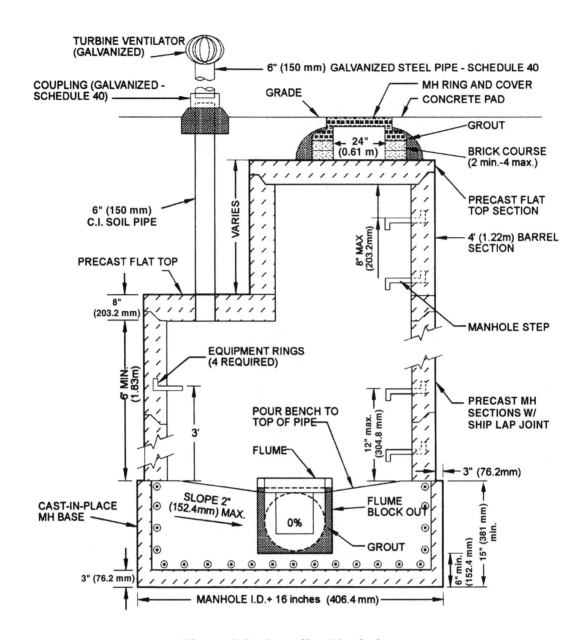

Figure 2-3   Sampling Manhole

etc., depending on local code and health-department regulations. (For more information, see *Data Book*, Volume 2, Chapter 2, "Gray-Water Systems.")

Water supply through a tank (suction or gravity type) should be considered by the plumbing engineer when the water-supply source may be subjected to some unusual demands, pressure fluctuations, and/or interruptions that will cause a sudden excessive draw and pressure loss on the main system. The tank will act as a buffer. Inadequate flow and pressure require the design of a water-storage tank and/or a booster pump for the water-supply system. Excessive pressure fluctuations are highly undesirable in medical-research laboratories. When such facilities are supplied from street pressure systems, the engineer may provide pressure-reducing valves on the branch lines, or a gravity tank system.

Use of diversity factors for sizing the water systems must be carefully analyzed by the designer. Medical-school laboratory classrooms have higher rates of simultaneous use than most research laboratories. Emergency rooms, out-patient treatment rooms, and operating-room wash-up areas also have high rates of simultaneous use.

Extreme care must be taken in order to protect the potable-water supply from contamination (cross connection). When an industrial (non-potable) system is not present, the engineer should specify the appropriate type of vacuum breakers (necessary for each fixture below the rim connection), hose-end outlet, and an aspirator or other serrated-tip laboratory outlet, whether they are required by the local plumbing regulations or not. The vacuum breakers provided for fume-hood outlets should be located outside the hood. Built-in (or integral) vacuum breakers are preferred to the hose-end type units.

Potable-Water Systems

Cold water should be provided at all required locations. The hot water should be generated with the most economical heating medium available.

With today's technology, several reliable methods can be applied to produce and store domestic hot water. Refer to ASPE's *Domestic Water Heating Design Manual* and *ASPE Data Book* Volume 2, Chapter 6, "Domestic Water-Heating Systems," for in-depth explanations of design methods for hot-water systems and a discussion of the various hot-water systems available. When large "dump" loads are anticipated (kitchens and laundries), storage of hot water is recommended. Hot-water usage in patient-care areas requires consideration of water temperature and bacterial growth. The most common water-borne bacterium of concern is Legionella pneumophila.

Recommended water temperatures for specific applications are as follows:

1. Patient-care and hospital general usage requires water temperatures between 105 and 120°F (40.5 and 49°C), except where the local plumbing codes or other regulations require other maximum temperatures. Hot-water distribution systems serving patient-care areas shall be under constant recirculation to provide continuous hot water at each hot-water outlet. The temperature of hot water for bathing fixtures and hand-wash lavatories shall be appropriate for comfortable use but shall not exceed 120°F (49°C).

2. Kitchen general usage requires 140°F (60°C) to fixtures, except the dishwasher's sanitizing cycle. The sanitizing cycle requires 180 to 190°F (82 to 88°C) to the dishwasher, with 180°F (82°C) minimum required at the dish rack. (Consult local health-department regulations.) Also, some health departments set a maximum temperature of 105 to 120°F (40.5 to 49°C) for hand-washing lavatories.

3. Laundry facilities should be supplied with two water temperatures, 140°F (60°C) for general usage and 160°F (71°C) minimum to washers/extractors for laundry sterilizations.

Providing a point-of-use booster heater for high-temperature applications instead of a central water-heater system is often more economical.

A closed system of chilled water may be required for the cooling of electron microscopes and x-ray tubes and should be of a recirculating design.

Film processors operate at a normal range of 40 to 30°F (4.4 to –1.1°C). Some models do require controlled water temperature for film processing. Depending on the quality of the water supply, a 5 to 75-µ filter may be required.

A thermometer should also be provided on the outlets of water heaters and thermostatically controlled valves. A pressure regulator, gauge, and flow meter may also be desired on the inlet side of pressure-sensitive equipment.

Non-Potable Water Systems

Non-potable water systems are usually employed in areas having multiple water requirements that could contaminate the potable-water supply. Areas in this category include: flushing-rim floor drains in animal rooms, all outlets in autopsy rooms, outlets in isolation rooms, and all outlets in infectious-disease and tissue-culture rooms. These systems normally use reduced-pressure-type backflow preventers as the means to protect the potable-water system. Hot water, when required, may be provided by a separate generator supplied from the non-potable water system.

Pure-Water Systems

"Pure water" is the term generally used to describe water that is free from particulate matters, minerals (soluble ions), bacteria, pyrogens, organic matters, and dissolved gases, which frequently exist in the potable water supply. Pure-water systems are usually required in the hospital's pharmacy, central-supply room, laboratories, and laboratory-glassware washing facilities.

There are two basic types of pure water available in hospital facilities: bio-pure water (water containing no bugs or other life forms) and high-purity water (pure water that is free from minerals, dissolved gases, and most particulate matters). Refer to *ASPE Data Book,* Volume 2, Chapter 11, "Water Treatment, Conditioning, and Purification," for additional information on water purity.

Water purity is most easily measured as specific resistance (in ohm-centimeter [Ω-cm] units) or expressed as parts per million (ppm) of an ionized salt (NaCl). The theoretical maximum specific resistance of the pure water is given as 18.3 MΩ-cm at 77°F (25°C). This water purity is difficult to produce, store, and distribute. This water is "starved" for impurities and constantly attempts to absorb contaminants. It is important to note that the specific resistance of the pure water is indicative only of its mineral contents and in no way shows the level of bacterial, pyrogenic, or organic contamination. An independent laboratory analysis should be made, whenever possible.

The five basic methods of producing pure water are as follows: distillation, demineralization, reverse osmosis, filtration, and recirculation. Depending upon the type of pure water required in the facility, one (or more) of these methods will be needed. Under certain conditions, a combination of several methods may be necessary.

1. *Distillation* produces bio-pure water, which is completely free from particulate matters, minerals, organics, bacteria, pyrogens, and most of the dissolved gases and has a minimum specific resistance of 300,000 Ω. An important consideration in this case is that the water is free from bacteria and pyrogen contamination, which is dangerous to the patients, particularly where intravenous solutions are concerned. Bio-pure water is needed in the hospital's pharmacy, central-

supply room, and other areas where there may be patient contact. Bio-pure water may also be desired in certain specific laboratories at the owner's request and as a final rinse in the laboratory's glassware washer.

The typical water-distillation apparatus consists of an evaporator section, an internal baffle system, a water-cooled condenser, and a storage tank. The best material for its construction is a pure block-tin coating for both the still and the tank. The heat sources, in order of preference based on economy and maintenance, are as follows: steam, gas, and electricity. The still may be operated manually or automatically. The distilled water may be distributed from the storage tank by gravity or by a pump. A drain is required for system drainage and flushing. On stills larger than 50 gph (189.3 L/h), a cooling tower should be considered for the condenser water.

2. *Demineralization,* sometimes called "deionization," produces high-purity water that is completely free from minerals, most particulate matters, and dissolved gases. Depending upon the equipment used, it can have a specific resistance ranging from 50,000 Ω to nearly 18 MΩ. However, it could be contaminated with bacteria, pyrogens, and organics (these contaminants may be produced inside the demineralizer itself). Demineralized water can be employed in most laboratories, the laboratory's glass-washing facilities (as a final rinse) and as the pre-treatment for still feedwater.

The typical demineralizer apparatus consists of either a two-bed deionizing unit (with a resistivity range of 50,000 Ω to 1 MΩ) or a mixed-bed deionizing unit (with a resistivity range of 1 to 18 MΩ). The columns are of an inert material filled with a synthetic resin, which removes the minerals by an ionization process. Since the unit operates on pressure, a storage tank is not required or recommended (as bacteria will grow in it). A demineralizer must be chemically regenerated periodically, and during that regeneration time no pure water is produced. If a continuous supply of pure water is needed, a backup unit should be considered by the engineer, as the regeneration process takes several hours. The regeneration process can be done manually or automatically. An atmospheric, chemical-resistant drain is required. High-flow water is required for backwash during the regeneration.

3. *Reverse osmosis (RO)* produces a high-purity water that does not have the high resistivity of demineralized water and is not bio-pure. Under certain conditions an RO process can offer economic advantages over demineralized water. In areas that have high mineral contents, an RO process can be used as a pre-treatment for a demineralizer or still.

   There are several types of reverse osmosis units currently available. Units consist of a semipermeable membrane, in either a roll form or a tube containing numerous hollow fibers. The water is then forced through the semipermeable membrane under high pressure. A drain is required with these systems.

   Note: Chlorine must be removed from the water, otherwise it will destroy the RO membrane.

4. *Filtration* Various types of filter are currently available to remove the particulate matters from the water as a pre-treatment. Depending upon the type of filter, a drain may be required. Bacteria may be eliminated through ultraviolet sterilization.

5. *Recirculation* High-purity systems should be provided with a circulation loop. Dead-end legs should be avoided whenever possible or limited to 50 in. (1.52 m). System design velocity should be between 4 and 7 fps (1.22 and 2.13 m/s) so as to discourage bacteria accumulation and provide transport back to an ultraviolet sterilizer and filtration for removal.

Pure-water piping system materials Water-treatment system components are selected to remove various impurities from the influent water. Connecting various system components together involves the use of interconnecting piping. The use of this piping should not contribute to adding any such impurity back into the treated water.

Selection of piping-system materials is determined by the application intended, the availability of the material, and the cost of the material. Pure-water applications, such as exist in the health-care industry, can be very sensitive to the piping methods selected.

General pure-water piping requirements include:

1. Inert materials—must not leach contamination into water.

2. Clean joining methods—avoid solvents, lubricants, and crevices.

3. No material erosion—must not flake off particles.

4. Material should not enhance microorganism growth.

5. Material should be smooth, crack and crevice-free, and nonporous.

6. Avoid dead legs—system should have continuous flow through piping.

7. Provide chemical cleaning connections.

8. Install (slope) with future cleaning and disinfection in mind.

A wide variety of piping materials are available on the market today. Their properties and cost cover a wide range.

Common pure-water materials

1. Stainless steel—various grades (304L & 316L).

2. Aluminum.

3. Tin-lined copper.

4. Glass or glass-lined pipe.

5. PVC/CPVC—Polyvinyl chloride/chlorinated polyvinyl chloride.

6. Polypropylene.

7. Polyethylene.

8. ABS—Acrylonitrile butadiene styrene.

9. PVDF—Polyvinylidene fluoride.

Metal pipe Aluminum, tin-lined copper, and stainless-steel pipe have all been used in pure-water treatment systems. Tin-lined pipe was once the material of choice in ultra-pure water systems. However, it does leach tin and eventually copper into the process fluid. Methods of joining tin-lined pipe can also leave non-smooth joints with crevices.

Aluminum pipe has also been used in pure-water systems. Pure water creates an oxide layer inside the pipe that continually erodes, producing particles and aluminum in the water.

Stainless steel has been used extensively in high-purity water systems. It can be joined with threads, butt welded, flanged, or manufactured with sanitary-type connection ends. Because it can use sanitary joints and can handle steam sterilizing, the sanitary-type connection method has been used in many pharmaceutical applications. However, experience has shown that even the best grades of stainless steel, with the best joints, still leach material from the metal that can cause problems in critical water systems.

Glass or glass-lined pipe Glass piping has been used in some special laboratory applications but, because it is fragile and does leach material into the water, it is not generally considered applicable for high-purity water systems.

PVC PVC pipe has been used on equipment and in piping systems successfully for many years. Advances in technology, especially in electronics, have now raised questions about the "true purity" or inertness of PVC.

PVC pipe contains color pigments, plasticizers, stabilizers, and antioxidants that can all leach out of the plastic and into ultra-pure water. Remember that 18,000,000-Ω quality water is highly aggressive. When PVC pipe is made (extruded), bubbles of air exist, some of which are covered over with a thin film of PVC on the interior walls of the pipe. As the pipe ages, these thin coverings wear away, exposing small holes which then serve as debris-collecting or micro-organism-breeding sites, not to mention the contribution of PVC particles and the potential release of organic dispersants, stabilizers, etc., originally trapped in these bubbles (holes).

Joints, either solvent welded or threaded, can leave crevices for the accumulation of particles and bacteria. Solvents from the weld can also leach into the water.

Premium grades of PVC, which reportedly have fewer leachables than standard PVC, are now being marketed.

CPVC is a special high-temperature PVC that has similar erosion and leachable characteristics.

Polypropylene Polypropylene is a very inert, strong piping material. However, in the manufacture of the pipe antioxidants and other additives are used to control embrittlement. These additives are potential sources of contaminants that can leach into the water. However, a virgin material with no leachable products is now available.

Polypropylene pipe shows good ability to withstand both corrosive chemicals and high temperatures, up to 220°F (104°C). The natural toughness of the material minimizes damage to pipe during installation and service.

Polypropylene is generally joined by the butt-fusion method, resulting in smooth joints.

ABS Acrylonitrile butadiene styrene (ABS) plastic pipe has been used in the primary stages of water-treatment systems because of relatively low cost and ease of installation.

ABS has some of the same contamination leach problems as PVC. In its manufacture, pigment dispersants, surfactants, styrene, and other additives are used that can leach into water over time. Hydrogen peroxide (used for system cleaning) will also attack ABS plastic.

PVDF There are numerous types of high-molecular-weight fluorocarbon pipes on the market, SYGEF, KYNAR, and HALAR, to name a few. Polyvinylidene fluoride (PVDF) plastic can be extruded without the use of additives that can leach out later. The different polymerization techniques used by each manufacturer can produce slightly different properties.

PVDF pipe is currently considered to be the state of the art in pure-water piping systems. It has exceptional chemical resistance; temperature range, –40 to 320°F (–40 to 160°C); impact strength; resistance to UV degradation; abrasion resistance; and smooth, clean, inside surfaces that discourage the collection of bacteria and particles. Most laboratory test reports show virtually zero leachables from PVDF piping systems.

PVDF pipe is joined by the butt-fusion method, resulting in clean, smooth joints.

When system pressures exceed 70 psig (482.6 kPa) or temperatures exceed 75°F (24°C), plastic piping system manufacturers should be consulted for compatibility. Polypropylene or PVDF-lined metal piping systems may be incorporated to meet pressures up to 150 psig (1034.2 kPa).

MEDICAL-GAS AND VACUUM SYSTEMS

General

Health care is in a constant state of change, which forces the plumbing engineer to keep up with new technology to provide innovative approaches to the design of medical-gas systems. In designing medical-gas and vacuum systems, the goal is to provide a safe and sufficient flow at required pressures to the medical-gas outlet or inlet terminals served. System design and layout should allow convenient access by the medical staff to outlet/inlet terminals, valves, and equipment during patient care or emergencies.

This section focuses on design parameters and current standards required for the design of nonflammable medical-gas and vacuum systems used in therapeutic and anesthetic care. The plumbing engineer must determine the needs of the health-care staff. Try to work closely with the medical staff to seek answers to the following fundamental design questions at the start of a project:

1. How many outlet/inlets are requested by staff?

2. How many outlet/inlets are required?

3. Based on current conditions, how often is the outlet/inlet used?

4. Based on current conditions, what is the average duration of use for each outlet/inlet?

5. What is the proper usage (diversity) factor to be used?

Medical-Gas System Design Checklist

As any hospital facility must be specially designed to meet the applicable local code requirements and the health-care needs of the community it serves, the medical-gas and vacuum piping systems must also be designed to meet the specific requirements of each hospital.

Following are the essential steps to a well-designed and functional medical-gas piped system, which are recommended to the plumbing engineer:

1. Analyze each specific area of the health-care facility to determine the following items:

   A. Which piped medical-gas systems are required?

   B. How many of each different type of medical-gas outlet/inlet terminal are required?

   C. Where should the outlet/inlet terminals be located for maximum efficiency and convenience?

   D. Which type and style of outlet/inlet terminal best meet the needs of the medical staff?

2. Anticipate any building expansion and plan in which direction the expansion will take place (vertically or horizontally). Determine how the medical-gas system should be sized and valved in order to accommodate the future expansion.

3. Determine locations for the various medical-gas supply sources.

   A. Bulk oxygen (O_2).

   B. High-pressure cylinder manifolds (O_2, N_2O or N_2).

   C. Vacuum pumps (VAC).

   D. Medical-air compressors (MA).

4. Prepare the schematic piping layout locating the following:

   A. Zone valves.

   B. Isolation valves.

   C. Master alarms.

   D. Area alarms.

5. Calculate the anticipated peak demands for each medical-gas system. Appropriately size each particular section so as to avoid exceeding the maximum pressure drops allowed.

6. Size and select the various medical-gas and vacuum supply equipment that will handle the peak demands for each system, including future expansions. If this project is an addition to an existing facility, determine the following:

   A. What medical gases are currently provided and what are the locations and number of the stations?

   B. Can the current gas supplier (or the hospital's purchasing department) furnish the consumption records?

   C. Are the capacities of the existing medical-gas supply systems adequate to handle the additional demand?

D. Are any existing systems valved that could be used for an extension? Are the existing pipe sizes adequate to handle the anticipated additional loads?

E. What type of equipment is in use and who is the manufacturer? Is this equipment state-of-the-art?

F. Is it feasible to manifold the new and existing equipment?

G. What is the physical condition of the existing equipment?

H. Is there adequate space available for the new medical-gas supply systems and related equipment at the existing location?

I. Is existing equipment scheduled to be replaced? (A maintenance history of the existing equipment may help in this determination.)

Number of Stations

The first step is to locate and count the outlet/inlets, often called "stations," for each respective medical-gas system. This is usually done by consulting a program prepared by the facility planner or architect. This program is a list of all the rooms and areas in the facility and the services that are required in each. If a program has not been prepared, the floor plans for the proposed facility shall be used.

There is no code that specifically mandates the exact number of stations that must be provided in various areas or rooms for all health-care facilities. In fact, there is no clear consensus of opinion among medical authorities or design professionals as to how many stations are actually required in the facility areas. Guidelines are published by the American Institute of Architects (AIA), National Fire Protection Association (NFPA), and ASPE that recommend the minimum number of stations for various services in specific areas.

The most often-used recommendations in determining the number of stations for hospitals are those necessary to be accredited by the Joint Commission for the Accreditation of Hospitals Organization (JCAHO). Accreditation is required for Medicare and Medicaid compensation. The JCAHO publishes a manual that refers to the AIA

guidelines for the minimum number of stations for oxygen, medical air, and vacuum that must be installed in order to obtain accreditation. If this is a factor for the facility, these requirements are mandatory. Other jurisdictions, such as state or local authorities, may require plans to be approved by local health or building officials. These approvals may require adhering to the state or local requirements and/or NFPA 99, *Health-Care Facilities*.

If accreditation or the approval of authorities is not a factor, the number and area locations of stations are not mandated. The actual count then will depend upon requirements determined by each individual facility or another member of the design team using both past experience and anticipated future use, often using the guideline recommendations as a starting point. Table 2-4 provides those recommendations.

Medical-Gas Flow Rates

Each station must provide a minimum flow rate for the proper functioning of connected equipment under design and emergency conditions. The flow rates and diversity factors vary for individual stations in each system depending on the total number of outlets and the type of care provided.

The flow rate from the total number of outlets, without regard for any diversity, is called the "total connected load." If the total connected load were used for sizing purposes, the result would be a vastly oversized system, since not all of the stations in the facility will be used at the same time. A diversity, or simultaneous-use factor, is used to allow for the fact that not all of the stations will be used at once. It is used to reduce the system flow rate in conjunction with the total connected load for sizing mains and branch piping to all parts of the distribution system. This factor varies for different areas throughout any facility.

The estimated flow rate and diversity factors for various systems, area stations, and pieces of equipment are found in Tables 2-5, 2-6, and 2-7.

Total demand for medical-gas systems varies as a function of time of day, month, patient-care requirements, and facility type. The number of stations needed for patient care is subjective and cannot be qualified based on physical measurements. Knowing the types of patient care and/or authority requirements will

Table 2-4   Inlet /Outlet Station Data

Room	O$_2$	VAC	N$_2$O	Air	N$_2$	EVAC	Typical Uses
Anesthesia workroom	1	1	a	1			Equipment repair testing
Animal oper. (research surgery)	1	1	a				Animal anesthesia and surgery
Animal research lab	1	1		1			Routine animal care
Autopsy	1	1					Suction waste materials from body
Bed holding	1	1					Cardiac arrest, O$_2$ therapy
Biochemistry	b	1		1			Standard lab use[a]
Biochem. lab	b	1		1			Standard lab use[a]
Biophysics / biochemical	b	1		1			Standard lab use[a]
Blood processing		1		1			Standard lab use[a]
Blood receiving (blood donors)	1	1		1			Emergency use
Cardiac catheterization room	1	2					Cardiac arrest and other emergencies
Chem analysis lab (sm. lab in hosp.)		1		1			Standard lab use[a]
Chemical lab		1		1			Standard lab use[a]
Cystoscopy	1	3				1	Emergency use
Decontamination room (attached to inhalation therapy dept.)	1	1		1			Equipment testilng
Deep therapy	1	2					Cardiac arrest and other emergencies
Demonstration room (in-service training)	1	1					Demo. equip. to new empl. & students
Dental repair	1	1		1	b		Power drills (dental)
Dispensary (minor surgery, first aid, student health & exams)	a			a			Emergency use
Ear-nose-throat exam	1	1		1			Aspiration; topical spray
ECG (electrocardiogram)	1	1					Cardiac arrest and other emergencies
EEG (electro-encephalograms)	1	1					Cardiac arrest and other emergencies
Electron microscopy	1	1		1			Standard lab use[a]
Emergency room	1	2		1			Cardiac arrest and other emergencies
EMG (electromyogram)	1	1					Cardiac arrest and other emergencies
Examination room	1	1		1			Drive air tools and vacuum cleaning
Exam room and proctoscopic	1	1		1			Cardiac arrest and other emergencies
Experimental lab	b	1		1			Standard lab use[a]
Eye examination	1	1					Stock and cardiac arrest
Fluoroscopy (x-ray)	1	2					Cardiac arrest and other emergencies
Heart catheterization lab	1	1		1			Cardiac arrest and other emerg. respir.
Hematology	1	1		1			Standard lab use[a]
Intensive-care areas	2	3		1			For critically ill
Isolation (infectious & contagious diseases)	1	1		1			Patient care
Isolation room (patient room for contagious diseases)	1	2		1			Oral, gastric or thoracic
Lab annex		1		1			Pull waste evac. tubing drying apparatus
Lab cleanup area		1		1			Drying glassware
Lab—workroom		1		1			Standard lab use[a]

(Continued)

(Table 2-4 continued)

Room	O$_2$	VAC	N$_2$O	Air	N$_2$	EVAC	Typical Uses
Labor rooms—O.B.	1	1	a				Analgesia, patient care
Linear accelerator vault	1	1		1			
Microbiology		1		1			Standard lab use[a]
Microbiology lab—constant temp room		1		1	b		Standard lab use[a]
Multi-service room	1	1					Cardiac arrest and other emergencies
Neurological pharmacy teaching lab	1		1				Standard lab use[a]
Neurological physiology teaching lab	1	1		1			Standard lab use[a]
Nursery (full-term)	1	2		1			Incubators, respirators
Nursing floor	1	2		1			Therapy, oral, gastric; IPPB, aerosols
Nursing, security (psychiatric violent patients use lock box)	1	1		1			Patient care
Observation	1	1					Cardiac arrest and other emergencies
Obstetrics (delivery room)	1	3	a				Analgesia, anesthesia, patient care
Operating room (surgery—major and minor	2	3	1	1	a	1	Patient care
Oral lab (dental)	a	1	a	1	a		Standard lab use[a]
Orthopedic exam room	1	1					Cardiac arrest and other emergencies
Pathology (Drs. office special lab tests)		1		1			Standard lab use[a]
Patient room	1	1		1			Patient care
Pharma. room (drug prep.)		1		1			Standard lab use[a]
Physiology lab—general	1	1		1			Standard lab use[a] plus teaching
Premature nursery and obs.	2	1		1			Incubators—respirators
Radiation, low-level (x-ray dept.)	1	2		1			Cardiac arrest and other emergencies
Radio-chemical lab		1		1			Standard lab use[a]
Radioisotope, high level (x-ray dept.)	1	2		1			Cardiac arrest and other emergencies
Radioisotope room (research room for animal lab)		1		1			Standard lab use[a]
Recovery beds	2	3		1			2 thoracic, 1 oral, 1 gastric or wound
Recovery room—private (same as regular recovery)	1	3		1			Note: Need 1 more VAC for thoracic
Respiratory therapy	1	1		1			For out-patient treatments IPPB
Scanning room (part x-ray)	1	2					Cardiac arrest and other emergencies
Serology		1		1			Standard lab use[a]
Sterilization (CS or OR)	1	1		1			Equipment testing
Surgical preparation room	1	1		1			Pre-medication for anesthesia
Teaching lab	1	1		1			Standard lab use[a]
Treatment room	1	1		1			Special therapy
Urinalysis		1		1			Standard lab use[a]
Standard x-ray rooms	1	2		1			Cardiac arrest and other emergencies

Source: Information furnished courtesy of Puritan-Bennett, modified by ASPE.

[a] One outlet per area.

[b] Consult owner for number and location.

Table 2-5   Medical-Air Peak-Demand Chart

Area	Free-Air Design Flow, scfm (L/min)			Simultaneous Use Factor (%)
	Per Room	Per Bed	Per Outlet	
Anesthetizing locations[a]				
Special surgery	0.5 (15)	—	—	100
Major surgery	0.5 (15)	—	—	100
Minor surgery	0.5 (15)	—	—	75
Emergency surgery	0.5 (15)	—	—	50
Radiology	0.5 (15)	—	—	25
Cardiac catheterization	0.5 (15)	—	—	50
Acute-care locations				
Recovery room	—	2 (60)	—	50
ICU/CCU	—	2 (60)	—	50
Emergency room	—	2 (60)	—	50
Neonatal ICU	—	1.5 (40)	—	75
Dialysis unit	—	—	0.5 (15)	10
Subacute-care locations				
Nursery	—	—	0.5 (15)	25
Patient rooms	—	0.5 (15)	—	10
Exam & treatment	1 (30)	—	—	10
Pre-op holding	—	—	1.5 (40)	10
Respiratory care	—	1 (30)	—	50
Pulmonary function lab	—	—	1 (30)	50
Other				
Anesthesia workroom	1.5 (40)	—	—	10
Respirator-care workroom	1.5 (40)	—	—	10
Nursery workroom	1.5 (40)	—	—	10
Equipment repair	—	—	1.5 (40)	10

[a]These design flows are based on the use of air in the patient breathing circuit only. If air is to be used to power equipment such as an anesthesia ventilator, the design flow should be increased accordingly.

Table 2-6 Outlet Rating Chart for Medical-Vacuum Piping Systems

Location of Medical-Surgical Vacuum Outlets	Free-Air Allowance, cfm (L/min) at 1 atmosphere		Zone Allowances— Corridors, Risers, Main Supply Line, Valves	
	Per Room	Per Outlet	Simultaneous Usage Factor (%)	Air to Be Transported, cfm (L/min)[a]
Operating rooms:				
Major "A" (Radical, open heart; organ transplant; radical thoracic)	3.5 (100)	—	100	3.5 (100)
Major "B" (All other major ORs)	2.0 (60)	—	100	2.0 (60)
Minor	1.0 (30)	—	100	1.0 (30)
Delivery rooms	1.0 (30)	—	100	1.0 (30)
Recovery room (post anesthesia) and intensive-care units (a minimum of 2 outlets per bed in each such department):				
1st outlet at each bed	—	3 (85)	50	1.5 (40)
2nd outlet at each bed	—	1.0 (30)	50	0.5 (15)
3rd outlet at each bed	—	1.0 (30)	10	0.1 (3)
All others at each bed	—	1.0 (30)	10	0.1 (3)
Emergency rooms	—	1.0 (30)	100	1.0 (30)
Patient rooms:				
Surgical	—	1.0 (30)	50	0.5 (15)
Medical	—	1.0 (30)	10	0.1 (3)
Nurseries	—	1.0 (30)	10	0.1 (3)
Treatment & examining rooms	—	0.5 (15)	10	0.05 (1)
Autopsy	—	2.0 (60)	20	0.04 (1)
Inhalation therapy, central supply & instructional areas	—	1.0 (30)	10	0.1 (3)

[a] Free air at 1 atmosphere.

allow placement of stations in usage groups. These groups can establish demand and simultaneous-use factors (diversities), which are used in the calculation for sizing a particular system. All medical-gas piping systems must be clearly identified using an approved color-coding system similar to that shown in Table 2-8.

Medical-Gas System Dispensing Equipment

Medical-gas outlet/inlet terminals Most manufacturers of medical-gas system equipment offer various types of medical-gas outlets. These medical-gas outlets are available in various gas orders (e.g., O_2-N_2O-Air), center-line spacing, and

Table 2-7 Medical-Vacuum Peak-Demands Chart (Medical-Surgical Vacuum System)

Area	Free-Air Design Flow, scfm (L/min) Per Room	Per Bed	Per Outlet	Simultaneous Use Factor (%)
Anesthetizing locations:				
Specialized surgeries (open heart, organ transplant, etc.)	4 (115)	—	1.5 (40)	100
Major operating rooms	3.5 (100)	—	—	100
Cystoscopy	2 (60)	—	—	100
Delivery room	1 (30)	—	—	100
Emergency operating room	3 (85)	—	—	100
Other anesthetizing areas (minor O.R., orthopedic O.R., cardiac catheterization, radiology, induction rooms, etc.)	1 (30)	—	—	50
Waste anesthetic gas evacuation	1 (30)	—	—	100
Acute care (non-anesthetizing locations):				
Post-operative recovery room	—	3 (85)	—	50
O.B. recovery room	—	2 (60)	—	50
Intensive care units (except cardiac)	—	2 (60)	—	75
Emergency room	—	1 (30)	—	100
Cardiac intensive care	—	2 (60)	—	50
Neonatal I.C.U.	—	1 (30)	—	50
Subacute patient care areas:				
Normal nursery	—	—	1 (30)	10
Premature nursery	—	1 (30)	—	20
Labor / birthing	—	1 (30)	—	10
Patient room (surgical)	—	1.5 (40)	—	50
Patient room (medical)	—	1 (30)	—	10
Exam & treatment rooms	—	—	1 (30)	10
Other areas:				
Autopsy			2 (60)	20
Central supply			1.5 (40)	10
Respiratory care department			1.5 (40)	5
Equipment repair, calibration, and teaching			1.5 (40)	10
Medical lab			1 (30)	10

Table 2-8 Color Coding for Piped Medical Gases

Gas Intended for Medical Use	United States Color	Canada Color
Oxygen	Green	Green on white[a]
Carbon dioxide	Gray	Black on gray
Nitrous oxide	Blue	Silver on blue
Cyclopropane	Orange	Silver on orange
Helium	Brown	Silver on brown
Nitrogen	Black	Silver on black
Air	Yellow*	White and black on black and white
Vacuum	White	Silver on yellow[a]
Gas mixtures (other than mixtures of oxygen and nitrogen)	Color marking of mixtures shall be a combination of colors corresponding to each component gas.	
Gas mixtures of oxygen and nitrogen 19.5 to 23.5% oxygen All other oxygen concentrations	Yellow[a] Black and green	Black and white Pink

Source: Compressed Gas Association, Inc.

[a] Historically, white has been used in the United States and yellow has been used in Canada to identify vacuum systems. Therefore, it is recommended that white *not* be used in the United States and yellow *not* be used in Canada as a marking to identify containers for use with any medical gas. Other countries may have differing specific requirements.

for exposed and concealed mountings. Outlet types and configurations must meet the requirements of the local jurisdictional authority and NFPA 99. All outlets must be properly identified and confirmed. Care should also be taken to accurately coordinate the various pieces of medical-gas dispensing equipment with the architect and medical staff involved in the given project. If the project is a renovation, the outlet types should match existing equipment. With prefabricated patient headwall units, the medical-gas outlets are generally furnished by the equipment manufacturer, and it is very important that coordination be maintained by the engineer so that unnecessary duplication of work is avoided. Also, with regard to the over-the-bed medical-gas service consoles, these consoles are often specified in the electrical or equipment section of the specification and medical-gas service outlets are specified, furnished, and installed under the mechanical contract.

Gas-outlet sequence, center-line spacing, and multiple-gang-service outlets are some of the considerations to be taken into account when requesting information from the various equipment manufacturers. It is more practical, in terms of both the cost of the equipment and the installation, to specify and select the manufacturer's standard outlet(s). Details and specifications regarding the individual standard outlets are usually available from all manufacturers upon request.

The existing outlets are compatible with the adapters found on the hospital's anesthesia machines, flow meters, vacuum regulators, etc. Care should be taken to make sure all future expansions in the same facility have compatible equipment.

Patient head-wall systems A recent and growing trend in hospital construction is the requirement for patient head-wall systems, which incorporate many services for the patient's care. These units may include the following:

1. Medical-gas outlets.

2. Electrical-service outlets (including emergency power).

3. Direct and indirect lighting.

4. Nurse-call system.

5. Isolation transformers.

6. Grounding outlets.

7. Patient-monitoring receptacles.

8. Vacuum slide and IV brackets.

9. Night lights.

10. Electrical switches.

Bed locator units are also available, which serve to provide power for the more advanced patient beds, telephone, night lights, and standard power. These units also function to protect the walls from damage as beds are moved and adjusted.

Head walls currently vary in shape, size, type, and cost from a simple over-the-patient-bed standard configuration to elaborate total-wall units. Most manufacturers of medical-gas equipment offer medical-gas outlets for all types of patient consoles available in today's market. When specifying head-walls outlets, the plumbing engineer should consider the following:

1. Is the service outlet selected compatible with the existing outlet component?

2. Does the patient head-wall manufacturer include the type of medical-gas outlets required as part of the product?

Special types of ceiling-mounted, medical-gas outlets In critical-care areas, which are generally considered by most individuals to be those locations of the hospital providing a special treatment or service for the patient (such as surgery, recovery, coronary, or intensive-care units), the designer's selection and placement of the medical-gas service equipment must be done very carefully in order to provide efficient work centers around the patient for the medical staff.

Manufacturers of medical-gas service equipment usually provide a wide range of equipment that is available for use in these areas. Depending upon the customer's preference and the available budget, the equipment is selected to provide the necessary individual gas services and accessories.

Table 2-9 provides a quick reference guide for the engineer to use as a basis for selecting the commonly used types of outlet dispensing equipment.

Example 2-1

The following illustrative example presents some of the most important critical-care area equipment and options for the selection of the equipment.

Surgery medical-gas services to be piped include:

1. Oxygen.

2. Nitrous oxide.

3. Nitrogen.

4. Medical compressed air.

5. Vacuum.

6. Waste anesthetic-gas disposal.

Providing medical-gas service outlets in the surgery room may be accomplished in several ways, such as the following:

1. *Ceiling outlets* Individual medical-gas outlets mounted in the ceiling with hose assemblies providing the medical staff with connections from the outlets to the administering apparatus.

    This method is considered by most to be the most economical means of providing an adequate gas service to the surgery areas. The ceiling gas-service outlets are generally located at both the head and the foot of the operating table in order to provide alternate positioning of the operating table.

2. *Surgical ceiling columns* Surgical ceiling columns are usually available in two designs: rigid (a predetermined length from the ceiling height above the floor) and retractable. Both surgical ceiling columns provide medical-gas services within an enclosure that projects down from the ceiling. The ceiling columns are usually located at opposite ends of the operating table in order to provide convenient access to the medical-gas outlets by the anesthesiologist. In addition to the medical-gas outlets, these ceiling columns can be equipped with electrical outlets,

Table 2-9 Types of Dispensing Equipment for Specific Areas

Hospital Areas	Medical Gas Outlet Dispensing Equipment						
	Wall-Mounted Outlets	Patient Care Head Wall	Ceiling-Mounted Outlets with Hose Stops	Rigid Ceiling Columns	Retractable Ceiling Columns	Ceiling with Gas Stacks	Nitrogen Control Cabinets
Autopsy rooms	●		●				
Delivery rooms	●		●				
Emergency examination and treatment rooms	●		●				
Emergency operating rooms	●						●
Induction rooms	●						
Labor rooms	●	●					
Major surgery rooms	●		●	●	●	●	●
Minor surgery, cystoscopy	●		●				●
Neonatal intensive care units	●	●					
Normal nursery rooms	●	●					
Nursery workrooms	●						
O.B. recovery rooms	●	●					
Patient rooms	●	●					
Pediatric and youth intensive care unit	●	●	●				
Post-operative recovery rooms	●	●	●				
Premature and pediatric nursery rooms	●	●	●				
Pre-op holding rooms	●	●					
Radiology rooms	●						
Respiratory care unit	●						
Specialized surgeries (cardiac and neuro)	●		●				

grounding receptacles, physiological monitor receptacles, and hooks for hanging intravenous-solution bottles.

Most manufacturers offering surgical ceiling columns allow for many variations in room arrangements of medical-gas services and related accessories, depending upon the specific customer's needs and the engineer's specifications. When specifying this type of equipment, it is necessary to specify carefully all medical-gas service requirements and their desired arrangement(s). Also, the engineer must coordinate all other required services with the electrical engineer and medical staff.

3. *Surgical gas tracks* Surgical gas tracks are forms of ceiling outlet and hose-drop arrangements that allow the movement of the hose drops from one end of the operating table to

the other on sliding tracks mounted on the ceiling. These products are currently available from various manufacturers and all provide the same basic services. The proper selection and specification of specific types are based on individual customer preference. Many variations in products and particular product applications are available in critical (intensive) care areas. Consultation with appropriate manufacturers for recommendations is always advisable.

4. *Articulating ceiling-service center* Articulated ceiling-service centers are moved by pneumatic drive systems and are designed for the convenient dispensing of medical-gas and electrical services in operating rooms. The medical-gas and electrical systems are complete for single-point connection to each outlet at the mounting support platform.

High-pressure nitrogen (N_2) dispensing equipment Special consideration must be given by the plumbing engineer to the placement of the nitrogen outlets. The primary use of nitrogen gas in hospitals is for driving turbo-surgical instruments. Variations of these turbo-surgical instruments, in both their manufacture and their intended use, will require that several different nitrogen-gas pressure levels be available. For this reason, it is necessary that the engineer provide an adjustable pressure-regulating device near the nitrogen gas outlet. A nitrogen control panel is usually located on the wall (in the surgery room) opposite the operating area sterile field. The installation should allow for the access and adjustment of pressure settings by a surgical nurse.

Piping from the nitrogen control panel to a surgical ceiling outlet will provide a convenient source of nitrogen for surgical tools. This will prevent hoses from being located on the floor or between the wall outlet and the operating table. Excess hose can be obstructive to the surgical team.

Medical-Gas Storage

After deciding the medical-gas services to be provided at the facility, the engineer should determine the storage capacity and the pipe sizing required and possible locations for the source. Local codes and references as well as the administrative authority having jurisdiction should be consulted for each medical-gas system.

Because of the unique characteristics of each medical-gas source, the gases are described separately in this section. Also, an explanation of the techniques currently employed to exhaust anesthetic gases is provided.

Figure 2-4 illustrates a typical layout of liquid oxygen, oxygen emergency reserve supply (equal to one day's supply), cylinder nitrous oxide supply, and cylinder nitrogen supply.

Oxygen (O_2) Several factors must be known when estimating the monthly consumption of oxygen in new or existing health-care facilities:

1. Type of medical care provided.

2. Number of oxygen outlets *or*

3. Number of patient beds.

4. Future expansion of facility.

5. In existing facilities, approximate consumption.

Two methods can be used by the plumbing engineer to estimate the consumption of oxygen. The more accurate method is to obtain a detailed consumption record from the health-care facility or obtain monthly oxygen shipment invoices from the supplier. If inventory records are not available from the health-care facility or the supplier, use consumption records from a comparably sized facility, with good judgment.

The second method is to apply the following rule of thumb to estimate the monthly supply of oxygen. This estimating method should be used with good judgment. Always coordinate estimated demand with the oxygen supplier during the design process.

1. In non-acute-care areas, allow 500 ft^3 (14 m^3) per bed per month for supply and reserve oxygen storage.

2. In acute-care areas, allow 1000 ft^3 (28 m^3) per bed per month for supply and reserve oxygen storage.

Oxygen supply sources are divided into two categories: (1) bulk-oxygen systems and (2) cylinder-manifold-supply systems. Bulk-oxygen systems should be considered for health-care facilities with an estimated monthly demand above 35,000 ft^3 (991 m^3) or equal to 70 oxygen outlets. Manifold systems are used in small general hospitals or clinics.

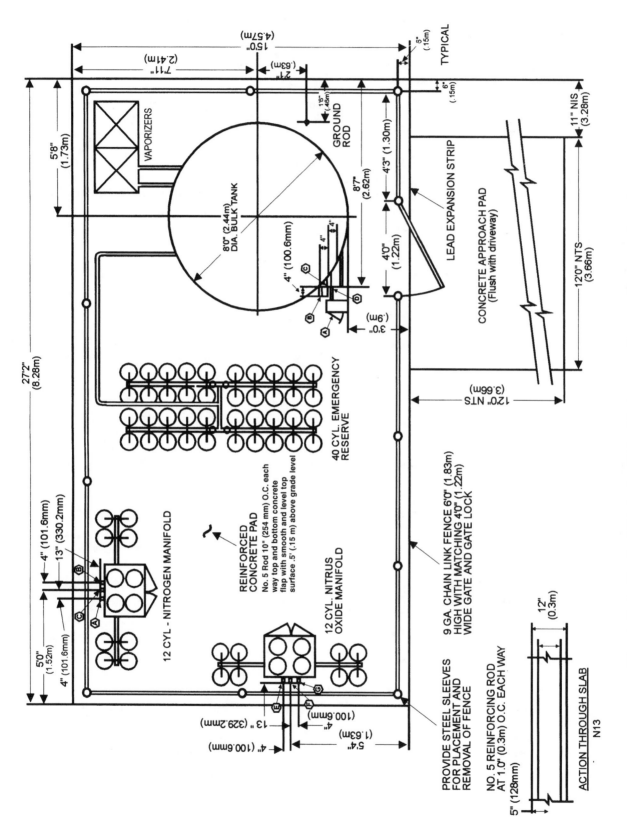

Figure 2-4 Typical Layout of Liquid Oxygen, Oxygen Reserve Supply, Cylinder Nitrous-Oxide Supply, and Cylinder Nitrogen Supply

Bulk-oxygen systems When selecting and placing bulk-oxygen systems, there are several factors to be considered: Oxygen transport truck size, truck access to bulk-storage tanks, and NFPA 50, *Standard for Bulk Oxygen Systems at Consumer Sites*. Bulk-oxygen equipment, construction, installation, and location must comply with NFPA 50 recommendations. If liquid oxygen is spilled or leaked, an extreme fire or explosive hazard could occur. NFPA has design standards to minimize fire exposure to and from surrounding structures. The location of bulk-oxygen storage tanks and equipment must be certain distances from specified structures and materials, as shown in Table 2-10.

Bulk-storage systems consist of cryogenic tanks that store liquid oxygen at low pressures (225 psi [1551.3 kPa] or less). Cryogenic tanks are ASME unfired, double-walled, vacuum-insulated, pressure vessels. Liquid oxygen has a boiling point (nbp) of $-297.3°F$ ($-182.9°C$) and a liquid density of 71.27 lb/ft^3 (1141.8 kg/cm^3). When vaporized into gas, it produces 900 times its liquid volume. Furthermore, since the tank is changed less often, process stability is maximized and the introduction of atmospheric impurities is reduced. Tank systems are furnished with an integral pressure-relief valve vented to the atmosphere should the liquid oxygen convert to a gas. Table 2-11 depicts currently available cryogenic tank capacities.

Most bulk-oxygen storage systems are furnished with vaporizers. Vaporizers are banks of finned-tube heat exchangers that convert the liquid to its gaseous state. The vaporizers come in several styles—including atmospheric, powered (forced-air, steam, and electric), waste-heat, and hybrid—and sizes. The selection of vaporizers should be based on demand, intermittent or continuous usage, energy costs, and temperature zones. Poorly ventilated sites or undersized heat exchangers can cause ice to form on vaporizers during the conversion process. Excessive ice formations can clog and damage the vaporizer. Also, ice could allow extremely cold gas or the cryogenic liquid to enter the piped system; damage the valves, alarms, and medical components; and even injure patients. Figure 2-5 illustrates a typical bulk-oxygen system schematic.

Table 2-10 Exterior Bulk Oxygen-Storage Installation Criteria

Bulk Tank Separation Distances, ft (m)	Item
1 (0.30)	Building structure (except wood frame)
5 (1.52)	Property line
10 (3.05)	Parked vehicles, sidewalk, structure openings
15 (4.57)	All classes of flammable and combustible liquids stored below ground. Class III B liquid, 1000 gal (3785 L) or less, above-ground storage.
25 (7.62)	Solid slow-burning material, coal, lumber, etc., underground tank vent or fill openings. Above-ground flammable and combustible liquids, 1000 gal (3785 L) or less, except Class III B liquids.
35 (10.67)	Clearance for ventilation one side.
50 (15.24)	Public assembly area, open or enclosed. Wood-frame structure. Non-ambulatory patient area.
75 (22.86)	Liquefied hydrogen storage above ground. Clearance for ventilation one side.
25 (7.62)	1000 gal (3785 L) liquefied gas or 25,000 ft^3 (700 m^3) non-liquefied gas.
50 (15.24)	Over 1000 gal (3785 L) of liquefied gas or over 25,000 ft^3 (700 m^3) of non-liquefied gas.

Source: NFPA no. 50.

Table 2-11 Cryogenic Storage Tank Capacities

Gross Volume, gal (L)	Net Liquid Capacity, gal (L)	Capacity Oxygen, ft³ (10⁶ L)	Approximate Weight Empty Vessel, lb (kg)	Approximate Weight Vessel Loaded with Oxygen, lb (kg)
330 (1249.1)	314 (1188.5)	36,200 (1.02)	4,000 (1816)	7,000 (3178)
575 (2176.4)	535 (2025)	61,500 (1.74)	5,800 (2633.2)	10,900 (4948.6)
975 (3690.4)	920 (3482.2)	105,700 (2.99)	9,300 (4222.2)	18,100 (8217.4)
1,625 (6150.6)	1,533 (5802.4)	176,100 (4.99)	10,400 (4721.6)	25,000 (11 350)
3,400 (1286.9)	3,250 (12 301.3)	374,000 (10.59)	18,500 (8399)	49,400 (22 427.6)
6,075 (22 993.9)	5,935 (22 463.9)	684,999 (19.40)	27,999 (12 711.5)	83,500 (37 909)
9,200 (34 822)	8,766 (33 179.3)	1,009,000 (28.57)	34,000 (15 436)	117,500 (53 345)
11,000 (41 635)	10,500 (39 742.5)	1,215,000 (34.41)	40,000 (18 160)	139,750 (63 446.5)

Note: Consult local supplier for available tank capacities.

Automatic controls furnished with the tanks regulate the flow of liquid through the vaporizers. When there is a demand for oxygen, the supply system draws liquid from the bottom of the cryogenic storage tank through the vaporizers. The gas moves through a final line regulator. Thus, a constant supply of oxygen at a regulated pressure is provided.

In case of mechanical difficulty or the depletion of the liquid-oxygen supply, the reserve supply will begin to feed into the distribution system automatically.

An alarm signal should alert appropriate hospital personnel when the liquid in the oxygen storage tank reaches a predetermined level. The alarm signals should indicate low liquid levels, reserve in use, and reserve low.

Cylinder-manifold supply systems Compressed-oxygen systems are comprised of cylinder manifolds that allow a primary supply

source of oxygen cylinders to be in use and an equal number of oxygen cylinders to be connected as a reserve supply. The controls of the cylinder manifold will automatically shift the flow of the oxygen gas from the service side to the reserve side when the service side is depleted. Refer to Figure 2-6 for a typical oxygen manifold-system schematic.

Manifold systems can be located indoors or outdoors. When manifolds are located indoors, the engineer should observe the following:

- *Location* Preferably, the manifold should be in a dedicated room on an outside wall near a loading dock and have adequate ventilation and service convenience.

- *Adjacent areas* There should be no doors, vents, or other direct communications between the anesthetizing location or the storage location and any combustible agents. If locating near or adjacent to an elevated temperature area is unavoidable, the engineer should specify sufficient insulation to prevent cylinder overheating;

- *Fire rating* The fire-resistance rating of the room should be at least 1 h.

- *Ventilation* Outside ventilation is required.

- *Security* The room (or area) must be provided with a door or a gate that can be locked and labeled.

Oxygen manifolds are sized taking into consideration the following:

1. The size of the cylinders, 244 ft³ (6909 L) H-cylinder (see Table 2-12 for a sizing chart).

2. The hospital's usage of oxygen, in ft³ (L) per month.

Table 2-12
Selection Chart for Oxygen Manifolds

Hospital Usage		Duplex Manifold Size	
Cu. Ft. (10³ L) per month		Total Cylinders	Cylinders per Side
5,856	(165.8)	6	3
9,760	(276.4)	10	5
13,664	(386.9)	14	7
17,568	(497.5)	18	9
21,472	(608.0)	22	11
25,376	(718.6)	26	13
29,280	(829.1)	30	15
33,154	(938.8)	34	17

Note: Based on use of 244 ft³ (6909.35 L) H-cylinders.

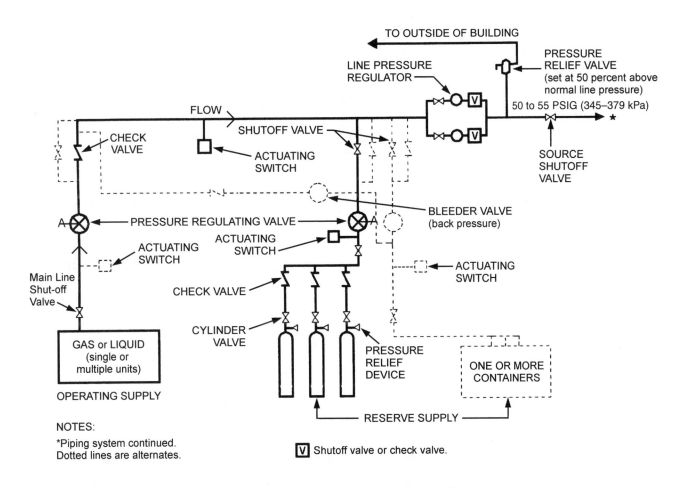

NOTES:
*Piping system continued.
Dotted lines are alternates.

[V] Shutoff valve or check valve.

Figure 2-5 Typical Bulk Supply System (Schematic)

Nitrous oxide (N₂O) The common source of nitrous oxide is a cylinder-manifold system. High-pressure manifold systems consist of two banks of cylinders, primary and reserve. (See discussion under "Oxygen," above.)

System demands for nitrous oxide can be more difficult to determine than they are for other medical gases. The number of surgeries scheduled, the types and lengths of surgery, and the administering techniques used by the anesthesiologists cause extreme variations in the amount of nitrous oxide used. Because of this variation,

considerations must be given to the size and selection of the nitrous-oxide manifold system.

Avoid locating the nitrous-oxide manifold system outdoors in areas with extremely cold climates. Nitrous oxide is supplied liquefied at its vapor pressure of 745 psi (5136.6 kPa) at 70°F (21.1°C). At extremely cold temperatures, the cylinder pressure will drop dramatically, reducing the cylinder pressure to a point where it is impossible to maintain an adequate line pressure. This is due to a lack of heat for vaporization.

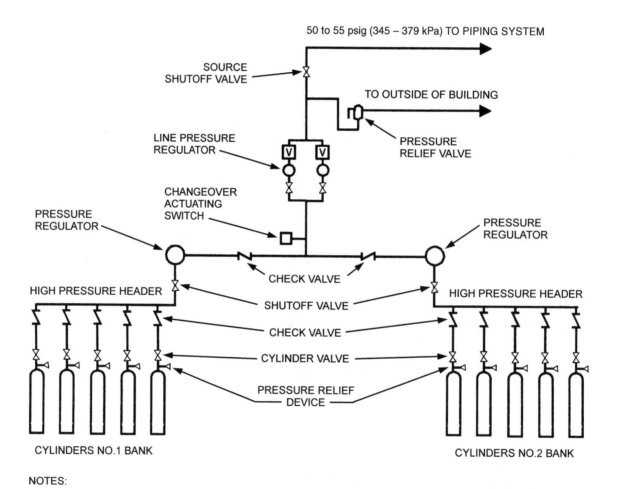

Figure 2-6   Typical Cylinder Supply System without Reserve Supply (Schematic)

Note: Supply systems with different arrangements of valves and regulators are permissible if they provide equivalent safeguards (Level 1 gas system).

For nitrous-oxide manifolds located indoors, the same precautions previously listed for oxygen systems must be observed.

The following should be considered when selecting and sizing nitrous-oxide manifolds and determining the number of cylinders required:

1. The size of the cylinders: 489 ft^3 (13 847 L) K-cylinders (see Table 2-13).

2. The number of anesthetizing locations or operating rooms.

3. Provide ½ of 1 cylinder per operating room for in-service and reserve supplies.

Table 2-13   Sizing Chart for Nitrous Oxide Cylinder Manifolds

Number of Operating Rooms	Duplex Manifold Size			
	Indoor		Outdoor	
	Total Cylinders	Cylinders per Side	Total Cylinders	Cylinders per Side
4	4	2	4	2
8	8	4	10	5
10	10	5	12	5
12	12	6	14	7
16	16	8	20	10

*Note:*Based on use of 489 ft^3 (13.85 X 10^3 L) K-cylinders.

Medical compressed air Medical compressed air may be supplied by two types of system: (1) a high-pressure cylinder-manifold system; and (2) a medical air-compressor system.

The manifold systems for compressed air are similar in configuration to those for oxygen and nitrous oxide (see discussion under "Oxygen," above). Air supplied from cylinders or that has been reconstituted from oxygen U.S.P. and nitrogen N.F. must comply, as a minimum, with Grade D in ANSI ZE86.I, *Commodity Specification for Air.*

Medical compressed air can be produced on site from atmospheric air using air compressors designed for medical applications. There are three major types of air compressor in the marketplace today: the centrifugal, reciprocating, and rotary screw. The reciprocating and rotary screw are "positive-displacement" type units, while the centrifugal compressor is a "dynamic" type compressor. The medical air compressor shall be designed to prevent the introduction of contaminants or liquid into the pipeline by one of two methods: Type 1 air compressors eliminate oil anywhere in the compressor. Type 2 air compressors separate the oil-containing section from the compression chamber. Examples of a type 1 compressor are the liquid ring, rotary screw, and permanently sealed bearing compressor. Type 2 compressors have extended heads.

A positive-displacement compressor is normally rated in actual cubic feet per minute (acfm). This is the amount of air taken from atmospheric conditions that the unit will deliver at its discharge. Within a broad range, changes in inlet air temperature, pressure, and humidity do not change the acfm rating of either the reciprocating or the rotary screw compressor. The centrifugal compressor's capacity, however, is affected slightly by the inlet air conditions due to the nature of the compression process. For example, as the air temperature decreases, the capacity of the dynamic compressor will increase. The capacity of a centrifugal compressor is normally defined in inlet cubic feet per minute (icfm) . In an effort to obtain an "apples to apples" comparison of various compressors, many manufacturers specify their capacity requirements in standard cubic feet per minute (scfm). This sometimes causes much confusion because many people do not fully understand how to convert from acfm or icfm to scfm. The design engineer specifying scfm must define a typical inlet air condition at the building site and their set of "standard" conditions (normally 14.7 psia [101.4 kPa], 60°F [15.6°C], and 0% relative humidity). Typically, the warmest normal condition is specified because as the temperature goes up scfm will go down.

To convert from acfm to scfm, the following equation is used.

Equation 2-1

$$scfm = acfm \times \frac{P_i - (P_{pi} \times \%RH)}{P_{std} - (P_{p\,std} \times \%RH_{std})} \times \frac{T_{std}}{T_i}$$

where

P_i = Initial pressure

P_{pi} = Partial initial pressure of water vapor in 100% humid air at the temperature in question

RH = Relative humidity

P_{std} = Pressure under standard conditions

$P_{p\,std}$ = Partial standard pressure of water vapor in 100% humid air at the temperature in question

RH_{std} = Relative humidity at standard conditions

T_{std} = Temperature at standard conditions, °F (°C)

T_i = Inlet temperature, °F (°C)

Equation 2-1a

This equation is derived from the Perfect Gas law, which is:

$$\frac{P_1 V_1}{T_1} = \frac{P_2 V_2}{T_2}$$

or:

$$V_2 = V_1 \times \frac{P_1}{P_2} \times \frac{T_2}{T_1}$$

where

P_1 = Initial pressure

V_1 = Initial volume

T_1 = Initial temperature

P_2 = Final pressure

V_2 = Final volume

T_2 = Final temperature

For a reciprocating or rotary-screw compressor, the conversion from acfm to scfm is simple. The inlet air conditions and standard conditions are inserted into the above formula and multiplied by the acfm capacity of the unit. It makes no difference what the design conditions are for that compressor, as these do not figure into the formula. In the case of a dynamic compressor, the icfm air flow at the given inlet conditions is inserted in place of the acfm in the formula. Another design issue that the engineer should be aware of is how altitude affects the output of the compressor. At altitudes above sea level, all medical-air systems have reduced flow. In these cases, the required sizing will need to be adjusted to compensate. To do this, multiply the scfm requirements by the correction factor in Table 2-14.

In other words, to correctly size the medical-air system, you would apply the correction factor

Table 2-14 Altitude Correction Factors for Medical-Air Systems

Altitude, ft (m)	Normal Barometric Pressure, in. Hg (mm Hg)	Correction Factor for SCFM (L/min)
Sea level	29.92 (759.97)	1.0 (28.31)
1,000 (304.8)	28.86 (733.04)	1.01 (28.6)
2,000 (609.6)	27.82 (706.63)	1.03 (29.16)
3,000 (914.4)	26.82 (681.23)	1.05 (29.73)
4,000 (1219.2)	25.84 (656.33)	1.06 (30.01)
5,000 (1524)	24.90 (632.46)	1.08 (30.58)
6,000 (1828.8)	23.98 (609.09)	1.10 (31.14)
7,000 (2133.6)	23.09 (586.48)	1.12 (31.71)
8,000 (2438.4)	22.23 (564.64)	1.15 (32.56)
9,000 (2743.2)	21.39 (543.3)	1.17 (33.13)
10,000 (3048)	20.58 (522.7)	1.19 (33.69)

listed in the chart above to the peak-calculated load (scfm) at sea level.

Example 2-2

A facility is located at 5000 ft (1524 m) above sea level and the system demand is 29.4 SCFM. Take the 29.4 scfm and multiply it by 1.08 (correction factor from Table 2-14) to get the adjusted scfm requirement of 31.8 scfm at 5000 ft above sea level. Therefore, a medical-air system of greater capacity is needed at higher altitudes.

Another handy formula for compressed-air systems is the following: to convert scfm to L/min multiply by 28.31685.

Each compressor must be capable of maintaining 100% of the medical-air peak demand regardless of the standby compressor's operating status. The basic compressor package consists of filter intakes, duplex compressors, after-coolers, receiving tanks, air dryers, in-line filters, regulators, dew-point monitors, and valves. The compressor components are connected by piping that allows equipment isolation, provides pressure relief, and removes condensate from receivers. Medical-air compressors must draw outside air from above the roof level, remote from any doors, windows, and exhaust or vent openings. Where the outside atmospheric air is polluted, special filters can be attached to the compressor's intake to remove carbon monoxide and other contaminants. Refer to NFPA 99 for proper location of medical-air intakes. Medical compressed air must comply with NFPA 99 and/ or Canadian Standards Association's (CSA's) definition of air-quality standards.

Where more than two units are provided for the facility, any two units must be capable of supplying the peak calculated demands (see Table 2-5). Provide automatic alternators (duty-cycling controls) to ensure even wear in normal usage. Alternator controls incorporate a positive means of automatically activating the additional unit (or units) should the in-service pump fail to maintain the minimum required pressure.

Medical compressed air produced by compressors may be defined as "outside atmosphere to which no contaminants (in the form of particulate matter, odors, oil vapors, or other gases) have been added by the compressor system." Not

every compressor is suitable for use as a source for medical compressed air in health-care facilities. Only those compressor units specifically designed and manufactured for medical purposes should be considered as a reliable source of oil-free, moisture-free, and low-temperature compressed air. Acceptable compressor types include oil-free, oil-less, and liquid-ring compressors. Separation of the oil-containing section from the compression chamber by at least two seals is required by the compressor manufacturers.

Air compressed for medical-breathing purposes are to be used for this purpose only and should not be used for other applications or cross-connected with other compressed air systems. See Figure 2-7 for a typical arrangement of a medical air-compressor system.

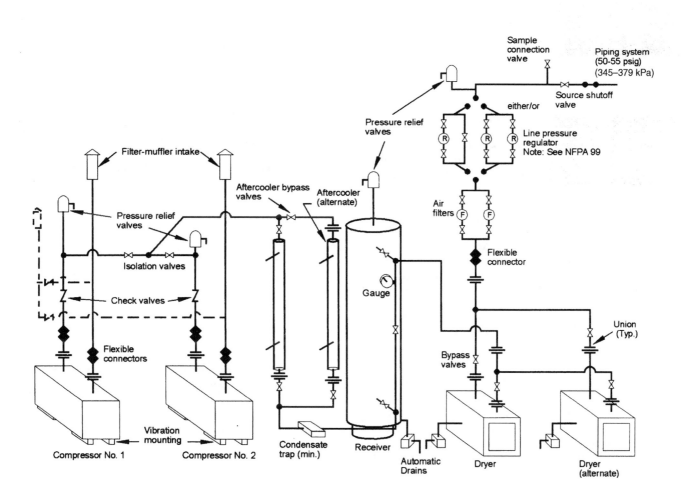

Figure 2-7   Typical Duplex Medical Air-Compressor System (Type 1 Gas System)

Table 2-15 provides the minimum pipe sizes for medical air-compressor intake risers. Consult with the compressor manufacturer on intake recommendations and allowable friction loss for the intake riser before finalizing the pipe size equipment selection.

Table 2-15 Minimum Pipe Sizes for Medical Air-Compressor Intake Risers

Pipe size, in. (mm)	Flow rate, cfm (L/min)	
2.5	(63.5)	50	(1416)
3	(76.2)	70	(1985)
4	(101.6)	210	(5950)
5	(127.0)	400	(11 330)

Nitrogen (N₂) The supply source for nitrogen is generally in the form of high-pressure cylinder manifolds (see discussion under "Oxygen," above). The primary use of nitrogen is to power surgical pneumatic instruments. The selection and size of nitrogen manifolds should be based on the instruments with the highest pressure requirements at the greatest gas consumption rate.

High-pressure gas (nitrogen) systems Surgical instruments are used to drill or cut bones and metals. Surgical applications include neurology, where instruments are used to cut the cranium; in orthopedic service for bone work and joint replacement; for facial reconstruction; and during open-heart surgery.

There is currently available a series of instruments with the highest pressure requirements and the greatest flow rates of all instruments: 200 psig (1379 kPa) at the instrument and a maximum flow rate of 15 scfm (7.08 L/s) to operate effectively. Recent developments have resulted in a new series of tools that requires only 120 psig (827.4 kPa) with a maximum flow rate of 12 scfm (5.66 L/s) to achieve the same effectiveness as the older, higher-pressure line of tools. Other manufacturers of pneumatically operated instruments commonly use a pressure of 160 psig (1103.2 kPa) and a maximum flow rate of 15 scfm (7.08 L/s). For the foreseeable future, there will be a mixture of instruments in use by various facilities.

The tools are operated by a foot pedal. The gas supply to the tool and discharge from the tool are both brought to the floor where the foot pedal is located.

Revisions in NFPA 99 made provisions for pressures up to 300 psig (2068.4 kPa), up from a maximum of 200 psig (1379 kPa) previously allowed. Care must be taken to ensure that all components of a proposed distribution system, including connectors, hose, etc., are rated and approved for the higher pressures.

The following should be considered when selecting and sizing nitrogen manifolds and determining the number of cylinders required:

1. The size of the cylinder: 224 ft³ (6343 L) H-cylinder (see Table 2-16).

2. The number of operating rooms served by the nitrogen gas.

3. Provide 1 cylinder per operating room for in-service and reserve supplies.

4. Determine the flow rate and pressure requirements of utilized instruments.

Table 2-16 Selection Chart for Nitrogen Cylinder Manifolds

Number of Operating Rooms Piped with Nitrogen	Duplex Manifold Size	
	Total Cylinders	Cylinders per Side
1	2	1
2–4	4	2
5–8	8	4
9–12	12	6
13–16	16	8
17–20	20	10
21–24	24	12
25–28	28	14

Note: Based on use of 224 ft³ (6343.35 L) H-cylinders.

Vacuum Systems

"Vacuum" is a negative pressure created by the vacuum pumps within the piping system. The evacuation of the air from the piping system allows ambient air to be pulled from station inlets and exhausted to the outside. The volume of air, in cubic feet per minute (cfm) (liters per minute [L/min]), in the piping is greater than the volume of the ambient air (cfm) (L/s) at atmospheric pressure entering the system, due to expansion under vacuum. In a vacuum system acfm is the air that has been expanded in a vacuum volumetric flow. Values of acfm are much greater than values of scfm. To convert acfm to scfm at 19 in. Hg (482.6 mm Hg), divide acfm by 2.73. For the ratio of scfm to acfm at other pressures, refer to Table 2-17.

At altitudes above sea level, all vacuum systems have reduced flow. In these cases, the required sizing will need to be adjusted to compensate. To do this, multiply the total demand in scfm by the appropriate multiplier shown in Table 2-18.

In other words, to size the medical vacuum system correctly in accordance with NFPA 99 recommendations of scfm at 19 in. Hg (482.6 mm Hg), apply the correction factor listed in Table 2-18 to the peak calculated demand in scfm at 19 in. Hg (482.6 mm Hg).

Table 2-18 Altitude Correction Factors for Vacuum Systems

Altitude, ft (m)		Normal Barometric Pressure	Multiplier used for required SCFM
0	(0)	29.92" Hg	1.0
500	(152.4)	29.39" Hg	1.02
1,000	(304.8)	28.86" Hg	1.04
1,500	(457.2)	28.33" Hg	1.06
2,000	(609.6)	27.82" Hg	1.08
2,500	(762)	27.32" Hg	1.10
3,000	(914.4)	26.82" Hg	1.12
3,500	(1066.8)	26.33" Hg	1.14
4,000	(1219.2)	25.84" Hg	1.16
5,000	(1524)	24.90" Hg	1.20
6,000	(1828.8)	23.98" Hg	1.25
7,000	(2133.6)	23.09" Hg	1.30
8,000	(2438.4)	22.23" Hg	1.35
9,000	(2743.2)	21.39" Hg	1.40
10,000	(3048)	20.58" Hg	1.45

Table 2-17 ACFM to SCFM Conversion Table

Vacuum Level (in. Hg)	Ratio at Sea Level (scfm:acfm)
0	1:1
15	1:2
18	1:2.5
19	1:2.73
20	1:3
21	1:3.33
22	1:3.75
23	1:4.28
24	1:5
25	1:6
26	1:7.5
27	1:10
28	1:15
29	1:30
29.5	1:60

Example 2-3

A facility total demand is 27.5 scfm to produce a 19 in. Hg (482.6 mm Hg) vacuum at sea level. If this facility is located at 5000 ft (1524 m) above sea level, you take the 27.5 scfm and multiply it by 1.20 (the correction factor from Table 2-18) to get the adjusted total requirement of 33.3 scfm at 5000 ft (1524 m) above sea level.

Be sure to use actual cubic feet per minute (acfm) (actual liters per minute [aL/min]) to size vacuum pumps. The patient vacuum system is intended to be a dry vacuum system. However, occasionally fluids enter the piping system accidentally. This should not affect the operations of the vacuum pumps, but it will eventually restrict flow, as the pipes' inner walls become coated with dry body fluids, dust, and debris. Some facilities use the vacuum system to remove airborne smoke particles from electrosurgical or laser-surgery areas. This is not a recommended application for the vacuum system. The smoke contains particulates, hydrocarbons, and water, which, if captured, will condense on the pipes' inner walls, producing a tar-like substance that will eventually restrict flow.

The vacuum-pump system includes duplex (or more) vacuum pumps, a receiver tank and automatic drain, controls, exhaust piping, muffler, and valves. System components are connected by piping that allows equipment isolation and drainage of a receiver tank. The receiver serves as a reservoir and an interceptor for fluids that may enter the vacuum system. Fluid must be periodically drained to the sanitary sewer from the receiver.

The vacuum pump system must be selected, sized, and specified to provide the estimated peak flow demand and a dependable source of medical vacuum at all required times.

Each vacuum pump of a duplex system must be sized for 100% of the estimated peak demand. When a triplex or quadruplex system is specified, each pump shall be sized so that in the event of one pump failing, the remaining pumps are capable of maintaining the required vacuum at 100% of the peak calculated demand. Provide automatic alternators (duty-cycling controls) to ensure even wear in normal usage. Alternator controls incorporate a positive means of automatically activating the additional unit (or units) should the in-service pump fail to maintain the minimum required vacuum.

Individual exhaust stacks should be straight and as short as possible. The collection of the duplex stacks to a single stack is permissible if it is assured that back pressure will not be a potential problem for the system in the future. The exhaust system should be piped to the outside environment, have a gooseneck termination, and be properly screened to prevent insects, leaves, and debris from entering. The exhaust vents should be a minimum distance of 25 ft (7.6 m) from any door, window, outside air intakes, or other opening and a minimum distance of 20 ft (6.1 m) above the ground. The prevailing wind currents and the proximity of the power vents and intake louvers are very important factors to be considered when locating the outdoor vacuum-pump exhaust.

Laboratories should be served by a dedicated vacuum line that is separate from the medical vacuum system; be equipped with drainable fluid traps; and be connected by separate laterals, risers, and mains to the receiver.

Because the vacuum requirements vary considerably in the different sections of a hospital, in both peak demands and in the frequency of use, the total demand for the entire vacuum system should be calculated by the following:

Equation 2-2

$$FR \times UF \times NI = EPF$$

where

FR = Room or station inlet flow rates (scfm)

UF = Simultaneous usage factors

NI = Number of rooms or station inlets

EPF = Estimated peak flow (scfm)

Table 2-19 provides minimum pipe sizes for vacuum exhaust risers. Consult with the vacuum-pump manufacturer on back pressure (friction loss) before finalizing pipe-size equipment selection.

Table 2-19 Minimum Pipe Sizes for Vacuum Exhaust Risers

Pipe Size, in. (mm)		Flow Rate, cfm (L/min)	
1¼	(31.75)	12	(340)
1½	(38.1)	23	(655)
2	(50.8)	40	(1 140)
2½	(63.5)	70	(1 990)
3	(76.2)	130	(3 685)
4	(101.6)	160	(4 535)
5	(127.0)	350	(9 915)
6	(152.4)	525	(14 875)

Figure 2-8 illustrates the schematic of a typical, duplex, medical-surgical, vacuum-pump system.

Waste Anesthetic-Gas Management

Anesthesia is as common to medical care as the antiseptic care of wounds. For too long, however, exposure to and control of waste anesthetic gases (WAGs) and vapors during surgical procedures have put health-care workers in jeopardy. At any given time, more than 250,000 people who work in hospitals, operating rooms, dental offices, and veterinary clinics might be exposed unnecessarily to harmful levels of WAGs.

The waste anesthetic gases and vapors of concern are nitrous oxide and halogenated agents (vapors) such as halothane, enflurane, methoxyflurane, trichloroethylene, and chloroform. The list of workers with the potential for exposure to

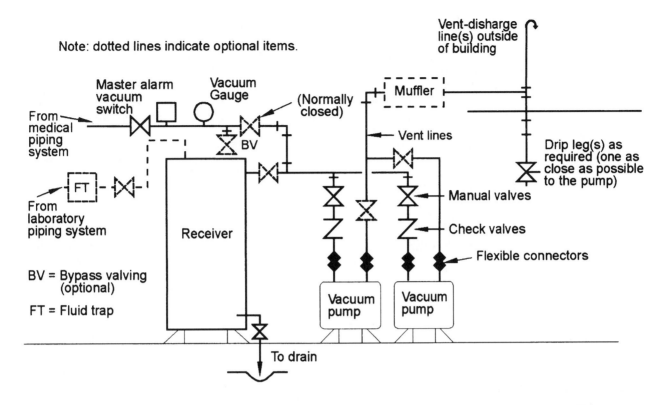

Figure 2-8 Schematic of a Typical, Duplex, Medical-Surgical, Vacuum-Pump System

WAGs includes nurses, physicians—surgeons, obstetricians, and gynecologists—operating-room technicians, recovery-room personnel, dentists and veterinarians and their assistants, and other auxiliaries. Hospital emergency-room personnel may also be exposed, but not on a regular basis.

A complete WAGs management program includes at the outset the application of a well-designed WAGs scavenging system. Such a system consists of a collecting device (scavenging adapter) to collect WAGs and vapors from breathing systems at the site of overflow, a ventilation system to carry WAGs from the operating room, and a method or device for limiting both positive and negative pressure variations in the breathing circuit that may be used by the scavenging systems. Most anesthesia equipment being manufactured today includes scavenging systems.

The remainder of the WAGs management program should include work practices minimizing gas leakage, the application of a routine equipment-maintenance program so that gas leaks are minimized, periodic exposure monitoring, and the provision of adequate general ventilation.

System-Control Valves

General After the proper selection of the medical-gas system source has been made by the plumbing engineer, the next step in the design of such a system is the specification and installation of the pipeline and controls. These typically include 1) source shut-off valves, 2) main shut-off valves, 3) in-line shut-off valves, and 4) zone valve-box assemblies. The purpose of including these intermediate valves in the medical-gas system is to provide the capability of isolating various portions of the systems, in total or by area. This is useful in case of an emergency and in order to allow for maintenance without interruption of the total medical-gas system. Often, future remodeling connections should be considered in the determination of valve placement. All valves in medical-gas systems must be totally accessible, labeled, and, if concealed, identified. This allows area shutdown, purge, and certification to be done while the remainder of the system stays in service. Based upon the latest recommendations of the NFPA, zone valves that are accessible to other than authorized personnel should be installed inside of valve boxes that are provided with breakable or removable windows. This valve is to be readily operable from a standing position in the corridor on the same floor it serves.

Shut-off valves should be located in medical-gas systems at the following locations:

1. Source equipment outlet shut-off valves.

2. The main supply line entering the building.

3. The base of each medical-gas riser adjacent to the riser connection.

4. Each floor distribution zone serving patient areas.

5. Each anesthetizing locations.

6. Each critical (intensive) care area, emergency room, and recovery room.

Valves, fittings, and other components The valve(s) and box assemblies should be full-port ball valve(s) with 90° from the open to the closed position. The size of the valves should be based upon the size of pipe they serve so as not to provide a reduction (or restriction) in the flow of the pipeline system.

A gauge, installed downstream of the zone valve, is required in the patient room.

The locations cited above are the minimum recommendations; local plumbing codes, NFPA standards, and site conditions should prevail in the final determination of the valve placement. All piping, except control-line tubing, shall be identified. All service-main, branch-main, and riser valves shall be tagged, and a valve schedule shall be provided to the facility owner for permanent record and reference.

Valves and fittings and other components shall be cleaned for oxygen service.

Warning Systems

The facility's gas-dispensing equipment is adjusted to deliver a particular gas at a given flow and pressure. Fluctuations in the given pressure may cause the dispensing equipment to stop functioning or to function inaccurately. For this reason, line-pressure sensing switches should be installed in all medical-gas lines immediately downstream from the source's main shut-off valve. Monitoring of the design conditions is extremely important because any alarms require a certain response from the maintenance engineers, nursing personnel, and supply personnel.

Warning systems are classified into two basic groups: (1) master alarms and (2) area alarms. Additionally, interface controls (relays) are now being provided in computerized signal equipment.

Master alarms NFPA requires that two master-alarm panels be provided, located (1) in the engineer's office and (2) in an area where a 24-hour surveillance is maintained. The master alarm provides its signals by a pressure switch (vacuum switch) located immediately downstream from the source's main shut-off valve or at the site of the source. For example, with a liquid-oxygen system, various pressure switches are located at the bulk site, which provide signals to main of reserve changeover, reserve in use, reserve failure, and low reserve. Additional oxygen signals needed for the master alarm are line pressure high and line pressure low.

Typical manifold gases, such as nitrous oxide, require signals to the master alarm to indicate line pressure high, line pressure low, and reserve supply in use.

Area alarms Area alarms are local alarms usually provided with a self-contained pressure switch and a gauge located in the panel. These area alarms monitor the line pressure in areas in order to indicate if the pressure increases or decreases from the normal operating pressure. Except in the operating or delivery area, locations where each operating or delivery room is valved, the area alarm signals are from the specific line supplying the area, with the individual room shut-off valve being the only one between the actuating switch and the room outlets.

Care should be taken by the engineer to locate the area alarm in convenient view of the nursing personnel who normally work in the area covered. In case of a stoppage of the medical gas or any other alarm condition, the proper personnel must take prompt and precise corrective actions. Area alarm signals for critical zones should be interfaced with the master-alarm panels.

Interface controls In order to advise total building maintenance systems of any malfunctions in the medical-gas systems, most manufacturers usually provide a relay interface control so that easy and compatible signals can be provided by the total building maintenance and control system.

Medical-Gas Piping

Installation guide The basic principles to be considered by the plumbing engineer and kept in mind during the design phase are as follows:

1. *Buried piping* Always protect against leakage, frost, corrosion, and physical damage. Conduit or castings may be used as necessary. Medical-gas piping may be installed in the same utility tunnel with fuel-gas pipelines, electrical lines, or stream lines, provided that there is adequate natural or forced-air ventilation. The medical-gas pipelines must not be placed in a tunnel, trench, or duct where they may be exposed to physical contact with oil or corrosive materials.

2. *Concealed locations* In concealed spaces, always protect against any physical damage by installation within a pipe or conduit. Openings for pipelines installed in combustible partitions must be fire stopped with a type of construction having a fire resistance equal to, or greater than, the original construction.

3. *Pipe shafts* Medical-gas systems may be installed in a pipe and duct shaft if suitably protected against any possible physical damage, effects of excessive heat, corrosion, or contact with oil. Shafts that penetrate multiple floors must meet local code requirements regarding fire rating and sealing of shaft penetrations.

4. *Prohibited piping locations* The following installation locations are prohibited by codes and must not be considered by the plumbing engineer:
   A. Elevator shafts.
   B. Kitchens.
   C. Electrical switch-gear rooms.
   D. Storage rooms for combustible materials.

5. *Exposure in an activity area (such as a corridor where movement of portable equipment may effect damage)* Installation in these lo-

cations should be avoided if possible. If unavoidable, use a hard-temper tubing and provide adequate identification, protective shields, and monitoring.

6. *Pipe hangers* Pipe and supports should be supported from the building structure in accordance with MSS or the schedule given in Table 2-20.

Table 2-20 Medical-Gas Pipe Support Schedule

Pipe Size, in. (mm)	Max. Span Between Hangers, ft (m)
¼ (6)	5 (1.52)
⅜ (10)	6 (1.83)
½ (12.5)	6 (1.83)
¾ (20)	7 (2.13)
1 (25)	8 (2.44)
1¼ (32)	9 (2.74)
1½ (40) and larger	10 (3.05)

Medical-gas pipe sizing criteria

General Pipe sizing is one of the most important aspects of designing medical-gas systems. Oversized piping is required for future expansions. However, undersized pipes will never provide adequate flow or pressure during peak-demand conditions. The friction loss or pressure drop between the supply source and outlets must be designed within acceptable limits. Each medical-gas system has a system operating pressure and maximum pressure loss (drop), which are given later in this section.

To determine the approximate pressure loss for a system, start by measuring the longest pipe run from the source to the last station outlet/inlet. Multiply the longest pipe run by a fitting factor (30 to 50% is normal) to establish the equivalent length. Divide the allowable pressure drop by the equivalent length, and multiply by 100 (30.48) to obtain an allowable friction loss per 100 ft (30.48 m). Friction-loss tables provided later in this chapter give the friction loss per 100 ft (30.48 m) of various sizes of pipe. The system's peak probable demand is calculated by multiplying the number of stations by the flow allowance by the simultaneous use factor. Pipe diameters are determined by reading the friction-loss tables at the proper correlating flow rate and friction loss per 100 ft (30.48 m) of pipe. Refer to the following equations:

Equation 2-3

$$EL = DM \times ff,$$

then

Equation 2-3a

$$PL = \frac{APD}{EL} \times 100$$

$$\left(PL = \frac{APD}{EL} \times 30.48 \right)$$

where

EL = Equivalent length, ft. (m)

DM = Longest pipe length/run, ft (m)

ff = Fitting factor

PL = Pressure loss, ft per 100 ft (m per 30.48 m)

APD = Allowable pressure drop, ft (m)

Acceptable pipeline-system design criteria require that the risers be sized larger than the laterals and the laterals larger than the drops to the outlets. In general, the diameters tend to reduce from the source to the end of the distribution system.

Oxygen The flow rate for oxygen outlets is 1 cfm (.47 L/s). A source pressure of 55 psi (379.2 kPa) and maximum pressure drop of 5 psi (34.47 kPa) should be used in the design. Adult and infant ventilators require volumes of oxygen that exceed the 1 cfm (.47 L/s) flow rate. The recommended flow rate for adult ventilators is 6.36 cfm (3.0 L/s) with no diversity factor. Infant ventilators require 1 cfm (.47 L/s) with no diversity factor. Refer to Table 2-21 for outlet rating and diversity factors.

The friction-loss data for oxygen-pipe systems are given in Table 2-22.

Nitrous oxide The flow rate for nitrous oxide outlets is 1 cfm (0.47 L/s). A source pressure of 55 psi (379.2 kPa) and maximum pressures drop of 5 psi (34.47 kPa) should be used in the design. Refer to Table 2-21 for outlet rating and diversity factors.

Base oxygen and nitrous-oxide pipe-size selection on the more stringent of the following requirements:

1. Maximum friction loss of 1 psi (6.90 kPa) per 100 ft (30.48 m).

2. Maximum friction loss of 5 psi (34.47 kPa) to the farthest outlet.

The friction-loss data for nitrous oxide pipe systems are given in Table 2-22.

Nitrogen The flow rate for nitrogen outlets is 15 cfm (7.1 L/s) per operating room. The source pressure range is 200 to 300 psi (1378.96 to 2068.44 kPa) and the maximum pressure drop is 10% of total system pressure. Specific pressue requirements for tools may dictate the pressure required at a specific point in the system. Refer to Table 2-21 for outlet rating and diversity factors.

Base nitrogen pipe-size selection on the more stringent of the following requirements:

1. Maximum friction loss of 2 psi (13.79 kPa) per 100 ft (30.48 m).

2. Maximum friction loss not to exceed 10% of total system pressure to the farthest outlet.

The friction-loss data for nitrogen pipe systems are given in Table 2-23.

Medical air The flow rate for medical-air outlets is generally 1 cfm (30 L/min), although this may vary. A source pressure of 50 psi (344.74 kPa) and a maximum pressure drop of 5 psi (34.47 kPa) should be considered. Specific pressure requirements for equipment may dictate the pressure required at a specific point in the system. Refer to Table 2-21 for outlet rating and diversity factors.

The friction-loss data for medical-air pipe systems are given in Table 2-24.

Vacuum The flow rate for vacuum inlets is different than it is for other systems because areas vary in demand. Table 2-21 provides outlet rating data and diversity factors. Consider a source vacuum of 19 in. (64.2 kPa) Hg at the service inlet with a maximum pressure drop of 5 in. (16.9 kPa) Hg.

The friction-loss data for vacuum-pipe systems are given in Table 2-25.

Piping materials Pipe and fittings installed in medical-gas systems shall be thoroughly cleaned suitably for oxygen service, with the removal of oil, grease, and other readily oxidizable materials. Such piping systems shall be plugged or capped to prevent contamination until final as-

Table 2-21 Medical-Gas Diversity (Simultaneous-Use) Factors

System	Abbreviation	Quantity of Outlets	Diversity (%)	Minimum Flow, cfm (L/min)	
Oxygen & nitrous oxide	O₂ and N₂O	1–3	100	—	—
		4–12	75	2	(56.64)
		13–20	50	4	(113.28)
		21–40	33	5	(141.60)
		41 & over	25	6	(169.92)
High-pressure nitrogen	N₂	1 & 10	100	—	—
		11–20	75	2.5	(70.8)
		21 & over	66	3.75	(106.2)
Medical laboratory compressed air	MA	1–2	100	—	—
		3–12	80	3	(84.96)
		13–38	60	10	(283.2)
		39–115	40	25	(708.0)
		116–316	30	50	(1 416.0)
		317–700	20	95	(2 690.4)
		701–1880	15	145	(4 106.4)
		1881–4400	10	285	(8 071.2)
		4401–16,000	5	445	(12 602.4)
		16,001–80,000	2	800	(22 656.0)
		80,000 & over	2	800	(22 656.0)
Laboratory vacuum	VAC	1–4	100	—	—
		5–12	80	5	(141.60)
		13–33	60	10	(283.20)
		34–80	50	21	(594.72)
		81–150	40	40	(1 132.80)
		151–315	35	61	(1 727.52)
		316–565	30	111	(3 143.52)
		566–1000	25	171	(4 842.72)
		1001–2175	20	251	(7 108.32)
		2176–4670	15	436	(12 347.52)
		4671 & over	10	701	(19 852.32)

Minimum recommended pipe sizes, in. (mm)

Service	O₂	N₂O	N₂	MA	MV
Minimum system pipe/tube size	½ (12.5)	½ (12.7)	½ (12.7)	½ (12.7)	¾ (19.1)
Minimum riser size	¾ (19.1)	¾ (19.1)	1 (25.4)	¾ (19.1)	1 (25.4)
Minimum branch size	½ (12.7)	½ (12.7)	½ (12.7)	½ (12.7)	¾ (19.1)
Minimum single outlet supply size	⅜ (9.5)	⅜ (9.5)	⅜ (9.5)	⅜ (9.5)	⅜ (9.5)

Table 2-22   Data for Sizing Oxygen and Nitrous Oxide Supply Piping

O₂ and N₂O, cfm (L/min)	Nominal Pipe Size, in. (mm)								
	½ (12.7)	¾ (19.1)	1 (25.4)	1¼ (31.8)	1½ (38.1)	2 (50.8)	2½ (63.5)	3 (76.2)	4 (101.6)
	Pressure Drop per 100 Ft (30.48 m) of Pipe, psi (kPa)								
1.76 (50)	0.04 (0.28)								
3.53 (100)	0.16 (1.1)								
4.41 (125)	0.25 (1.72)								
5.3 (150)	0.33 (2.27)	0.04 (0.28)							
6.18 (175)	0.48 (3.31)	0.06 (0.41)							
7.06 (200)	0.63 (4.34)	0.07 (0.48)							
8.83 (250)	0.99 (6.83)	0.11 (0.76)							
10.89 (300)	1.41 (9.72)	0.16 (1.1)	0.04 (0.28)						
14.12 (400)	2.51 (17.31)	0.29 (2.0)	0.07 (0.48)						
17.66 (500)	3.92 (27.03)	0.45 (3.1)	0.11 (0.76)						
26.48 (750)		1.02 (7.03)	0.24 (1.65)						
35.31 (1 000)		1.80 (12.41)	0.42 (2.9)	0.13 (0.9)	0.05 (0.34)				
44.14 (1 250)		2.81 (19.37)	0.66 (4.55)	0.21 (1.45)	0.09 (0.62)				
52.97 (1 500)			0.95 (6.55)	0.30 (2.07)	0.12 (0.83)				
70.62 (2 000)			1.05 (7.24)	0.67 (4.62)	0.22 (1.52)	0.05 (0.34)			
88.28 (2 500)				0.83 (5.72)	0.34 (2.34)	0.08 (0.55)			
105.93 (3 000)				1.19 (8.2)	0.49 (3.38)	0.11 (0.76)			
141.24 (4 000)				2.11 (14.55)	0.88 (6.07)	0.20 (1.38)	0.06 (0.41)		
176.55 (5 000)				3.30 (22.75)	1.36 (9.38)	0.32 (2.2)	0.10 (0.69)		
264.83 (7 500)					3.10 (21.37)	0.71 (4.9)	0.22 (1.52)	0.09 (0.62)	
353.11 (10 000)						1.27 (8.76)	0.40 (2.76)	0.16 (1.1)	
529.66 (15 000)						2.82 (19.44)	0.89 (6.14)	0.35 (2.41)	0.08 (0.55)
706.21 (20 000)						5.00 (34.47)	1.58 (10.9)	0.63 (4.34)	0.15 (1.03)
882.77 (25 000)							2.47 (17.03)	0.98 (6.76)	0.23 (1.59)
1059.32 (30 000)							3.55 (24.48)	1.40 (9.65)	0.31 (2.14)
1412.43 (40 000)								2.48 (17.1)	0.59 (4.07)
1765.54 (50 000)								3.90 (26.9)	0.92 (6.34)

sembly. Piping materials allowed by code, subject to local requirements, shall be hard-drawn, seamless medical-gas tube, type K or L (ASTM B819), cleaned and capped, and shall bear one of the following markings: "oxy, med"; "oxy/med"; "acr/oxy"; or "acr/med." Mains and branches in piping systems shall not be less than ½ in. (12.5 mm) in nominal size. For systems operated at pressures between 200 and 300 psig (1379 and 2068.4 kPa), ASTM B819, type K copper shall be used. Joints in medical-gas tube shall be brazed except that "memory metal" couplings having temperature and pressure ratings not less than those of a brazed joint are also acceptable. Unions are not permitted in any distribution pipeline system.

Hoses and flexible connections Metallic and nonmetallic hoses or flexible connections are to be no longer than required and should not be permanently concealed in walls, floors, ceilings, or partitions. Hoses are to have a flame-spread rating of 200 in accordance with NFPA 255.

Certification of Medical-Gas Systems

Testing shall be in strict accordance with state and local regulations, NFPA 99-1996, and the following:

Note: The alternative test specified in NFPA 99-1996 4-3.4.1.3(a)2 is not recommended for our purposes. Because of the possibility of line-pressure drops, malfunction of test gauges, and/or

Table 2-23 Data for Sizing Nitrogen Supply Piping

cfm	(L/min)	½ (12.7)		¾ (19.1)		1 (25.4)		1¼ (31.8)		1½ (38.1)		2 (50.8)	
		Pressure Loss, psi per 100 ft (kPa per 3.48 m) of 160 psi (1103.2 kPa) Piping											
5	(145)	0.11	(0.76)	0.01	(0.07)								
10	(284)	0.43	(2.96)	0.07	(0.48)	0.02	(0.14)	0.01	(0.07)				
15	(425)	0.96	(6.62)	0.12	(0.83)	0.04	(0.28)	0.01	(0.07)				
20	(567)	1.70	(11.72)	0.26	(1.79)	0.07	(0.48)	0.02	(0.14)	0.01	(0.07)		
25	(708)	2.66	(18.34)	0.42	(2.90)	0.11	(0.76)	0.03	(0.21)	0.01	(0.07)		
30	(850)			0.59	(4.07)	0.17	(1.17)	0.04	(0.28)	0.02	(0.14)		
35	(992)			0.81	(5.58)	0.22	(1.52)	0.05	(0.34)	0.02	(0.14)		
40	(1133)			1.06	(7.31)	0.29	(2.00)	0.07	(0.48)	0.03	(0.21)		
45	(1275)			1.34	(9.24)	0.37	(2.55)	0.09	(0.62)	0.04	(0.28)	0.01	(0.07)
50	(1416)			1.65	(11.38)	0.46	(3.17)	0.11	(0.76)	0.05	(0.34)	0.01	(0.07)
60	(1700)			2.37	(16.34)	0.66	(4.55)	0.15	(1.03)	0.07	(0.48)	0.02	(0.14)
70	(1984)					0.90	(6.21)	0.21	(1.45)	0.09	(0.62)	0.02	(0.14)
80	(2266)					1.17	(8.07)	0.27	(1.86)	0.12	(0.83)	0.03	(0.21)
90	(2550)					1.48	(10.20)	0.34	(2.34)	0.15	(1.03)	0.04	(0.28)
100	(2833)					1.83	(12.62)	0.43	(2.96)	0.19	(1.31)	0.05	(0.34)
110	(3116)					2.21	(15.24)	0.51	(3.52)	0.23	(1.54)	0.06	(0.41)
120	(3400)							0.62	(4.27)	0.27	(1.86)	0.07	(0.48)
130	(3683)							0.72	(4.96)	0.32	(2.21)	0.09	(0.62)
140	(3966)							0.83	(5.72)	0.37	(2.55)	0.10	(0.69)
150	(4250)							0.96	(6.62)	0.42	(2.90)	0.11	(0.76)

Header: Nominal Pipe Size, in. (mm)

Table 2-24   Pressure Loss, psi per 100 ft (kPa per 30.48 m) in 50 psi (344.74 kPa) Compressed-Air Piping

		Nominal Pipe Size, in. (mm)								
cfm	(L/s)	½ (12.7)	¾ (19.1)	1 (25.4)	1¼ (31.8)	1½ (38.1)	2 (50.8)	2½ (63.5)	3 (76.2)	4 (101.6)
5	(2.36)	0.30 (2.07)	0.03 (0.21)	0.01 (0.07)						
10	(4.72)	1.15 (7.93)	0.18 (1.24)	0.05 (0.34)	0.01 (0.07)					
15	(7.08)		0.40 (2.76)	0.11 (0.76)	0.03 (0.21)					
20	(9.44)		0.69 (4.76)	0.20 (1.38)	0.05 (0.34)	0.02 (0.14)				
25	(11.80)		1.14 (7.86)	0.31 (2.14)	0.07 (0.48)	0.03 (0.21)				
30	(14.16)			0.44 (3.03)	0.10 (0.69)	0.05 (0.34)				
35	(16.52)			0.61 (4.21)	0.14 (0.97)	0.06 (0.41)				
40	(18.88)			0.80 (5.52)	0.18 (1.24)	0.08 (0.55)				
45	(21.24)			1.00 (6.89)	0.23 (1.59)	0.10 (0.69)	0.03 (0.21)			
50	(23.60)				0.29 (2.00)	0.13 (0.90)	0.04 (0.28)			
60	(28.32)				0.42 (2.90)	0.18 (1.24)	0.05 (0.34)			
70	(33.04)				0.56 (3.86)	0.25 (1.72)	0.07 (0.48)	0.03 (0.21)		
80	(37.76)				0.74 (5.10)	0.33 (2.28)	0.09 (0.62)	0.03 (0.21)		
90	(42.48)				0.93 (6.41)	0.41 (2.83)	0.11 (0.76)	0.04 (0.28)		
100	(47.20)				1.15 (7.93)	0.51 (3.52)	0.14 (0.97)	0.05 (0.34)		
110	(51.92)					0.62 (4.27)	0.17 (1.17)	0.06 (0.41)		
120	(56.64)					0.73 (5.03)	0.20 (1.38)	0.08 (0.55)		
130	(61.36)					0.86 (5.93)	0.23 (1.59)	0.09 (0.62)	0.03 (0.21)	
140	(66.08)					1.00 (6.89)	0.27 (1.86)	0.11 (0.76)	0.03 (0.21)	
150	(70.80)						0.31 (2.14)	0.12 (0.83)	0.04 (0.28)	
175	(82.60)						0.42 (2.90)	0.16 (1.10)	0.05 (0.34)	
200	(94.40)						0.54 (3.72)	0.21 (1.45)	0.07 (0.48)	
225	(106.20)						0.69 (4.76)	0.29 (2.00)	0.08 (0.55)	
250	(118.00)						0.85 (5.86)	0.33 (2.28)	0.10 (0.69)	
275	(129.80)						1.03 (7.10)	0.40 (2.76)	0.13 (0.90)	
300	(141.60)							0.48 (3.31)	0.15 (1.03)	
325	(153.40)							0.56 (3.86)	0.18 (1.24)	
350	(165.20)							0.65 (4.48)	0.20 (1.38)	
375	(177.00)							0.74 (5.10)	0.23 (1.59)	
400	(188.80)							0.84 (5.79)	0.27 (1.86)	
450	(212.40)							1.06 (7.31)	0.32 (2.21)	
500	(236.00)								0.42 (2.90)	
550	(259.60)								0.50 (3.45)	0.12 (0.83)
600	(283.20)								0.60 (4.14)	0.14 (0.97)
650	(306.80)								0.70 (4.83)	0.17 (1.17)
700	(330.40)								0.82 (5.65)	0.19 (1.31)
750	(354.00)								0.94 (6.48)	0.22 (1.52)
800	(377.60)								1.06 (7.31)	0.25 (1.72)
850	(401.20)									0.28 (1.93)
900	(424.80)									0.32 (2.21)
950	(448.40)									0.36 (2.48)
1000	(472.00)									0.39 (2.69)
1100	(519.20)									0.48 (3.31)
1200	(566.40)									0.57 (3.93)
1300	(613.60)									0.67 (4.62)
1400	(660.80)									0.77 (5.31)
1500	(708.00)									0.89 (6.14)
1600	(755.20)									1.00 (6.89)

Table 2-25 Data for Sizing Vacuum Piping Systems

Air Flow, cfm (L/s)	Nominal Pipe Size, inches (mm)							
	¾ (19.1)	1 (25.4)	1¼ (31.8)	1½ (38.1)	2 (50.8)	2½ (63.5)	3 (76.2)	4 (101.6)
	Pressure Drop per 100 Ft (30.48 m) of Pipe, in. Hg (kPa)							
1 (0.5)	0.15 (0.51)							
2 (0.9)	0.39 (1.32)	0.10 (0.34)						
3 (1.4)	0.77 (2.60)	0.19 (0.64)						
4 (1.9)	1.24 (4.19)	0.31 (1.05)	0.10 (0.34)					
5 (2.4)	1.78 (6.01)	0.44 (1.49)	0.14 (0.47)					
6 (2.8)	2.40 (8.10)	0.60 (2.03)	0.19 (0.64)					
7 (3.3)		0.77 (2.60)	0.24 (0.81)	0.12 (0.41)				
8 (3.8)		0.95 (3.21)	0.31 (1.05)	0.15 (0.51)				
9 (4.3)		1.17 (3.95)	0.38 (1.28)	0.18 (0.61)				
10 (4.7)		1.38 (4.66)	0.45 (1.52)	0.22 (0.74)				
15 (7.1)		2.80 (9.46)	0.88 (2.97)	0.44 (1.49)	0.12 (0.41)			
20 (9.4)			1.46 (4.93)	0.72 (2.43)	0.19 (0.64)			
25 (11.8)			2.20 (7.43)	1.09 (3.68)	0.29 (0.98)	0.10 (0.34)		
30 (14.2)				1.52 (5.13)	0.41 (1.38)	0.14 (0.47)		
35 (16.5)				2.00 (6.75)	0.54 (1.82)	0.18 (0.61)		
40 (18.9)				2.50 (8.44)	0.67 (2.26)	0.22 (0.74)	0.10 (0.34)	
45 (21.2)					0.81 (2.74)	0.27 (0.91)	0.12 (0.41)	
50 (23.6)					0.99 (3.34)	0.33 (1.11)	0.14 (0.47)	
60 (28.3)					1.34 (4.53)	0.45 (1.52)	0.19 (0.64)	
70 (33.0)					1.79 (6.04)	0.60 (2.03)	0.26 (0.88)	0.07 (0.24)
80 (37.8)					2.30 (7.77)	0.77 (2.60)	0.32 (1.08)	0.09 (0.30)
90 (42.5)						0.96 (3.24)	0.41 (1.38)	0.11 (0.37)
100 (47.2)						1.17 (3.95)	0.50 (1.69)	0.14 (0.47)
125 (59.0)						1.71 (5.77)	0.74 (2.50)	0.20 (0.68)
150 (70.8)						2.30 (7.77)	0.99 (3.34)	0.27 (0.91)
175 (82.6)							1.28 (4.32)	0.35 (1.18)
200 (94.4)							1.61 (5.43)	0.44 (1.49)

human error, it should not be allowed in cross-connection testing of vital life-support gases.

Medical-gas certification checklist It is recommended that a step-by-step checklist be followed to ensure that every aspect of the medical-gas and vacuum system is tested properly.

Prior to having the system certified, the plumbing contractor should perform items 1, 2, 3, 4, 5, and 6 below. Typically these are inspected by local inspectors.

1. Clean the piping system by clearing it with pressurized, oil-free, dry air or nitrogen. This cleaning shall be performed just after the installation of the piping system but before the installation of the alarm switches, manifolds, pressure gauge, and other "peripheral" components.

2. Visually inspect each brazed joint. This inspection shall be done to make sure that the brazing alloy has been properly applied to the joint and that there are no discernible defects. During the inspection, excess flux shall be removed.

3. Before the wallboard application, pressurize each section of the piping system to 150 psig (1034.22 kPa) using oil-free, dry air or nitrogen. After the system has been pressurized, each joint shall be checked for leakage using a soap-water solution or another nontoxic leak-detecting agent. If leaks are detected, the system shall be repaired and retested.

4. After testing each individual medical-gas system, the completely assembled station outlets and all other components shall be installed and subjected to a 24-h standing pressure test at 20% above normal operated line pressure. This test gas shall be oil-free, dry nitrogen. The source valve shall be closed. Leaks, if any, shall be located, repaired, and retested.

5. Each dedicated gas system shall be tested with oil-free, dry nitrogen, to verify that there are no cross-connections to any other system. To determine the presence of cross connections, pressurize only one system to 50 psig (344.74 kPa) at a time, and then test each outlet to verify that the gas exists only at each of the expected outlets. (See item no. 7.)

6. Each gas piping system shall be purged of contaminants by flushing it with the appropriate source gas while under system pressure. The piping system for each gas shall be purged by successively opening each outlet in progressive order, starting with the outlet that is nearest the pressure source and ending at the outlet that is farthest from the pressure source. The gas shall be purged through a white cloth material at a flow rate of at least 3.5 cfm (100 L/min) until there is no longer any evidence of discoloration or particulates. It is also important to purge for a sufficiently long time so that all of the test gas previously used is removed from the system. (See item no. 11.)

Start-up, testing, and certification of the medical-gas systems shall be conducted by an independent, third-party, trained representative with a minimum of 5 years experience in medical-gas pipeline testing and certification. Proof of liability insurance should be requested by the owner/general contractor.

After successful start-up of all systems and components, vital information regarding the proper operation of the equipment shall be made a part of the medical-gas certification. This shall include, but not be limited to:

*   The medical air compressors, dryers, purifiers, filters, regulators, and dew-point and carbon-monoxide monitors.

*   The medical-vacuum pumps.

*   The bulk liquid-oxygen field and oxygen, nitrous-oxide, nitrogen, and carbon-dioxide manifolds.

*   The master and area alarms and their signal devices.

*   The medical-gas valves and zone-valve boxes.

*   The outlets, nitrogen-control panels, columns, and hose drop assemblies.

7. *Cross-connection test*

    A. After the closing of walls and the completion of requirements of NFPA 99-1996 4-3.4.1.2, it shall be determined that no cross connection of piping systems exists. All medical-gas systems shall be reduced to atmospheric pressure. All sources of test gas from all of the medical-gas systems, with the exception of the one system to be checked, shall be disconnected. This system shall be pressurized with oil-free nitrogen to 50 psig (344.74 kPa gauge). With appropriate adapter matching outlet labels, each individual station outlet of all medical-gas systems installed shall be checked to determine that test gas is being dispensed only from the outlets of the medical-gas system being tested.

a. The source of the test gas shall be disconnected and the system tested reduced to atmospheric pressure. Proceed to test each additional piping system in accordance with 7A.

b. Where a medical-vacuum piping system is installed, the cross-connection testing shall include that piped vacuum system with all medical-gas piping systems.

B. The presence and correctness of labeling required by this standard for all components (e.g., station outlets, shut-off valves, pipelines, and signal panels) shall be verified.

8. *Valve test* Valves installed in each medical-gas piping system shall be tested to verify proper operation in rooms or areas of control. Records shall be made listing the rooms or areas controlled by each valve for each gas. The information shall be utilized to assist and verify the proper labeling of the valves.

9. *Flow test*

A. All outlets shall be tested for flow. Tests shall be performed with the use of oil-free, dry nitrogen as described in CGA P-9, *Inert Gases: Argon, Nitrogen and Helium.*

B. Oxygen, nitrous-oxide, and air outlets shall deliver 3.5 scfm (1.65 L/s) with a pressure drop of no more than 5 psig (34.47 kPa) and static pressure of 50 psig (344.74 kPa).

C. Nitrogen outlets shall deliver 5.0 scfm (2.36 L/s) with a pressure drop of no more than 5 psig (34.47 kPa) and static pressure of 160 psig (1103 kPa).

10. *Alarm testing*

A. *General* All warning systems for each medical-gas piping system shall be tested to ensure that all components function properly prior to placing the piping system in service. Permanent records of these tests shall be maintained.

Warning systems that are part of an addition to an existing piping system shall be tested prior to the connection of the new piping to the existing system.

B. *Warning systems* Tests of warning systems for new installations (initial test) shall be performed after the cross-connection testing discussed in item 7 but before the purging and verifying in item 12. Initial tests of warning systems that may be included in an addition or extension to an existing piping system shall be completed before connection of the addition to the existing system. The test gas for the initial tests shall be oil-free, dry nitrogen.

C. *Master alarm systems*

a. The master alarm system test shall be performed for each of the nonflammable medical-gas piping systems. Permanent records of these tests shall be maintained with those required under NFPA 99-1999 4-3.5.3.

b. The audible and noncancellable visual signals of NFPA 99-1999 4-3.1.2.1(b)3e shall indicate pressure in the main line increases or decreases 20% from the normal operating pressure.

D. *Area alarm systems* The warning signals for all medical-gas piping systems supplying anesthetizing locations and other vital life-support and critical-care areas, such as post-anesthesia recovery, intensive-care units, and coronary-care units shall indicate the pressure in the piping system if it increases or decreases 20% from the normal operating pressure.

11. *Piping purge test* To remove any traces of particulate matter deposited in the pipelines as a result of construction, a heavy, intermittent purging of the pipeline shall be done. The appropriate adapter shall be obtained from the facility or manufacturer, and high purge rates of least 8 cfm (225 L/min) shall be put on each outlet. After the purge is started, it shall be rapidly interrupted several times until the purge produces no discoloration in a white cloth loosely held over the adapter during the purge. In order to

avoid possible damage to the outlet and its components, this test shall not be conducted using any implement other than the proper adapter.

For each positive-pressure gas system, cleanliness of the piping system shall be verified. Filter a minimum of 35 ft³ (991.1 L) of gas through a clean, white 0.45-μ filter at a minimum flow of 3.5 scfm (99.12 L/min). Filter shall show no discoloration and shall accrue no more than 0.1 mg of matter. Each zone shall be tested at the outlet most remote from the source. Test shall be performed with the use of oil-free, dry nitrogen described in CGA P-9.

12. *Piping purity test* For each positive-pressure system, the purity of the piping system shall be verified. Test each zone at the most remote outlet for dew point, total hydrocarbons (as methane), and halogenated hydrocarbons, and compare with source gas. The two tests shall in no case exceed variation as specified in the the maximum allowable variation table that follows. Test shall be performed with the use of oil-free nitrogen gas as described in CGA P-9.

Maximum Allowable Variation Table

Dew Point	41°F @ 50 psig (5°C @ 375 kPa)
Total hydrocarbons as methane	±1 ppm
Halogenated hydrocarbons	±2 ppm

13. *Final tie-in test* Prior to connection of any work or any extension or addition to an existing piping system, the tests in items 7 through 12 shall be successfully performed. After connection to the existing system and before use of addition for patient care, the tests in 14 through 16 shall be completed. Permanent records of these tests shall be maintained in accordance with NFPA 99-1996 4-3.5.3.

The final connection between the addition and existing system shall be leak tested with the gas of system designation at the normal operating pressure. This pressure shall be maintained until each joint has been examined for leakage by means of soapy water or another equally effective means of leak detection safe for use with oxygen.

14. *Operational pressure test*

A. Piping systems, with the exception of nitrogen systems, shall maintain pressure at 50 +5/-0 psig (345 +35/-0 kPa gauge) at all station outlets at the maximum flow rate in 14D and 14E.

B. A nitrogen system shall be capable of delivering at least 160 psig (1103 kPa gauge) to all outlets at flow in 14E.

C. Piping systems that vary from the normal pressures in 14A and 14B shall be capable of delivering flows and pressures consistent with their intended use.

D. Oxygen, nitrous oxide, and air outlets shall deliver 3.5 scfm (1.65 L/s) with a pressure drop of no more than 5 psig (34.47 kPa) and static pressure of 50 psig (344.74 kPa).

E. Nitrogen outlets shall deliver 5.0 scfm (2.36 L/s) with a pressure drop of no more than 5 psig (34.47 kPa) and static pressure of 160 psig (1103 kPa).

15. *Medical-gases concentration test*

After purging each system with the gas of system designation, the following shall be performed:

A. Each pressure gas source and outlet shall be analyzed for concentration of gas, by volume.

B. Analysis shall be with instruments designed to measure the specific gas dispensed.

C. Allowable concentrations shall be within the following ranges:

Oxygen	99+% oxygen
Nitrous oxide	99+% nitrous oxide
Nitrogen	<1% oxygen or 99+% nitrogen
Medical air	19.5 to 23.5% oxygen
Other gases	Concentration as specified by their labeling ±1%, unless otherwise specified.

16. *Medical-air purity test (compressor)* Analyze medical air source for concentration of contaminants, by volume. Take samples for air system test at a sample point. The compared tests shall in no case exceed variation as specified under the maximum allowable

variation table below. Allowable concentrations shall be as follows:

Maximum Allowable Variation Table

Dew point	+39°F @ 50 psig (3.9°C @ 375 kPa)
Carbon monoxide	≤10 ppm
Carbon dioxide—air	±500 ppm
Gaseous hydrocarbons—air	≤25 ppm (as methane)
Halogenated hydrocarbons—air	≤2 ppm

Codes and Standards

This section on medical gases was limited to the pressurized gases generally piped throughout a hospital and to vacuum systems, including evacuation vacuum (which is a common method of exhausting the anesthetic gases from an operating room). It also included the diverse methods of providing the gases under pressure, including air compressors (designed and manufactured for supplying medical breathing air), cylinder gases via automatic manifolds, and liquid gas stations.

Care must be taken by the plumbing engineer to investigate and review the most recent local plumbing code and NFPA 99 provisions pertaining to the piping of nonflammable medical-gas systems. The plumbing engineer should note that, in many areas, state and/or local codes exist that may take precedence over the nationally recognized, voluntary standards.

GLOSSARY

ACFM (actual cubic feet per minute) The unit used to express the measure of the volume of gas flowing at operating temperature and pressure, as distinct from the volume of a gas flowing at standard temperature and pressure. (See "SCFM.")

Air, oil-free, dry (air for testing) Air complying, as a minimum, with Grade D in CGA, Inc., Pamphlet G-7.1, *Commodity Specification for Air,* and having a maximum dew point of –20°F (–28.9°C) at line pressure.

Alarm system, Level III An area alarm system for a patient nonflammable medical-gases system,

typically oxygen, nitrous oxide, and medical air in dental-care facilities and medical-care facilities.

Alarm system, local A warning system that provides visible and audible signals for the monitoring functions of medical-gas and vacuum system source equipment at the equipment site.

Alarm system, master A warning system that provides visible and audible signals for the monitoring of medical-gas and vacuum sources and systems; it consists of alarm panel(s) and associated actuating device(s).

Ampacity Current-carrying capacity of electric conductors, expressed in amperes.

Anesthetic As used in this chapter, applies to any inhalation agent used to produce relative analgesia or general anesthesia.

Anesthetizing location Any area of a facility that has been designated to be used for the administration of nonflammable, inhalation, anesthetic agents in the course of examination or treatment, including the use of such agents for relative analgesia (see "anesthetic").

Authority having jurisdiction The organization, office, or individual responsible for approving equipment, an installation, or a procedure.

Clinic A health-care facility where patients are seen on an ambulatory basis, but where surgery involving general anesthesia is not performed.

Combustible A substance that, if ignited, will react with oxygen and burn.

Combustion products The gases, volatilized liquids and solids, particulate matter, and ash generated by combustion.

DISS connector A threaded medical-gas connector complying with the CGA Pamphlet V-5. *Diameter Index Safety System—Non-Interchangeable Low Pressure Connections for Medical Gas Applications.*

Flammable gas Any gas that will burn when mixed in any proportion with air, oxygen, or nitrous oxide.

Flash point The minimum temperature at which a liquid gives off vapor in sufficient concentration to form an ignitible mixture with air near the surface of the liquid within the vessel, as specified by appropriate test procedures and apparatus.

Health-care facilities Buildings or portions of buildings in which medical, dental, psychiatric, nursing, obstetrical, or surgical care is provided. Health-care facilities include, but are not limited to, hospitals, nursing homes, limited-care facilities, clinics, medical and dental offices, and ambulatory-care centers, whether permanent or movable.

Hyperbaric Pressures above atmospheric pressure.

Hypobaric Pressures below atmospheric pressure.

Laboratory A building, space, room, or group of rooms intended to serve activities involving procedures for investigation, diagnosis, or treatment in which flammable, combustible, or oxidizing materials are to be used. These laboratories are not intended to include isolated, frozen-section laboratories; areas in which oxygen is administered; blood-donor rooms in which flammable, combustible, or otherwise hazardous materials normally used in laboratory procedures are not present; and clinical-service areas in which hazardous materials are not used.

Limited-care facility A building or part thereof used on a 24-hour basis for the housing of four or more persons who are incapable of self-preservation because of age; physical limitation due to accident or illness; or mental limitations such as mental retardation/developmental disability, mental illness, or chemical dependency.

Medical air For the purposes of this chapter, air that (1) is supplied from cylinders, bulk containers, or medical air compressors or has been reconstituted from oxygen USP and nitrogen NF, and (2) complies with the following:

1. Medical Air USP.
2. Total hydrocarbons
   Liquid: Nondetectable
   Gaseous: <25 ppm
3. Pressure dew point
   at 50 psig: <39°F (4°C)
4. Permanent particulates: 5 mg/m³ at normal atmospheric pressure of particulate at 1-μ size or greater

Note: Air supplied from an on-site compressor and associated air-treatment systems (as opposed to medical air USP supplied in cylin-

ders) that complies with the above limits is considered medical air.

Hydrocarbon carryover from the compressor into the pipeline distribution system could be detrimental to the safety of the end user and to the integrity of the piping system. The mixing of air and oxygen is a common clinical practice, and the hazards of fire are increased if the air is thus contaminated.

Compliance with these limits is thus considered important to fire and patient safety. The quality of local ambient air should be determined prior to its selection for compressors and air-treatment equipment.

Medical compressed air has many uses in the health-care field. It is used in respiratory therapy applications in conjunction with high-humidity treatments using nebulizers in pediatrics and the nurseries. It is also used to power pneumatic surgical instruments that have a pressure range of 120 to 200 psi (827.4 to 1379 kPa).

Medical air compressor A compressor that is designed to exclude oil from the air stream and compression chamber and that does not under normal operating conditions or by any single fault add any toxic or flammable contaminants to the compressed air.

Miscellaneous gases Occasionally, in a teaching institution or in a hospital specializing in cardiovascular surgery, it is common to find the need for piping other gases, such as carbon dioxide (CO_2), helium (He), and mixtures of each of these two gases with oxygen.

Nitrogen (N_2) An element that, at atmospheric temperatures and pressures, exists as a clear, colorless, odorless, and tasteless gas. It is a nontoxic and inert gas that inhibits combustion by displacing the air. The principle use of nitrogen gas in a health-care facility is for powering pneumatic surgical instruments.

Nitrous oxide (N_2O) Nitrous oxide is a nonflammable gas commonly used as an analgesic and, in combination with one or more agents, for the production of a balanced anesthesia.

Oxidizing gas A gas that supports combustion. Oxygen and nitrous oxide are examples of oxidizing gases. There are many others, including halogens.

Oxygen (O_2) The most widely used of all the medical gases, oxygen is colorless, odorless, and tasteless. Of the three basic essentials for the maintenance of life—oxygen, water, and food—the deprivation of oxygen leads most rapidly to death. Tissue cells have no reserve; they must be continually supplied with oxygen by the body's circulation system. Oxygen is a nonflammable gas used for respiratory therapy and in surgery for anesthesia.

Note: Its outstanding properties are its ability to sustain life and to support combustion. Although oxygen is nonflammable, materials that burn in air will burn much more vigorously and create higher temperatures in oxygen or in oxygen-enriched atmospheres.

Oxygen, gaseous A colorless, odorless, and tasteless gas; also, the physical state of the element at atmospheric temperature and pressure.

Oxygen, liquid Exists at cryogenic temperature, approximately –300°F (–184.4°C) at atmospheric pressure. It retains all of the properties of gaseous oxygen, but, in addition, when allowed to warm to room temperature at atmospheric pressure, it will evaporate and expand to fill a volume 860 times its liquid volume.

Note: If spilled, the liquid can cause frostbite on contact with skin.

Oxygen-delivery equipment Any device used to transport and deliver an oxygen-enriched atmosphere to a patient. If an enclosure such as a mask, hood, incubator, canopy, or tent is used to contain the oxygen-enriched atmosphere, then that enclosure is considered to be oxygen-delivery equipment.

Oxygen-enriched atmosphere For the purpose of this chapter, and only for the purpose of this chapter, an atmosphere in which the concentration of oxygen exceeds 23.5% by volume.

Oxygen index The minimum concentration of oxygen, expressed as a percent by volume, in a mixture of oxygen and nitrogen that will just support combustion of a material under conditions of ASTM D2863, *Method for Measuring the Minimum Oxygen Concentration to Support Candle-like Combustion of Plastics (Oxygen Index)*.

Oxygen toxicity (hyperbaric) Physical impairment resulting from breathing gaseous mixtures containing oxygen-enriched atmospheres at elevated partial pressures for extended periods of time. Under the pressures and times of exposure normally encountered in hyperbaric treatments, toxicity is a direct function of concentration and time of exposure.

Patient vacuum (VAC) Patient vacuum is typically used to provide a source for patient drainage, aspiration, and suction in order to remove body fluids (such as saliva or blood) from an affected patient area. The body fluid is normally trapped in a container near the patient. The vacuum source only provides a source of subatmospheric pressure.

Piping The tubing or conduit of the system. There are three general classes of piping, as follows:

Main lines Those parts of the system that connect the source (pumps, receivers, etc.) to the risers or branches, or both.

Risers The vertical pipes connecting the system main line(s) with the branch lines on the various levels of the facility.

Branch (lateral) lines Those sections or portions of the piping system that serve a room or group of rooms on the same story of the facility.

Psia (pounds per square inch absolute) A unit of pressure measurement with zero pressure as the base or reference pressure.

Psig (pounds per square inch gauge) A unit of pressure measurement with atmospheric pressure as the base or reference pressure (under standard conditions, 0 psig is equivalent to 14.7 psia).

SCFM (standard cubic feet per minute) The unit used to express the measure of the volume of a gas flowing at standard conditions—a temperature of 68°F (20°C) and a pressure of 1 atmosphere (29.92 in. Hg).

Station inlet An inlet point in a Type I medical-surgical piped vacuum distribution system at which the user makes connections and disconnections.

Station outlet An outlet point in a piped medical-gas distribution system at which the user makes connections and disconnections.

Vacuum system, Level 1 A system consisting of central-vacuum-producing equipment with pressure and operating controls, shut-off valves, alarm warning systems, guages, and a network of piping extending to and terminating with suitable station inlets at locations where patient suction might be required.

Vacuum system, Level 3 A vacuum system, either a wet or dry piping system, designed to remove liquid, air/gas, and solids from the treated area.

Notes: (1) The system is not intended for Level 1 vacuum applications. (2) A wet piping system is designed to accommodate liquid, air/gas, and solids through the service inlet. (3) A dry piping system is designed to accommodate air/gas only through the service inlet. (Liquids and solids are trapped before entering the service inlet.)

Waste anesthetic gas disposal (WAGD) A surgical vacuum system that is used to evacuate the anesthetic gases from the operating room after the gases have been exhaled by the patient. Also, the process of capturing and carrying away gases vented from the patient breathing circuit during the normal operation of gas anesthetic equipment.

REFERENCES

1. Canadian Standards Association (CSA). *Non-flammable medical gas piping systems*, Z-305.1.

2. Compressed Gas Association, Inc. (CGA). *Characteristics and safe handling of medical gases*, CGA-P-2.

3. ——. *Commodity specification for air*, CGA-G-7.1/ ANSI ZE 86.1.

4. ——. *Commodity specification for nitrogen*, CGA-G-10.1.

5. ——. *Compressed air for human respiration*, CGA-G-7.0.

6. ——. *Diameter-index safety system—Non-interchangeable low pressure connections for medical gas applications*, CGA-V-5.

7. ——. *Inert gases: Argon, nitrogen and helium*, CGA-P-9.

8. ——. *Standard for color-marking of compressed gas cylinders intended for medical use*, CGA-C-9.

9. ——. *Standard for the installation of nitrous oxide systems at consumer sites*, CGA-G-8.1.

10. National Fire Protection Association International (NFPA). *Standard for bulk oxygen systems at consumer sites*, NFPA-50.

11. ——. *Standard for health-care facilities*, NFPA-99.

RESOURCES

1. Canadian Standards Association (CSA), 178 Rexdale Boulevard, Rexdale, Ontario, CANADA, M9W-1R3.

2. Compressed Gas Association, Inc. (CGA), 1725 Jefferson Davis Hwy., Arlington, VA 22202.

3. National Fire Protection Association International (NFPA), 1 Batterymarch Park, P.O. Box 9101, Quincy, MA 02269.

3

Industrial Waste-Water Treatment

INTRODUCTION

"Industrial waste water" is a generic term used to describe nonsanitary (plumbing) effluent, such as that typically found in chemical, pharmaceutical, and other manufacturing facilities. The definition also includes storm-water runoff discharged from any industrial activity site considered harmful by the Environmental Protection Agency (EPA).

This chapter describes the regulatory framework governing industrial waste water, hazardous substances, and hazardous wastes, and the impact of these regulations upon industrial-process plumbing design. It also contains a listing of design considerations, describes a few of the more common treatment technologies, and provides a list of resources from which more detailed information can be obtained. For information on laboratory-waste piping, refer to other *Data Book* chapters, such as looseleaf Chapter 10, "Piping Systems."

Whether discharged to municipal sewers, surface waters, deep wells, or the environment (land, ground water, air, etc.), industrial waste water and some storm-water runoff are subject to government permitting requirements. In most cases, these wastes must be treated before discharge to abate pollution. Permits specify the maximum allowable concentrations of pollutants in the discharge and the frequency and type of monitoring required to show compliance. Pollution abatement by dilution is no longer allowed. The segregation of incidental water streams, such as noncontact cooling water or storm water runoff, from process waste water is almost

universally required. Even clean, incidental waste-water streams require a permit.

Most nonaqueous liquids (including solvents, oils, and sludge) and some solids and gases are regulated as hazardous substances or hazardous wastes during their generation, use, collection, storage, transportation, treatment, and disposal. Some aqueous wastes that are not regulated under a waste-water permit are regulated as either hazardous substances or hazardous wastes.

As a result of these regulations, plumbing designers must either consult with an experienced environmental engineer or become familiar with the various environmental requirements to ensure an acceptable installation. New facilities must meet both environmental and plumbing code requirements. For novel manufacturing processes, the designer, environmental engineer, and owner may be required to work with regulatory authorities during the design stage to ensure compliance with the intent of the various codes and regulations. The designer is responsible for producing an installation with a low probability of failure. For plumbing design, this means minimizing the possibility of leaks and providing a means to limit the impact of spills upon the public safety and the environment.

REGULATORY FRAMEWORK

The most important pieces of environmental legislation affecting the design of plumbing systems for hazardous material and waste facilities serving industrial plants are the Clean Water Act (CWA), the Resource Conservation and Recovery

Act (RCRA), and the Comprehensive Environmental Response Compensation and Liability Act (CERCLA or "Superfund"). These regulations, promulgated by the EPA and enforced by either EPA or counterpart state agencies, provide a comprehensive framework of pollution control. *National Pollutant Discharge Elimination System* (NPDES) has recently been revised to include the discharge of storm water from selected industrial sites. Current EPA regulations can be found in the *Code of Federal Regulations* (CFR), which is an annually updated compendium of all federal regulations. CWA regulations are contained in the sections beginning with 40 CFR, Part 100, and 40 CFR, Part 400; RCRA regulations begin at 40 CFR, Part 300. Any updates or regulation changes after the last publication date of the CFR can be found in the *Federal Register* (FR), a daily government newspaper in which all agencies and departments publish their notices, proposals, and final regulations. Most states with counterpart regulations have similar codifications and newspapers.

The great body of codes and regulations can easily be a labyrinth, even for those persons with a good understanding of the overall outline and purpose of the statutes. Anyone with questions should not hesitate to seek advice from trade groups, regulatory officials, environmental engineers, lawyers, and other specialists, as needed. There are also numerous "current events" reporting services that digest federal and state regulatory actions and publish readable evaluations as well as reprints of important regulations, policies, and case notes.

Definitions

Hazardous substances Under Section 311 of the Clean Water Act, the EPA has compiled a list of hazardous substances (40 CFR 116). If the substances on this list are spilled or discharged, it must be reported to the EPA.

Priority pollutants The Natural Resources Defense Council and the EPA decide what are priority toxic pollutants. These pollutants have been incorporated into several regulatory programs, including NPDES permits (40 CFR 261), pre-treatment standards (40 CFR 403), hazardous wastes (40 CFR 261), and CERCLA (40 CFR 541).

Hazardous wastes The EPA has adopted regulations to control hazardous wastes under the Resource Conservation and Recovery Act (RCRA). These regulations (40 CFR 2651) list hazardous wastes, including specific chemicals and mixtures defined by their characteristics. It should be noted that controls under RCRA apply to waste only and not to hazardous substances that are being stored prior to use in product manufacturing or that are to be reclaimed, recycled, or reused. RCRA regulates the generation, transportation, storage, treatment, and disposal of hazardous wastes.

Hazardous materials This term means substances or materials that have been determined by the Secretary of Transportation, under 49 CFR 172, to be capable of posing an unreasonable risk to health, safety, and property when transported in commerce. Chemicals included in this definition are hazardous substances, hazardous wastes, most of the priority pollutants, and many other chemicals in commerce that are too numerous to mention here. In this chapter the term "hazardous materials" is used to describe all the previously defined materials and substances.

For detailed listings of these and other regulated chemicals and wastes, refer to the regulations cited in the above definitions.

The Clean Water Act

The CWA establishes a mechanism for setting uniform national standards for discharge to surface waters and to sewers. The EPA has established categorical effluent standards, usually prorated to production volume, for 28 industrial classifications under the Effluent Guideline program. The affected industries are listed in Table 3-1. EPA has also promulgated general standards for discharge to public sewer systems. These standards restrict pollutants that interfere with sewage treatment, pass through the system untreated, damage sewer lines or treatment facilities, or overload the treatment processes.

State laws and regulations follow the federal format, with a few important differences. All states are allowed to make their regulations more stringent than the federal standards. Additionally, some states regulate discharges to the land (and hence to the ground water). States also set goals for water-quality levels in streams, lakes, and coastal waters. They then determine the allowable loading of each pollutant and allocate portions of that loading based on low-flow conditions where dilution is minimal. Water-quality based, discharge-permit limits are almost always

Table 3-1 Categorical Standard Summary Status

1.   Aluminum forming.
2.   Battery manufacturing.
3.   Coal mining.
4.   Coil coating.
5.   Copper forming.
6.   Electrical & electronic components I.
7.   Electrical & electronic components II.
8.   Electroplating.
9.   Inorganic chemicals manufacturing I.
10. Inorganic chemicals manufacturing II.
11. Iron and steel.
12. Leather tanning & finishing.
13. Metal finishing.
14. Metal molding & casting.
15. Nonferrous metals forming.
16. Nonferrous metals manufacturing I.
17. Nonferrous metals manufacturing II.
18. Ore mining & dressing.
19. Organic chemical, plastic, & synthetic fibers.
20. Pesticide chemicals.
21. Petroleum refining.
22. Pharmaceuticals.
23. Plastics molding & forming.
24. Porcelain enameling.
25. Pulp, paper, & paperboard.
26. Steam electric.
27. Textile mills.
28. Timber products.

Source: EPA, Feb. 1986.

more stringent than the industry-wide limits of the categorical effluent standards.

There are two types of water-discharge permit that may require treatment processes. Permits for a direct discharge into a surface water (stream, lake, ocean, etc.) are called National Pollutant Discharge Elimination System (NPDES) permits. These permits may be issued by the EPA, by a state, or jointly, depending on location. Application is required well in advance of initiating a discharge.

The other type of industrial discharge permit is obtained from a Publicly Owned Treatment Works (POTW), the modern name for the local sewage/waste-water treatment plant. Industrial discharges to a POTW are called "indirect discharges" and are regulated by pre-treatment ordinances to ensure that the POTW meets the conditions of its NPDES permit. The ordinances are usually administered by the POTW, except when the industrial discharge is large, the POTW fails to meet its permit requirements, or the discharge is from an industry regulated under the Effluent Guidelines program.

RCRA and CERCLA

These two laws, together with the federal and state regulations derived from them, have had a major impact upon the industrial management of hazardous substances and hazardous wastes. Almost all nonaqueous liquids, many aqueous mixtures, and many solids and gases are regulated when they become wastes or are spilled.

The purpose of CERCLA is to limit the uncontrolled releases or threats of release of hazardous substances into the environment and to provide for a coordinated and effective response to mitigate actual releases. CERCLA requires industrial-risk evaluations, in the form of contingency plans, and establishes a mechanism for governmental response to environmental and health hazards. CERCLA does not require any permits and does not force changes in current hazardous-substances handling methods. Nevertheless, a great deal of publicity can result when the mishandling of hazardous substances leads to an environmental incident. There can also be an enormous cost to dispose of the hazardous wastes generated during a spill. These are strong inducements to chemical manufacturers and users to install process systems that minimize risk.

RCRA's purpose is similar to CERCLA's, except that RCRA regulates hazardous waste from ongoing manufacturing activities. The goals of RCRA are accomplished through strict licensing and operational standards for every aspect of hazardous-waste management.

RCRA requires identification numbers and/or permits for every hazardous-waste activity. The permit application requirements are lengthy and technical for some of the regulated activities. In some cases, the regulations give performance standards that the designer must meet to obtain a permit for the facility. In other cases, the compliance method is almost completely specified. Obtaining RCRA permits for the facility may take six months and include public hearings and disclosure of detailed process and waste information, including chemical material safety data sheets (MSDS).

When evaluating waste streams to determine if they are regulated as hazardous wastes, it is important to check both the federal and state regulations. This is because states are allowed to be more stringent than the EPA. States may define certain wastes as hazardous when EPA doesn't consider them so; for example, waste oil is considered hazardous by many states but not by the EPA.

The relationship between RCRA and CERCLA is shown by the following example. A tank containing a hazardous substance begins to leak onto the ground. Under CERCLA, the owner must notify EPA and the state, stop the leak, and clean up the spilled material. If the owner fails to take action, the regulatory agency may act under CERCLA then seek reimbursement up to triple the cost of its expenses. Under RCRA, the spilled hazardous substances and any contaminated soil become hazardous waste. The hazardous waste must then be removed, stored, transported, and disposed of in accordance with RCRA requirements.

DESIGN CONSIDERATIONS

For plumbing designers, the challenge is to design systems that minimize the chance of leaks, contain any spills that might occur, and segregate hazardous substances from both non-hazardous process streams and incompatible hazardous process streams. The design of a system that anticipates the potential for leaks and spills must include suitable materials, reliable jointing, good fabrication, and provision for the secondary containment of liquids on high spill-risk areas and systems.

Many leaks occur as a result of material incompatibility between the equipment and either the hazardous substances handled or the atmosphere in which the equipment is utilized. The incompatibility can be physical, such as PVC pipes melting at high temperature or plastic pipes dissolving in solvents they were not designed to contain. Table 3-2 lists general properties of the most common tank and pipe materials. Specific

applications should be checked with the appropriate chemical compatibility references from the manufacturer.

Even the best designed liquid-handling systems are subject to occasional failure, particularly during liquid-transfer operations. Secondary containment is an important aspect of any hazardous-material system design to protect employees and the environment. Secondary containment may include a dike around a tank or tank farm or pipes within pipes for systems handling extremely hazardous liquids. Common secondary-containment systems typically have the following features:

1. Containment floors, pads, ponds, and dikes constructed of materials impervious to the substance stored.

2. Perimeter diking and storage reservoirs sized to contain 110% of the largest tank plus the maximum rainfall predicted to occur over 24 h once in 10 years, in exterior areas (or 20 min of sprinkler water flow for interior areas).

3. Pumps, drain valves, or siphons to empty the secondary containment area to either a storage tank or treatment facility.

4. Controls and procedures to prevent the accidental release of contained spills and an alarm system to notify operations should a spill occur.

Minimal equipment and practices for preventing transfer spills should include: overfill prevention, including level sensors; gauges and high-level alarm; automatic valve and pump shutdown; established transfer procedures, including an operator on duty; proper curbing and containment; redundant valves and controls; vapor recovery; alarms; regular inspections; and a maintenance program. The equipment used in water treatment is operated to achieve the following: mixing and flocculation, sedimentation, clarification, filtering, removing turbidity, removing metals, and disinfection.

Historically, underground tanks up to 10,000 gal (37 854 L) capacity, and occasionally larger, have been preferred for hazardous materials, primarily to minimize fire risks. Unfortunately, many of these tanks were kept in service too long and, because of corrosion, have leaked and contaminated drinking water supplies. As a result, designers now must compare the environmental and fire risks of the

Table 3-2 General Properties of Materials Used for Storage Tanks and Piping

Containment Materials	Advantages	Disadvantages
Carbon steel	Compatible with petroleum products and dry organics but incompatible with many aqueous solutions.	Subject to attack by corrosive chemicals and corrosive soils.
Stainless steel	Better corrosion resistance than carbon steel and higher structural strength—There are more than 70 standard types of stainless steel and many special alloys.	Corroded by chloride and exposure to reducing environments.
Fiberglass-reinforced plastic (FRP)	Compatible with a wide range of petroleum and chemical products, if proper resin is selected.	Lacks the structural strength and impact resistance of steel tanks.
Polyvinyl chloride	Excellent chemical resistance to acids, alkalis, and gasoline.	Lower structural strength than steels, generally not suited for the storage or handling of organic solvents such as benzene, carbon tetrachloride, and acetone, or use at temperatures above 140°F (60°C).
Concrete	Generally good resistance to alkaline chemicals, epoxy coatings often applied to concrete to increase chemical resistance.	Subject to cracking and spalling with changes in temperature such as during freeze/thaw cycles, uncoated concrete absorbs solvents.
Polypropylene	Resistance to all aqueous solutions except strong oxidizers.	Low structural strength, temperature limit of 248°F (120°C).
Lined steel	Chemical resistance of plastic and structural strength of steel.	Relatively high cost for material and installation.

above-ground tank. In either case, more attention must be given in the design to ensure an installation resistant to leaks and capable of containing spills. Soil conditions and groundwater levels, which affect the design, must be evaluated for each installation. Secondary containment of these tanks is the primary method of insuring against leakage.

ELEMENTS OF AN INDUSTRIAL WASTE-WATER HANDLING SYSTEM

pH Control

Neutralization for pH control involves the chemical reaction of an acid with alkaline substance (a base), resulting in the formation of a salt and water. In an aqueous solution, the acid or base molecules dissociate and form ions. Sulfuric acid is presented in the solution as H^+ and $SO_4^=$ ions and caustic soda as Na^+ and OH^- ions. The H^+ ions of the sulfuric acid and the OH^- ions of the caustic soda have a strong attraction for each other and combine to form H_2O, which is water. For example, in the neutralization reaction of H_2SO_4 and NaOH, the following process occurs:

$$H^+_2SO_4^= + 2(Na^+OH^-)$$
$$Na^+_2SO_4^= + 2H_2O$$

If excess hydrogen (H^+) ions remain, the liquid will be acidic, and with a surplus of hydroxide (OH^-) ions, the liquid will be alkaline.

The acidity or alkalinity of a solution is expressed on the pH scale, with neutral water at a pH of 7, in the middle of the range between extremely acid (pH = O) and extremely alkaline (pH = 14). The scale is logarithmic, so a pH of 3 is ten times more acidic than a pH of 4. There are also buffers, like bicarbonate/carbonate, which undergo a chemical change when strong acids or bases are added to a solution and thereby act like capacitors that must be filled before the pH will change.

A typical two-stage, continuous-flow pH neutralization process is shown in Figure 3-1. For flows less than 10 gpm (37.85 L/min), it is sometimes preferable to neutralize in a batch basis,

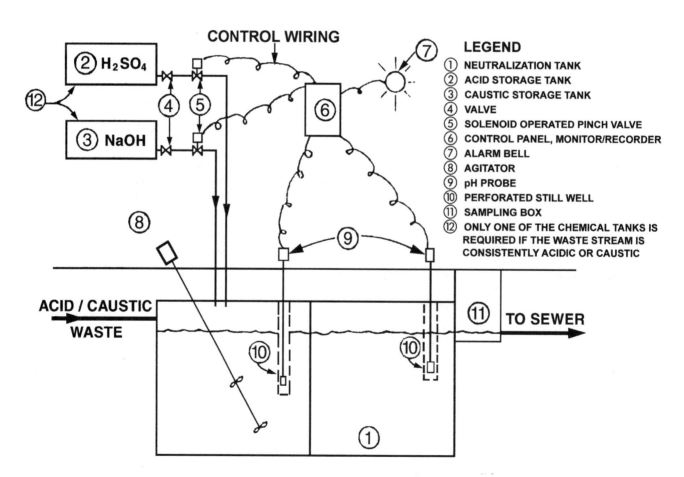

Figure 3-1   Acid/Caustic Neutralization Diagram

Note: Not to scale.

with two tanks alternating between collection and treatment.

The most critical feature of the pH adjustment system is the controller that activates the chemical feed pumps. The controller must have the ability to prevent overfeeding of either acid or base, which would cause wide pH swings and subsequent repetitive chemical additions. Overfeeding is most probable in waste water with no buffering capacity near the pH set point, e.g., deionized and soft water. Controllers with multi-rate response adjustment should be specified for each application.

Sulfuric acid is the most costly method for pH adjustment purposes, although in some cases the commercial 93% acid must be diluted prior to use. The manufacturer's recommendations for materials of construction, control of the heat of dilution, and safety precautions should be carefully followed. Carbon-steel pipe and tanks are commonly used for 93% sulfuric acid, with stainless alloy 20 (a high nickel alloy) valves, as well as polyvinyl chloride (PVC) and chloropolyvinyl chloride (CPVC). For sulfuric acid at concentrations below 93%, polypropylene (PP), fiberglass-reinforced plastic (FRP), PVC, CPVC, and lined steel are preferred.

Sodium hydroxide (caustic or caustic soda) in 50% solution is the most convenient commercial alkaline material for pH adjustment. Unfortunately, 50% caustic freezes at 54°F (12.2°C), so indoor storage or heated tanks are necessary. (Note that 20% caustic freezes at –18°F [–27.7°C].) Caustic solutions may be handled in carbon steel, stainless steel, and PVC tanks and pipe. Lime and hydrated lime are considerably less expensive than caustic but must be fed with dry feeders and/or slurry tanks, which require considerable maintenance. Consequently, lime is favored in applications where the cost outweighs the convenience of caustic.

Dissolved and Suspended Metals Removal

Another common industrial waste-water treatment requirement is the removal of dissolved and suspended metals. The most popular method is to desegregate cyanide and chromium VI waste-water sources from each other and all other metal-bearing waste waters. The cyanide is destroyed by oxidation with chlorine (or sodium hypochlorite solution) at a pH of 9 to 11 and the chromium VI is reduced to chromium III with sulfur dioxide or sodium bisulfate at a pH of 2. Various treatment methods are shown in Figures 3-2, 3-3, and 3-4.

Oil–Water Separation

Oil–water separation may involve free-floating oils, mechanical emulsions or diversions, and chemical emulsions. The size of oil droplets in emulsions may range from below 20 μ to above 150 μ. In selecting separation equipment, the designer must consider the oil quantities, the droplet size, the presence of emulsifiers, the temperature of the water and oil, the difference in the specific gravity of the fluids, their viscosity, the pH, and other waste-water constituents.

There are separators on the market to suit every situation, including simple settling tanks (e.g,. American Petroleum Institute [API] separators), tanks with coalescing media to promote the agglomeration of dispersed oils, and tanks with chemical pre-treatment to promote the separation of chemically emulsified oils. Equipment options include sludge removal and automatic oil skimming. In special conditions, such as where oil is mixed with and adheres to suspended solids, dissolved air flotation separators may be necessary. Figure 3-5 shows a unit designed to remove free and mechanically emulsified oil.

Biological Treatment

Waste water discharging directly to surface or ground water must be treated to remove organic compounds, which would deplete the dissolved oxygen in the receiving water. Typically, permits allow an average of 30 mg/L or 5-day biological oxygen demand (BOD). Treatment is accomplished by processes that convert soluble organic compounds to biological cell mass, which can be separated from the effluent by gravity in a clarifier. Colloidal material and some nondegradable compounds are normally absorbed in the settled solids.

Biological waste-water treatment plants are expensive to build and operate, and specialized experience is necessary to produce a successful design. Consequently, an industry faced with a biological treatment requirement should first compare the feasibility and economics of discharging to a municipal treatment system to building its own facility. If the build alternative is indicated, a choice must be made between the

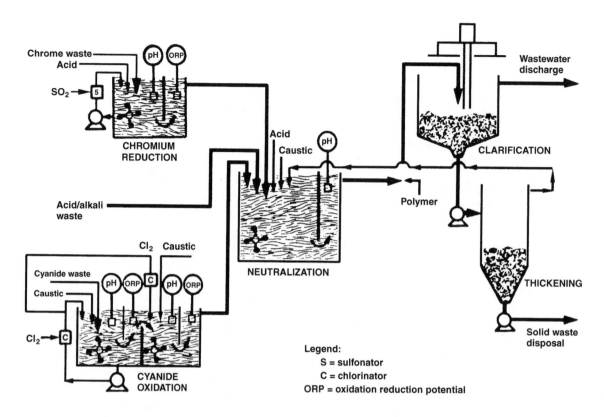

Figure 3-2   Conventional, Electroplating, Industry Waste-Water Treatment

Note: Not to scale.

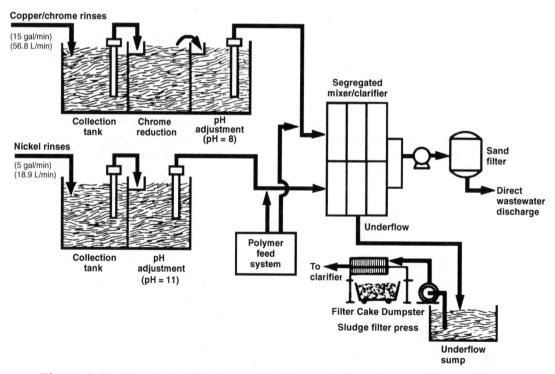

Figure 3-3   Treatment System with Waste-Water Stream Segregation

Note: Not to scale.

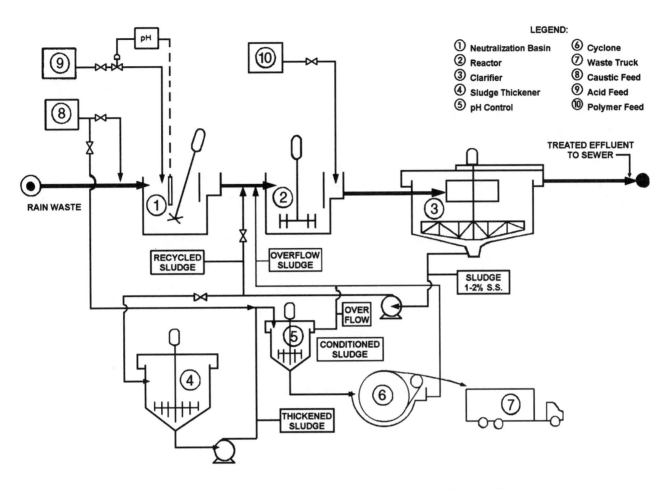

**Figure 3-4 Typical Continuous Treatment of Waste Water
and Solid-Handling System for Heavy Metals**

Note: Not to scale.

available application methods, including activated sludge, aerated lagoons, trickling filters and rotating filters, and the anaerobic process. Expert advice is warranted.

REFERENCES

Codes and standards

1. American National Standards Institute (ANSI). *Chemical plant and petroleum refinery piping*, Standard B3.13. New York: ANSI..

2. American Petroleum Institute (API). *Large welded petroleum tanks*, Specification 12D. Washington, DC: API.

3. ——. *Small welded petroleum tanks*, Specification 12F. Washington, DC: API.

4. ——. *Steel tanks for oil storage*, Standard 250. Washington, DC: API.

5. American Society of Mechanical Engineers (ASME). *ASME boiler and pressure vessel code.* New York: ASME.

6. National Fire Protection Association (NFPA). *Flammable and combustible liquids code*, NFPA 30. Quincy, Massachusetts: National Fire Protection Association.

7. Underwriters' Laboratory (UL). *Steel above ground tanks for flammable and combustible liquids*, UL 142. Northbrook, Illinois: UL.

8. ——. *Steel underground tanks for flammable and combustible liquids*, UL 58. Northbrook, Illinois: UL.

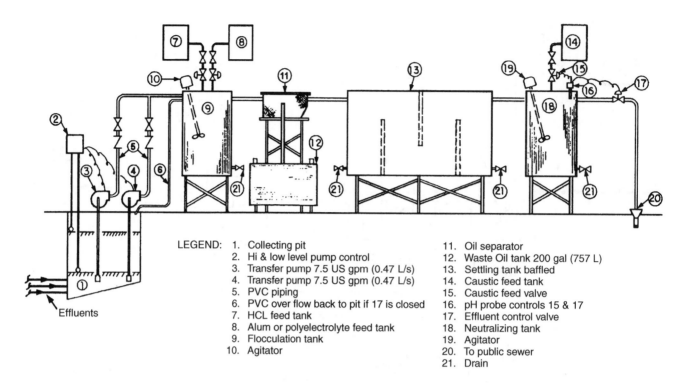

LEGEND:
1. Collecting pit
2. Hi & low level pump control
3. Transfer pump 7.5 US gpm (0.47 L/s)
4. Transfer pump 7.5 US gpm (0.47 L/s)
5. PVC piping
6. PVC over flow back to pit if 17 is closed
7. HCL feed tank
8. Alum or polyelectrolyte feed tank
9. Flocculation tank
10. Agitator
11. Oil separator
12. Waste Oil tank 200 gal (757 L)
13. Settling tank baffled
14. Caustic feed tank
15. Caustic feed valve
16. pH probe controls 15 & 17
17. Effluent control valve
18. Neutralizing tank
19. Agitator
20. To public sewer
21. Drain

Figure 3-5 Emulsified-Oil Removal Flow Sheet

Note: Not to scale.

Government publications

1. Environmental Protection Agency (EPA). *Activated carbon process for treatment of wastewater containing hexavalent chromium,* EPA-600/ 2-79-130.

   Contains technical analysis and/or comparison of environmental problem solutions, equipment, or control strategies. It is available through the National Technical Information Service (NTIS) (see "Resources" below).

2. ——. *The EPA effluent guidelines series,* EPA-440.

   Contains in-depth analysis of specific industrial groups, including waste characterizations, control and treatment technologies, and applicable regulatory standards. The industrial groups covered by these guidelines are listed in Table 3-1 of this chapter. These publications are available through the National Technical Information Service (NTIS) (see "Resources" below).

3. ——. *Treatment of organic chemical manufacturing wastewater for reuse,* EPA-600. 2-79-184.

   See note for reference no. 1 above.

4. New York State Department of Environmental Conservation. 1983. *Technology for the storage of hazardous liquids: A state-of-the-art review.* Albany, New York: New York State Department of Environmental Conservation.

5. US Government. *Code of federal regulations,* Clean Water Act, 40 CFR 100. Washington, DC: US Government Printing Office.

   The code is available from the Superintendent of Documents, US Government Printing Office (see "Resources" below); local government bookstores; and most public libraries.

6. ——. Op. cit. Clean Water Act, 40 CFR 400. Washington, DC: US Government Printing Office.

7. ——. Op. cit. Comprehensive Environmental Response, Compensation and Liability Act (Superfund), 40 CFR 300. Washington, DC: US Government Printing Office.

8. ——. Op. cit. Resource Conservation and Recovery Act, 40 CFR 260. Washington, DC: US Government Printing Office.

Technology and industry handbooks

1. Ciba-Geigy Pipe Systems, Inc. *Piping specifications and installation practices.* Houston, Texas: Ciba-Geigy Pipe Systems, Inc.

2. Mellar. 1976. *Corrosion resistant materials handbook.* 3d ed. Park Ridge, New Jersey: Nuyes Data Corp.

3. n.a. 1978-1980. *The encyclopedia of chemical technology.* 2d ed. New York: Interscience Publishing.

4. n.a. 1984. *Perry's chemical engineering handbook.* 6th ed. New York: McGraw-Hill.

5. Shweitzer. 1985. *Handbook of corrosion resistant pipeline.* 2d ed. Malabar, Florida: Robert E. Krieger Publishing.

RESOURCES

1   American National Standards Institute (ANSI), Inc., 1430 Broadway, New York, NY 10018.

2. American Petroleum Institute (API), 2101 L Street NW, Washington, DC 20037.

3. American Society of Mechanical Engineers (ASME), United Engineering Center, 345 East 47th Street, New York, NY 10017.

4. National Fire Protection Association (NFPA), Battery March Park, Quincy, MA 02269

5. National Technical Information Service (NTIS), Springfield, VA 22151.

6. New York State Department of Environmental Conservation, 50 Wolf Road, Albany, New York.

7. Superintendent of Documents, US Government Printing Office, Washington, DC 20402.

8. Underwriters' Laboratory, Inc., Publications Stock, 333 Pringsten Road, Northbrook, IL 60062.

Irrigation Systems

INTRODUCTION

The function of irrigation systems is to provide and distribute a predetermined amount of water in order to economically produce and/or maintain ornamental shrubs, cultivated lawns, and other large turf areas. This chapter discusses the basic design criteria and components of irrigation systems for ornamental lawns and turf. Among the factors considered are water quality and requirements, soil considerations, systems concepts, and components. A design information sheet is also provided, as Appendix A, to assist the plumbing engineer in the orderly collection of the required field information and other pertinent data.

WATER QUALITY AND REQUIREMENTS

In urban areas, where the source of the water supply is often the municipal water system, the plumbing designer does not need to be concerned with the quality of the water. In cases where private sources are used and the water quality is unknown, the water should be analyzed by the appropriate, local health authority having jurisdiction prior to use. The three main areas of concern are as follows: (1) any silt content that, if high, may result in the baking and sealing of soils, (2) any industrial waste that may be harmful to good growth, and finally (3) any soluble salts that may build up in the root area. The most common solution currently available for handling excessive amounts of silt is the construction of a settling basin, usually in the form

of a decorative lake or pond. In those areas where the salt content is excessive, 1000 ppm and beyond, the inability of the soil to cope with the problem may require the use of special highly salt-tolerant grasses.

The quantity of water required for an effective irrigation system is a function of the type of grass, the soil, and the local weather conditions. The quantity of water is usually expressed as the depth of the water applied during a given period of time over the area to be covered. The amount of water applied to a given area can be controlled easily by adjusting the length and frequency of operation of the irrigation system. An efficient irrigation system takes into consideration the rate of the application of the water, usually expressed in terms of inches/hour (in./h), and the attempt to match the application rate with the absorption rate of the soil. Often, this condition is achieved through frequent short watering cycles.

SOIL CONSIDERATIONS

Sandy, porous soils have relatively high absorption rates and can handle the high output of the sprinklers. Steep slopes and very tight, nonporous soils require low precipitation rates to avoid erosion damage and wasteful runoff.

A sufficient amount of water must be applied during each irrigation period in order to ensure a penetration to the root zone. Table 4-1 suggests guidelines for several soil profiles (net amount of water to apply per irrigation cycle). In the absence of any specific information on the soil and local weather conditions, the irrigation system may be designed for 1½ in. (38.1 mm) of water per week. The plumbing engineer, however, should consult with the local administrative authority to determine compliance with the applicable codes in the jurisdiction. The designer can obtain specific information on the soil and local weather conditions by contacting a local weather bureau, a university, or a state engineer.

Table 4-1   Net Amount of Water to Apply per Irrigation Cycle

Soil Profile	Amount, in. (mm)
Coarse, sandy soils	0.45 (11.43)
Fine, sandy loams	0.85 (21.59)
Silt loams	1.10 (27.94)
Heavy clay or clay loams	0.90 (22.86)

Note: Net amount of moisture required based on 12 in. (304.8 mm) root depth.

SYSTEM CONCEPTS

The three basic system concepts that can be used by the engineer in the design of an irrigation network are (1) the block method, (2) the quick-coupling method, and (3) the valve-per-sprinkler method.

The block system is an approach in which a single valve controls the flow of water to several sprinkler heads; it is ideal for residential and other small turf areas. Either manual or automatic valves may be used in the block system. As the irrigation area increases or where high-volume sprinkler heads are employed, the block system becomes less attractive to the designer because of the large valves and pipe lines required. Numerous sprinkler heads can be installed or reasonably sized lines and selected sprinkler heads operated without exceeding the available demand or an alternate technique. Examples of the block system are shown in Figure 4-1.

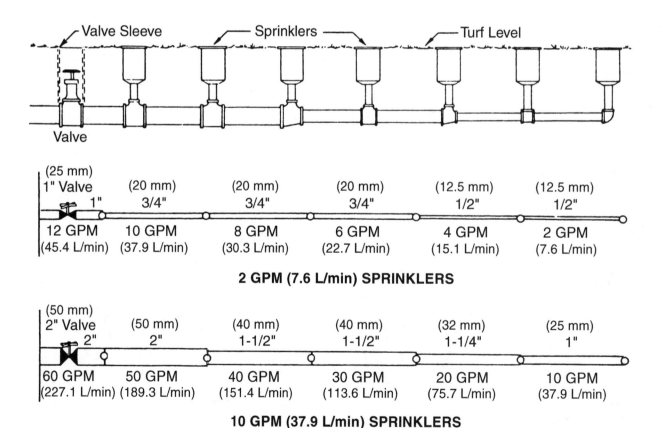

Figure 4-1   Examples of a Block System

The quick-coupling irrigation system is an answer to the high cost incurred on large block-system projects. Development of the quick-coupling valve provided a more flexible irrigation system. The valve is located underground but can be activated from the surface. Where manpower is not critical and security is reasonable, the quick-coupling irrigation system may be considered by the designer. An example of a quick-coupling valve is illustrated in Figure 4-2.

The last concept in sprinkler-system design is the valve-in-head method. Small actuator valves, operated at low voltage, provide great flexibility and control. Sprinklers in diverse areas having the same (or similar) water requirements may be operated concurrently. In other applications, such as quarter applications covering quarter circles or half circles, the irrigation sprinklers may be piped, wired, and operated together through system programmers. The valve-in-head system provides the opportunity to standardize the pipe sizes by selecting the appropriate sprin-

klers to be operated at any given time. Figure 4-3 illustrates this design.

SYSTEM COMPONENTS

Sprinkler Heads

One of the most important considerations for the plumbing engineer when designing an underground sprinkler system is the selection of the sprinkler heads. Many different types of sprinkler heads are currently manufactured for a variety of system applications. The plumbing engineer should become knowedgeable of the various types before selecting the sprinkler heads because the application rates and operating pressures must be nearly the same in each of the system's circuits.

Spray heads Surface-type spray and pop-up-type spray sprinkler heads (see Figure 4-4) produce a single sheet of water and cover a relatively small area, about 10 to 20 ft (3.05 to 6.10 m) in radius. These sprinkler heads can operate on a low-pressure range of 15 to 35 psi (103.4 to 241.3 kPa). They apply the water at a high rate of application—1 to 2 in./h (25.4 to 50.8 mm/h)—and are most economical in small turf or shrub areas and in irregularly shaped areas.

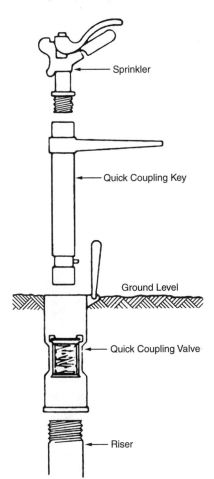

Figure 4-2   Quick-Coupling Valve

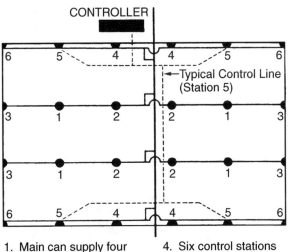

1. Main can supply four 20 gpm (75.7 L/min) sprinklers at one time.
2. 60' (18.3 m) square spacing
3. Maximum loss per station = 2.3 psi (15.9 kPa)
4. Six control stations required.
5. Similar numbered heads on same control station.
6. All lateral pipe is 1¼" (32 mm).

Figure 4-3   Valve-in-Head System

Due to the fine spray design, the pattern can be easily distorted by the wind and, therefore, should be installed in protected areas.

Impact heads Impact heads (see Figure 4-5) can be permanent or movable and either the riser-mounted type (see Figure 4-2) or the pop-up rotary type (see Figure 4-6). Impact heads have an adjustable, revolving water stream and are available in both single-nozzle and double-nozzle heads. These devices can operate at a higher pressure (25 to 100 psi [172.3 to 689.5 kPa]) and cover larger areas (40 to 100 ft [12.2 to 30.5 m] in radius). The water is applied at a lower rate (0.20 to 0.5 in./h [5.08 to 12.7 mm/h]). Because of its larger, more compact stream of water, this sprinkler head is not easily distorted by the wind and is most economical in large, open turf areas.

Free-standing sprinkler heads are not desirable where they are exposed. In such cases, the pop-up, rotary-type heads shown in Figure 4-6 may be used. These nozzles rise above the ground level only when the water is being delivered to the unit.

Part-circle, rotary sprinkler heads can discharge the same volume of water as full-circle units. A half-circle, rotary sprinkler head can provide the same amount of water as a full-circle unit over half the area, doubling the application rate. Quarter-circle sprinkler heads can quadruple the application rate. Some equipment manufacturers use different nozzles to compen-

Figure 4-5   Impact Sprinkler

Note: Photo courtesy of Rain Bird Corporation

**Figure 4-6   Rotor Sprinkler—
Arcs and Full Circles**

Note: Photo courtesy of Rain Bird Corporation

Figure 4-4   Pop-Up Spray Heads

Note: Photo courtesy of Rain Bird Corporation

sate for the reduced area and, thereby, provide a uniform application rate. If compensating nozzles are not used in part-circle sprinkler heads, these units must be valved and operated separately for a balanced application of the water.

Shrub heads Shrub heads are presently available, including bubblers (see Figure 4-7), flat-spray heads, and stream-spray heads. Shrub heads can be mounted on risers to spray over plants. If the plants are tall and not dense near the ground, shrub heads can be used on shorter risers and the spray can be directed under the plants. The spray can also be kept below the plant. Flat-spray shrub heads are best employed for these applications.

Trickle irrigation Trickle irrigation is commonly used in vineyards and orchards and routed through tubing with special emitters installed at each planting. Most emitters have flexible orifices and may have provisions for adding fertilizer. These irrigation systems have a low-volume usage and are usually not installed in conjunction with conventional lawn sprinkler systems.

Valves

Remote-control valves are generally classified into three basic categories: electric, hydraulic, and thermal-hydraulic. The electrically operated valve receives an electric signal from the controller and actuates a solenoid in the valve. This solenoid opens and closes the control valve. The hydraulic control valve is operated with the water pressure and has control tubing from the controller to the valve. The thermal-hydraulic control valve uses an electric signal from the controller to heat up the components of the valve in order to open the unit. The most common use of this valve is to control the water usage to the different zones.

These devices should be installed with access for maintenance. Most control valves have some provisions for manual operation. In some systems, manual control valves are installed in pits or vaults with a long T-handle wrench used for the activation of each circuit.

An irrigation system may be installed with an automatic check valve on the sprinkler heads. When a zone is installed on sloping terrain, these valves will close when they sense a low pressure at turnoff, preventing the drainage of the supply pipe through a sprinkler head installed in a lower area.

Atmospheric vacuum breakers (see Figure 4-8) must be installed on every sprinkler circuit downstream from the control valve to eliminate the possibility of back-siphonage into the potable water system. Many (if not all) local jurisdictions have codes that require this type of valve. The plumbing designer should consult with the local administrative authority and check all applicable codes for their requirements.

Pressure-reducing valves are installed where higher street pressures are involved and are also commonly used to maintain a constant pressure where the inlet pressures may vary. Some manufacturers offer remote-control valves with pressure regulation.

Low-flow control valves may be installed to avoid damage to the piping or tubing from pressure surges during the filling of a (dry) system. This control valve allows a slow filling of the piping or tubing until the pressure is established.

In climates where freezing conditions may occur, automatic-type drain valves should be installed at the low points of the system to allow for drainage of the system. This control valve will automatically open when the water pressure

Figure 4-7 Nozzles—Adjustable Arcs and Patterns

Note: Photo courtesy of Rain Bird Corporation

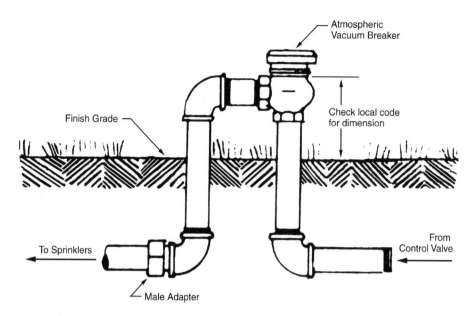

Figure 4-8   Installation of Atmospheric-Type Vacuum Breakers

drops below a set point. In heavy or dense soils, a pit of gravel should be provided for quicker drainage.

Controllers

Presently, many types of controllers for irrigation systems are available. Selection of this device is based on the specific application involved. Controllers are programmed to activate each irrigation zone at a specific time and will also control the length of time that each zone is activated. Some controllers have a "calendar," which allows the irrigation system to be used only on certain days. Other types of controllers have manual (or automatic) overrides to shut down all systems during rain or to turn on specific zones for extra water. Some controllers have soil-moisture monitors, which turn on zones only when needed. Controller panels can be surface mounted, recessed mounted, or pedestal mounted. Figure 4-9 shows a typical illustration of a surface-mounted and a pedestal-mounted irrigation-system programmer.

DESIGN INFORMATION

When designing an underground sprinkler system, the plumbing engineer should consider the following factors: the site plan, the type of plants, and the type of soil.

Site Plan

An accurate site plan, preferably laid out on graph paper and showing all buildings, shrubs, trees, hedges, walks, drives, and parking, should be drawn as closely as possible to scale. Areas where overspray is undesirable, such as on walkways and buildings, should be clearly noted. Property lines should also be shown on the site plan. The heights and diameters of shrubs and hedges should be noted to determine which sprinkler head would best suit their needs.

Types of Plantings

The designer should show the areas that will be irrigated on the site plan as well as the areas that will be omitted. Those areas that require a different style of sprinkler head and separate zoning should also be indicated. Some plantings require more frequent watering than others and, therefore, require a separate zone and a control valve of their own. The designer should determine whether the plantings should have spray on their leaves (or any other special type of spray) and should select the heads accordingly.

Type of Soil

The type of soil determines the proper rate of application of water to the soil. The length and

Figure 4-9 Irrigation Sprinkler Programmers

Note: Photo courtesy of Rain Bird Corporation

frequency of the applications can be determined by considering the soil and the types of plants.

A sufficient amount of water must be applied during each irrigation period to ensure penetration to the root zone. Table 4-1 recommends acceptable guidelines for several types of soil profile. Where available, the designer should secure local soil and weather conditions by contacting the local state extension engineer, university, or weather bureau. The local weather bureau usually publishes an evapotranspiration guide, which shows the deficit water required to maintain turf grass. This value is compiled by measuring the rainfall minus the evaporation taking place during a particular period. The balance would be the amount of water required. In the absence of any specific information on local soil and weather conditions, the irrigation system should be designed for a minimum of 1½ in. (38.1 mm) of water per week.

Sandy, porous soils (as previously indicated) have relatively high absorption rates and can handle the high output of sprinklers. Steep slopes and very tight, nonporous soils require low precipitation rates in order to avoid erosion damage and runoffs.

Type and Source of Water

The source of the water should be located on the site plan. If the water source is a well, the pump capacity, well depth, pump discharge pressure, and other pertinent data should also be recorded. If the water source is a city water main, the locations, size, service-line material, and the length of piping from the service line to the meter should be researched by the plumbing engineer. The water-meter size and the static water pressure of the city main are also needed. The designer should determine whether special meter pits or piping arrangements are required by the utility company.

System Location

Due to the influence of physical and local climatic conditions, the general area may require specific design considerations, such as drain valves on systems subjected to freezing temperatures. Windy areas require a closer spacing of sprinklers, and the wind velocity and the direction must be considered. For areas on sloping terrain, there will be a difference in the outlet pressure, and consideration must be made for system drainage.

The designer must review local codes to determine acceptable piping materials, installation, requirements, and the approved connection to municipal water works.

REFERENCES

1. Irrigation Association. *The ABC's of lawn sprinkler systems.* Fairfax, Virginia: Irrigation Association.

2. Pair, Claude H., ed. *Sprinkler irrigation.* 4th ed. Silver Spring, Maryland: Sprinkler Irrigation Association.

3. The Rainbird Company. *Architect-engineers turf sprinkler manual.* Glendora, California: The Rainbird Company.

4. The Toro Company, Irrigation Division. *Design information for large turf irrigation systems.* Riverside, California: The Toro Company.

5. Young, Virgil E. *Sprinkler irrigation systems.* Auburn, Washington: Mister Rain, Inc.

RESOURCE

1. Irrigation Association, 8260 Willow Oaks Corp. Dr., no. 120, Fairfax, VA 22031.

APPENDIX 4-A
SUGGESTED INFORMATION SHEET FOR SPRINKLER SYSTEM DESIGN

All available information should be contained on this sheet, plot plan, or both.

1. Project name_____ Address_____

2. Water supply:

    a. Location and size of existing tap, meter, pump, or other._____

    b. Existing meter, pump, or tap capacity: Residual Pressure_____GPM_____

    c. Power supply: Location_____ Voltage_____

    d. Length, type, location, and size of existing supply line. (Identify on plan.)

3. Area to be watered. Identify all planted areas whether shrubbery or trees; indicate clearance under trees. (Identify on plan.)

4. Soil type: Light_____ Medium_____ Heavy_____

5. Hours per day/night allowed for irrigation:_____

6. Amount of precipitation required per week:_____

7. Area to be bordered or not watered. (Identify on plan.)

8. Elevations and prevailing wind conditions. (Identify on plan.)

9. Type of system: (a) automatic electric_____ (b) automatic hydraulic_____

    (c) manual pop-up_____ (d) manual quick-coupling_____ (e) other_____

10. Indicate equipment preference:_____

11. Indicate preferred location for valves and controllers:_____

    _____

12. Indicate vacuum breaker and/or drain valve requirement:_____

    _____

13. Indicate pipe material preference: 2½" and larger_____ 2" and smaller_____

14. Indicate any preference for sprinkler riser types:_____

    SPECIAL NOTES (Use additional sheet if necessary.):

    _____

    _____

    _____

    _____

    _____

    _____

    _____

    _____

    _____

    _____

5

Reflecting Pools and Fountains

INTRODUCTION

Reflecting pools and fountains provide visual and auditory pleasure, add charm to garden areas, and provide a retreat area in which to rest and relax. Fountains generate sound and provide a cooling effect on hot summer days. Fountains may be self-contained units or pre-engineered kits or they may be custom designed and built. Self-contained fountains, consisting of pools, pumps, valves, lights, and other hardware, are shipped assembled, and the addition of water is all that is necessary to put the fountain into normal operation. No permanent connections to the plumbing system are required. Pre-engineered fountain kits, complete with equipment, need only assembly and hook-up to the water-supply, drainage, and power sources.

Plumbing engineers, architects, and landscape architects are all involved in the creation of display fountains and reflecting pools. The architects are concerned with the overall aesthetics, whereas the engineers must be familiar with the available fountain equipment and the technical details of each component if they are to design systems that will achieve the desired display effects. The plumbing engineer should work closely with the architect and the landscape architect to achieve the desired display. In addition, the systems should be designed with provisions for cleaning, water treatment, and maintenance. Custom fountains providing small or large water displays with almost any desired decorative effects are discussed in this chapter. Also included are the technical details of pool design; mechanical equipment, including spray systems; and operation and maintenance.

The engineer must also be aware that the fountain is usually represented on a set of architectural drawings as an undefined space or a rendering. It is also usually the last item to be coordinated. What this means is that the engineer usually designs the fountain in its entirety, including the water effect and its influence on the surrounding area. Then, he/she needs to quickly (and accurately) select the nozzles, determine flow rates, select the equipment, try to get space for the equipment, coordinate with the other disciplines involved, then coach contractors, who look upon a fountain as a glorified swimming pool. When all this is done, however, the engineer can look upon a beautiful piece of engineered art that will most likely never be duplicated and can be proud to claim it as his/her work.

POOL DESIGN

General Considerations

A number of general items of information should be kept in mind when designing a fountain.

For an engineer or designer, the most important issue surrounding any body of water is safety. There is always a risk attached to a water feature. It is not the intent of this chapter to acquaint the engineer with drowning and entrapment issues, but the engineer is encouraged to study the available codes and standards regarding swimming pools and spas and apply them as necessary. Many jurisdictions regard 18 in. (457.2 mm) of water as the maximum depth allowed without severe access restrictions, such as railings, fences, and gates.

From a mechanical, operating perspective, the most important thing is to locate all pumps to ensure flooded suction lines. If at all possible, locate the pumps so that the operating water level of the fountain is above the suction inlet of the pump. This helps to prevent cavitation and to ensure that the pump primes quickly.

Painting the pool interior a dark color helps to conceal piping, lighting, cable, junction boxes, and other equipment located in the pool, and, in addition, provides reflective qualities. But the dark color tends to cause an increase in water temperature by absorbing the sun's heat. This, in turn, creates a requirement for more chlorine. Thin or fine-mist spray effects are difficult to see against light colors, mixed colors, or lace-type backgrounds. A massive display should be used under these conditions.

The construction of pools at or below grade level creates a potential problem with leaves and other debris blowing into the pool, therefore, this should be avoided. Reflecting pools and fountains may be installed above or below grade. Above-grade fountains offer the advantage of adding more height to the water display. Multilevel pools provide the possibility of having numerous waterfall displays with only one water source.

Aerating nozzles that use a venturi action to entrain air into the water stream can cause a wave action in circular pools. In such cases, surge collars or underwater baffles should be installed to minimize this action.

Water will splash horizontally approximately one half the height of the water display except where wind is a problem. Since wind can push water long distances, it is important to locate nozzles so that the splash and wind effect will not create undue problems. It may be advisable to provide a wind control to lower the height of the display or to shut off the system when there is too much wind.

Water hitting water creates a lot of noise. There are times and locations when this is desirable. When the noise is too loud, however, it can be reduced by locating various types of planting around a pool.

Multilevel Pools

Multilevel and multiple pools involve special considerations, which, if taken into account, do not present any difficulty. If these considerations are

not taken into account, however, disaster can result.

The amount of flow over a waterfall is determined by the height of the water flowing over the weir. This height over the weir is the same as the height of the pool behind the weir. When the pumps stop, this water will all come over the weir and spill into the pool below. The water in the air (i.e., the waterfall) will also come to rest in the lower pool. The lower pool must be sized to accommodate this extra water. For the water in the air, the depth over the weir times the height of the water is sufficiently accurate to calculate the volume.

Multilevel pools should have some method of draining the upper pools. A small drain line with a screw plug at the upper pool can be used. The drain line should be a maximum of 1¼ in. (31.75 mm) to restrict the discharge rate into the lowest pool.

For multiple pools with different elevations, a common reference must be established to drain the basins. An example would be waterfalls at several different elevations with basins at several different elevations served by a single pump system. If the pumps were turned off, the water in the basins would all drain to the lowest basin through the common suction header. To prevent this, either check valves must be installed in all suction and discharge lines or all basins must drain to a surge pit. The surge pit provides a common reference for the pumps and allows each basin to drain independently of the others. The surge pit method is also much easier to balance than the method with check valves. (See Figure 5-1.)

For multiple pools at the same elevation, an equalizer line should be run between the pools. No matter how accurate the calculations and installation, two identical pools will have varying flow rates. The equalizer line should not tie into any other line except a valved drain. The equalizer should be sized so that it is as large as the largest line coming into the pools. If each pool receives the discharge through a 4-in. (100-mm) line, the equalizer should be a 4-in. (100-mm) line.

Preliminary Display Selection and Determination of Flow Rates

Spray jets and nozzles The flow rates for spray

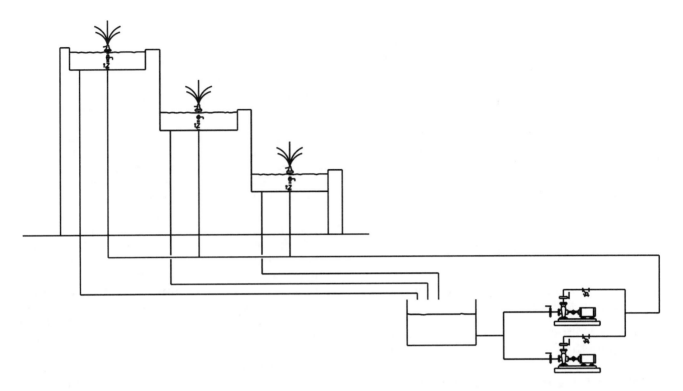

Figure 5-1 Multilevel Pools with a Surge Pit

jets and nozzles should be determined by the manufacturer's data. Most manufacturers publish catalogs showing the various types of jet in operation. The client should be given the opportunity to select the jets from a subjective standpoint; the selection should then be reviewed by the engineer for practicality.

Weirs Weirs are normally sized by the length of the weir and the depth of the water flowing over the weir edge. The engineer may have to assist the client in determining the effect desired. It is useful to have the client see an existing water feature then actually measure the depth over a weir. If the client desires an unbroken sheet of water over the weir into the pool, a rule of thumb is about ¼ in. (6.35 mm) of water over the weir per 4 ft of vertical drop.

The four most common types of weir are the rounded edge; the upward-tapered weir; the downward-tapered weir; and the downward-tapered, metal-edge weir. The rounded-edge weir is used when it is desired to have the water run down the wall surface. The upward-tapered weir requires more water than the other types and should not be used for waterfalls exceeding 5 ft

in height. The downward-tapered weir is very effective in creating smooth sheets for waterfalls up to 15 ft in height. The downward-tapered, metal-edge weir achieves the same effect as the downward-tapered weir with the added advantage of being easier to level.

The waterfall or weir is normally supplied from a trough behind the weir edge. The trough can be supplied with water by many methods as long as the surface disturbance is kept to a minimum. A header can be installed with holes drilled along the length of the header to supply water equally along the length of the trough. Hydrophilic well piping, precut with slots along the length of the pipe, makes a very smooth supply method. Oversized inlets (to lower the water velocity) in the bottom of the trough with diverter plates can also be used.

Weir lips must be level. This is difficult to achieve with poured concrete, therefore, a metal or plastic lip should be provided. If the spill lip is in the shape of an overhang, a drip lip in the shape of a ¼ in. (6.35 mm) deep rectangular slot should be provided under the slot. This will prevent the water from running down the wall.

Filtration turnover The filtration turnover rate is determined by the volume of the pool and the desired number of hours per complete water change. The filtration turnover can vary from 4 to 12 h per complete water change. This needs to be determined by the engineer. For areas with blowing dust and debris, a faster water change is needed. For cleaner areas, such as those indoors, a slower water change can be used. The filtration flow rate is determined by dividing the pool water volume, in gallons (liters), by the turnover time, in minutes.

Example 5-1

An 8000-gal pool divided by (12 h x 60 min) equals 11.1 gpm flow rate.

(A 30 283-L pool divided by [12 h x 60 min] equals 45.42 L/min flow rate.)

Therefore, a filtration system sized for a flow rate of 12 gpm (45.42 L/min) would be adequate.

Inlet/Outlet and Device Location

By convention, an "inlet" is defined as a device allowing water to flow into the pool. An "outlet" is defined as a device allowing water to leave the pool.

Main drains Main drains are provided for pump suction and draining the pool. Main drains should be located at the lowest point of the pool. There should be at least one main drain for the lowest basin. Main drains should be located so that there is not more than 20 ft between drains or more than 15 ft from the sidewall of the pool. The main drains should be sized to accommodate the full flow of the system. Main-drain gratings should be sized at no greater than 1.5 fps through the grating. See the manufacturer's listings for the approved flow rate through anti-vortex gratings.

Main drains used for pump suction must have some method of preventing entrapment: either they must be the anti-vortex type or they must be installed in pairs at least 4 ft apart to prevent suction entrapment. Although reflecting pools and fountains are not intended to be occupied by humans, people do accidentally (and on purpose) fall into them. Pairing drains and using anti-vortex drains minimizes the risk of suction entrapment and disembowelment. If paired drains are used, they must be connected

to a common suction line without any intervening valves. (See Figure 5-2.)

Main drains are used to empty the pool for cleaning and to drain storm water when the pool is empty. A drain line is run to the nearest storm drain line and a valve is installed in this line.

Skimmers Skimmers are necessary in all pools to collect windblown debris and dust. Even indoor pools can collect an amazing amount of floating debris that must be cleaned out periodically. Skimmers normally consist of a skimmer body that is cast into the pool wall, a floating weir, and a strainer basket. The floating weir draws a thin layer of water into the skimmer. With a thin layer, the water's velocity is higher and its influence extends farther out into the pool. Skimmer strainer baskets need to be cleaned out periodically, and access to the strainer defines the type of skimmer used. Top-access skimmers, while easiest to maintain, are very visible. Since architects prefer to hide every component possible, front-loading skimmers are preferred. In addition, front-loading skimmers are less prone to vandalism.

Skimmers should be located so that there is 1 skimmer provided for each 500 ft² (46.45 m²) of lower basin, with a minimum of 1 skimmer. The skimmer system should be sized to accommodate the full filtration flow. A 2-in. (50.8-mm) skimmer can accept about 30 gpm (113.56 L/min), but skimmers can be ganged together to increase their capacity. A majority of the skimmers should be located such that the prevailing winds and current blow the debris toward them.

Filtration return inlets Filtration return inlets come from the filters and return clean water to

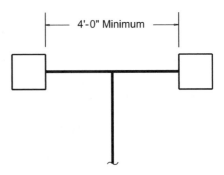

Figure 5-2 Main Drains

the pool. Return inlets should be placed at least 12 in. (304.8 mm) below water level to minimize surface disturbance. If the pool is too shallow, increase the inlet pipe size to reduce the velocity into the pool. Each pool should have a minimum of 2 inlets, with a sizing criteria of 1 inlet per 600 ft^2 (0.093 m^2) of basin. Inlets should be sited to direct flow toward the skimmers.

Mechanical space or vault The pumping equipment can be located in the building, in an underground equipment vault, or outdoors above ground in a protected area. The determination as to whether or not to provide a vault depends on the following factors: (1) the distance from the pool to the mechanical space in the building vs. the distance from the pool to an underground vault; (2) the difference in cost for piping, electrical wiring, and conduit between the two locations; (3) the cost of the mechanical space vs. the cost of a vault; and (4) whether or not mechanical space is available.

If the equipment is installed in an area remote from the fountain, it is advisable to have a remote-control panel located within view of the fountain.

Provide adequate space for all fountain equipment, including electrical panels. Observe all code-mandated clearance requirements. Allow some method of removing motors and pumps that will not require the removal of parts of the building. This could be an overhead crane rail or merely an eye bolt attached to the structure over each motor for lifting.

A floor drain is required near the equipment. Specify a floor drain with a backwater valve if there is any possibility of water backing up through the drain, especially in a vault. If a floor drain cannot flow by gravity to the sewer, a sump pit and pump is required. If the equipment is installed in a vault, a battery-operated, backup sump pump may be desirable.

In a vault, provide an electric receptacle; a light; a hose bibb; a ventilating blower; intake and exhaust vents; an access ladder; and a lockable, spring-loaded access hatch big enough for all equipment to pass through. A heavy manhole cover is not recommended because the maintenance personnel become annoyed with lifting the cover and tend to *forget* their maintenance duties. In some cases, a 3-ft deep vault with an access hatch covering the entire vault is adequate.

FOUNTAIN SYSTEMS AND COMPONENTS

The fountain system consists of the following major systems:

1. Display system.
2. Piping system.
3. Water-treatment system.
   A. Mechanical-filtration system.
   B. Chemical-treatment system.
4. Makeup-water system.
5. Overflow and drainage system.
6. Lighting system.
7. Other miscellaneous systems.

The reflecting pool may or may not have a display system, depending on the desired effect.

Each of these systems often overlaps or relies on another system to function correctly. For instance, if the filtration system is not working properly, the spray heads will load up with debris and not function correctly. If the water is not kept at the proper level with an autofill, the lighting system may overheat.

Display System

There are two distinct display types: static and dynamic. Static displays have a constant or nearly constant volumetric flow rate at all times. Examples include a waterfall weir and constant-height jets. Dynamic displays vary the flow through the system. Examples are dancing fountains, where the fountain appears to react to music or lights, and waterfalls and rivers that are part of a simulated storm scenario. For either type of display, the typical system consists of the following components: suction outlets and suction piping, pump(s), return piping, and discharge device(s). The display system for each type of effect, e.g., nozzles, weirs, whirlpools, and waves, should have a different pump system dedicated to it.

Piping System

Two separate types of piping systems are defined for any fountain. These are the display systems and the filter system. The piping for these systems can normally share suction outlets but should remain separate from there until returning to the pool. An example of a poor design is a fountain system where the display water and the filter water are combined such that a single pump draws from the pool and pumps through the filter then back to the nozzle. When the filter is clean, this system will work fine. As soon as the filter gets dirty, however, the flow from the nozzle will gradually drop until the filter is backwashed. Then the cycle will begin again.

Water-Treatment System

The water-treatment system consists of two separate processes. First, mechanical filtration removes the solids and some of the suspended organics from the water. Second, the chemical filtration disinfects and balances the water to provide clean, sparkling clear, odor-free water that is pleasing to the eye and not detrimental to the pool and equipment.

Makeup-Water System

It is essential to maintain the proper water level in the pool. The reasons are threefold. First, certain spray nozzles require that the water level vary no more than ½ in. (12.7 mm) in order to achieve the desired display. A variation in the water level causes the nozzle display to become erratic and to differ from the original design. Second, underwater lights must be submerged to a specific depth to both protect the lights and to remove heat. Third, a substantial water-level drop could cause the suction line to entrain air, resulting in pump cavitation and possible damage.

Overflow and Drainage System

The fountain must be equipped with an overflow system to handle storm water and the possible malfunction of the makeup-water system. In addition, mundane reasons, such as draining the pool for winter and cleaning, mandate that a drain system be installed.

Water-Heating System

If a fountain is to be kept in operation during the winter months and it is possible for the water to freeze, an aquastat-controlled pool heater should be provided. The heater should be sized to maintain pool water at about 35 to 40°F (1.67 to 4.44°C).

Lighting System

Underwater lights are used to provide illumination for the various displays. The number of lights depends on the overall size of the pool, the depth of the water, the height and width of the water display, and possible interference from ambient lighting. Lights can be white or another color as desired.

SYSTEM AND COMPONENT SELECTION AND DESIGN CRITERIA

Filter Systems

Types of filter There are many types of filter on the market today. Some of these are specialty filters for water treatment, RO systems and the like. For fountains, swimming pool and spa filters best fit the application. Mechanical filtration is required to remove suspended particulates down to about 50 μ. In this range, cartridge filters and high-rate, pressure sand filters are the best choice for fountains.

There is a division in filter sizes that occurs around the 120 gpm (454.25 L/min) flow rate. Above that rate are the commercial filters used on larger pools and fountains and below are the residential filters used on smaller pools and fountains. Many manufacturers do not make a distinction regarding quality at the different levels, but some do. Check with the distributors and pool contractors as to which filters cause the least trouble.

When sizing filters, it is good practice to use more than one filter when the flow rate is above 120 gpm (454.25 L/min). For example, a system that requires 280 gpm (1059.92 L/min) of filtration would do better with two filters sized at 140 gpm (529.96 L/min) each than one filter sized at 280 gpm (1059.92 L/min). The reason is cleaning time. Whether the filter selected is a cartridge, sand, or diatomaceous earth (DE), it will have to be cleaned at some time. With multiple filters, the filtration process continues while one filter is being cleaned. In the case of sand filters, the filter type of choice for most large systems, the backwash flow rate is lower, necessitating a smaller backwash pit and sewer line.

With multiple filters, use multiple pumps. Although the pumps are not to be piped individually to each filter, a pump can be shut down while a filter is serviced. This will prevent over-running the other filters while one filter is down.

Cartridge filters Cartridge filters are lower in first cost than the other types of filters and are relatively easy to maintain. The filter consists of a body constructed of plastic or stainless steel that contains a polyester element. The cartridge filter element is cleaned by removing the filter top and pulling out the element. It can then be hosed clean and reinstalled in the body. These filters are available in sizes ranging from 150 gpm down to 5 gpm. The small-size filters are of the inline type made for filtering spas and are excellent for small fountains.

Cartridge filters must be removed from the body to be cleaned and require some space to be hosed down. This is a consideration when the fountain is indoors and requires that the cartridges be taken away to be cleaned. A second set of cartridges will be necessary for a swap.

Cartridges should be sized at 0.375 gpm/ft^2 maximum flow rate.

High-rate, pressure sand filters A pressure sand filter consists of a body constructed of plastic, fiberglass, or stainless steel that contains sand to filter the water. The term "high rate" comes from the flow rate per square foot of sand bed. If the flow rate is above about 10 gpm (37.85 L/min), the filter is classified as "high rate." There are sand filters that are considered "low" or "slow" rate, but they are seldom specified today. Water enters the filter at the top and is pumped down through the sand to an underdrain manifold with slots narrow enough so that the water will pass but the sand will not. The water is piped to the sand filter through a series of valves (see Figure 5-3) or a multiport valve. A multiport valve is a single-handle control with four ports that can be configured to either filter, backwash, rinse, shutoff, bypass, or drain. They are limited to filters with 3-in. (80-mm) or smaller connections. Either the valve series or the multiport valve may be automated.

As the filter accumulates debris, the differential pressure across the filter will increase. When the differential pressure has increased to a specific point, normally about 15 psi, the filter has reached the limit of its effective filter run and requires cleaning. Cleaning is accomplished by backwashing.

Backwashing a sand filter is exactly what it sounds like. Backwashing reverses the flow so that the pump now forces water through the underdrain manifold with enough flow to lift the sand bed and stir it around. The debris is floated out of the sand and flows out the inlet pipe to a drain. A backwash sight glass should be installed to allow the operator to see when the effluent is clear.

Provisions must be made with the project plumbing engineer if a sand filter is to be used. Many jurisdictions require that a sand filter be backwashed into a sand trap to prevent sand from entering the sewer system. Some jurisdictions require that a sand filter backwash as an indirect waste into a pit. The ultimate destination of the backwash effluent must also be determined. Some jurisdictions allow effluent to flow to the storm sewer, others require it to go to the sanitary sewer. Provision must be made to handle the large flow rates that are customary with a sand-filter backwash. Although the backwash only lasts 5 min at maximum, an enormous amount of water can be used in that time. Backwash rates are generally 20 gpm/ft^2 of filter area.

A high-rate, pressure sand filter is generally sized at 12 to 15 gpm/ft^2 of filter area, although the filter may be rated up to 20 gpm/ft^2.

Sizing filters To size a filter, first determine the filtration rate through the pool. Once this is established, divide the filtration rate by 0.375 for cartridge filters or 12 to 15 for sand filters. This will determine the required filter area. For filtration rates over 120 gpm (454.25 L/min), dual filters should be considered, with the flow divided equally between them. Filters should never be sized at their maximum allowed flow rate. This will cause higher pressure drops through the filter over the filter run and will substantially increase the energy used by the pump.

Pumps

Display pumps Display pumps can be the dry type, the self-priming dry type, or the submersible type. When it is necessary to locate the pump above water level, a self-priming pump should be used. If the size and cost of a self-priming pump preclude its use, a foot valve or check valve may be installed in the suction line.

Submersible pumps are more expensive than dry-type pumps and may require additional water

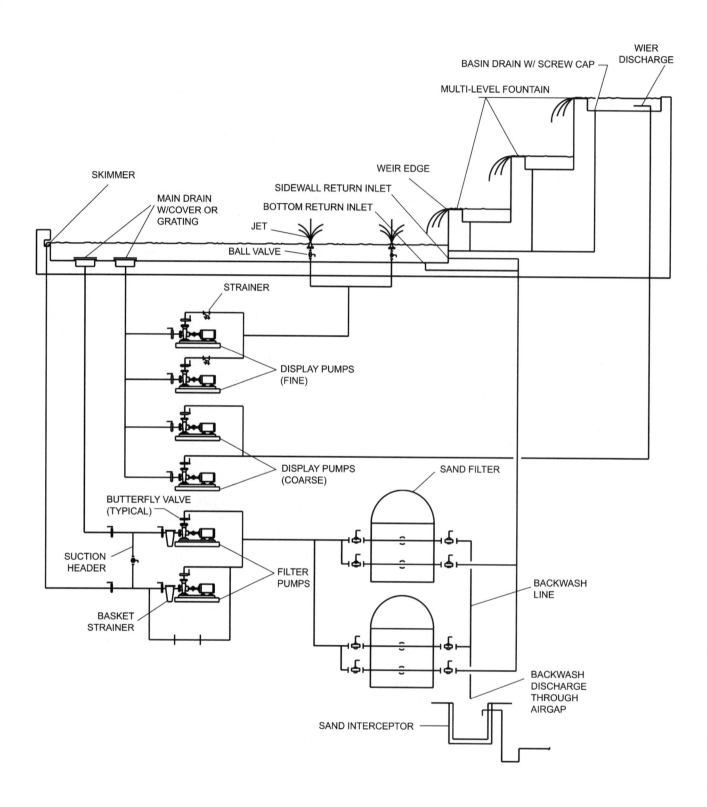

Figure 5-3   Fountain Components

depth in the pool. This can be accomplished by providing a pump pit in the water and installing a fiberglass grating over the pit. The grate offers protection from vandals and also hides the pumps from view. The advantage of using a submersible pump is that it can eliminate the need for long runs of pump suction and discharge piping, thereby saving on horsepower. Since there is less piping and corresponding friction loss, the required pump head is lower. In some cases, this can mean a substantial difference in horsepower. The *National Electric Code* does not allow submersible pumps over 230 V to be installed in fountains.

Dry-type pumps are installed in a vault adjacent to the pool or a mechanical equipment room within the building. The preferred installation is one where the pump-suction inlet is located below the pool's operating water level. If this is not allowed, a self-priming pump may be used. In most projects, an end-suction, close-coupled, centrifugal pump is used, but there are some projects where a horizontal, split-case, centrifugal pump is necessary. This can occur where the flow rate is high and the required pump head is low. In all cases, the pump selection should be made using the manufacturer's pump curves. Multiple pumps in parallel are preferred to one large pump. Redundancy, wind control, and opportunities for different displays are excellent reasons for multiple pumps. Some fountains have displays that require high-pressure, low-flow nozzles; low-pressure, high-flow nozzles; and waterfall discharges. Where there are multiple types of display, a separate pumping system should be used for each type.

Display pumps are sized according to the hydraulic calculations for friction loss and flow rate. Pumps can be cast iron, bronze or plastic. Pump materials should be suitable for contact with fresh water. Since vaults and mechanical spaces are frequently tight, it should be possible to remove the pumps' motors and impellers without disconnecting the piping. Pumps should be equipped with suction basket strainers with removable baskets, suction and discharge gauge taps, isolation and balancing valves, eccentric and concentric reducers as required, and flexible connectors. Proper pump piping practices, as described elsewhere in the *Data Book,* should be followed.

To size the display pump the following steps should be followed:

1. Determine the static head required between the lowest water level and the highest water level. This is important for multilevel fountains.

2. Determine the head required at the discharge point. Manufacturers provide charts that give the gpm and pressure required at the nozzle. If the discharge is for a waterfall effect with the discharge point submerged, use 10 ft of head.

3. Calculate the friction loss in the piping, fittings, and valves.

4. Add the results to obtain the required pump head.

5. Determine the total gpm as required for the nozzles, using the manufacturer's charts (or the gpm for a weir, as calculated using the weir length and depth).

6. Select the pump using the manufacturer's pump curves. If the exact flow rate and head cannot be obtained, select the next larger size pump. In almost all cases, the pump selected should have a flat pump curve. Select the motor that will provide a nonoverloading condition for the entire length of the pump curve. Wide-open conditions are common in water effects.

Filter pumps Filter pumps may be of the same type as the display pumps. (See discussion above.) There are few reasons why all the pumps cannot be of the same type.

Filter pumps are sized to match the gpm (L/min) required for a proper filtration rate and the head required to give that rate with a dirty filter. Components in the filter system that contribute to head loss include: skimmers and main drains (piped in parallel so that the longest run must be determined), valves, basket strainers, face piping (the piping connecting the pump to the filter), return piping, and return inlets. Elevation changes need to be accounted for and added or subtracted. Generally, since return inlets are below the water level, there is no net elevation change.

It is important that the pump be sized to give the proper flow rate with a dirty filter, but it is also important that the engineer calculate the operating point on the pump curve with a clean filter. There can be a substantial difference between these two conditions in pump flow, and a variable flow-control device might be considered for evening out the flow rates.

Pump strainers and suction screens As a general rule, suction strainers protect the pumps and discharge strainers protect the nozzles. Display pumps are not as likely to pick up waterborne debris as are filter pumps, which are connected to skimmers and main drains. Provisions can be made for display pumps to have gratings over their suction outlets in the fountain.

Basket strainers on the pump suction protect the pump from waterborne debris, which could get caught in the impeller. Although display pumps can be protected somewhat from debris large enough to damage the pump, filter pumps should always have basket strainers.

Y-type strainers are mostly used to protect nozzles with small openings. They are installed on the discharge side of display pumps to intercept waterborne debris before it jams inside an actuator or orifice. The strainer should be equipped with a valve and hose connection to allow for easy blowdown.

Suction diffusers are installed on the suction inlet to the pump and allow for rapid changes in the direction of piping close to the pump. The diffuser slows the water down and straightens it so that it enters the pump with less turbulence. Suction diffusers are also equipped with screens but they are very difficult to remove for cleaning and should probably not be used when other methods are available.

Piping and Valves

Most piping for fountains is made of Schedule 40 PVC plastic. Easy handling, light weight, and low friction losses make it the piping of choice in most fountains. Although PVC seems to be the perfect choice, there are some caveats pertaining to its use. Piping installed through pool walls and floors and into the pool should be copper or brass. PVC piping exposed to sunlight will become brittle, unless it is specifically made to withstand the effects of ultraviolet rays. Pump suction and discharge piping installed underground or within a building can be PVC where allowed by the local authorities. Be aware that smooth holes have been found in plastic piping installed underground. The University of Illinois and the University of Florida both determined that the holes were caused by termites. They do not eat the PVC; they chew through it when it gets in the way of their continued foraging for food. Also, be aware that most codes do not allow plastic piping to be installed in a plenum. Ductile iron, galvanized steel pipe, or stainless-steel pipe can be used if large pipe sizes are required and PVC cannot be used. Carbon-steel piping should never be used in a fountain due to the highly oxygenated water running through the piping.

All buried piping should be treated as a water-service application. Specifically, piping needs to be bedded in sand or clean, rock-free backfill. All changes of direction in piping 3 in. (76.2 mm) and larger need to be restrained with poured concrete thrust blocks. Starts and stops in fountain systems can cause severe water hammer and resultant failure in unrestrained systems.

All piping penetrations into the pool wall should be water stopped in some fashion. A common method is to use a "puddle flange" attached to the pipe itself. For penetrating walls into mechanical rooms, a mechanical pipe seal can be used. (See Figure 5-4.)

Unions or flanges should be used at the final connection to all equipment so that the equipment can be easily removed for repairs. Drainage lines from the overflow and drain lines should be either PVC or cast iron, as required by local code. Water makeup and fill lines should be copper tubing. Different metal pipes carrying water or installed underground must not come into contact with each other (dielectric isolation).

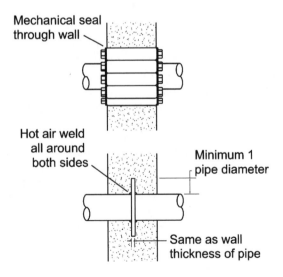

Figure 5-4   Wall Penetrations

All piping systems should be pressure tested immediately after installation, and the test should be left on until the piping is ready to be connected to the inlet and outlet devices and equipment. This way, a glance at a pressure gauge can indicate immediately if a pipe has been broken during another phase of the construction. The test pressure should be limited to 50 psi (344.74 kPa), since the fountain piping systems are operated at relatively low pressures. If the system requires higher pressure, the pressure test should be made at a pressure that is 25 psi (172.37 kPa) higher than the operating pressure. Make sure that plastic piping is tested within the pressures recommended by the manufacturer.

Prior to connecting the devices and equipment, piping systems should be flushed and cleaned. Caps should be left on until ready to make the final connection to prevent debris from entering the piping. More than one pump has been damaged or had reduced flow due to debris that was in the pipe before the pump was connected.

Suction-line piping Size the suction line at a velocity not to exceed 6 fps for copper piping and 10 fps (3.05 m/s) for plastic piping. Provide a suction inlet designed so that the drain will not trap a person in the pool. This is accomplished by having dual drains spaced at least 4 ft apart or dual drains located in different planes (such as a bottom drain and a sidewall drain) or by using anti-vortex drains. Some means of preventing vortexing should be used to prevent cavitation of the pumps. If a minimum of 18 in. (457.2 mm) of water cannot be provided over a suction drain, size the drain for ½ of the manufacturer's recommended maximum flow and add more drains as necessary. Suction-line piping should be installed without vertical loops, which can become air bound. In addition, it is critical that suction piping pass a 25 psi (172.37 kPa) pressure test because a void as small as a pinhole can prevent a self-priming pump from pumping.

Return piping Return piping should be sized at 6 fps maximum for copper piping and 10 fps maximum for plastic piping. Return piping, especially piping close to the discharge of the pump, should be properly braced within the mechanical room. Fire-protection bracing methods may be used. Return piping to multiple inlets (nozzles, etc.) must be hydraulically balanced. Filter return piping terminates in either adjustable or nonadjustable return fittings. Return fittings can be wall or floor mounted and should be adjusted to direct flow to the main drain and skimmers. Dead spots should not be allowed in a pool.

Hydraulic balancing Suction and return headers should be hydraulically balanced as closely as possible to ensure even flow throughout the fountain. (See Figure 5-5.) For applications where the fountain can be encircled by a header, this provides an excellent balancing tool. Nozzle patterns and return inlet headers can be sized using the following equation:

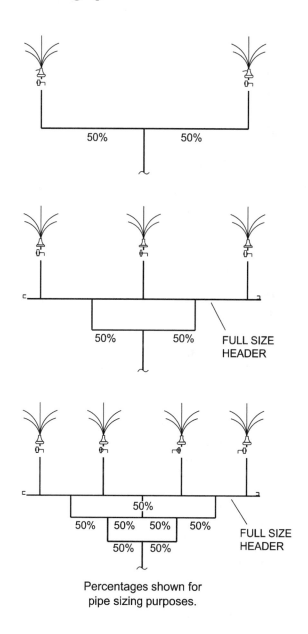

Percentages shown for pipe sizing purposes.

Figure 5-5 Hydraulic Balancing

Equation 5-1

$$q_n = 2.45C(D^2)(2gh_n)$$

where

q_n = Discharge from orifice n, gpm (L/min)

2.45 = Conversion factor used to express the discharge in gal/min (L/min) when the diameter is expressed in inches (mm) and the velocity is expressed in fps (m/s).

C = Orifice discharge coefficient (usually = 0.61 for holes drilled in the field)

D = Diameter of orifice, in. (mm)

g = Acceleration due to gravity, 32.2 ft/s² (9.81 m/s²)

h_n = Head on orifice n, ft. (m)

The head on orifice n is equal to:

Equation 5-2

$$h_n = \left[\frac{1}{(2.45CD^2)^2\,2g}\right]q_n^2$$

$$= kq_n^2$$

$$= k(mq_1)^2$$

$$= m^2h_1$$

where

k = Constant

h_1 = Head on orifice 1, ft (m)

m = Mass flow rate

The head loss between orifice 1 and n, which corresponds to the head loss in the distribution pipe between orifice 1 and n, is:

Equation 5-3

$$\Delta h_{(1-n)} = h_1 - h_n$$

Now it can be shown that the head loss between the first orifice and the last orifice in a distribution pipe with multiple, evenly spaced orifices is approximately equal to one-third of the head loss that would occur if the total flow were to pass through the same length of distribution piping without orifices. Thus,

Equation 5-4

$$h_{fdp} = \tfrac{1}{3}\,h_{fp}$$

$$= \Delta h_{(1-n)}$$

where

h_{fdp} = Actual head loss through distribution pipe, ft (m)

h_{fp} = Head loss through pipe without orifices, ft (m)

The head loss through the pipe can be computed using the Hazen-Williams equation:

Equation 5-5

$$h_{fp} = 10.5\,(L_{1-n})\left(\frac{Q}{C}\right)1.85D - 4.87$$

where

h_{fp} = Head loss through the pipe from orifice 1 to orifice n, ft (m)

L_{1-n} = Length of pipe between orifice 1 and n, ft (m)

Q = Pipe discharge, gpm (L/min)

C = Hazen-Williams coefficient (150 for plastic pipe)

D = Inside diameter of pipe, in. (mm)

The difference in discharge between orifice 1 and n for a given distribution pipe and orifice size can now be determined using Equations 5-1 through 5-5. If the computed value of m is too low (<0.98), the size of the distribution pipe can be increased. The percent difference in flow between 1 and n will be [(1 − n) × 100]. A good value would be less than 2%.

Valves

Shutoff valves Most valves for fountains are of a type that allows throttling. Since adjusting the fountain is very subjective, almost every valve in the system could be involved in the final adjustments. This limits the selection to ball-and-globe valves for the smaller pipe and butterfly valves for the larger pipe. Lug-type, butterfly valves are normally used in applications where equipment needs to be disconnected while still under water pressure. A pump room that is much lower than the fountain will be best served by lug valves at the equipment connections so that the equipment can be serviced without draining the fountain.

Check valves There are several types of check valve, but most are of two types: gravity and spring loaded. The gravity, or swing-check, valve must be installed in a prescribed manner. The gravity check should be installed where water pressure will help provide a positive closure. Where a check valve must be installed on a horizontal line, a spring check should be installed. A foot valve is a special type of check valve that is installed in the pump-suction line. The purpose of a foot valve is to prevent the suction line from draining back into the pool and causing the pump to lose prime. A valved line from the makeup system should be installed between the pump and the foot valve to aid in priming. It would be prudent also to install a drain in that section of pipe.

Pressure-regulating valves   Dynamic fountains are designed using pressure-regulating valves. The regulating valve maintains a selected downstream pressure regardless of the changes in the upstream pressure. Therefore, when the spray height of one set of nozzles is raised or lowered, the regulating valve keeps a second set of nozzles at the same spray height.

Actuator-control valves   In addition, actuator-controlled, motorized, or pneumatic valves can be controlled using a 4 to 20-milliamp (mA) electrical signal. The valve can be set to be fully closed at 4 mA and fully open at 20 mA. At any point in between, the valve will be open an amount corresponding to the position of the point within this range. For example, at 6 mA, the valve will be slightly open and at 15 mA it will be almost fully open. A computer can be programmed to provide signals to open and close the valves in any pattern desired.

Materials   A sample schedule of piping materials is shown in Table 5-1.

Discharge Devices

Many return methods are used to return the water into the pool. The designer must choose which method either creates the least disturbance to the desired water effect or creates the desired water effect.

Weir pools   Common methods of return into upper weir pools are: diverter plates (often anti-vortex drains used on the return side), well screens, and double tees. (See Figure 5-6.)

Spray jets   Numerous types of nozzle are manufactured. The designer should select the type of that will provide the desired spray effect. This can only be done by referring to the data listed in the manufacturer's catalogs. Nozzles are available to provide solid or aerated columns of water, pyramid-like columns of water, aerated mounds of water, mushroom shapes, floating dandelion effects, fan-shaped sprays, finger-like fan sprays, bell-like shapes, twirling jets, and numerous other effects.

All aerating jets of various types fall into two categories: water-level dependent and water-level independent. The water-level dependent type of jet relies on the water level in the pool being constant. This constant level allows the jet to aspirate air into the water to give a pleasing, frothing effect. There is a range of depths for most manufacturer's jets with a zone of 1-2 in. wherein the jet will function. These jets are slightly less expensive than the independent type but require

Table 5-1   Sample Schedule of Materials

System	Indoor/Outdoor	Abv/Blw Grade	Size, in. (mm)	Pipe Material	Fittings	Joints
Static display piping	Either	Either	½–24 (12.5–600)	Sch. 40 PVC	Socket	Solvent weld
Dynamic display piping	Either	Either	½–16 (12.5–400)	Sch. 80 PVC	Socket	Solvent weld
Filtration piping	Either	Either	½–24 (12.5–600)	Sch. 40 PVC	Socket	Solvent weld
Makeup water	Either	Either	½ –4 (12.5–100)	Type L copper	Wrot copper	Solder
Makeup water	Either	Either	6+ (150+)	Type 302 stainless steel	Type 302 stainless steel	Mechanical groove

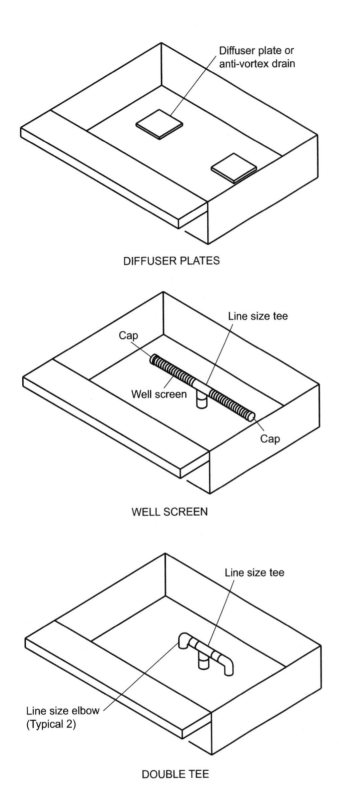

DIFFUSER PLATES

WELL SCREEN

DOUBLE TEE

Figure 5-6   Discharge Devices

that the level be maintained very accurately. Using jets in a pool that empties over a weir is a very good application of this jet. Using jets to surround a geyser that erupts every few seconds is not a good application, as the water will surge a great deal. In the latter case, a water-level independent jet would be the answer.

Controls

Remote control   Display pumps and filter pumps should be controlled from a point within view of the fountain. This can be achieved with a remote, hard-wired control panel and key switches or a radio signal. Radio remote-control units that control several separate electrical loads by means of a hand-held transmitter and a manual switching panel are available. These enable a doorman or concierge to quickly shut down the fountain in the event of a problem, such as someone jumping into the fountain.

Pump starters   All pumps should have starters with overload protection to protect their motors. A disconnect switch must be installed within view of the pump. The engineer should verify that these items are provided for under the scope of electrical work.

Wind controls   Wind controls reduce the height of a fountain display or shut off the display pump. A time-delay relay keeps the pump off for at least 3 min to avoid the problem of pump cycling. Three methods are used to reduce the height of the fountain display:

1. The wind control opens or closes a solenoid or motorized valve, thereby bypassing water from the nozzles back into the pool and reducing the spray height of the nozzles. The valve and bypass line must not be undersized, or the required flow will not be bypassed.

2. A pressure-regulating valve can be installed in the discharge line of the display pump, and a reduced-pressure setting is used to lower the spray height. This method is somewhat more expensive than the bypass-control valve.

3. If the display pumps consist of two or more pumps in parallel, shutting down a pump will reduce the height by slightly less than the proportional amount produced by the shut down pump. Reduced friction in the discharge line will slightly increase the discharge of the remaining pump.

With all these methods, hydraulic calculations are required to determine that the capacities and friction losses are adequate to achieve the desired effect. A two-stage wind control is often used, in which the first stage reduces the height of the display and the second stage turns the system off completely.

Time switches Various types of time switches are available, from electric motor operator to electronic. Time switches can be used to operate the pumps at the desired times. In addition, cycle timers can be used to turn solenoid valves on and off at preset intervals of 5 s or more.

Pressure and flow switches Pressure and flow switches are used to shut pumps off in the event that the pressure or flow drops too low in the pump discharge. They are also used to signal water-treatment systems of flow/no flow conditions. Start/stop switches are equipped with time-delay relays to allow the pump to be started and also to keep the pump off for a programmable delay to prevent pump cycling.

Lighting

Lights are available in low-voltage as well as normal line voltage. Some jurisdictions, such as the City of New York, require only low-voltage lighting and approval of all lights and transformers used in the jurisdiction. Most lights can be obtained with colored lenses if desired. Rock guards are required. Maintain the water level over the lights as required by the manufacturer. The *National Electrical Code* (NEC) must be followed when installing underwater lights, transformers, and submersible pumps. All electrical systems that supply power to equipment or lights in the pool must have ground-fault interrupter circuit breakers.

Fountain lights should be installed directly under the water display to illuminate the general pool area as well as the water display. The number of lights and the wattage depend on the overall size of the pool, the height and width of the water display, and possible interference from ambient lighting.

Free-standing lights are wired through a bronze, underwater junction box. The box must be listed by a nationally recognized testing agency and approved for underwater use. The cable from the light is fed through a compression seal that is connected to the junction box. When the ar-

chitect wants to conceal the cable, the cable is fed through a compression seal to an adjacent brass conduit to a remote junction box. The cable must be long enough to reach the remote junction box without splices.

Niche lights that are installed in pool walls have conduit directly connected to the niche and extended to a remotely located switch box. The cable must be long enough to reach the remote junction box without splices.

Lights are usually controlled by either astronomical time switches or regular time switches and a photocell. It is advisable to design the control system so that maintenance personnel are not required to adjust the light timers for daylight savings time and changing sunset times.

In general, selecting colors for the lights should be done with care because of the subjective nature with which each person views the fountain. If blue, red, amber, and other dark colors are used, the lights should have a higher wattage.

Water Heating Equipment

If a fountain is to be kept in operation during the winter months and it is possible for the water to freeze, a pool water heater should be provided. The pool heater can be a steam heat exchanger, a hot-water heat exchanger, an electric water heater, or a gas-fired water heater. The heater should be sized to maintain the pool water at a minimum of 35°F (1.67°C).

Overall heat loss due to surface evaporation, radiation, conduction, and convection for concrete pools where the water temperature is 35°F (1.67°C) and the air temperature is 10°F (–12.2°C) can be obtained as follows:

* *25 mph wind velocity*

   Total Btu/h heat loss = [203 × surface area of the pool in ft² (m²)] + [34 × sidewall area in ft² (m²)]

* *20 mph wind velocity*

   Total Btu/h heat loss = [176 × surface area of the pool in ft² (m²)] + [33 × sidewall area in ft² (m²)]

* *15 mph wind velocity*

   Total Btu/h heat loss = [145 × surface area of the pool in ft² (m²)] + [32 × sidewall area in ft² (m²)]

It is also necessary to include the heat loss from the piping. Select a heater with an output equal to the Btu/h heat loss. In many large buildings, the heating medium can be the heating hot water or steam. The heater is controlled by a temperature control with the sensing bulb located in the inlet pipe to the heater. The control will turn on the heater if the incoming water from the pool is below 35°F (1.67°C) and shut it off if the temperature is above 37°F (2.78°C). A flow switch in the inlet to the heater will prevent operation of the heater if there is insufficient or no flow. The heater should be located on a bypass line, as shown in Figure 5-7. The piping within 3 ft of the heater should be Type L copper tubing.

Water-Treatment System

A properly engineered water-treatment system will allow the operator to maintain a sparkling clear, odor- and algae-free pool. Certain water-treatment methods should be engineered into the system and certain water-treatment methods can be administered by the operator. Water-treatment parameters include:

1. *Disinfectant residual*—measured in parts per million (ppm).

2. *Oxidation reduction potential (ORP)*—a measure of the cleanliness of the water. Measured in millivolts (mV).

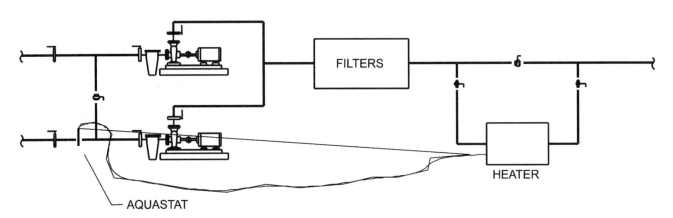

BYPASS HEATER SYSTEM

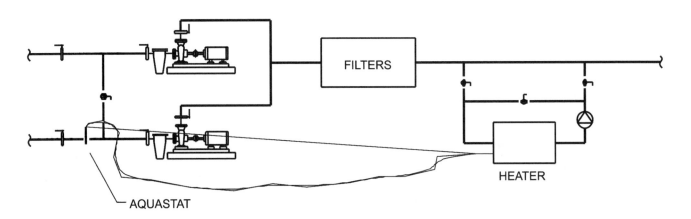

HEATER SYSTEM WITH PUMP

Figure 5-7 Piping Schematics

3. *pH*—a measure of the acidity or causticity of the water.

4. *Alkalinity*—a measure of the resistance of the water to change in pH, a dimensionless number.

5. *Total dissolved solids*—a measure of the total dissolved solids in the water, measured in ppm.

6. *Calcium Saturation Index (CSI) or Langelier's Index*—a dimensionless number.

7. *Cyanuric acid level*—Cyanuric acid is used to prevent the dissipation of chlorine by sunlight. It is also toxic at higher levels. Measured in ppm.

Engineered systems include:

1. *Mechanical filtration*—sand or cartridge filters, which remove particulates from the water.

2. *Disinfection systems*—including chlorine and bromine feeders and ozone. Provide control of organics and algae.

3. *pH control systems*—gaseous CO_2 contact tanks and acid/base feeders.

4. *Oxidation reduction potential (ORP) monitors*—provide an overall measure of the cleanliness of the water.

Operator-administered treatments include:

1. *Water chemistry*—Although some chemistries can be done electronically, most must be done by the operator and the data recorded.

2. *Shock or hyperchlorination*—used to destroy chloramines formed when chlorine destroys organic compounds in the water. Chloramines give pools that distinctive chlorine smell. A massive dose of chlorine (10 ppm) will destroy the chloramines.

3. *Dechlorination*—After shock treatments, the water is often dechlorinated with sodium thiosulfate.

4. *pH adjustment*—Different chlorine compounds will either raise or lower the pH. Gaseous chlorine (rarely used) will lower the pH and soda ash will need to be added. Powdered or liquid chlorine will raise the pH and muriatic acid will have to be added.

Although proper water chemistry is important from a disinfection standpoint, resulting in an algae-free pool, water balance is equally im-

portant. The Calcium Saturation Index or Langlier's Index is a measure of the corrosiveness of the water. If the CSI is below 0, the water is corrosive and will start to corrode the pool walls, fittings, and equipment. If the CSI is above 0, the water is saturated and will begin to plate out calcium deposits on the pool wall, fittings and equipment.

Disinfection in reflecting pools is necessary to control algae and to destroy organics in the water. Common methods of disinfection are chlorine, bromine, and ozone. Chlorine can be used indoors or out with equal success. If used outdoors, the chlorine should be combined with cyanuric acid as a stabilizer. The cyanuric acid will enable the chlorine to last much longer in direct sunlight. Bromine is not recommended for outdoor pools because there is currently no way to stabilize it and it dissipates rapidly.

Chlorine comes in three forms: gaseous, liquid, and solid. Gaseous chlorine is the most efficient method of delivery but can be very dangerous when mishandled. Liquid chlorine is the preferred method when dealing with multiple bodies of water or a single body of water in excess of 75,000 gal (283 905 L). A chemical proportioning pump and 50-gal (189.27-L) chlorine solution tank is used to administer the disinfectant. The injection point should be downstream of the filter. Solid or dry chlorine comes in many forms: solid pellets, granular, or powder. It is administered using an erosion feeder that is installed in parallel with the filter and works on the differential pressure across the filter.

Caution: Two types of dry chlorine, sodium hypochlorite and calcium hypochlorite, are both currently used. If these two compounds are mixed together, a violent explosion can result. Chlorine use varies from 1 to 5 oz/day/1000 gal (0.03 to 0.15 L/day/3785.4 L), depending on the temperature of the water and the amount of sunlight. Both warm water and sunlight dissipate chlorine rapidly.

Ozone is an excellent method of disinfection for water but does have limitations. The ozone gas should be applied in a contact tank and the off gas from the tank should be directed to an unoccupied area. In addition, ozone does not leave a residual in the water. A small chlorine feeder should be added to pools receiving a high organic load, such as outdoor pools. As a final note, certain manufacturers will not warranty their products for use in an ozone-treated pool.

Makeup-Water System

The fountain should be provided with both a manual and an automatic fill system piped in parallel (see Figure 5-8). The manual fill line should be at least 1½ to 2 in. (40 to 50 mm) and the automatic fill line be ¾ in. (20 mm) for small and medium fountains and as large as 4 in. (100 mm) for large fountains. A good rule is to determine the makeup-water rate for cooling towers in the area. The information should be in gpm (L/min) of makeup water per gpm (L/min) of condenser water. This will translate directly to gpm (L/min) of makeup water per gpm (L/min) of effect water. For reflecting pools, the local water authority should have information regarding evaporation rates from swimming pools. When designing the makeup-water system, it may be advantageous to connect the makeup-water line to the filter-pump suction line. If this is done, make sure that there are no valves between the makeup-water inlet and the pool. This is to ensure that the filter system does not become pressurized to domestic-water line pressure. Most pool equipment is not built to withstand the higher pressure.

In all cases, backflow preventers are required on makeup-water piping to float valves. They are also required on solenoid-operated, makeup lines unless the inlet pipe is at least 2 pipe diameters or more above the pool wall. Verify all methods of backflow prevention with the local authority having jurisdiction.

Multilevel pools require that a water-level sensor (not a float valve) be located in the lowest pool and the makeup inlet be located in the highest pool. Low-water cutoff sensors are required in the lowest pool and, if the underwater lights do not have individual low-water cutoffs, then every pool level must have a low-water cutoff.

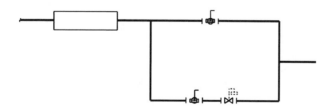

Figure 5-8   Makeup-Water Devices

Makeup-water devices

Stilling wells or chambers   Stilling wells or chambers are an important part of any makeup-water system. With a stilling well, the level in the well is an accurate representation of the level in the pool. The advantage to the stilling well is that it remains relatively calm inside the well and does not reflect the surface disturbances that may occur in the pool itself. A stilling well can also incorporate an overflow drain.

Mechanical methods   Mechanical water makeup is the cheapest method and is least prone to maintenance problems. In this method, a float valve installed in the wall of the pool provides automatic makeup. The top of the pool water must be at least 5 in. above the water level for the float box to fit in the pool wall. A method of remotely maintaining the water level is to install a float valve in an open tank or connected to the pool by a pipe and rooted to a remote location. There should be no connection to this pipe except for a valved drain. With the pipe open at either end, the water level in the tank will be the same as the water level in the pool. The problem encountered with this application is finding a location for the tank.

Another method, commonly used on large pools, uses a pilot-operated makeup valve. With this method, a small float valve is installed in a stilling well and the pilot water for the larger valve is routed through it. When the level drops, the pilot float valve opens and water is allowed to open the larger valve. The advantage to this method is that a small stilling chamber can be located near the pool while the larger valve can be located near the pumps in the mechanical room.

Electrical method   Where the above methods cannot be used, water makeup can be provided by using electrical sensors that open or close a solenoid valve on the makeup-water line. A manual fill valve is ordinarily installed in a bypass around the solenoid valve. The sensors use low voltage or induced voltage that precludes any electrical danger. Sensors that utilize a reed switch, activated by a permanent magnet, are also available. The sensors can be mounted in the wall of the pool, accessible from the front. (See Figure 5-9.) They can also be located in the top of the wall with the sensors hanging down into a 1¼-in. (32-mm) brass pipe that has an air vent and a horizontal leg extending into the pool water. Where it is not feasible to mount the sen-

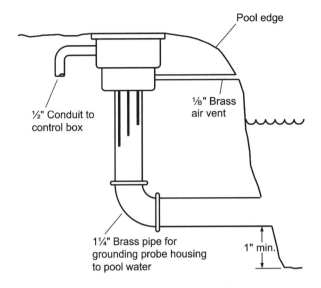

Pool edge

½" Conduit to control box

⅛" Brass air vent

1¼" Brass pipe for grounding probe housing to pool water

1" min.

Figure 5-9   Electronic Makeup-Water Device

sors in the pool wall, they can be located anywhere in the pool water by mounting the sensor box on top of a brass conduit wherever it enters the pool. The sensor will generate a small amount of current from the sensor tip, through the water and into the brass pipe. If water is not present, the current flow stops and the control panel opens the solenoid valve. Brass piping must be used as it provides the electrical ground path. Electrical wiring has to be extended to the sensors in the pool area as well as to the control panel and the solenoid valve.

Dual sensors are available that will provide for water makeup and low-water cutoff (so that pumps will be shut off in the event of low water level). They can also shut off the underwater lights, which can be damaged by operation without adequate water cover.

Overflow and Drainage System

Overflow drains   Overflow drains are required for two reasons: to provide a means to remove water if the makeup-water valve malfunctions and to provide a means to remove storm water and maintain a fixed water level so that nozzles will work properly. The size of an overflow drain for an indoor pool should be 2 in. If the makeup-water line is larger than 1 in., increase the size of the overflow drain to prevent flooding. Sizing for an outdoor pool should be based on the area

of the pool, in ft^2 (m^2), as required by the local plumbing code for storm drainage.

The preferred location for an overflow drain is in the pool wall, because it is less obtrusive there. There are times though when the pool wall is insufficient for the installation of an overflow drain. In such cases, a removable overflow standpipe can be provided. A dome or screen should be placed on top of the standpipe. The overflow drain also acts as the main drain when the standpipe is removed. Overflow standpipes are subject to vandalism and should be located so that they are not easily accessible to the public. Another method is to install an overflow pipe on a bypass around a main drain valve. The overflow pipe invert must be slightly higher than the high water level and have an air opening to prevent siphonage.

Emergency drains   Emergency drains are needed to drain the pool if the outside temperature drops below freezing. This is achieved by providing an aquastat that controls a solenoid valve located in the drain line. The aquastat should be set to open the solenoid valve if the temperature drops too low. The solenoid valve must have a manual override in the event of a power failure and must not require differential pressure to open the valve. An Ongontz valve is another emergency drain valve that mechanically starts to open when the temperature drops to 38°F (3.33°C) and fully opens at 34°F (1.11°C). In the above cases, electrical sensors, as described above under "Makeup-Water Devices," should be provided to shut off the electrical power to the pumps and lights. The makeup-water valve should be wired to close if the emergency drain valve is open. It may also be advisable to have an alarm ring to indicate that the emergency drain valve has opened.

REFERENCES

1.   American National Standards Institute/National Spa and Pool Institute. 1991. *Standard for public swimming pools,* ANSI/NSPI-1 1991. Alexandria, VA: National Spa and Pool Institute.

2.   Kowalsky, L. 1990. *Pool/spa operators handbook.* San Antonio, TX: National Swimming Pool Foundation.

3.   Tchobanoglous, George, and Franklin L. Burton. 1991. *Wastewater engineering: Treatment, disposal, and reuse.* 3d ed. New York: McGraw-Hill.

Public Swimming Pools

INTRODUCTION

This chapter discusses public indoor and outdoor swimming pool size and the selection of pool plumbing, piping components, and equipment required for operation in conformance with the health and other codes of the authorities having jurisdiction (AHJ).

CODES AND STANDARDS

In addition to the plumbing code, swimming pool construction and operation are usually governed by state health department regulations and the requirements of local authorities. Publications of the National Spa and Pool Institute are often referenced standards. The codes usually govern recirculating rates; types of filter and filtration rates; the spacing of main drains, grate areas, and inlets; the spacing and capacity of gutter drains and surge tanks or skimmers; and heating, disinfection system, draining, and fill and makeup requirements. In addition to the standards noted above, if the pool is to be used for competition, the rules and regulations of the Federation Internationale de Natation Amateur (FIFA) need to be reviewed to ensure that the pool meets international standards.

PRELIMINARY DESIGN PARAMETERS

Before the plumbing for a swimming pool project can be designed, the following information should be obtained: occupant capacity, the size of the facility (including pool volume), the facility's location and configuration, the style of pool(s), times of use, availability to infants/children (may necessitate a separate pool), tournament/racing requirements, toilet requirements, concession/vending requirements, and bathhouse requirements.

Occupant Capacity and the Size of the Facility

Assuming that the swimming pool is part of a complex that includes other outdoor facilities (such as ball fields, tennis courts, and basketball courts), the following are generally accepted criteria for estimating the number of swimmers:

1. The total membership of the facility can be estimated to be 10% of the total population of the community it will serve.

2. The maximum attendance on the peak day can be estimated to be 68% of the total membership.

3. Maximum attendance at the public swimming pool facility can be estimated to be 40% of the projected maximum attendance on the peak day.

4. The maximum number of swimmers is approximately 33% of maximum attendance.

This method of determining the maximum number of swimmers cannot be applied to all swimming pools. The social and economic conditions of a particular local community must be taken into account when designing a public swimming pool facility. Swimming pool occupancy, or capacity, restrictions are subject to local regulations and vary from one locality to another. Supervision capability may also limit pool capacity.

The desirability of accommodating competitive swimming should be considered when designing a swimming pool. The requirements for such events are 25 and 50-yard lengths for United States competitive meets and 25 and 50-meter lengths for international events. Normal competition pools are divided into a minimum of 6 swimming lanes, with each lane having a minimum width of 7 ft (2.0 m). An additional 3 ft (0.9 m) should be divided equally between the 2 outside lanes to aid wave quelling. The shallow-end depth should be a minimum of 4 ft (1.2 m) for competitive pools and 3.5 ft (1.1 m) for recreational pools, depending on codes. The deep-end minimum depth of pools with spring boards is between 9 and 12 ft (2.7 and 3.7 m) for a 3-ft (1-m) board and 11.5 and 13 ft (3.5 and 4.0 m) for a 10-ft (3-m) board, depending on local codes. Platform diving is performed in specially designed pools, which are outside the scope of this chapter.

Location of the Public Swimming Pool Facility

There are no generally accepted rules for choosing the location of a public swimming pool facility. Only careful investigation of the available sites and the use of common sense will result in a suitable location.

First, consideration must be given to the accessibility of the location. A public swimming pool will be used in direct proportion to the convenience for the local population of reaching the facility. Distance is a barrier, and so are stop lights and railroad tracks. The engineer must also consider the traffic flow in the area and the relative safety for pedestrians and bicycle riders of the routes normally taken to and from the public swimming pool facility.

Equally important at this stage are the physical properties of the proposed swimming pool site, including its soil quality, ground water locations, and subsurface obstructions such as rocks. Attention also must be given to the availability of water, gas, sewers, and electricity. If all utilities are not available or extensive clearing, grading, or difficult excavation is required at or near the proposed site, significant additional expenses may be incurred.

General Physical Character of the Public Swimming Pool(s)

Deciding on the general physical character of a proposed public swimming pool facility involves determining such things as the type of swimming pool, its style, the pool's intended use, its shape and dimensions, indoor vs. outdoor design, bathhouse planning, and the location and type of equipment. A swimming pool complex with separate recreation pool, diving well, and wading area accommodates all possible uses, including recreation, training, diving, water sports, exercise, therapy, and competitive swimming. There is a definite aesthetic trend toward luxury in the contemporary design of swimming pools. The use of color, walks, deck areas, and plantings creates a pleasant and interesting personality but also substantially increases costs.

Before commencing the design, it is important to determine the style of pools the facility requires and the impact this will have on the space available for mechanical systems. Many facilities are now being designed with a multipool or a multi-use pool. Pool styles can range from leisure pools, to swimming pools with a wave-pool component, to 25/50-m competition pools with diving facilities.

Many leisure pools are now being designed in conjuction with other pool facilities that allow families and younger children to enjoy the water while playing with interactive water toys and water slides. These pools usually have water depths that range from 1 to 4 ft and may have an uneven bottom, depending on the location of the interactive play toys. The number of toys and the size of the pool will have an impact on the space requirements for pumps and filters.

Wave pools have been introduced to public swimming facilities in the last few years, which allow swimmers to experience the sensation of swimming in ocean-like conditions. Many wave pools are designed so that the wave generator can be set to come on at certain times of the day and/or night or when requested by the swimmers. Wave pools usually have a beach component at one end of the pool, which requires that special consideration be given to the gutter systems and water pickup at the beachhead. The wave-generation equipment requires additional space within the mechanical room, and this needs to be taken into consideration when planning a facility with this component.

Competition pools have very specific regulations that govern the water quality, clarity, turnover rates, temperature, size, depth, and marking that are permitted within the pool. These requirements may be more stringent than the local health-department requirements and may require that more or larger components be located within the mechanical rooms.

There are many alternatives of shape and dimension available to the designer. However, public pool configurations most commonly use straight lines and right angles. Often there are good reasons for unconventional designs and shapes in private swimming pools and, perhaps, in motel swimming pools where architectural interest (or uniqueness) may be of prime consideration.

The question of indoor versus outdoor swimming pool design is considered during the preliminary planning of the facility. It is well established that, although about 10% of the public likes to swim outdoors in the summer, less than 1% is interested in swimming in the winter, even if indoor facilities are provided.

Therefore, the need for outdoor swimming is addressed first. Then, if the budget permits, indoor facilities can be added. An indoor swimming pool facility costs approximately three to four times what a comparable outdoor swimming pool facility does. If the total cost is of little consideration, the same swimming pool facility can be used for both indoor and outdoor swimming.

A possible solution to the problem of providing indoor swimming is the cooperative funding, planning, and construction of a swimming pool facility adjacent (or connected) to a school. This requires the cooperative effort of the school board, the park district, the recreation department, and any other taxing body. The engineer should plan such a swimming pool facility to have the following: (1) an indoor swimming pool of sufficient size to meet the needs of the school and the local community, (2) an outdoor swimming pool complex planned and constructed to meet the needs of the local community, (3) a central shower and toilet area, and (4) mechanical equipment for water treatment designed to serve both the indoor and the outdoor swimming pools. During winter, the indoor swimming pool can be used for the school's and community's training and recreational needs. During summer both indoor and outdoor swimming pools can be scheduled and used. This arrangement allows one pool to be out of service for maintenance while the other remains operational. A facility of this type saves a considerable amount of money and provides a swimming pool facility for year-round comprehensive scheduling with a revenue sufficient to cover the operational and maintenance costs.

There are many technical problems involved in the design of an indoor swimming pool facility. First, there is the obvious problem of maintaining the proper relationship between air and water temperatures (to control condensation and fogging), then there are the lesser considerations of acoustics, ventilation, and air movement. To be properly balanced, the water temperature should be in the range of 75 to 80°F (23.8 to 26.7°C) and the air temperature in the building should be maintained 3 to 5°F (1.6 to 2.6°C) above the water temperature. If this relationship is inverted, the swimmers will become uncomfortable and both fogging and condensation are likely to occur. The rules for the design of the local bathhouse are generally specified in great detail by the local governing public health authorities. The preliminary planning of the bathhouse facility must be carried out within the limits of these established regulations. Apart from these rules, however, the designer may exercise imagination with a considerable latitude in several areas: (1) achieving a pleasing and aesthetic architectural balance; (2) providing an adequate floor area for traffic and storage and management facilities; and (3) providing an open dressing area with ample sunshine and air but some roof cover protection for use during inclement weather.

Equipment locations should be established during the preliminary design phase. It must be decided, for example, whether equipment is to be located in the bathhouse or in a separate enclosure (keeping in mind that it is usually desirable to combine all these facilities under a single enclosure). The filter assembly should be housed in an area with heat for the off season and with ample storage space. The filter equipment also should be located in the filter room for easy and efficient operation and maintenance. Consideration needs to be given to the location of the pumps in relation to the water levels in the pools. Wherever possible, the pool pumps should be located so that they are below the water level determined by the gutter system or surge tank so that the pumps will have positive suction. Self-priming pumps are used for a number of pool applications, but the use of this style of pumps is subject to greater start-up problems and maintenance issues.

The construction of a major swimming pool facility with the filter equipment located outdoors or under drop lids to save costs is false economy. This will result in the rapid deterioration of the pumps, hoses, motors, and other specialized equipment during the off season as well as make operation during the season difficult and costly.

Finally, the designer must select the type of filtration and purification equipment to be used. The most obvious considerations are pool size; available space; the type, location, and availability of sewer facilities; soil, rock, and ground water conditions; and the location, availability and cost of the water. If the water is plentiful and inexpensive and space is not a problem, sand filtration should always be given first consideration. Scarce or costly water and limited space might dictate the use of diatomite filtration. The size of the swimming pool facility will usually determine the type of disinfection equipment to be used.

Bathhouses, Toilets, and Showers

Adequate dressing and toilet facilities must be provided. Each swimming pool complex must have separate facilities for male and female bathers, with no interconnections between them. The rooms must be well lighted, drained, and ventilated. They must be constructed of impervious materials, finished in light colors, and developed and planned so that good sanitation can be maintained throughout the building at all times.

The partitions used in dressing rooms, showers, and toilets must be made of durable materials and not subject to water damage. They should be designed so that there are spaces under the partitions to permit a thorough cleaning of the walls and floors. If these partitions are subject to vandalism, block walls and vandalproof devices should be considered.

The showers and dressing booths for females should have curtains or some other means of providing privacy. This rule may may not apply for schools and other institutional facilities where a swimming pool may only be open to one sex at a time or where supervision is necessary.

Facilities for the physically challenged must also be provided that meet all local and state regulations for private and public facilities.

The floors of a bathhouse must be free of joints or openings, be continuous throughout the area, have a slight texture to minimize slipping but also be relatively smooth to ensure positive drainage of all parts of the building, and have an adequate slope toward the drains. An adequate number of floor drains shall be provided. Floor drains should be positioned based on the requirements of the plumbing and building codes, but in no case should the floor slopes be designed for less that ¼ in./ft to ensure proper drainage of all floor areas.

An adequate number of floor drains shall be provided. An adequate number of ¾ in. (20 mm) hose bibbs must be provided for the washing of the dressing rooms and the bathhouse interior. At least 1 drinking fountain should be provided for the bathers of each sex in the bathhouse, with additional drinking fountains provided at the pool.

The minimum sanitary plumbing facilities, as mandated by the local plumbing code, should be provided. These minimum criteria for bathhouse plumbing facilities must be based upon the anticipated maximum attendance.

If the local code does not address swimming pool facilities, the following minimum facilities should be provided: 3 shower heads for the first 150 male users and 1 shower head for each additional 50 male bathers; 2 shower heads for the first 100 female users and 1 shower head for each 50 additional female bathers.

Tempered water at a temperature of approximately 90-100°F (32.2-37.8°C) should be provided to all shower heads. Water heaters and thermostatic mixing valves should be inaccessible to the bathers.

Soap dispensers, providing either liquid or powdered soap, must be furnished at each lavatory and between each pair of shower heads. The dispensers should be constructed of metal or plastic; no glass is permitted. Mirrors must be provided over each lavatory. Toilet paper holders must be furnished at each water closet combination. As previously stated, vandal-proof devices should be considered, if applicable.

POOL OPERATING SYSTEMS AND COMPONENTS

Most provincial and state regulations now require that pool-system components have the certification of an independent testing agency, such as the National Sanitation Foundation (NSF). This certification ensures that all the components meet a national standard for quality of materials in the piping and components and that public health-and-safety issues are addressed. This standard also ensures that the equipment meets consistent quality controls and builds a level of confidence in the product.

Water Supply and Drainage

The water supply system provides the means to fill the pool initially with water and to make up water lost through wastewater discharge and evaporation. The preferred supply source for filling the pool and maintaining adequate volume is potable water. In areas with limited water supply, or where the system capabilities are in doubt, consideration should be given to minimum backwash water filtration equipment and to an off-peak filling and servicing schedule. Well water is often of good quality and may be used directly; however, the mineral content may be sufficiently high to require treatment. All water should be given a detailed chemical analysis in the early planning stages of the swimming pool to determine whether treatment, e.g., softening or pH control, is required. Protection of the potable water supply system through air gaps or backflow prevention equipment is mandatory. The type required must be determined by checking with the local AHJ.

The rate of water evaporation from the pool should be obtained to determine the average makeup water required.

Direct discharge of swimming pool water into the local storm sewer system or a watercourse without proper treatment may not be allowed since chlorinated water is harmful to the environment. The chemistry of the proposed effluent should be approved by the AHJ.

In areas where freezing temperatures are possible, and if the pool is not used year-round, provision must be made for draining the water lines, exposed drains, and plumbing fixtures to prevent damage by freezing. Alternatively, all areas must be provided with minimum heating equipment.

Refer to other *Data Book* chapters for water pipe, sanitary sewer, storm drainage, and private sewage disposal system design and details.

Filtration System

The filter system is an assembly of several components that removes or reduces particulates (dirt particles, solids, and algae) in the water to a level acceptable to swimmers. The components are the filter medium and tanks, backwash subsystem, circulation pump, water inlets, skimmers (if used), surge tank (if used) and the interconnecting piping. This system must conform to the requirements of the AHJ.

Filters The filter assembly is very important because it makes the water clear by removing the small suspended particles in the water that cause turbibity (cloudiness). Although pool chemicals are also necessary to control the purity of the water, and skimming, brushing, and vacuuming play a significant part in proper pool maintenance, the filter's role is the most important one.

Filter tanks For years, sand filter tanks have been made of bare, coated, or galvanized steel with PVC or ABS plastic under-drains and have traditionally been constructed in a vertical configuration. Fair-to-good performance is obtained from these tanks. Magnesium anodes provide cathodic protection if required. In general, excellent performance is reported with these alloys. Of the stainless steels, Type 304 is predominant, even though a fair amount of Type 316 appears to be in use. Filter elements in diatomite filters made of bronze, stainless steel, and plastic are reported to give good service. Coated and galvanized steel filters generally give good performance and are an economical selection, especially for larger units. In recent years, filters have also been constructed from either laid mat or bobbin-wound fiberglass in both vertical and horizontal configurations.

The designer of pool systems needs to assess the requirements of pool flow rates, water quality, mechanical-room location, and space before deciding on the style and material of the filter system. In systems where it is deemed that water clarity is important, the designer may choose a vertical filter with a greater depth of sand bed, but where space is limited and the flow rates are large, the designer may choose either single or double-stacked, horizontal filters to conserve space.

Filter media types Filter types fall into two general classifications: granular and diatomaceous earth. Sand-and-gravel filters are further divided into gravity and pressure systems. The gravity system is more suitable for very large water pools; the pressure type is the most popular choice for other pool sizes. Diatomite filters also are divided into two types: pressure and vacuum. The latter is sometimes combined with a skimmer to form a skimmer filter.

There are numerous types of granular medium. Sand is the most common. Anthracite and proprietary synthetic media are also available. Media beds consisting of alternating layers of granular media are marketed as "high-rate" filters. The following general discussions provide a background for understanding the engineering concepts involved.

Granular filter media   Historically, sand is the oldest filter medium known. It performs its intended function today exactly as it did 1000 years ago. As the water flows through a sand bed, a high percentage of its solids and visible impurities either are trapped in the voids among the sand particles or adhere to the sand particles. The result is an effluent of good quality. A pressure sand filter is illustrated in Figure 6-1.

Several factors affect the efficiency of a sand filtration system: (1) the inlet flow rate, (2) the media particle size, (3) the inlet water solids load, (4) the depth of the media bed, and (5) the underdrain system. The rate at which the media become clogged and the quality of the effluent are affected by the rate at which the water flows through the filter medium. Therefore, accepted practice is to operate pressure sand filters at rates of 2 to 3 gpm/ ft^2 (1.4 to 2.0 L/s/m^2) of filter area with backwash flow rates of 12 to 15 gpm/ft^2 (8.1 to 10.2 L/s/m^2) for 2½ min. Few jurisdictions allow the use of gravity sand filters without prior authorization and most generally restrict flow rates to 1.0 to 1.5 gpm/ft^2 of filter area.

The sand particle size, particularly in the top layer of the filter bed, is of critical importance. Effective grain size should be 0.012 to 0.02 in. (0.30 to 0.50 mm) and the uniformity coefficient should not exceed a ratio of 1.6:1 from smallest to largest. The actual particle size distribution may vary, and the safest rule is to follow the directions of the sand filter manufacturer, who publishes detailed loading charts. Departure from these directions can lead to problems, such as when an exceptionally fine top filter layer becomes quickly compacted by the pressurized

stream of water (sometimes in a matter of a few minutes) and the system stops functioning altogether.

Another condition that affects the overall efficiency of a sand filter system is the initial solids loading of the filter bed. A clean sand bed is relatively inefficient at the outset of the cycle. During the first few hours of operation, the top 2 to 3 in. (50.8 to 76.2 mm) of sand accumulates a gelatinous layer, which then brings the solids-removing efficiency into a range roughly comparable to that of the diatomaceous earth.

With the advent of mass swimming pool construction and the mass production of swimming pool equipment, the swimming pool industry began to experiment with ideas about filtration. The net result has been the development of granular media filters that operate at flow rates up to 20 gpm/ft^2 (13.6 L/s/m^2), have beds of less depth, and totally eliminate the gravel medium that traditionally has been used to support a sand bed. Mixed media filters, consisting of layers of materials of differing granular size, have been developed for swimming pool use. These filters are commonly described as "high rate." To date, their greatest acceptance has been in the private swimming pool field. The end results of their use have been encouraging, though design and reliability vary from one equipment manufacturer to another. Public health officials have already approved high-rate filtration methods in many areas.

Finally, the underdrain must also be considered, pertaining more to the backwash cycle than to the filter cycle. To filter efficiently, the underdrain system must deliver uniformly distributed backwash water to expand the entire bed. This permits all the sand particles to be agitated and scrubbed clean. This uniform distribution is a function of both the underdrain piping configuration and the coarse gravel media, which exist for the purpose of uniformly distributing the flow of the backwash water.

Defective underdrain piping is seldom experienced. When underdrain problems occur, the water develops a high-velocity escape route through the filter bed in several directions. Eventually, the sand bed may be washed to waste or be channeled through the filter into the swimming pool. This situation can produce the familiar problems of mudballing and calcification, although these conditions are more often the result of inadequate backwash rates.

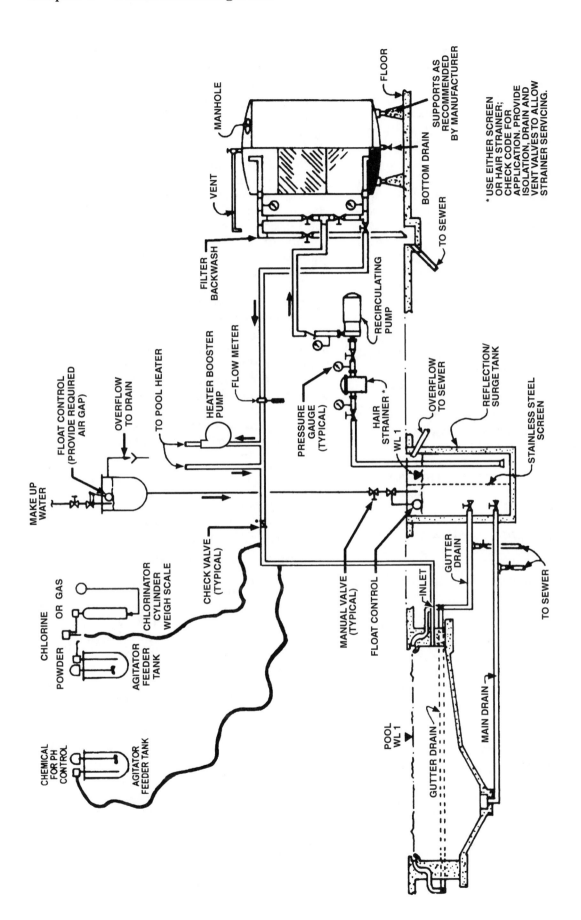

Figure 6-1   Pressure Sand or Mixed Granular Filter Conditional Flow

An often used filter material is anthracite coal, which may be substituted for the sand layer. Anthracite is hard coal that has been crushed and graded to a particle size roughly equal to that of the filter sand. It functions exactly as sand does and has the same efficiency. Anthracite is used less frequently than sand because it is not as commonly available.

In some respects, anthracite may be considered superior to sand since it is about half the weight and it expands more readily at lower flow rates during the backwash cycle. These characteristics make it the ideal medium for the single-tank, residential system where backwash velocities are low. This same argument also may apply to aluminum silicate, a light-weight aggregate used in private swimming pool filters in some areas.

Although granular filters can be of either vacuum or pressure type, the pressure tank, rapid sand system is the most popular system, accounting for at least 95% of the current granular filter business. It should be noted that the gravity (or suction) sand system is equally efficient and is probably the least complicated of all the filters from an operational viewpoint. It has several other advantages, but gravity sand filter installations are seldom proposed today due to space, weight, and cost considerations and code restrictions.

Diatomaceous earth filter medium

Diatomaceous earth is the remains of diatoms, microscopic single-cell plant forms having a siliceous shell. The diatomaceous earth filtration process uses a support mat or septum, upon which a light, thin coating called a filter coat, or mat, of the filter medium is first placed. Dirt particles are removed by becoming entrapped in the filter cake. The main difference between this and a sand system is that the sand bed filters in its depths while the diatomaceous earth cake filters on its surface. Thus, the sand filter has much greater dirt-holding capacity per unit of filter surface area. At the outset of the cycle, diatomaceous earth filters are much more efficient than sand filters in terms of the size of the particles removed.

The diatomaceous earth filter is much smaller and lighter than its sand equivalent. It has, therefore, been less costly in terms of purchase price and installation. This was particularly true for the larger systems used in commercial and public swimming pool installations. Diatamaceous

earth is becoming more expensive to mine, ship, and handle, however.

In terms of operation, the diatomaceous earth filter is much more complicated and sophisticated. It requires knowledgeable maintenance personnel who know how to handle the material. Standards are becoming more stringent for the handling of this type of media, and personnel who handle it must now wear respirators. As noted earlier, the diatamaceous earth filter's several radical departures from the traditional sand filter system (flow rates, depth and type of bed and underdrain design) can be accomplished without adversely affecting the original system performance. On the other hand, the diatomaceous earth filter requires close control. For example, the relationship between the flow rates and the filter cycles is important in diatomaceous earth filtration systems. The maximum recommended flow rate is 2.5 gpm per square foot (1.7 L/s/m^2) of filter surface area. Some states and localities limit the flow rates through the systems to 1 gpm per square foot (0.68 L/s/m^2) of filter area. Flow control added to the filter system will provide customers with a filter plant requiring backwashing or servicing only three or four days per swimming season.

Diatamaceous earth is viewed by some jurisdictions as solid, contaminated waste, and the cost of the disposal of this material is climbing. Not all jurisdictions permit the material to be discharged directly to the sanitary sewer.

From an operational viewpoint, there are several rules the designer should note. First, an adequate precoat cake is essential to good performance. The diatomaceous earth filter should be charged with a precoat of not less than 10 lb of filter aid per square foot (48.8 kg/m^2) of surface area over any 24-hour period. A fact that is often overlooked is that this precoat serves not only to provide a filter cake for dirt entrapment but to protect the filter system elements against clogging and contamination. A cake of the proper depth guards against system element clogging.

Second, with particular reference to public swimming pools (where bathing loads are substantially higher than in private swimming pools), the pool filter cycle should be supported by slurry feeding. Slurry feeding is the continuous addition of diatomaceous earth to the filter inlet water. Slurry feeding is mandatory in some states and localities. By this procedure, the filter cake is kept porous as the cycle progresses, the dirt holding capacity of the system is greatly increased, and the system cycle is often extended to two to three times what it would be without slurry feeding. The rate of feed of the filter powder must be determined by the conditions prevailing from hour to hour or from day to day. The heavier the bathing load, the heavier the slurry feed.

The slurry charge itself is usually mixed as a one or two-day supply. If it is mixed to cover a longer period of time, the constant agitation of the powder mixture and the water will tend to break up the diatomaceous earth particles and lower their efficiency as a filter medium. Since the slurry has the tendency to pack and clog the slurry feeder and the feed tubes at low velocity and in heavy concentrations, it is good practice to mix a dilute solution and feed it at a rapid rate rather than to feed a heavy slurry solution at a slower rate.

In terms of system design, the diatomaceous earth filter offers greater latitude to the engineer. There is a wide selection of both tank design (shapes) and construction materials. There are several alternatives in the choice of filter backwashing or cleaning techniques and there are two major filtration alternatives: pressure and vacuum.

There are no important differences in particle removal efficiency between the pressure and the vacuum systems. The choice is made based primarily upon hydraulic and operational considerations. The pressure diatomaceous earth filter can be conveniently located above or below the swimming pool level and can be operated efficiently with a single recirculation pump. In this respect, it is the more versatile of the two systems. The vacuum system, ideally, should be located above the water level; two pumps are required. A typical vacuum diatomite filter is illustrated in Figure 6-2. The vacuum system's controls are more complicated and costly. Control failures could result in the flooding of the equipment area.

The vacuum system offers some operational advantages over the pressure system, principally in respect to the servicing and the cleaning of the equipment. Obviously, the backwashing of a pressure system depends entirely upon the hydraulic efficiency of the system. Because the flow rate and pressure of the backwash are undefined, the water that cleans the septum cannot be precisely controlled. On the other hand, the vacuum filter is an open tank readily accessible to the individual who must manually clean the elements. The maintainability of the vacuum system is its primary advantage.

Another theory has been developed in support of the vacuum diatomaceous earth system. Tests indicate that there are some important hydraulic differences between vacuum and pressure systems in the manner in which the filter cake responds to the dirt loading. At the present time, the vacuum system seems capable of delivering longer cycles than its equivalent pressure system.

Finally, neither the pressure nor the vacuum system can be said to have a clear advantage in terms of cost. The particular design situation will determine which system has a cost advantage. The vacuum filter will usually operate at a lower cost due to its lower horsepower requirements and power cost.

Granular and diatomaceous earth filter comparison summary   The following comparison between sand filters and diatomaceous earth filters is appropriate:

1. Diatomaceous earth filters are smaller, more compact, and less costly to purchase and install than sand filters.

2. Sand filters are easier to operate, less prone to complicated system problems and less demanding of skill and judgment on the part of the operator than diatomaceous earth filters.

3. The operating costs of the two filter systems are approximately equal. The cost of the filter media lost in the diatomaceous earth system is about equal to the cost of the water discharged in the high-volume backwashing of sand filters. However, the diatomaceous earth must be separated from the backwash effluent and properly disposed of.

4. The choice of a system in a particular situation depends upon such factors as equipment room space, the budget, the relative cost of the water, the proximity to manufacturing sources, the local availability of the media and the local availability of trained operators.

The aim of every swimming pool project, large or small, is user satisfaction. The user judges by one criterion: water clarity. The best job of pool and deck construction cannot overcome poor water quality. This fact is too often overlooked. The cost difference between a correctly

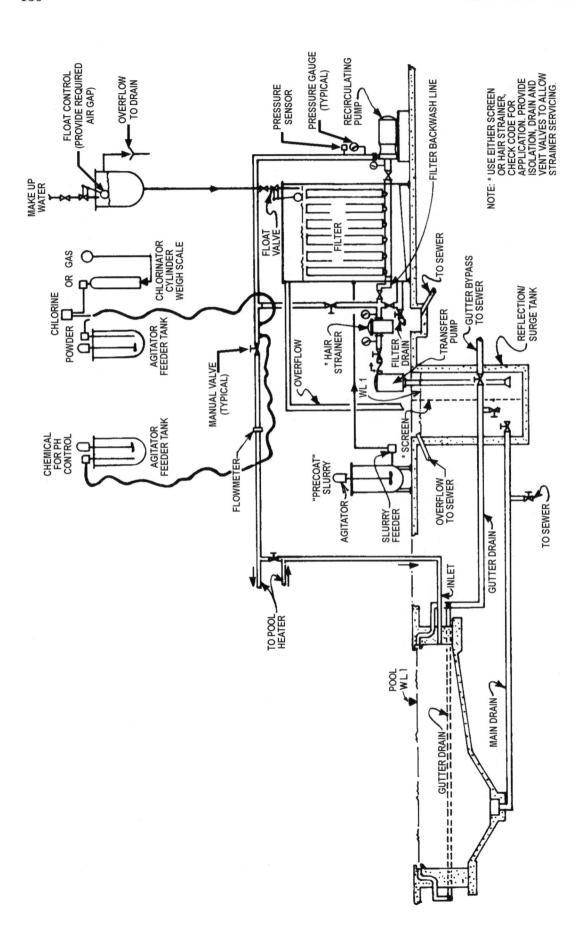

Figure 6-2 Vacuum Diatomite Filter Conventional Flow

designed, sized, and installed filtration system and one that is barely adequate (or inadequate) is normally less that 10% of the mechanical cost. The return in satisfaction and the savings in call-back time can be very high.

Filter backwash As the filter cycle progresses, the filter bed becomes increasingly soiled and offers a greater resistance to the flow of the water. Eventually a point is reached (indicated by the system pressure gauges) when the filter bed must be cleaned by reversing the flow of the water (backwashing) to waste. The backwash water must be disposed of to a sanitary sewer and not reused.

Backwash pit Since the flow rate of water used for backwashing may be greater than the discharge capacity of the drain, a backwash pit or tank is used to store or accumulate the backwash water from the swimming pool filters until the drain can carry it away. Any backwash piping from the filter directed into the backwash pit needs to maintain an air gap to ensure the impossibility of cross contamination from the sewer system.

Surge tank A surge tank, or chamber, is one popular method of accommodating the additional pool water that is displaced by swimmers entering the pool. Another method is to increase the depth and configuration of the pool gutter system. (The hydraulics of the pool system need to be reviewed with this type of system, but it is an economical way of accommodating the additional space requirements.) Both methods serve to maintain a constant swimming pool water level. Surge tanks are not usually required with vacuum diatomite filters, skimmers, or patented, continuous-flow gutters.

Gutter A gutter is an integral and continuous collection system, located on the pool perimeter, that takes pool water overflow and recirculates it back into the pool. The pool gutter system is an integral part of the pool recirculation system and must be designed to accommodate the style of skimmer system selected for the particular pool.

Skimmer The function of the skimmer is to set up a surface current that removes floating leaves, debris, and other foreign objects from the pool and brings them to the filter and recirculating system. There are many different skimmer-system styles available for installations in pools. The designer needs to work with the architectural

and sport consultants to ensure that the selected gutter/skimmer system is appropriate for the intended activities in the pool. Depending on the size and function of the pool, there are three main styles of skimmer that may be selected:

- The first is the most basic style skimmer, the premanufactured skimmer that is predominantly installed in residential pools. It is placed around the perimeter of the pool and piped back to the mechanical room. This style of skimmer usually has a built-in basket strainer and equalization fitting that prevent the system from sucking air in low pool-water conditions.

- The second style of skimmer/gutter is a built-in, continuous gutter set below the deck of the pool with a continuous grate of slot at the water level. This is the style traditionally found in community pools where the water level is set 8 to 12 in. below the deck level. This style is hard to access for cleaning purposes and requires that swimmers lift themselves out from the water level.

- The third style, called a "roll-out gutter," is the most popular style for competition pools. This style of gutter sets the grating of the skimmer at the water level and extends the pool water surface 12 to 14 in. behind the edge of the pool wall. This style of gutter allows the swimmer to slip out of the water and on to the pool deck without much lifting. This system also allows the top of the grating to be removed for easy access and cleaning of the gutter system.

Main drain Located at the deepest point(s) of the swimming pool, the main drain draws the water from the bottom of the swimming pool and permits the entire pool to be drained. It may also be used to draw water from the bottom of the pool back to the filter.

Inlet fittings Pool inlet fittings can be separated into two basic styles: The first and most common is the eyeball inlet fitting, which can be located in the side wall of the pool and be directed to provide circulation within the pool. This style of inlet is usually limited to residential and smaller commercial pools. The second style of inlet is the adjustable floor inlet fitting. This style of fitting is usually installed in larger pools, with widths greater than 40 ft. The fittings are placed in a regular pattern along the bottom of the pool to ensure even distribution of the return water throughout the pool system.

Swimming Pool Water Heaters

Pool heaters are a very specialized variety of water heater. The conditions of operation are different than those for any other water heating application. It cannot be too strongly emphasized that pool heaters be installed and operated strictly as recommended by the manufacturer.

Types of heating system The following are five different types of water heater commonly used in public swimming pools:

1. *Direct fired, gas heater.* Most popular and practical are the direct fired, gas heaters in which swimming pool water is fed directly through and out the heat exchanger tubes. The direct type has the advantages of simplicity and low cost when designed with high-velocity flow through the tubes and an internal automatic bypass valve. It eliminates scaling and condensate problems, which plague ordinary boilers and water heaters in pool heating applications.

2. *Indirect fired, gas heater.* The indirect heater is a conventional heating boiler that has been fitted with a coil or heating bundle. The coil is immersed in boiler water, and pool water is pumped through it. In this type of heater, condensate is eliminated and the rate of scale is sometimes slower than with an ordinary direct type boiler; however, some indirect heaters are difficult to clean. The indirect heater has generally proven to be quite satisfactory. Its disadvantages are a higher initial cost and the complexity of its control systems since it contains two separate water heating systems, each with control devices. The main advantage is that a secondary heating function can be accomplished by the primary system.

3. *Central heating boiler.* This is used where a central heating boiler is available or planned for general heating service. Consideration should be given to the possibility of heating with hot water or steam by using a heat exchanger. In determining whether this system should be used, consideration should be given to the following:

   A. The cost of adding to the capacity of the central heating boiler plus the costs of a heat exchanger, additional controls, and a pump, as compared the cost of a separate pool heater;

   B. The requirements for pool heat during late spring and summer, which might necessitate operating a large boiler under uneconomical part-load conditions when the boiler might be otherwise shut down;

   C. The possibility that a larger boiler would require the presence, during the summer months, of an operating engineer whose services might not be necessary if a separate automatic pool heater were used.

4. *Radiant heating.* With this method, small diameter tubing is affixed to the inside of the pool structure, away from swimmers, in a serpentine fashion. Hot water is circulated through the tubing, which in turn heats the pool water through the inside walls of the pool. The main advantage of this system is that it operates as a closed system and raw pool water does not pass through the boiler or radiant tubing, so there is minimum maintenance. Disadvantages are a high cost of installation plus an extra pump. Also, some difficulties have been experienced due to the cracking of the pool finish in the vicinity of the hot water tubes.

5. *Solar heating.* Solar energy should be considered where appropriate. (See *Handbook: Solar Energy System Design.*)

Important points that are frequently overlooked are (1) the need to protect the heater from debris, (2) the need to protect the heater from chlorine compounds, and (3) the necessity of interlocking the electrical system of the heater with the filter pump:

1. Heaters must be protected from dirt and debris by being installed downstream of the filter. Where filter cleaning, backwashing, or pool vacuuming may bring debris into pipes supplying the heater, the heater should be protected with suitable valving and provisions for flushing.

2. The discharge of the chlorinator should connect to the filter system downstream of the heater. Discharging chlorine or chlorinating compounds through the heater can do great damage in a surprisingly short time.

3. Heaters that require an outside electrical connection should always be wired into the filter pump circuit in such a way as to prevent the heater from operating unless the filter pump is energized.

Design temperatures The following design temperatures for pool water have been generally established as acceptable for various activities:

- Minimum acceptable: 75°F (24°C)
- Competitive swimming and diving: 78-82°F (25.6-27.5°C)
- Commercial (club, motel, apartment): 82-90°F (27.8-32.2°C)
- Residential: 75-85°F (24-26.7°C)

Cost The cost of a pool water heating system adds approximately 10% to the original cost of the swimming pool equipment. By the time other improvements (such as decking, fencing, landscaping, and dressing rooms) are added, this cost becomes 5% or less of total project costs.

SYSTEM AND COMPONENT SELECTION AND DESIGN CRITERIA

Indoor vs. Outdoor Pools

In addition to the standard design considerations that need to be addressed for all pool systems, consideration has to be given to the effect of rainwater on outdoor pools. Rainwater can change a pool's chemistry if the storm is excessive, and excess rainwater needs to be drained off into the nearest storm system. Provisions need to be made in the gutter or surge tank to install a standpipe to permit storm water to be drained. The designer of the pool system also needs to check with the local authority having jurisdiction to ensure that chlorinated pool water can be dumped directly into the local storm system.

Selection of Filter Systems

General The type of water filter system used is usually determined by the cost and availability of space; the location, depth, and size of existing sanitary sewers; and the availability and cost of water.

It is preferable to locate the filter system in an enclosed, heated area with ample room for maintenance and have the filters mounted at the normal operating water level of the pool. If circumstances force the filters to be installed at pool deck level, automatic control valves on the filters' inlets and outlets should open and close with the starting and stopping of the pool circulating pump. This prevents the drainage of the filter tanks into the pool when the pump stops, which would result in surging and water hammer when the pool circulation pump restarted. A check valve should be installed on the inlet side of the pump.

Types of filter and their flow rates The filtering medium used in filters is usually sand, diatomaceous earth, or mixed granular media prepared specifically for high-velocity filters. Certain states and localities do not allow the use of high-velocity-rate filters, therefore, local codes should be consulted. Any of the media discussed are good, but good filter efficiency depends upon proper pool maintenance.

Sand filters The following types of sand filter are available:

1. *Pressure sand, low-velocity.* Flow rate 3 gpm/ft^2 (2.0 L/s/m^2) of filter media up to a pressure differential through the media of approximately 25 psi (172.4 kPa), with a backwash rate of approximately 15 gpm/ft^2 (10.2 L/s/m^2) of media for approximately 2½ minutes.

2. *Pressure sand or mixed granular, high-velocity.* Flow rates up to 20 gpm/ft^2 (13.6 L/s/m^2) of filter media up to a pressure differential through the media of approximately 25 psi (172.4 kPa) for approximately 2½ minutes.

Diatomaceous earth filters The following are the types of diatomaceous earth filter:

1. *Vacuum diatomaceous earth.* Flow rate 1 gpm/ft^2 (0.68 L/s/m^2) of filter media up to a pressure differential of 6 psi (41.4 kPa). Washing is accomplished by draining the tank and washing the screens with a hose. Screens are precoated after cleaning with a slurry of diatomaceous earth and water. Filter efficiency is maintained by the continual addition of a metered amount of diatomaceous earth until the filter differential pressure indicates a need for washing.

2. *Pressure diatomaceous earth.* Flow rate 1 gpm/ft^2 (0.68 L/s/m^2) of filter media up to a pressure differential of 12 psi (82.7 kPa), with a backwash rate of 1 gpm/ft^2 (0.68 L/s/m^2) of filter media for 3 minutes. Filter efficiency is maintained by the continual addition of a metered amount of diatomaceous earth until the pressure differential indicates a need for backwashing.

Design considerations Some design considerations for filter selection and operation are:

1. The available sewer may not be capable of receiving the additional full flow rate of the filter backwash. Local authorities should be consulted regarding the capacity of the existing sewer. It may be necessary to install a backwash surge tank to store the full volume resulting from filter backwash, with the surge tank having an orifice to limit the outlet volume to the capacity of the available sewer. A backwash pit with a drain specifically sized to discharge the calculated flow is another solution.

2. Consideration should be given to providing knockout panels, or some other means of installing and possibly replacing the filters. Provision should be made for removing and replacing the sand in sand filters.

3. Flow meters and inlet and outlet pressure gages (mounted at the same elevation) on each filter washing should be provided for both sand filters and diatomaceous earth filters.

4. The designer should provide flow meters and inlet and outlet pressure gages (mounted at the same elevation) on each filter as well as throttling-type valves to isolate and regulate the flow to each filter.

5. The architect and structural engineers should be advised of the operational weight of the filters and the weight of the suspended connecting piping.

6. Floor gravity drains with discharge to public sewers should be provided for pool equipment rooms to avoid flood damage from improper pool maintenance and/or overflows due to electric power failure.

Filter hydraulic design Schematic piping diagrams of typical systems for granular media and pressure-type diatomaceous earth filters are shown in Figures 6-1 and 6-2, for vacuum-type diatomaceous earth filters in Figure 6-3. Discussion of the main elements of these systems, water supply and drainage, filters, gutters and surge tanks, follows.

Turnover Rate

Sometimes referred to as the recirculation rate, the turnover rate is defined as the time it takes for the entire water volume of a swimming pool to be circulated through the purification system. Though generally expressed in hours, some individuals also refer to this rate on a times-per-day basis.

A generally accepted turnover rate is once every 6 hours. The engineer should check local code requirements. Often, a design is determined mostly by budget limitations, at the expense of good design practices. Naturally, there is valid reasoning behind code provisions; however, a swimming pool site is often in difficult surroundings. The designer may need to insist on a higher turnover rate than the code-required minimum. Sandy, desert areas that are subject to high winds are classic examples of situations calling for turnover rates that are higher than the code-specified minimum. The engineer must use good judgment in selecting turnover rates.

Pumps

Swimming pool pumps are generally of two types: horizontal centrifugal and vertical turbine. The pumps are usually manually operated. The net positive suction head (NPSH) requirements should be carefully checked, and pumps drawing water from tanks should be provided with low-water shut-off switches and alarms. Except for recirculating pumps serving diatomite filters, all recirculating pumps should be provided with full-line-size, quick-opening basket strainers in their suction piping.

With sand filter systems, it is sometimes possible to use the recirculating pump as the vacuum cleaning pump by providing 2 half-size recirculating pumps.

The head on the pump in a bottom-recirculating system with a pressure filter and no surge tank would be the sum of the pressure required at the outlet plus the discharge friction, the loss through the heater, the loss through the filter, the suction friction, and the loss through the strainer. The head on the pump with a surge tank would be the sum of the pressure required at the outlet, the lift from the pump to the pool water level, the discharge friction, the loss through the filter, the friction in the suction piping from the tank, and the loss through the strainer.

Horizontal centrifugal pumps may be used for swimming pool circulation where the liquid level in the pool is above the pump unit in order to ensure a flooded suction. This condition may

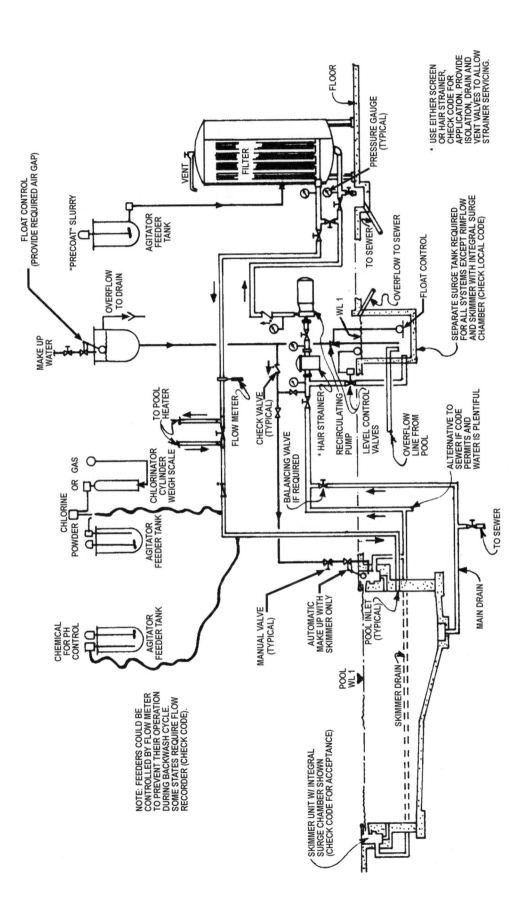

Figure 6-3 Pressure Diatomite Filter Conventional Flow

be accomplished by the installation of the pump in a dry pit next to the swimming pool.

For small capacities, an end-suction pump may be used; for larger applications, a horizontal split-case pump may be employed.

Horizontal, self-priming centrifugal pumps are used when the units must be above the water level in the swimming pool. These units must first be primed. These self-priming pumps utilize a built-in check valve and an air chamber to ensure that once a pump is primed it will continue to operate satisfactorily.

Vertical turbine pumps operate in much the same manner as standard centrifugal pumps, except that it is possible to attain much higher heads by adding stages. Designed for use in wells, the turbine pump may be constructed of one or more stages, with each subsequent stage adding head to the liquid and feeding it to the next stage. More pumps may be added while retaining a single shaft and driver. Proper installation requires a wet pit adjacent to the swimming pool. Sufficient head room must be provided for removing the unit for service or repairs. The area must be well lighted and electrical power should be readily available. Vertical turbine pumps offer significant advantages where floor space is at a premium or where special arrangements for priming are impractical.

Flow Indication

Accepted engineering practices, and most local codes, require that every swimming pool be equipped with a device that measures the flow of the swimming pool water directly in either gallons per minute or liters per second.

Many types of flow indicator are generally available and all have various advantages. It is recommended that the design engineer select a gauge with a capacity that is 50% greater than the design flow rate. Some state and local codes require that the flow indicator be equipped with a chart recorder and/or flow rate totalizer; check local code requirements.

Gutters

The capacity of the main gutter line should be 100% of the recirculation/turnover rate. The local administrative authority should be contacted for any other requirements.

Gutter drains should be spaced a maximum of 15 ft (4.6 m) apart. Grate areas should be at least 1.5 times the area of the outlet pipe. The outlet pipe size should be 2 in. (50 mm) minimum for commercial pools.

The sizing of the main gutter line depends on the static difference between the gutter line and the water level in the surge chamber when the swimming pool is occupied by the maximum number of bathers. The design of the surge chamber should allow this static difference to be at least 2 to 3 ft (0.6 to 0.9 m). With the flow rate and static head required to return the swimming pool water from the gutter to the surge chamber (since no pressure is required at the surge chamber), all of the static head will be used in the pipe friction loss. The friction loss calculations should include an allowance for the fittings and the entrance losses discussed previously. Normally, these obstructions are converted into equivalent lengths of pipe for calculations. The entrance of the main gutter line into the surge chamber should be below the operating swimming pool water level in the surge chamber.

Special patented, continuous-flow gutters, with adjusting weirs, and supply assemblies are sometimes requested. Check with local code authorities about the acceptability of these assemblies.

Skimmers

A skimmer is a single opening at the pool perimeter receiving pool overflow. Skimmers are generally used in lieu of a gutter system in an effort to reduce costs. Occasionally, they may be used in conjunction with gutters but, as a rule, one system replaces the other. Some jurisdictions prohibit the use of skimmers on commercial swimming pools or place limitations on the size of swimming pools allowed to utilize skimmers. The engineer should check local code requirements on this point.

Local codes, of course, vary; in general, however, 1 skimmer is required for each 400 to 500 ft² (37.2 to 46.5 m²) of swimming pool surface area. The skimmers should be sized for 80 to 100% of the turnover rate and/or for a flow rate of 30 gpm (1.9 L/s) or 3.75 gpm/in. (6.0 L/s/m²) of weir length. Pipes interconnecting the skimmers should be provided to equalize the flow. Some skimmers also include integral vacuum cleaning connections.

Surge Chamber

A surge chamber is a balancing tank storing water displaced by bathers. In sizing a surge chamber, the engineer must first determine the maximum bathing load of the swimming or diving pool. Allow 15 ft^2 (1.4 m^2) of swimming pool area per swimmer where the pool depth is less than 5 ft (1.5 m) and 25 ft^2 (2.3 m^2) of swimming pool area per swimmer where the pool depth is in excess of 5 ft (1.5 m). In locations where diving boards are provided, the number of swimmers will be reduced by 6 for each 3-ft (1-m) board and by 10 for each 10-ft (3-m) board. The nationally accepted average displacement per bather is 2.25 ft^3 (0.63 m^3). The top of the surge chamber must always be at or above the overflow elevation of the swimming pool. Failure to install the surge chamber at or above this elevation will result in flooding when the swimming pool circulating system is not in operation.

Backwash Pit

The volume of water used to backwash filters often exceeds the capacity of the drainage system to remove it. A backwash pit, therefore, is used to collect and store backwash effluent for disposal into the drainage system. The backwash pit is usually sized by determining the normal period of backwash time, at the rated gpm (L/s) of the swimming pool circulating pump. Using this process, the backwash pit will vary in size according to the size of the swimming pool, the type of filter medium used for water filtration, and the carrying capacity of the drainage system.

The required approval(s) must be obtained from the local code enforcement agencies having jurisdiction. Normally, sanitation districts in rural areas having small treatment plants will not allow a drain pipe from the backwash pit greater than 3 or 4 in. (76.2 or 101.6 mm) (normal size) to discharge into the sewer system. They will, therefore, insist on a reduction in the peak discharge flow rate and may require a separation chamber to remove the suspended diatomaceous earth particles in the backwash water.

Main Drain

For commercial swimming pools and, particularly, those installations where the main drain is directly connected to the pump suction, two separate main drains should be used to prevent bathers from being drawn toward a drain by the action of the pump suction. The drains should be covered with grates having an area of at least 4 times the area of the outlet pipe, or an area that creates a velocity of less than 1 ft/s (0.305 m/s). Main drains should be sized for 100% of the turnover rate.

The grates should have slots (or openings) not exceeding ⅜ in. (9.5 mm) in width. The velocity through the drain should not exceed 1 ft/s (0.305 m/s). The drain covers are to be designed so that they cannot be removed except with the use of specific tools. The drains should be located a maximum of 15 ft (4.6 m) from the side wall with a maximum of 30 ft (9.2 m) between drains.

The selection of the material for the main drain piping is up to the designer, though economics plays a part. Copper, cast iron, stainless steel, and plastic are suitable materials, which have all been used with varying amounts of success.

Where perimeter gutters are installed, antivortex main drain covers should be used to prevent bather entrapment due to excessive suction when the water level drops below the lip of the gutter.

Return System

The following design criteria for locating the swimming pool inlets are presented as a guide:

1. A minimum of 1 inlet per 10,000 gal (37 850 L) of swimming pool capacity should be provided.

2. Inlets should be spaced uniformly throughout the swimming pool in order to effect the proper distribution.

3. Inlets should be spaced less than 20 ft (6.0 m) apart and within 5 ft (1.5 m) of a corner.

4. Where practical, floor inlets should be used to improve the distribution of the filtered, heated, and chlorinated water, especially when the pool is used primarily for diving.

5. The piping should be sized so that the design flows do not exceed a velocity of 9 ft/s (2.74 m/s). However, velocities this high have caused excessive pipe corrosion and water hammer damage in some systems. A maximum velocity of 5 ft/s (1.5 m/s) should be considered in these systems.

6. The selection of materials of construction is the same as it is for the main drain piping.

7. Inlets should be equipped with integral throttling damper devices to simplify system balancing.

Vacuum Cleaning Lines

Two very distinct types of swimming pool vacuum cleaning system are currently available:

1. *Portable vacuum.* In this system configuration, there is no piping around the swimming pool. The system consists of a portable pump (either gasoline or electric), a suction hose, and a hand-held vacuum tool. A discharge line is directed into either the gutter system or the deck drains. These systems are less expensive than the plumbed systems but are more labor intensive and may cause objections due to the pump noise.

2. *Plumbed system.* In this type of arrangement, one or more separate inlet connections to the main pump (or separate pump suctions) are provided. The cleaning equipment is connected to these inlets. The vacuum connections must be located on the swimming pool wall, below the water level, and kept plugged except when in use. Discharge piping must be provided, connected either through the filter system or directly to waste for handling heavy dirt problems. Vacuum cleaning outlets should be located so that a maximum of 50 ft (15.0 m) of hose is used. The type of cleaning tool should be selected based on the size and shape of the pool.

Swimming pools using skimmers in lieu of gutters may be able to pipe such skimmers in such a manner that a vacuum cleaner can be connected to the skimmer instead of a separate piping system.

Pool Fitting Considerations

Makeup connections should be provided with a solenoid valve or pilot-operated valve that is interlocked with a high-water alarm and the recirculation pump to prevent overflow or flooding if the pump is not running.

When makeup water is introduced through an air gap, there should be open-and-closed type flow control at the valve with opening and closing speed controls.

There should be a full-sized, valved line for filling, and a smaller-sized bypass, including a float valve and throttling valve for makeup.

Pressure gauges should be provided on the discharge and suction sides of all recirculating pumps and on the strainer inlet. Compound type gauges should be installed at each strainer. Deck drains should discharge into the sanitary system for inside pools and the storm system for outdoor pools, with the approval of the AHJ.

In-ground pools (except small residential ones) should be provided with a tunnel chase for piping around them, which allows access.

Hydrostatic relief valves should be provided in the bottom of any swimming pool that has the bottom near or below the ground-water table. These valves may be obtained as an integral part of the body of the main drain units.

Drains should not have weep holes. The swimming pool membrane may require lead flashing soldered, not clamped, to a bronze body drain. Elastomeric and liquid waterproofing requires that the main drain be equipped with a wide flange and clamping collar. Carefully check this point on shop drawings.

Supply and return piping to the pumps should have a maximum velocity of 5 to 6 ft/s (1.5 to 1.8 m/s).

Heater Sizing

The sizing procedures for pool heaters are based only on the surface area of the swimming pool, since once the pool water has been brought up to the desired temperature substantially all the heat loss is from its surface. It is safe and practical to neglect the heat losses to the ground through the sides of the pool. In areas with deep frost penetration of the ground, an analysis may be required of the sidewall heat losses. The heat loss from the surface is available from standard engineering texts.

Two methods are commonly used for sizing the heaters. One is to size the heater to maintain the swimming pool at a given temperature without regard to the required initial warm-up time. When this method is used, initial warm-up time may be significant. The other approach uses the time element, providing oversized heaters that raise the water temperature within a specific period of time. This could be accomplished with multiple step heaters, which cycle the elements on and off as required.

Since most commercial-type swimming pools are maintained at a general temperature and started up once a season, the first method is recommended. However, on small residential swimming pools, where it has become fashionable to run the swimming pool filters on short cycles and to turn off the swimming pool heaters when the facility is not being used, the oversized or intermittent heating approach should be used. This method requires larger swimming pool heaters, and higher capital expenditure, for fast spot heating.

MATERIAL SELECTION[1]

Pool Ladders

These are usually offered in stainless steel, chromium-plated brass, and galvanized steel. About two-thirds of all returns in a recent survey expressed dissatisfaction with chrome-plated brass; by far the biggest problem was blackening, peeling, pitting, and dechroming, especially near the water line. Life ranged between 6 months and 3 years. Poor nickel-chromium plating was laid to blame. Fair performance is obtained from galvanized steel ladders. Stainless steel is the favored selection.

Underwater Lights

The majority of pool lights are the wet-niche type—lights that are set into the pool wall with water completely surrounding them, which allows the light units to be lifted to the pool deck for re-lamping or service without disturbing the electrical connections.

Copper and brass appear to be the most prevalent material selections for light bodies and niches, with silicon bronze used for the watertight rings. All of these give good to excellent performance. Aluminum light rings are subject to corrosion. Faceplates are usually made of chrome-plated brass and give fair to good performance, black discoloration being the chief complaint. Stainless steel faceplates are an alternate selection. The required minimum wattage per square foot of surface area is subject to local codes and competitive regulatory guides; however,

[1]The information on material selection was taken from National Spa and Pool Institute, Report no. 18, *Corrosion in swimming pools and general guide to materials selection.*

1 W/ft^2 (0.1 W/m^2) is generally accepted practice.

Pool Fittings

Of all the equipment used in a pool, the fittings represent the smallest percentage of the overall cost. They are critical to pool performance, however, and deserve attention. They include the inlet fitting, main drain fitting, vacuum wall fitting, rope anchors, and fill spout. Chrome-plated brass is the nearly universal selection, with performance reported as fair to excellent. Frequent black discoloration and occasional pitting are the chief complaints. Stainless steel, nickel silver, and plastic are favored as alternate selections and good results have been reported.

Piping

The piping material used most often is PVC plastic with an NSF International rating. This material has excellent resistance to most pool chemicals. It is of great importance to support the pipe as recommended by the manufacturer to avoid sagging when the water is heated. The expansion and contraction of plastic piping must also be considered.

Where copper piping is used, good to excellent life has been reported. Survey results indicate that in as many as one out of ten pools per year improper use of pool chemicals results in problems related to the release of protective corrosion films into the piping system. Poor control of pH or improper acid addition techniques is believed to be the cause for the introduction of copper salts into the pool and the resultant staining of the walls and corrosion of the piping and fittings.

Some velocity, impingement, and cavitation problems have been reported, but the incidence is not unduly high. Even though many local codes permit a velocity of 10 ft/s (3.05 m/s), the majority of pools operate in a range of 6 to 8 ft/s (1.8 to 2.4 m/s).

Valves and Pumps

Where copper tubing is used, valves should be bronze with a synthetic coating. Pumps should be bronze with a stainless steel shaft. Another possible selection is cast iron for the pump case and impeller, which gives a fair to good performance. Plastic valves are used with plastic piping systems and with a variety of pump types— bronze, cast iron, and plastic.

Surface Skimmers

The automatic skimmer has found universal acceptance among pool builders. The materials most commonly used for skimmer bodies are stainless steel, copper, plastic, and precast concrete, all of which give an excellent performance. PVC plastics and molded fiberglass have been reported as fair to good performers; cycolac skimmers have been reported as good performers.

Weirs are usually made of ABS or PVC plastic, are mounted in the front of the neck, and have a free-swinging hinge. Their performance is only fair and the need for design improvements has been noted. Skimmer baskets are usually made of perforated brass, stainless steel, molded polyethylene, or plastic-coated steel mesh. The skimmer lid is set flush with the pool deck and is made mostly of either aluminum (which gives a good performance) or the same material used in the skimmer body.

Cleaning Equipment

For the vacuum head and handles, chrome-plated brass is widely used, with excellent results. Alternate selections are anodized aluminum, which gives a good to excellent performance, and PVC or ABS plastic, which gives a fair performance (the chief complaint being ease of abrading).

The hose is made of plastic or rubber. Brushes are generally made of nylon, with performance reported as fair to excellent.

Heaters

There are two main types of heater: direct fired and radiant. There appears to be very limited experience with radiant heaters; direct fired heaters are much more common. From a corrosion and performance standpoint, most people feel that indirect heaters are by far the best. Copper or coated steel are employed for combustion chambers and copper or brass for the heating tubes or heat exchanger.

Problems experienced include: tubes plugging, tubes or coils burning out, corrosion when pH control is neglected, and external corrosion due to condensation.

POOL WATER CHEMISTRY

Untreated pool water is an environment that encourages the rapid growth of organisms. Continual treatment of this water is necessary to prevent the development of a health hazard. Water quality must equal or exceed the standards set by the appropriate authorities.

While filtration makes the water clear and attractive by removing suspended matter, the chemical treatment of microbial contamination is vital to the safe operation and proper maintenance of the pool. The purpose of chemical treatment is to disinfect the pool water by killing algae, bacteria, and viruses. As this process upsets the chemical balance, secondary treatment is necessary to prevent discomfort to bathers and damage to the pool and its equipment. Additional treatment may be necessary to precipitate dissolved minerals for removal by either the filter or the vacuum cleaner. The following discussion relates principally to the application of chlorine and its compounds for disinfecting swimming pools because these are the chemicals in common use.

The initial dose of chemicals must exceed the chlorine demand of the pool, which is the amount required to perform the following functions:

1. Kill all bacteria originally present.

2. Oxidize all other organic matter.

3. Promote chemical reactions with inorganic substances.

This phase of treatment is complete when tests show the existence of a stable chlorine residual for addressing the continual recontamination by bathers and other sources. This residual is comprised of very active, uncombined chlorine (the free residual) and less active chlorine in chemical combination with other substances (the combined residual). Chlorine must be added continually to maintain the chlorine residual, but the amount varies considerably from day to day depending on the weather and the bathing load.

The addition of chlorine gas to water results in the formation of hypochlorous and hydrochloric acids. Hypochlorous acid is very unstable and breaks down readily to release free chlorine for disinfection purposes. Hydrochloric acid contributes nothing to the treatment process, but is stable and so increases the acidity of the water. This change in acidity is a typical side effect of any process of disinfection and requires the addition of chemicals for counteracting purposes. Excessive counteraction in this case would result in too much alkalinity.

Acidity and alkalinity are measured by the pH value. This is a logarithmic system providing a numerical expression of pH in a series of numbers between 1.0 and 14.0, with values below 7.0 for acidity and above 7.0 for alkalinity, with 7.0 being neutral. Acid water fosters the corrosion of metal parts, which can lead to the expense of replacing heaters, filters, and other equipment. Alkaline water causes mineral deposits and interferes with disinfection. Cloudy water, which irritates bathers' skin, eyes, and breathing passages, is typical of a pool where the pH value is too high or low.

The foregoing shows that correct levels of chlorine residual and pH value are essential to satisfactory pool operation. Pool owners must use simple test kits to check chlorine residual and pH value daily.

A third factor in pool chemistry is total alkalinity. This refers to the quantity of alkaline materials in the water, which should be from 80 to 100 parts per million (ppm). It becomes significant in a pool only when a chronic condition persists in spite of normal levels of chlorine residual and pH value. Total alkalinity must not be confused with pH value, which refers to the balance between alkaline and acid substances/solutions.

pH Value

Salt water pools, with water of natural origin, have a high pH value due to the mineral content (approximately 3.5% by weight). As a result, the reduction of the pH to recommended levels may not be economical or desirable.

Adjusting the pH value in a new pool may be difficult for the following reasons:

1. The raw water may have a low or high pH value by nature.

2. New concrete is very alkaline, sacrificing lime to the more neutral water.

3. Many of the alkaline salts on the walls of an unpainted concrete pool will dissolve in the first fill of water.

Mineral Deposits

Scale formation by minerals causing "hardness" is a common problem for pool owners. The scale that accumulates on the pool structure, pipes, heat exchangers, filters and ladders includes the insoluble carbonates, aluminates, silicates, and sulfites of calcium, iron, and magnesium. Calcium carbonate (lime) is the largest component.

Water with a high temperature and high levels of pH, dissolved solids, and calcium hardness encourages scale formation. The pH value is the easiest factor to control. A pool heater should handle a large flow of water with a low temperature rise to avoid mineral deposits within the heat exchanger.

Red water   This is usually caused by iron oxide (rust). It is sometimes due to a low pH (acid) level, which fosters the corrosion of steel pipes, fittings, and tanks. Where the concentration of iron in swimming pool water exceeds 0.3 ppm, damage to the pool equipment and finish is likely to occur. Most iron-bearing waters are clear as they flow from the source; the discoloration occurs when the iron is oxidized, by either exposure to air or chlorination. The method of removing this discoloration by using alum has already been described.

Where the local water supply stains sinks and bathtubs, either fill the pool from another source that is iron-free or install an iron-removal filter. A portable iron-removal filter may be used during the filling operation, and the removal of iron from the subsequent makeup water could be effected by precipitation in a surge tank connected to the suction of the filter pump. (However, this requires a regular maintenance program to remove the sediments from the tank.) Alum and a heavy dosage of chlorine are fed continually into the surge tank to cause precipitation of the iron, which is retained on the sand bed as the water passes through the filter. If it is clear, the water from the source may be used for backwashing, provided that chlorine and alum are not supplied to the surge tank during the process. Where a gas chlorinator is in use, the raw water used to operate the chlorinator may be sufficient for makeup purposes.

Brown water   This is usually caused by tannin, an organic acid found in swamp water. Tests of brown water have shown low chlorine residual levels. The remedy is superchlorination followed by adjustment of the pH value as necessary.

Green water   This condition is usually caused by algae and a low level of chlorine residuals. The remedy is superchlorination, followed by adjustment of the pH value and the use of an effective algaecide.

Blue water   Blue or clear green water is due to the presence of copper salts formed by the acid corrosion of copper pipes and fittings. The actual color varies with the pH value and the types of ion in the water.

DISINFECTION

Pool water contains varying amounts of naturally occurring bacteria and bacteria introduced by bathers and airborne sources. Disinfection is the chemical process of killing disease-causing bacteria as well as other types of microorganism. In a swimming pool, this process is accomplished by maintaining a uniform residual in the water of some chemical (usually chlorine) capable of killing the bacteria. Chemical manufacturers provide detailed, written instructions concerning the quantities of chemicals required and the methods of injection.

To ensure a steady level of chlorine residual, there must be a continuous addition of chemicals to replace the chlorine expended during disinfection and dissipated by evaporation and reaction to sunlight. The methods of feeding chlorine into the water to meet the chlorine demand vary with the chemicals used and the forms in which they are supplied. Several systems of chlorine delivery and pH control are described in the following paragraphs.

Chlorine Gas

Chlorine gas is the most concentrated and inexpensive form of chlorine. For reasons such as safety, cost of equipment, the need for trained personnel for handling, and the type of secondary treatment required, however, its use is limited to large pools. A gas chlorinator allows the chlorine to flow at a constant rate from a high-pressure cylinder into the return pipe from the filter. The chemical reaction between the chlorine gas and the water produces hypochlorous and hydrochloric acids. Hypochlorous acid is a useful disinfectant. Hydrochloric acid, which is an unwanted byproduct, requires secondary treatment because of its adverse effect on the pH value. This treatment entails a chemical pot

feeding a solution of soda ash (sodium carbonate, Na_2CO_3) into the water downstream from all equipment at a rate of approximately 1.25 lb (0.57 kg) of soda ash per single pound of gas consumed. The alkaline soda ash neutralizes the acid, which would otherwise reduce the pH value. The gas cylinder is usually mounted on a platform scale for checking the weight of gas used each day.

Be sure to check local codes for special requirements for gas chlorinators, as some local codes do not permit its use. In the absence of specifics, the following is recommended:

1. The chlorinator should be housed in a separate, ventilated room with a door that opens away from the pool. The door should be provided with a glass panel so the chlorinator can be observed from outside without opening the door.

2. A self-contained breathing apparatus should be provided outside the chlorinator room for use by the operator.

3. Scales should be provided so that the amount of gas can be determined.

4. Restraining chains, wall racks, or anchors should be provided to hold cylinders in place and prevent the accidental tipping over of the cylinders.

Calcium Hypochlorite

This is a dry, white compound available in granular and tablet form under various trade names. It releases 70% of its weight in free chlorine when dissolved in water but has a different effect on the pH value than chlorine gas does. As a result of the alkalinity of the calcium byproduct, the pool water becomes alkaline and requires the addition of muriatic (20 deg. Baume hydrochloric) acid or sodium bisulfate to restore the balance.

The granular form is prepared for use by being dissolved in water. As this results in a precipitation of calcium carbonate, an extra container is necessary for mixing purposes, so that only the clear liquid is allowed to pass through the chemical feed pump (hypochlorinator) for discharge into the return line. It is important to use only the clear liquid because the calcium carbonate residue would clog the feeder system and form lime scale on the walls and floor of the pool.

Another method, which reduces calcium deposits in the pool, is to add soda ash to the container with the calcium hypochlorite. This converts the calcium hypochlorite into sodium hypochlorite. The same precaution noted above is necessary to ensure that only the clear liquid passes through the chemical feed pump (hypochlorinator). The heavy residue of calcium carbonate should be discarded. Tablets of calcium hypochlorite dissolve more slowly than the granules and have the advantage of providing a more constant and even supply of chlorine when thrown into the pool or used in a dissolving basket. These slowly dissolving tablets may also be placed in the skimmer basket.

Sodium Hypochlorite

This is the principal constituent of liquid household bleaches, which are usually 10 to 15% available chlorine by weight or roughly 1 ¼ lb/gal (2.15 kg/L). It can be either fed through a hypochlorinator (in commercial strength or diluted) or poured directly into the pool.

Commercial solutions of sodium hypochlorite contain sodium hydroxide to prevent the loss of chlorine during storage. As sodium hydroxide is alkaline, it reacts with acids in the pool to make the use of soda ash unnecessary. If the pool is already alkaline, the sodium hydroxide will increase the pH value and require counteraction by muriatic (20 deg. Baume hydrochloric) acid or sodium bisulfate.

Cyanurates

These are complex compounds for cyanuric acid, which are readily soluble in water. They have a slightly acidic effect so that the addition of acid for pH control is seldom necessary. As cyanurates are more expensive than conventional chemicals, initial treatment of the pool with 30 ppm cyanuric acid is essential to prevent the dissipation of chlorine residual due to exposure to ultraviolet sunlight. In an untreated pool, this dissipation may account for the loss of as much as 70% of the chlorine on hot, sunny days. When cyanurates are used, the free chlorine residual is maintained between 1.0 and 2.0 ppm. This level of stable chlorine residual is very effective against algae. The advantages of cyanurates make them ideal for residential pools.

The pool owner should use a test kit that shows values of free chlorine residual up to 3.0 ppm. The person who services the pool should also have a test kit for cyanuric acid up to 100 ppm.

Super Chlorination

This is the application of heavy doses of chemicals to raise the chlorine residual to 5.0 ppm or more, with the excess residual allowed to dissipate overnight. It is necessary when the pool water becomes cloudy or discolored, when a false residual test is discovered, or when signs of algae appear. The pool must be closed during this process. Testing to ensure proper chlorine residual must be performed before the pool is reopened.

Breakdown Chlorination

This usually applies to outdoor pools with a high organic content. When the initial dose of chemicals reacts with the pool water for the purpose intended, chloramines and other chlorine compounds may be formed. These substances are responsible for chlorine odors and tastes. The addition of small amounts of excess chlorine are necessary for normal pool operation, but in order to eliminate tastes and odors it is sometimes necessary to raise the free chlorine residual (say to 5.0 ppm). The free chlorine then starts to oxidize the chloramines and other chlorine compounds. As these reactions absorb much of the excess free chlorine, the residual falls suddenly to a lower value and the chlorine compounds disappear—together with their tastes and odors. The point at which this occurs is called the break point. At this point most of the chlorine in the water is in the free state.

Other chemicals for the disinfection of swimming pools include bromine, iodine, and certain other compounds.

Other Pool Chemicals

Aluminum sulfate   This chemical is used as a coagulant with sand filters to give improved clarity to the water. It dissolves slowly to make an acid solution which neutralizes in reaction with the pool water to form aluminum hydroxide. Under the right conditions, aluminum hydroxide precipitates in white flocs, which accumulate as a gelatinous mat on the filter bed. This mat will catch particles that would otherwise pass through the sand. The successful use of alum for flocculation requires alkaline conditions with a pH of 7.4 to 7.6. The alum should be put in the basket of the skimmer or of the hair and lint strainer after the backwashing of the filter.

During the initial disinfection of a pool containing water with a high iron content, the chlorine will cause the iron to precipitate as red iron oxide, which will discolor and cloud the water. If powdered alum or a saturated alum solution is sprinkled on the surface of the water and left overnight, it will coagulate the suspended particles and hasten the settling process, so that the precipitate can be vacuumed from the pool bottom in the morning. The pool should not be used during treatment and the water should be tested before use is allowed.

Algaecides   The safest chemicals for controlling algae in swimming pools are proprietary preparations made for this purpose. The ideal algaecide kills existing algae, prevents new algae growth, creates no problems with filter or pool operation. and is harmless to pool users.

Chemicals for cleaning filters   An inspection of the filter bed of a sand and gravel filter during cleaning may reveal the formation of mud balls. This condition can be corrected by purging the bed with lye (sodium hydroxide, NaOH) or calcium hypochlorate. The top of the filter should be opened and the water below the top of the sand drained. The sand and mud balls should be broken up and the top layer allowed to dry before the chemical is spread evenly over the bed.

Care should be taken that the top of the sand is dry before the chemical is applied, otherwise the chemical will emit dangerous fumes. The filter should be closed and the water level raised to about 2 in. (50.88 mm) above the sand. The chemical should stand in the filter between 4 and 6 hours; then the filter should be backwashed thoroughly, with backwashing continuing for at least 10 minutes after the water runs clear.

When the sand bed is partly calcified due to hard water, the use of muriatic (20 deg. Baume hydrochloric) acid or sodium bisulfate as an acid wash may correct the condition. The acid is applied the same way the purging chemicals are. Proprietary preparations are also available for this purpose and may include detergents and sequestering agents for removing oils and cosmetics.

If calcification is so bad that the bed is no longer porous, changing the sand is recommended rather than using an acid wash, which would corrode the tank and fittings.

Heat loss retardants   These are proprietary products that spread across the pool surface in molecular thickness to retard evaporation and conserve the heat of the pool water. They serve to reduce steaming and condensation around indoor pools. The ideal retardant should be colorless, odorless, nontoxic, and noncorrosive, and it should have no adverse effect on disinfection.

Sequestering agents   These are usually proprietary preparations that separate the in-soluble scale and scum-forming minerals in pool water and convert them into harmless soluble forms. An important application is preventing the accelerated corrosion, scale formation, and staining that may occur with heated pools.

Muriatic acid   This is the commercial name for 20 deg. Baume hydrochloric acid (HCl). It is used for reducing the pH value of pool water but requires careful handling by trained people. It is also used as an acid wash for calcified sand filters and for scrubbing the pool walls to get rid of established algae.

Sulfuric acid (H_2SO_4)   This acid salt is used for pH control and cleaning purposes. It is also known as "dry acid" because it serves as a safe alternative to muriatic acid; it is available in the pure form and in combination with other chemicals under various trade names.

Other chemicals for disinfecting pool waters include bromine, iodine, and certain other compounds, but these are employed relatively infrequently.

Manufacturers have designed equipment using ultraviolet radiation, silver salt, common table salt, etc. for pool use but with limited success. As of this writing, these methods cannot be recommended.

At pH readings greater than 7.0 (neutral), chlorine dissipates rapidly and may cause objectionable odors.

Chemical Feeding Equipment

Sterilization of the pool water using sodium or calcium hypochlorite solution is accomplished by the use of a hypochlorinator (chemical feeder). In public pools, hypochlorinators are usually required to be duplex units. Hypochlorinators are small, adjustable, positive displacement pumps, built specially for the service, drawing hypochlorite from a container and injecting it into the filter discharge piping to the pool after the water heater connections. An additional chemical feeder for pH control may be required. The equipment should be automated to control chlorine residual and the pH of the pool water.

Hypochlorinators are provided with plastic containers that hold the required hypochlorite solution and the acid and/or alkali required for pH control. The units selected must have a discharge pressure greater than that in the piping that they are connected to. Hypochlorinators should be interlocked with the filter recirculating pump so that they operate only when the pump is running. Table 6-1 gives recommended capacities for hypochlorinators.

Table 6-1
Hypochlorinator Capacity Recommended

System Volume,		Suggested Maximum Size	
gal	(L)	gph	(L/h)
10,000	(37 850)	0.15	(0.6)
18,000	(68 130)	0.25	(1.0)
42,000	(159 000)	0.60	(2.3)
72,000	(272 500)	1.0	(3.8)
114,000	(431 500)	1.6	(6.0)
180,000	(681 300)	2.5	(9.5)
360,000	(1 363 000)	5	(20)
720,000	(2 726 000)	10	(40)

REFERENCES

1. Gabrielson, M. Alexander, ed. 1975. *Swimming pools: A guide to their design and operations.* Fort Lauderdale, Florida: Hoffman Publications.

2. National Spa and Pool Institute. *Standard for public swimming pools.* ANSI/NSPI-1, 1991. Alexandria, VA.

3. National Spa and Pool Institute. *Standard for residential, in-ground swimming pools.* ANSI/NSPI-5, 1995. Alexandria, VA.

SOURCES OF ADDITIONAL INFORMATION

1. Amateur Athletic Union (AAU), 3400 West 86th St., Indianapolis, IN 46468

2. Council for National Cooperation in Aquatics (CNCA), 1301 16th St., NW, Washington, DC 20036

3. Federation Internationale de Natation Amateur (FINA), 555 N. Washington St., Naperville, IL

4. National Collegiate Athletic Association (NCAA), P.O. Box 757, Grand Central Station, New York, NY 11017

5. National Spa and Pool Institute (NSPI), 2111 Eisenhower Ave., Alexandria, VA 22314

6. United States Public Health Service USPHS, Department of Health, Education and Welfare, Washington, DC 20020

Gasoline and Diesel-Oil Systems

INTRODUCTION

This chapter describes the design, selection, and installation requirements for shop-fabricated, atmospheric storage tanks and distribution and dispensing networks for new and replacement systems for liquid, petroleum-based fuels. Although mentioned several times in this chapter, rail type tanker cars are not considered a primary method of fuel delivery. For the purposes of this chapter, trucks are considered the primary method of delivery.

DEFINITIONS AND LIQUID FUEL CLASSIFICATIONS

A "storage tank" for liquid fuel is any stationary receptacle designed to contain an accumulation of regulated substances. Tanks can be constructed of materials such as steel, concrete, and fiberglass-reinforced plastic, or of various combinations of materials that provide structural support.

A storage tank is considered "underground" if 10% or more of the total tank volume of single or multiple tanks, including all of the associated and interconnecting piping, is below grade or covered with earth.

A "regulated substance" is any designated chemical that includes hydrocarbons derived from crude oil such as motor fuels, distillate fuel oils, residual fuels, lubricants, used oils, and petroleum solvents.

Occupational Safety and Health Administration (OSHA) 29 CFR 1926 further defines storage tanks according to operating pressure ratings:

1. Atmospheric tanks—atmospheric pressure to 0.5 psig (3.45 kPa).

2. Low-pressure tanks—atmospheric pressure from 0.51 to 15 psig (3.451 to 103.42 kPa).

3. Pressure tanks—atmospheric pressure greater than 15 psig (103.42 kPa).

Liquid fuels are governed by the requirements of National Fire Protection Association (NFPA) Standard no. 30. This standard classifies liquids as either flammable or combustible based on their flash points. The flash point of a liquid is the temperature at which the liquid can give off vapor in sufficient concentration to form an ignitable mixture with air at or near the surface. In short, the flash point is the minimum temperature at which a fire or explosion could occur. The following definitions are only for the purpose of fire protection.

Beside classifying liquids as either flammable or combustible, the NFPA divides them into Class IA, B, and C; Class II; and Class IIIA and B.

Flammable liquids are only Class I. They have a flash point below 100°F (37.8°C) and a vapor pressure no higher than 40 psia (2086 mm hg) at 100°F (37.8°C). Class IA liquids (which include gasoline and gasoline blends) have a flash point below 73°F (22.8°C) and a boiling point below 100°F (37.8°C).

Combustible liquids are only Class II or III. They have a flash point at or above 100°F (37.8°C). Diesel fuel, light heating oil, and kerosene are Class II combustible liquids with a flash point at or above 100°F (37.8°C) but below 140°F (60°C). Class III liquids include motor lubrication and waste oil.

"Liquid petroleum" and "petroleum products" are defined as hydrocarbons that are liquid at atmospheric pressure and at temperatures between 20 and 120°F (-29 and 49°C), or are discharged as liquid at temperatures in excess of 120°F (49°C). For the purposes of this discussion, these products include gasoline, gasoline blends, and diesel oil used as fuel for motor vehicles or internal combustion engines. These fuels are classified as hydrocarbons. They are also considered flammable liquids.

"Specific gravity" is the direct ratio of a liquid's weight to the weight of water at 62°F (16.7°C).

The "viscosity" of a liquid is a measure of the internal friction between particles that resists any force tending to produce flow. The higher the viscosity, the more slowly the liquid will flow under gravity conditions. Viscosity is obtained by measuring the amount of time a given quantity of liquid at a specified temperature takes to flow through an orifice. Viscosity is expressed in Seconds Saybolt Universal (SSU), used primarily for pump work, as well as Kinematic Viscosity Centistrokes or Centipoises, Seconds Saybolt Fucol, and Seconds Redwood.

The vapor produced by the evaporation of hydrocarbons is in a category known as "volatile organic compounds" (VOC), which are environmentally controlled emissions. Vapor produced by gasoline and gasoline blends is required by code to be recovered. "Phase I systems" refer only to storage tanks where vapor is displaced when the tank is filled with product. The recovered vapor is returned to the delivery truck or rail tanker car. "Phase II systems" refer only to vapor recovery from automobiles when their tanks are filled with product. The recovered vapor is returned to the storage tanks. Kerosene and diesel oil storage and dispensing systems do not require vapor recovery at this time. Codes concerning environmentally controlled substances are changed and improved frequently. It is essential that the designer stay abreast of current code requirements.

CODES AND STANDARDS

The US Environmental Protection Agency (EPA) has written basic, minimum regulations to protect the environment and people's health from the leakage of hydrocarbons and VOCs from underground storage tanks (USTs), above-ground storage tanks (ASTs), and associated piping. The basic purpose of these regulations is to ensure the proper installation of the various system components, to prevent leaks or spills from occurring and, should a leak or spill occur, to ensure that the leak is quickly found, corrected, and reported.

Other organizations regulate component testing and make general provisions for system components and installation with regard to fire prevention.

In almost all jurisdictions where these systems are installed, specific requirements are mandated by local and state agencies. They concern permits, registration, fees, and record keeping, as well as specific technical rules and regulations regarding system installation, maintenance, materials, and leak detection. Very often, these requirements are more stringent than the federal EPA regulations cited here. A thorough code search is necessary to ensure complete compliance with all applicable federal, state, and local regulations.

The following is a list of commonly used codes, regulations, and guidelines. This list is not complete and must be verified in the locality where the project is constructed.

1. NFPA Standard nos. 30, 30A, 385, and 329.
2. Federal Regulation 40 CFR 112, Spill Containment Control and Countermeasures.
3. Regional fire codes such as SBCCI, BOCA, and UFC. Also state fire marshal regulations as applicable.
4. Underwriters Laboratories UL-142, Standard for Safety, and UL-2085, Fire Resistance. Also UL listings.
5. Federal Resource Conservation and Recovery Act (RCRA), Subtitles 1 and C.
6. Steel Tank Institute (STI) regulations.
7. Public Laws (PL) 98 and 616.
8. Clean Air Act Amendments (CAAA).
9. SARA Title III, 1986.

SYSTEM COMPONENTS

Liquid fuel storage and dispensing, whether in an AST or a UST, require many interrelated subsystems and components for proper operation and for compliance with applicable codes and standards. They are:

1. Storage tanks:
   A. Tank filling and accidental spill containment.
   B. Atmospheric tank venting.
   C. Overfill protection.
   D. Storage tank vapor recovery system.
2. Leak detection and system monitoring.
3. Motor vehicle vapor recovery system, if applicable.
4. Pump and piping systems for dispensing and distributing product from the storage tank into motor vehicles or directly to engines.

Because there are significant differences between a UST and an AST in terms of materials, installation, and operation, these systems are discussed separately.

UNDERGROUND STORAGE TANK SYSTEM

Storage Tanks

General Storage tanks are designed and fabricated to prevent product releases due to structural failure and/or corrosion of the tank from the time of installation to the end of the expected useful life of the system. This requires that the tank manufacturer fabricate the tank in conformance with applicable codes and nationally recognized standards for structural strength and corrosion resistance. Since the tank must be installed in a manner that prevents distortion and stress, the installation of the specific tank must be done by contractors trained and approved by the manufacturer. The tank foundation, bedding, and backfill must be done only with material and methods approved by the manufacturer, local code authorities, and nationally recognized standards.

Prior to tank installation, the ground-water conditions, soil composition, and potential for corrosive action should be determined. When deemed necessary, tests should be made to determine the allowable soil pressure. The excavation for the storage tank should be sufficiently large to permit safe installation and proper backfilling on all sides of the tank with a minimum of 18 in. (0.46 m) of noncorrosive inert materials, such as clean sand or gravel. The suggested backfill material should be a naturally rounded aggregate such as pea gravel, with particles ranging from ⅛ to ⅜ in. (3.2 to 9.5 mm) in diameter, clean and free flowing.

Other conditions that should be considered when installing tanks include:

1. High water-table levels.
2. The possibility of flooding from an adjacent water body or source.
3. Established flood plains for the local area.
4. Seismic or earthquake conditions.
5. Corrosion protection (soil conditions).

Since tank dimensions for the same size tank differ among manufacturers, consult the manufacturers of the proposed tank for exact dimensions.

Tank materials The materials used to manufacture primary and secondary tanks include:

1. Steel, with thin coating or thick cladding depending on the corrosion protection method selected by the manufacturer. Cathodic protection may be required.
2. Fiberglass-reinforced plastic (FRP). No corrosion protection is required.
3. Steel and fiberglass-reinforced plastic composite.
4. Pre-engineered, cathodically protected steel.

Clad steel is manufactured by applying a layer of plastic, usually FRP, over the exterior surface of the steel tank. This offers the strength of steel with the corrosion protection of FRP. Great care must be taken to prevent damage to the cladding during shipping and installation. Since cracks and crevices in the cladding may allow corrosion to occur, some authorities require the installation of sacrificial anodes.

FRP tanks are manufactured by several proprietary processes from thermoset plastic reinforced by fiberglass. Reinforcing ribs are built into the tank for increased structural strength. Generally, there is a resin-rich layer that contacts the product. The specific plastic materials are listed by the manufacturer as being suitable for the intended product. These tanks are completely resistant to corrosion; however, they have the disadvantage of being more susceptible to damage from mishandling and distortion during backfill installation.

The composite tank is manufactured by having the steel tank "wrapped" in a jacket of high-density polyethylene that is not bonded to the tank itself. This provides a very thin interstitial space that can be monitored. Experience has shown that the jacket is the portion of the assembly that fails most often.

Pre-engineered, steel tanks are constructed by putting an insulating coating on a steel tank and welding sacrificial anodes to the tank side. The coating is usually coal tar epoxy, although FRP and polyurethane are also used. If steel piping is used, it must be isolated from the tank by special dielectric bushings or unions. This is the least costly material but it has the disadvantage of requiring that the cathodic protection be constantly monitored.

Tank construction Typical tanks are cylindrical with a round cross section. FRP tanks have half-dome ends and steel tanks have dished ends. Tanks are available in either single-wall or double-wall construction. In double-wall construction, the inner tank containing the product is called the "primary tank" and the outer tank is called the "secondary containment tank." This system of double-wall tanks is often referred to as being "double contained." The outer tank may be manufactured from the same material as the primary tank, or, as approved by the jurisdictional agency, it may be a different material.

A space between the primary and secondary tank is called an "interstitial space." The width of the space varies among manufacturers and types of construction. It is this space that is monitored for leakage from the primary to the secondary containment tank. Monitoring systems may sense product leakage from the primary tank or ground-water leakage into the secondary tank, or both.

Tank connections and access Reference applicable codes and standards—local, state, and federal—for mandated connections, access requirements, and overfill/spill prevention regulations. The following are generic, standard features recommended for all installations.

There must be a convenient and leakproof method of providing connections directly into the primary tank to allow for filling, venting, product dispensing, gauging, and leak detection. For larger tanks, access directly into the tank for personnel may also be desired. Allowance for this is made by providing a "manway," which is formed at the factory during manufacturing. This opening is provided with a bolted and gasketed cover. (It should be noted that a tank is considered a confined space, and entrance is specifically regulated by OSHA standards, which require, minimally, the use of self-contained breathing apparatus and an outside assistant/observer. Also, the tank must be marked per OSHA requirements. See current standards.) In addition to the manway, individual half couplings are usually provided for direct connection to piping to the tank.

The manway is often used for installing equipment and several piping connections. A manway cover on the tank with multiple piping connections in a variety of sizes can be provided. (This is done to eliminate the need for secondary containment, and, if the pipes are installed inside the manway, to allow for easier maintenance of them.) Standard fittings are 3 and 4 in. (80 and 100 mm) national pipe thread (NPT). Standard inside diameters (IDs) of manway openings are generally 22, 30, and 36 in. (0.56, 0.76, and 0.91 m), the size depending on the size of the tank and code or OSHA requirements. These connections can be arranged in a straight line or in circular configuration, as illustrated in Figure 7-1.

Where only piping connections are provided, an enclosure connected to all pipes and including an extension to grade should be installed to allow leakage monitoring and access to the connections for maintenance. This arrangement is commonly called a "containment sump" because there is no direct connection of the sump to the wall of the tank.

Tank filling USTs are filled from delivery trucks or, in rare cases, rail tanker cars. When done by gravity, this is commonly called a "gravity drop" or simply a "drop." When gravity filling is not possible, truck-mounted pumps are used. If the fill port is located directly over the UST, the assembly is called a "direct fill port." If there is any horizontal piping from the fill port to the tank, it is considered a "remote fill port." The fill port covers must be water tight. Where multiple

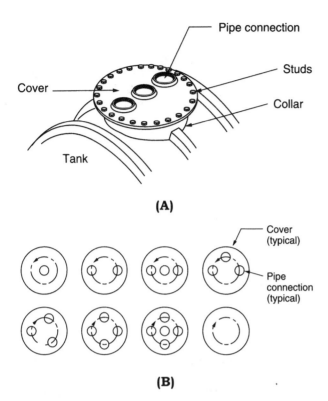

Figure 7-1 (A) Typical Manway into FRP Tank with Pipe Connections, (B) Typical Available Manway Cover Fitting Configurations.

Source: Courtesy of Xerxes.

tanks containing different products are installed, the fill port covers should be color coded to distinguish among the various product ports and the vapor recovery ports. The cover plates should be installed a minimum of 1 in. (25 mm) above the level to minimize the possibility of storm water entering the port.

Another integral part of the filling system is the drop tube or piping inside the tank. The drop tube provides a submerged inlet for product during filling. This reduces the fluid turbulence inside the tank.

Overfill protection must be provided.

Spill prevention The purpose of spill prevention is to provide a safe filling method that is capable of catching spills from delivery hose disconnections. A typical 20-ft, 0-in. (6.1-m) length of 4-in. (100-mm) delivery hose holds 15 gal (56.8

L). Spilled product must be prevented from entering the soil adjacent to the fill port through the provision of safeguards that are code mandated and recommended as good practice.

This is accomplished by installing a below-grade catchment basin with a capacity of 3.5 to 15 gal (13.2 to 56.8 L) to catch spillage of product from truck delivery hoses. An optional device that could be part of the basin is a drain valve that, when opened, empties the product into the tank fill line. Any water accumulating in the sump must be removed manually and properly treated elsewhere.

A dry disconnect coupling on the delivery truck hose could also be used to prevent spills.

The fill port assembly is designed to accomplish the following:

1. Provide a water-tight grade cover allowing access to the fill hose connection.

2. Provide a fill hose connection for the tanker truck delivery hose; the hose end has a standard end connection. An adapter may be required on the fill pipe leading to the tank. The gravity drop delivers approximately 200 gpm (756 L/min). The flow rate of a truck-mounted pump is generally 50 gpm (189 L/min).

3. Allow any fuel spillage from the fill hose to be contained and returned to the tank.

4. Allow for any storm water to be removed.

Another fill method involves the use of a coaxial truck delivery hose to both fill the tank and recover vapor. This requires only one connection from the truck to the tank fill port and a different type of adapter than is used for a fill connection alone.

Atmospheric tank venting The USTs are at atmospheric pressure and require continuous tank venting to ensure that no pressure or vacuum is built up inside the tank when it is filled or emptied. These vents are not to be confused with vapor recovery vents, which serve a different purpose.

Since all of the vapors produced from products are heavier than air, the vapors normally do not escape. A release of vapor can occur as the tank is filled (vapor is displaced by the product added), as product is removed, or as a result of a buildup of vapor pressure caused by the evaporation of product at times of high temperature.

Each tank is vented by means of a dedicated vent pipe, typically 2 in. (50.8 mm) in size.

The vent pipe is directly connected to the top of each primary tank and should be extended to a safe location above the highest level of any adjacent building or to a minimum of 12 ft (3.66 m) above grade. The vent discharge must be directed either vertically or horizontally away from buildings and other tanks.

When not in conflict with other regulations, general practice is to have the vent terminate in a pressure/vacuum cap that protects against the entrance of rain and birds and only opens when the pressure exceeds 2 to 15 oz/in.^{2} (0.86 to 6.46 kPa) or when a vacuum pressure of 1 oz/in.^{2} (0.43 kPa) is exceeded. If a cap is not provided, a flame arrestor should be installed, if permitted by regulations.

Overfill prevention   All UST systems must be provided with overfill protection by the installation of one or more of the following devices or by other methods approved by the local authorities. The individual or combination of acceptable devices and methods in any specific location should be obtained from local authorities.

1. A device that alerts the operator when the tank is no more than 90% full by restricting the flow of product into the tank or by sounding an audible alarm, which is activated by a high-level alarm probe.

2. A mechanical device that shuts down flow into the tank when the product level reaches 95% full.

The best method of overfill protection is the second—installation of an automatic device on the fill tube that reduces flow into the tank when the tank is 90% full and stops it entirely when it is 95% full. There are a number of approved mechanical devices from different manufacturers that perform this function. This is the method most often required by local authorities.

The first method listed above is installation of an audible alarm, activated by the level gauge, that automatically sounds when the liquid level in the tank reaches 90% full. Often a visible alarm is included. This alarm must be located in clear sight of the fill port and the operator.

In addition, tanks that do not require a vapor recovery system can have a floating ball device installed on the atmospheric vent line that closes the vent when the product reaches a pre-

determined point (usually the 90% full level), at which additional filling may cause a spill. When the vent is closed, the air pressure increases inside the tank and restricts the inflow, alerting the operator that the tank is approaching the full level. If such a device is used, an extractor fitting is required to allow access into the line for maintenance or removal of the float assembly.

Leak Detection and System Monitoring

General   Leak detection is required by code. The three basic requirements for leak detection are:

1. Leakage must be capable of being detected from any portion of the tank or piping that routinely contains petroleum.

2. The leak detection equipment meets the performance requirements described in Federal Regulations, sections 280.43 and 280.44.

3. Leak detection equipment is installed, calibrated, operated, and maintained in accordance with manufacturers' instructions.

The EPA has established various options, combinations of which may be used, depending on project conditions, initial or long-term costs, and product. In addition, state and local requirements may differ from EPA requirements in terms of the number and application of these options. A schematic diagram indicating methods of detecting leaks from tanks and piping is illustrated in Figure 7-2.

The options are:

1. Leakage from tanks.
    A. Manual tank gauging. (Many states no longer allow this method.)
    B. Automatic tank gauging. (Many states no longer allow this method.)
    C. Tank secondary containment interstitial monitoring.
        a. Vapor monitoring.
        b. Liquid monitoring.
        c. Hydrostatic monitoring.
        d. Pressure monitoring.
    D. Tank tightness testing with inventory control. (Many states no longer allow this method.)
2. Leakage outside of tanks.

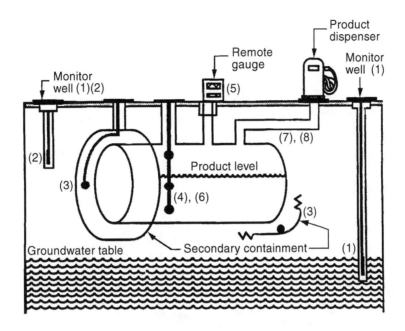

**Figure 7-2 Schematic Diagram of Leak
Detection Methods for Tanks and Piping**

(1) Groundwater monitoring, (2) Vapor monitoring, (3) Secondary containment with interstitial monitoring, (4) Automatic tank gauging, (5) Tank tightness testing with inventory control, (6) Manual tank gauging, (7) Leak detection for suction piping, and (8) Leak detection for pressurized piping [or (7) Vapor recovery, and (8) Pressure product supply].

A. Ground-water monitoring.

B. In-ground vapor monitoring.

C. Piping leak detection.

Leakage from tanks[1] Measuring leakage from tanks is accomplished by gauging the level of product in a tank and measuring the amount of product dispensed and the amount of product delivered. If the dispensed and remaining product figures agree with the amount of product delivered, there is no leakage.

Manual tank gauging In manual gauging, referred to as "sticking," a long gauge stick calibrated to 8 in. (203.2 mm) is lowered directly into the tank until it rests on the bottom. This requires that straight, direct access into the tank be provided. The liquid leaves a mark on the stick that is read by the operator after the stick is removed from the tank. This method is generally limited to tanks of 2000 gal (7570 L) or less

and is used only in conjunction with tightness testing for tanks with capacities greater than 550 gal (2082 L).

With this method, the tank being measured must be completely idle for at least 36 hours. Two separate readings must be taken, one at the beginning and one at the end of that period, and the readings must be taken once per week. If the readings do not meet or match weekly or monthly standards, the tank is leaking.

It is common to provide manual tank gauging as a check of mechanical or electronic methods and to allow measurement if electrical power is out or if the automatic devices fail.

Automatic tank gauging Automatic tank gauging is accomplished by the permanent installation of a probe, or monitor, into the storage tank. The probe can be mechanical, pneumatic, or electronic.

Mechanical tank gauging The least costly tank gauging is a mechanical device, such as a float, that rides on the surface of the liquid. By its movement the float transmits a reading of the

---

[1]Many states no longer allow manual or automatic tank gauging or tightness testing with inventory control as methods of leak detection.

liquid level by mechanical or other means to a remote indicator. General accuracy is about 2%.

Pneumatic tank gauging Another, slightly more accurate method is a pneumatic tank gauge that uses a bubbler pipe extending down into the liquid. A permanent source of compressed air or a hand-operated air pump forces air out of the bubbler pipe. The operating principle is a measurement of the pressure required to force air out of the bubbler pipe—the more pressure required to produce the bubbles, the deeper the depth of liquid.

Electronic tank gauging An electronic tank gauging system consists of a probe mounted in a tank opening and extending to the bottom of a tank and a remote panel that is microprocessor controlled and can be programmable. The probe, which is capable of monitoring several parameters, extends from the primary tank bottom to a termination point above the tank that both anchors the probe and acts as a junction box for the wiring. For USTs this point is below grade. Access to the box through a small manhole is required. For ASTs, the probe terminates in a junction box on top of the tank.

The advantage to the electronic gauging system is it has the capability of being programmed to automatically record many functions. The probe can monitor such parameters as product and water level inside the tank and product temperature. In addition, probes extending from various locations can be electronically linked together to monitor vapor and liquid leakage from many sources such as monitoring wells, piping, containment sumps, and tank interstitial spaces. Probes from multiple tanks can be linked to a single panel. Overfill and low-product levels are also capable of being monitored.

The types of electronic probe that are commonly available are the magnetostrictive and the ultrasonic. The magnetostrictive type uses changes in the magnetic field produced by movable product sensor floats, one for water and one for product. Each float has an integral magnet and is free to ride on the probe shaft as the product and water levels change. Ultrasonic devices use ultrasound waves from the probe on the shaft to a receiver on the top of the probe to signal a change in product level.

Capacitance type probes are no longer recommended, having been replaced by less expensive, more accurate, electronic probes.

Interstitial monitoring The interstitial space between tanks is used to contain and detect any leakage from the primary tank. Many states now require some form of this type of monitoring of tanks and connected piping. The monitoring of interstitial space is divided into two general categories: wet and dry.

Dry methods use vapor monitoring for the presence of hydrocarbon vapors. Wet methods monitor for the presence of liquid product using either air pressure or vacuum.

Vapor monitoring Vapor monitoring is achieved by placing a probe sensitive to product vapor in the dry interstitial space. The probe is generally placed one half the distance into the interstitial tank space. When leakage occurs, the vapor produced by the product is detected and a signal is given. This method has the advantage of being unaffected by condensed water.

Liquid monitoring Liquid monitoring is achieved by placing a probe capable of detecting liquid at the bottom of the dry interstitial space. When leakage occurs, it is detected and a signal is given. A shortcoming of this method is that water condensation in the interstitial space is detected as leakage. However, external ground-water leakage through the secondary containment tank is also detected. Monitors that are sensitive only to product, based on specific gravity, are available.

Hydrostatic monitoring system This is more expensive than other methods but it is the most accurate method of interstitial monitoring. It is a wet system in which a liquid, usually brine, which is installed at the factory, completely fills the interstitial space. The system is at atmospheric pressure with the liquid carried above the tank into a reservoir that contains a level probe. Since normal product temperature differences will cause the liquid level to fluctuate, the level probe is set to annunciate only when there are unacceptable changes.

Water from a high water table leaking into the interstitial space from a hole in the secondary tank will cause the level to rise. Product leaking out of the primary tank into the interstitial space will also cause a change in the brine level, as will a hole in the secondary tank. A typical hydrostatic leak detection system is illustrated in Figure 7-3.

To maintain atmospheric pressure, holes must be made in the standpipe cap. If the possibility of water entering the holes exists, a

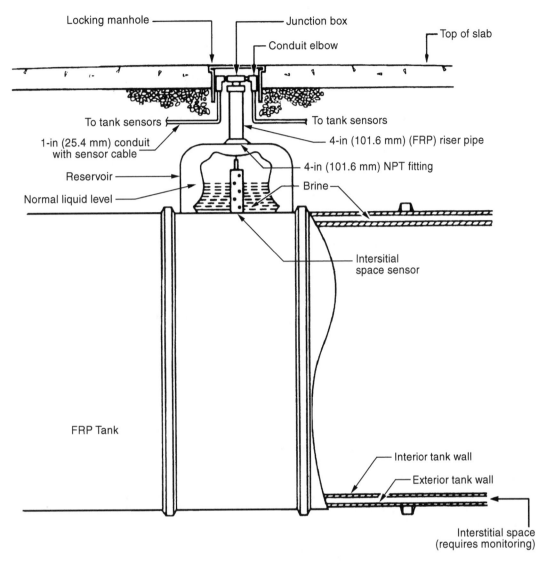

Figure 7-3   Detail of Hydrostatic Interstitial Monitoring

separate vent line, extended to a point safely above grade, must be installed.

Pressure monitoring Pressure monitoring of the interstitial space is accomplished by applying air pressure (1.5 psig, 10.34 kPa) or creating a vacuum in the space. Any increase or reduction of pressure/vacuum indicates a leak, and a signal is sent to a remote panel for annunciation. Pressure systems are rarely used due to the level of experience and maintenance required.

Tank tightness with inventory control This is a combination method using periodic tank tightness testing and monthly inventory control;

it is allowed only for the first 10 years of operation. Many states no longer allow the use of this method in new tank installations. (Check local code requirements.)

Tank tightness testing requires that the tank be taken out of service and temporary testing equipment be installed. One method uses volumetric testing to exactly measure the change in the level of product over a period of several hours. Another method uses ultrasound or tracer gas detection techniques to detect leaks in the tank wall.

The monthly inventory requires that an exact measurement be taken each month of the amount of product delivered; that measurement must then be compared to the total of the amount stored in the tank and the amount dispensed. If the two figures do not balance, there is a leak.

Leakage remote from tanks

Ground-water monitoring Ground-water monitoring involves sensing the presence of product floating on the surface of ground water. It can only be used where water and the products to be measured are immiscible. This method requires the installation of monitoring wells in the ground water at several strategic locations near the tank. The wells must be properly designed and sealed to eliminate surface contamination. A geotechnical report may be required to determine the flow of underground water and the direction a pollution plume might travel were the ground water to become contaminated.

The wells can be checked either manually or automatically, by electronic methods. Manual methods require the use of a "bailer" to collect liquid samples from inside the well and bring them to the surface. Samples must be sent for analysis once a month. Electronic methods use probes suspended in the well to continuously monitor for the presence of contamination in ground water. If there is contamination, an alarm is annunciated at a remote panel. Monitor wells are limited to sites where the ground-water level is 20 ft (6.1 m) or less below the surface, with the best results obtained from depths of between 2 and 10 ft (0.60 and 3 m).

In-ground vapor monitoring In-ground vapor monitoring involves measuring the "fumes" in the soil around a storage tank to determine whether spilled product is present. This method, like ground-water monitoring, requires the installation of monitoring wells.

The wells can be checked either manually or automatically, by electronic equipment. Manual methods require monthly air sample gathering and laboratory analysis. Electronic methods use a probe suspended in the well and a remote, finely calibrated analyzer. Vapor monitoring should be considered only where backfill is sand, gravel, or some other material that allows vapor to move readily from the tank through the backfill to the monitor. It is not recommended where high ground water and excessive precipitation might interfere with the operation of the system for more than 30 days.

Leakage from piping

Underground pressurized delivery systems Pressurized piping must have one automatic leak detection method and one additional leakage detection method, as described below:

1. Automatic leak detection entails a permanently installed, automatic flow restrictor or automatic flow shut-off device installed in the product discharge piping, and/or a continuous alarm system. The continuous alarm system could be a probe installed in the secondary pipe that continuously monitors the liquid or vapor release of the secondary containment piping system. If the secondary containment terminates in a manway or containment sump, the lower end of the secondary containment pipe should be open to the sump and allow any leaking liquid to spill into the sump to be detected.

   The following accuracy must be provided for automatic detection: a pressurized shutdown monitoring device that prevents the flow of product when a line tightness test indicates a minimum leakage of 0.10 gph (0.063 L/h). In addition, the device must be capable of shutting down the system when a leak of 3 gpm (0.19 L/s) at 10 psi (68.95 kPa) is detected. One commonly used type of device is installed on the discharge of the submersible pump in the manway. It must act independently of any other pressurized shut-down monitoring device.

2. An additional method of leak detection may be any one of the following, performed monthly: ground-water monitoring, secondary pipe vapor monitoring, or secondary pipe liquid monitoring. Annual pipe tightness testing also meets the requirement for an additional method, as does a continuous alarm to detect spillage as described above.

Underground suction delivery systems Underground suction piping leak detection is not required if the piping is sloped back to the tank from the dispenser and if a check valve is installed in the dispenser as close as possible to the vacuum pump. Because increased use of alcohol additives with gasoline is anticipated, it is general practice to provide double-contained suction piping for gasoline systems. Double-contained piping is not required for diesel fuel, but it is highly recommended.

When the tank is higher than the dispenser, it is necessary to use double-contained piping. A sump is installed at the low point of the piping and a probe is installed to detect leakage from the secondary pipe.

Leakage into sumps, pans, etc. Any product leaking from the primary pipe will spill into the secondary containment pipe and flow by gravity to the low point. The piping is pitched downward to a bulkhead, sump or manway. Double-contained piping penetrates the side of the bulkhead using special fittings called "bulkhead fittings." These fittings are used to terminate double-contained piping so that the secondary containment is open and free to have liquid from between the two pipes spill into the sump to be detected.

Leakage within containment sumps and manways is monitored by means of probes sensitive to liquid or vapor. They are suspended in or attached to the sides of the containment sump. The liquid probe level is adjusted to signal the presence of liquid. Probes that discriminate between water and petroleum products are available. They are connected by wires to a remote panel for annunciation.

Inductive sensors that do not require penetration of the secondary containment pipe are also available. These attach directly to the outside of the secondary pipe to detect leakage by interruption of the inductive path of the sensor.

Vapor Recovery Systems

It is a code requirement that VOC vapors resulting from the displacement of gasoline and gasoline-blended products be prevented from entering the atmosphere. VOC vapors occur when storage tanks and motor vehicles are filled. Diesel fuel, kerosene, waste and motor oil, and heating oil do not require vapor recovery.

Vapor recovery is divided into two phases. Phase I is recovery from gasoline storage tanks; phase II is recovery from gasoline dispensers used to fill motor vehicles.

Phase 1 vapor recovery Phase 1 vapor recovery entails a separate and independent, closed system installed at the storage tank for use only during the filling of the storage tank. The product flowing into the tank displaces an equal volume of vapor, which must be recovered. The purpose of phase 1 vapor recovery is to prevent the escape of VOCs from the UST into the atmosphere. It can be achieved by means of a two-point or coaxial system.

Two-point system The two-point vapor recovery system consists of a separate fill line to and vent from the UST, each piped directly to the tanker truck. A separate hose from the truck is connected to an outlet accessed through a vapor recovery fill port adjacent to the product fill port.

It is common practice for the vapor recovery pipe to be the same size as the fill line. Typically, this size is 3 in. (80 mm), and the vapor recovery pipe does not require double containment.

Coaxial vapor recovery This is a combination system that uses a single connection point. It is similar in principle to the phase 2 vapor recovery used with dispensers. It consists of a drop tube having a pipe within a pipe and a delivery hose of the same construction.

Product is delivered through the center pipe of the delivery hose and the vapor passes through the outer pipe of the drop tube, which returns vapor directly to the delivery truck through the coaxial delivery hose as the product fills the tank.

Phase 2 vapor recovery Phase 2 vapor recovery is a separate and independent closed system installed at the dispenser only for use during the dispensing of gasoline. Its purpose is to prevent the escape of VOCs from the motor vehicle tank into the atmosphere during tank filling. Phase 2 vapor recovery can be achieved by use of either a balanced or a vacuum type system. The balanced is the type most often used.

Product Dispensing Systems

Product dispensing concerns only transferring product from the storage tank into the fuel tanks of motor vehicles.

Two methods are used to transfer product from the UST to the motor vehicle: pressure and vacuum systems. The pressure system uses a submerged pump immersed in the UST to create the pressure needed to transfer product from the UST to the vehicle. (See Figure 7-4.) The vacuum system uses a pump installed in the dispenser enclosure to create the suction pressure needed to draw product from the UST into the vehicle.

For USTs, the pressure system is preferred for the following reasons:

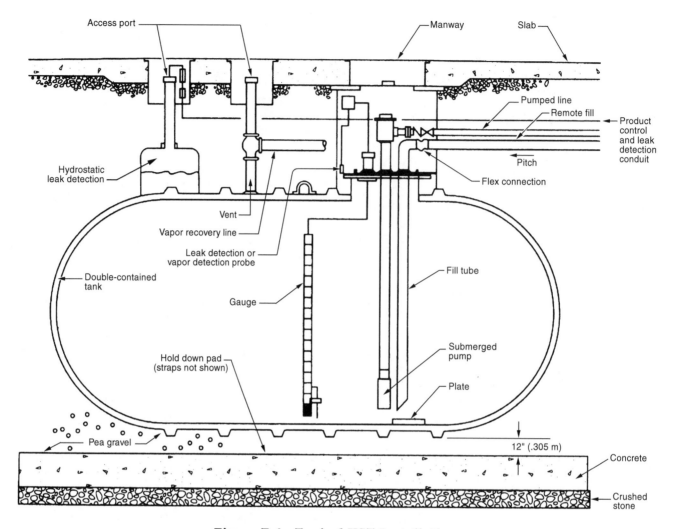

Figure 7-4 Typical UST Installation

1. Maintenance is much lower compared to that for vacuum systems.

2. Lower initial cost.

3. For vacuum dispensers, there is a practical upper limit of 10 ft (3 m) suction lift from the UST bottom to the highest point of the dispensing system. **Note**: The vacuum system is no longer recommended.

4. A submersible pump can supply multiple dispensers. Vacuum pumps must be installed in each individual dispenser.

5. Submersible pumps can deliver higher flow rates than vacuum pumps.

6. Vapor lock is eliminated with a submersible

pressure pump system, as the pump suction is always flooded.

Pressure dispensing system The pressure system consists of a small-diameter, submersible pump installed in the product storage tank that provides the required flow rate and pressure. The submersible pump is sized to fit inside a 4-in. (100-mm) tank connection. Other sizes are also available.

Product dispenser Dispensers are commonly available in two flow rates: standard speed for cars, which delivers at a flow rate in the range of 7 to 15 gpm (0.44 to 0.95 L/s), and high speed for trucks, which delivers as much as 45 gpm (2.84 L/s). For passenger cars, the average dispenser discharges approximately 10 gpm (0.63 L/s) and requires approximately 30 psi (207 kPa). The size of the hose from the dispenser to the nozzle could be either ½ or ¾ in. (15 or 20 mm), ¾ in. (20 mm) being the most often used. High flow rates for large fuel tanks require a 1-in. (25-mm) sized hose.

Dispensers have a wide variety of features. The following are the major components generally found in a dispenser:

1. The register. How will it display the amount of product?

2. A meter. Used to register the total gallons.

3. Location of the hose outlet. Available in a side or front location.

4. Hose. Coaxial type for phase 2 vapor recovery. Twelve-ft (3.66-m) length is average, but 15-ft (4.57-m) length is available, with breakaway fittings.

5. A high hose retriever will keep the hose off the floor/driveway.

6. A high-capacity product filter.

7. An emergency shut-off that will stop flow in the event of a supply or dispenser hose line break.

8. A dispenser containment mounting pan for installing the dispenser.

9. A nozzle, with a vapor recovery feature where required and an automatic shut-off feature. Two sizes are generally available: ½ in. (15 mm) and the more commonly used ¾ in. (20 mm).

Dispenser pan   A dispenser pan is required to attach the dispenser to a concrete pad or island. The pan provides a liquid-tight entry for both single and double-wall product piping and electrical conduit. It is also designed to collect and monitor spills and to prevent product from leaking below the dispenser into the environment.

Figure 7-4 is an illustration of a typical UST with various equipment installed. Figure 7-5 illustrates the entire UST storage and dispensing system installed in a typical service station.

ABOVE-GROUND STORAGE TANKS

Tank Materials

The primary tank most often used is factory constructed of steel and intended for atmo-spheric pressure conditions. Such a tank must conform to UL-142, standard for safety. Materials such as FRP, reinforced concrete, and FRP clad steel are seldom used for smaller tanks. Stairs or ladders are generally provided to allow inspection and delivery truck operators to reach connections located on top of the tank.

Tank Construction

ASTs are factory fabricated in both round and cylindrical configurations. Primary tanks are often manufactured with compartments capable of storing different products. NFPA Standard no. 30 limits motor fuel AST capacity to 6000 gal (22 710 L). All ASTs must be provided with some form of product leakage and overfill containment conforming to Spill Containment Control and Countermeasures (SPCC) regulations. This containment can be achieved by having a dike or an impoundment capable of holding 110% of the tank contents or by providing integral secondary containment of the primary tank.

Many smaller tanks are provided with integral secondary containment and an interstitial space. The width of the space varies among manufacturers. There are several proprietary methods used to construct the secondary containment vault around the primary tank. An often used material is plastic-lined concrete, which, if sufficiently thick, provides a 2-hour fire rating, as required by UL-2085.

It is a code requirement that the outside of a concrete vault be protected against corrosion, weather, and sunlight. Another material used for external secondary containment vaults is steel. Insulation between the primary and secondary tank is provided by some manufacturers to protect the primary tank from temperature extremes. This may also be used to meet fire safety requirements for a 2-hour fire rating.

Corrosion Protection

Since the tank is above ground, the only corrosion protection required for the tank is weather resistance on the tank exterior. This is a code requirement, and each manufacturer has a proprietary method of protecting the outside of the AST.

The exposed piping must be either a corrosion-resistant material such as FRP (which must also be impervious to UV light), stainless steel, or protected (painted or coated) black steel.

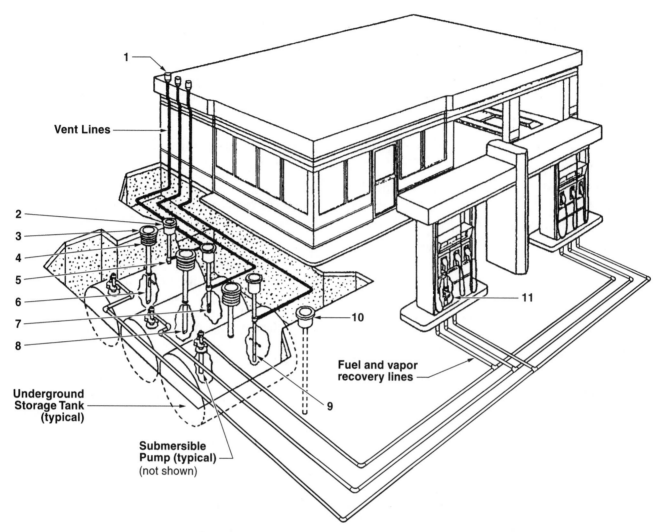

Figure 7-5 Typical Service Station Piping

(1) Vapor vent cap, (2) Vapor recovery port, (3) Tank fill hose adaptor, (4) Spill containment sump, (5) Extractor fitting, (6) Overfill prevention, (7) Ball float overfill prevention, (8) Drop tube, (9) Tank gauge, (10) Monitor well, (11) Emergency shut-off.

Tank Connections and Access

Connections are located only on top of the tank and extend through the vault or secondary containment into the primary tank. Except for larger tanks, there is usually no direct access for personnel entry into the primary tank. Standard connections include:

1. Tank vent.

2. Emergency vent.

3. Product dispenser outlet.

4. Product fill (either coaxial or single as required).

5. Phase 1 vapor recovery.

6. Tank gauging.

7. Leak detection.

Tank Filling and Spill Prevention

Tank filling   The tank is filled using a fill port assembly built into the tank encasement or containment at the top of the tank. The delivery truck must have a pump and the operator is often required to climb stairs to make the connection. The fill port cover could be locked if desired. In order for the operator to reach the top-mounted connection with the hose, stairs are provided as part of the installed tank. If a coaxial vapor recovery system is used, only one connection to the tank is required. If a two-point system is used, two connections are required. An optional, ground-level remote tank filling station is usually available as a separate piece of equipment to allow convenient filling without the necessity of connecting to the top of the tank. The remote fill station could have a self-contained pump or the built-in fuel truck pump could be used.

Spill containment   For tanks with integral secondary containment there is a containment sump surrounding the fill pipe. The size of the sump ranges from 5 to 15 gal (18.9 to 56.8 L). For tanks with external secondary containment, spills enter the containment and are manually removed. The remote fill station could be provided with an integral spill containment sump to catch any hose spills. A small hand or electric pump could be provided to empty the containment sump into the primary tank.

Atmospheric Tank Venting

An AST requires two vents. One is the standard atmospheric vent used to keep the tank at atmospheric pressure. This is commonly a 2-in. (50-mm) size and must extend to a point 12 ft 0 in. (3.66 m) above grade. The end typically terminates in a pressure/vacuum cap.

The second is an emergency vent required to depressurize a tank if there is a fire close to or under the tank that raises the temperature to a point where product vapor is generated faster than the atmospheric vent can pass it. Such a vent is commonly 6 or 8 in. (150 or 200 mm) in size, based on the tank size and the volume stored. The tank manufacturer provides the required emergency vent, with size based on American Petroleum Institute (API) standards.

Overfill Prevention

Overfilling is prevented by automatic or manual means installed directly on the tank.

Automatic overfill prevention employs an overfill preventing valve similar to that described previously in the discussion of USTs. Manual methods include a direct reading level gauge installed in sight of the operator and/or an audible high-level alarm activated by a separate probe installed inside the tank. Alarms shall sound when the product level reaches 90% of capacity and product delivery will be stopped when the level reaches 95%.

Leak Detection and System Monitoring

Leakage from tanks   Use of above-ground tanks requires a method of containing any possible product release and preventing contamination of the adjacent environment. Product releases can result from small leaks or the catastrophic failure of the tank. Containment methods that meet requirements include a dike completely surrounding the tank, remote secondary containment, and integral secondary containment.

For ASTs without secondary containment, a dike must be provided. Dikes are required to be capable of containing 110% of tank capacity and to be constructed of materials such as concrete, steel, or impermeable soil designed to resist the full head of liquid. Dikes must be constructed in conformance with NFPA Standard no. 30. For discharge from the dikes there must be a separator along with the necessary control valves—which may have to be self actuating to conform with local codes. It is recommended that an additional impoundment basin be constructed at least 50 ft (15.2 m) from the AST and at a safe distance from other buildings, property lines, or tanks. The purpose is to capture and isolate any flammable liquids released during a fire or tank failure and remove them to a safe distance from the AST. For ASTs, dikes are seldom used because remote and integral secondary containment have far lower initial costs.

Remote secondary enclosures are usually made of steel. They are totally enclosed and sealed in a manner that prevents the entrance of rainwater. They are required by code to have a capacity that is 110% of the nominal capacity of the primary tank.

Tank integrity is achieved by enclosing the primary tank with an integral secondary containment, usually of steel or reinforced concrete. This type of tank has an interstitial space that is monitored for leakage in the same manner used for the USTs, which was discussed previously.

System monitoring   System monitoring consists of product level gauging and leakage annunciating. AST systems can be monitored either manually or electronically; however, manual reading is no longer allowed in some states.

Product level gauging in the tank can be achieved by use of a visual level gauge or an electronic gauge, either mounted on or immediately adjacent to the tank or at a remote location. Level gauges similar to those installed in USTs can be used. Remotely mounted electronic gauges capable of recording and placing in memory many functions using probes similar to those installed in USTs are commonly used.

Leak detection for ASTs is much easier than that for USTs because leakage from the tank can be easily observed manually. Automatic means of system monitoring include a stand-alone alarm panel and alarms that are integral to an electronic panel used for product level indication.

Vapor Recovery

Phase I and phase II vapor recovery for gasoline and gasoline blends is required. For phase I recovery, similar to USTs, either coaxial or two connections from a delivery truck are necessary during the filling operation. Phase II vapor recovery for tank-mounted dispensers is usually integral. For remote dispensers, a separate vapor recovery line, connecting from the dispenser to the tank, is required.

Product Dispensing Systems

For ASTs, the dispenser is usually directly connected to the tank or located a very short distance from it. For remote dispensers, the vacuum system is usually preferred for these installations because it is lower in initial cost, and, due to the short piping runs and single dispenser, most of the objections discussed previously, in the UST section, do not apply. It is important to include an antisiphon valve to all AST dispensing systems.

For ASTs, the dispenser can be mounted either on the tank or as a separate, remote dispenser (similar to those used for a UST). Dispensers are available with vacuum or pressure type systems.

The tank-mounted dispensing system consists of a submersible pump, the complete dispenser (nozzle, hose, integral phase II vapor recovery system, means of base-mounting, and safety features), product pump, and interconnecting piping. This arrangement has the lowest initial cost.

Figure 7-6 illustrates a typical AST with piping for an attached dispenser.

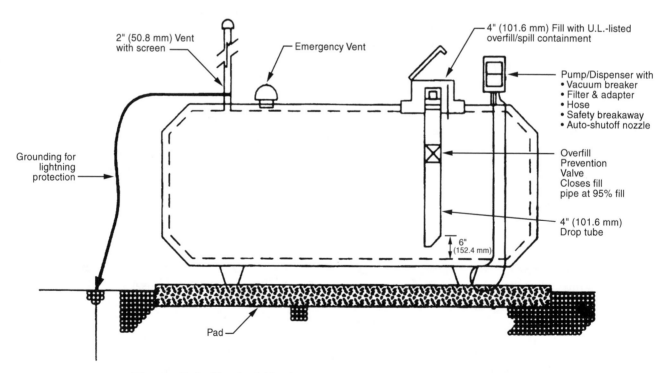

Figure 7-6   Typical Tank-Mounted, Above-Ground Dispenser

Source: Courtesy of Convault.

Tank Protection

All ASTs located adjacent to a road or subject to a possible automotive collision must be adequately protected. Acceptable means of protection are concrete barriers and bollards. Bollards similar to those used to protect fire hydrants are the means most often used. The entire assembly—tank, fill station, etc.—should be placed within fencing with a lockable gate.

SYSTEMS DESIGN

Piping Materials

Piping above ground from an AST is for the vent and product delivery. The most common piping material is A-53 steel with threaded joints and factory-applied corrosion protection. The pipe must be coated at the factory with an accepted and proven corrosion paint or coating. A common practice is to use a baked-on powder. Another material used where a higher degree of corrosion protection and strength is required is stainless steel. FRP with ultraviolet protection added to the pipe is another often-used material. Galvanized steel pipe is not considered acceptable. Adapters are used to connect steel pipe to FRP if an underground run to a remote dispenser is necessary.

For new and replacement USTs, interconnecting piping is almost exclusively plastic or FRP with plastic or FRP secondary containment. Requirements regarding approval of the specific piping material and connections selected, and cathodic protection, if applicable, must be checked with the jurisdictional authority.

Plastic piping is commonly divided into two general types, flexible and rigid. Flexible pipe is generally manufactured from proprietary materials. If it is UL listed and/or FM approved, it is generally acceptable. Flexible piping materials have found limited use and acceptance. In addition, the joints and connections should be selected to provide the greatest strength, ease of installation, and corrosion resistance.

Rigid FRP piping with an epoxy interior lining has been widely used and accepted, and is considered the piping material of choice. The primary pipe is assembled with socket type fittings and epoxy cement. The outer (secondary containment) pipe is the same material as the primary pipe and is manufactured in two half sections with a longitudinal flange. It is assembled after the primary pipe is tested using cement placed on the adjacent flanges with nuts and bolts installed to hold the two half sections together until the cement dries.

Flexible pipe connectors are used to connect piping runs to sumps and manways to allow for settlement. In addition, because submersible pumps are screwed into a tank connection, the product discharge will not always face the direction of the piping run to the dispenser when tightened. Flexible connectors are necessary inside manways to connect the submersible pump discharge to the dispenser supply piping.

Because leakage is visible, double-contained piping is not required for ASTs if the tank is located within a dike or inside a remote containment. If pipe is run underground or above ground outside diked areas, it must be double contained and provided with leak detection.

Gasket materials must be either Buna-N (nitrile butadiene) or NBR (acrylonitrile butadiene rubber).

Pipe Sizing

Pipe sizing is based on the flow rate of the product, the allowable friction loss of the fluid through the system, and fluid velocity. This is an iterative procedure done in conjunction with selecting the size of the product pump.

Information required Before the pipe can be sized, the following procedure for sizing the dispensing system must be done:

1. Select the dispenser location, type, and ancillary devices.

2. Select the pipe material.

3. Lay out the piping system, including length, fittings, and elevations in the layout.

4. Select the storage tank size and location.

5. Select a suction or pressure product pump system.

Flow rate For ordinary applications, the typical discharge flow rate to a motor vehicle from an average dispenser is 8 to 10 gpm (0.50 to 0.63 L/s). High-rate dispensers with discharge rates of up to 45 gpm (2.84 L/s) are available for buses and trucks.

Simultaneous use factor The number of dispensers likely to be used at once is usually determined by experience. Where this can't be determined by experience, the following rule of thumb may be used: For multiple dispensers up to four, normally use a 100% use factor. For more than four, use a 75% simultaneous use factor.

Velocity For FRP piping, the recommended maximum velocity should be kept at or below 7.5 ft/s (2.3 m/s). This figure keeps the pressure rise from water hammer to a safe level of 150% of design pressure. This is necessary due to the quick closing of the dispenser valve. For steel pipe, a maximum velocity of 8 ft/s (2.44 m/s) has been found acceptable.

Piping friction loss Friction loss of product through piping is found by checking with the manufacturers of the submersible pump or dispenser. Using the established flow rate, the allowable friction loss can be selected based on pipe size and the selected product.

For preliminary sizing purposes only, and if specific tables are not available, most products are close enough in viscosity to water that standard water charts can be used to obtain a friction loss figure that is sufficiently accurate. For FRP pipe, the friction loss should be decreased by 10% for a more accurate figure.

Submersible Pump Sizing

The pump is sized using the total gpm (L/s) flow rate and the total head required.

The submersible pump is suspended in the product storage tank with the impeller near the bottom of the tank and the motor, piping connections, and electrical work exposed in a manway at the tank top. Pump curves from the manufacturer are used for the selection of the most appropriate pump.

To find the flow rate:

1. Calculate the total gpm (L/s) from each section of the product line. This is done using the flow rate from the selected dispensers and the simultaneous use factor for the number of dispensers that may be used at the same time. This gives the gpm (L/s) figure for the pump.

To find the total pump head required:

1. Calculate the height from the bottom of the storage tank to the high point of the dispenser hose, including the elevation of the high hose dispenser.

2. Find the friction loss of the product flow through the distribution piping up to the dispenser, based on the flow rate calculated. This figure must include the equivalent length of run and other losses through fittings and all other connected devices. Most figures are obtained from manufacturers. For pressure loss through a submersible pump leak detector, the dispenser assembly, and dispenser hose, refer to manufacturers' information.

3. Obtain the recommended pressure required for proper operation of the selected dispenser. A typical figure used is in the range of 25 to 30 psi (172 to 207 kPa). This figure includes losses through the nozzle, hose, strainer, etc.

4. Add all of the above figures together to calculate the total head required.

5. For a system head loss calculation sheet containing a checklist of all fittings and devices, refer to Figure 7-7. This checklist contains many items that may not be necessary for all installations.

From the manufacturer of the selected pump, obtain the pump curves and select the pump based on the calculated head and flow rate.

General Design Considerations

For pressurized product pipe, it is common practice to use a minimum of a 2-in. (50-mm) size, increasing it only if the system under design requires a larger size based on a higher flow rate or if the difference in friction loss will allow the selection of a lower horsepower submersible pump. Generally accepted practice is not to use pipe sizes smaller than 1¼ in. (32 mm). A larger size product pipe is generally used in order to lower the head requirements of the pump selected.

Tests

Testing of all piping and the UST at the time of installation is critical to ensure that no leakage of product can occur and to check the integrity of the pressure-bearing components. In addition, tests of the UST for deformation after installation and corrosive coating damage are also necessary. Testing must be performed in accordance with code and local jurisdictional authority

Project _____ Specific gravity _____ Temp. _____
Liquid _____ gpm (L/s) Range _____ Viscosity _____

Static Losses		
Tank Diameter	_____	ft (m)
Bury Depth	_____	ft (m)
Height High Hose Reel	_____	ft (m)
Total Static Height	_____	ft (m)
A. Run of Pipe, Pipe Size (in diameter)	_____	in. (mm)
Measured Run	_____	ft (m)
Fittings — equivalent length (E.L.)	_____	ft (m)
Valves — equivalent length (E.L.)	_____	ft (m)
Reducers and Enlargements (E.L.)	_____	ft (m)
B. Total Equivalent Length	_____	ft (m)
C. Pipe Friction Loss	_____	× friction loss/100 ft (30.5 m)
Total Friction Loss	_____	ft (m)
Equipment Loss (in feet head)		
Meter	_____	ft (m)
Dispenser	_____	ft (m)
Filter and Leak Detector	_____	ft (m)
Hose and Nozzle	_____	ft (m)
Strainer	_____	ft (m)
D. Total Equipment Losses	_____	ft (m)
E. Total Head Loss (A + C + D)	_____	ft (m)

Figure 7-7 System Head Loss Checklist

requirements. As a minimum, the following guidelines should be utilized:

Testing of the storage tank   The UST must be pressure tested before the tank is placed into the excavation and again after backfilling is complete. Certification must be obtained from the manufacturer that the inner and outer tank walls were leak free prior to shipment. The certification must be based on a factory-performed tank tightness test. If a factory-installed hydrostatic interstitial monitoring system is used, a test before installation is not required since a visual check of the leak detection system will disclose any problem.

The pressure test prior to installation consists of applying 5 psig (34.5 kPa) air pressure in the tank for 2 hours with no lowering of pressure permitted. At this time, all tank openings should be sealed and a soapy water solution applied to all connections so that any bubbles indicating leakage can be observed. If the tank has a coating for corrosion protection, this must be checked with an electronic device that discloses imperfections in the coating, called "holidays," which must be repaired.

After installation, a hydrostatic test of the tank should be performed at a pressure of 5 psig (34.5 kPa) for a period of 30 minutes, with all piping isolated so that only the tank is under pressure. (It is important to remove all traces of water prior to filling with product.)

Testing of the piping network   All piping containing product must be tested hydrostatically at a pressure of 100 psig (689.5 kPa) for a period of 30 minutes with no leakage allowed. Containment piping must be tested with air at 10 psig (68.9 kPa) for 30 minutes with no leakage permitted.

Vent and vapor recovery piping must be tested hydrostatically at a pressure of 30 psig (206.8 kPa) for 30 minutes with no leakage permitted.

Tightness testing Tightness testing is a general term used for testing and evaluating existing tanks and piping systems that contain product. Tightness testing is required periodically, following a schedule obtained from local authorities. Generally, periodic tightness testing is not required for the following:

1. Tanks and piping containing no. 5 and no. 6 fuel oil.

2. Tanks and piping with a capacity of 1100 gal (4163.5 L) or less, unless authorities have a reason to believe leakage is occurring.

3. Tanks and piping that are corrosion resistant and have an approved leak detection system.

4. Tanks and piping installed in conformance with requirements for new construction.

5. Tanks larger than 50,000 gal (189 250 L) where it is technically impossible to perform a meaningful series of tests. An alternative test or inspection approved by local authorities must then be conducted.

All tests must conform to EPA and local requirements and the technicians performing them must be trained and qualified by the test equipment manufacturer.

The tightness test must detect a leak of 0.1 gph (0.38 L/h) from the system with a detection probability of 95% and a false alarm probability of 5%. Acceptable leakage amounts are variable and depend on values established by the local jurisdictional authorities.

Many types of test are capable of achieving this precision and various manufacturers make equipment suited for making these tests. The following should be considered prior to selecting the type of test:

1. Vapor pockets.

2. Thermal expansion of product.

3. Temperature and temperature stratification.

4. Groundwater level.

5. Evaporation.

6. Tank end deflection.

7. Pressure.

System Installation Considerations

Tank installation The installation of the tank is critical to the longevity and proper functioning of the system and to the prevention of leaks over time. It is a requirement that the contractor or installer be trained and certified by the specific tank manufacturer as qualified to install any tank manufactured by that manufacturer.

FRP type UST tanks rely on the quality of the backfill for long-term support to resist distortion and resulting failure. Experience has shown that carefully compacted, washed pea gravel that is free from any organic matter and has no sharp edges is the best backfill material. FRP tanks must be installed in conformance with API 1615. If there is a remote possibility of the tank floating, such as exists in areas subject to flooding or where there may be a high water table, the tanks must be installed over a reinforced concrete ballast pad heavier than the buoyant force of the tank and anchored to that pad by means of hold-down straps. The weight of backfill over the pad, which also resists floating, should not be added but used instead as a safety factor. It is recommended that the calculated load on each hold down strap have a safety factor of 5. FRP tanks do not require corrosion protection.

Steel UST tanks are structurally stronger and do not depend as much on backfill for support. The backfill must prevent all but very minor shifting or settling of the tank over time. Tanks must be installed in conformance with NFPA Standards 30 and 31. The requirements for ballast pad and hold-down straps are the same as those for FRP tanks.

When steel tanks are used, they need to be protected against corrosion by coating or cladding. Coatings must be tested for faults (called holidays) while the tank is on the truck and after its initial placement in the excavation. All defects found must be repaired in strict conformity to the manufacturers' recommendations.

Tanks should not be stored on the site prior to installation due to the possibility of damage. Arrangements should be made to deliver the tank on the day installation is to be made.

ASTs should be placed on saddles on a level concrete pad of sufficient thickness to adequately support the tank and product. Bollards must be placed around the tank to protect it from vehicle damage.

Piping installation Pipe should be installed in a flat and level trench, far enough underground to prevent vehicular and frost damage. Initial backfill should be pea gravel, clean sand, or some other acceptable material. A generally accepted minimum depth from grade surface to the top of the pipe is 18 in. (450 mm) where there is no slab, 12 in. (300 mm) below asphalt slabs, and 6 in. (150 mm) under concrete slabs. It is also accepted practice where electrical conduit is installed in the same trench as piping to protect the conduit with a concrete encasement and to provide 4 in. (100 mm) minimum separation.

The following is a typical installation checklist:

1. Is the installation in compliance with federal and local or municipal ordinances?

2. Have specifications and drawings been submitted to regulating bodies for approval?

3. Are all permits for construction compatible with liquid to be stored?

4. Is tank material construction compatible with liquid to be stored?

5. Are there surrounding structures that might create excessive loading on the tank?

6. Are clearances from adjacent buildings, property lines, roads, sidewalks, and surroundings in accordance with NFPA and insurance underwriter requirements?

7. Have groundwater tables, flood plains, and adjacent water bodies been investigated?

8. Does the piping system, as designed, create undesirable pressure or vacuum on the tank?

9. Have the chemical and physical properties of the soil been checked?

10. Has the depth of the tank installation been established with respect to traffic conditions over the tank?

11. What is the local seismic zone, and are other earth movements possible?

12. Are there existing underground utilities or structures in the area?

13. Do the vent pipe locations pose hazards to buildings or personnel?

14. If a non-metallic tank is installed, have the ballast pad weight and size been adjusted?

15. Has the frost-line depth in the area been checked for possible tank depth adjustment?

16. As regards secondary containment, have the natural lay and slope of the land been considered?

17. Has the tank location been provided with restrictive fencing, lightning protection, maintenance lighting and power, and delivery truck access?

18. Can visual and audible alarms be observed/heard by operators?

REFERENCES

1. American Petroleum Institute. *Bottom loading and vapor recovery for MC-306 tank motor vehicles.* AOIRP 1004.

2. American Petroleum Institute. *Installation of underground gasoline tanks and piping at service stations.* API Bulletin no. 1615.

3. American Petroleum Institute. *Service station tankage guide.* API Bulletin no. 1611.

4. Frankel, M. 1996. *Facility piping systems handbook.* New York: McGraw-Hill.

5. National Fire Protection Association (NFPA). *Flammable and combustible liquids code.* NFPA Standard no. 30.

SOURCES OF ADDITIONAL INFORMATION

American Petroleum Institute
1801 K Street NW
Washington, DC 20006

Environmental Protection Agency
Office of Air and Water Programs
Room 943, Waterside Mall
Washington, DC 20460

Steam and Condensate Systems

INTRODUCTION

Steam system piping differs from other piping because it can carry three different fluids: steam, air, and water. The proportions of steam, air, and liquid expected in a given steam system pipe depend upon the type of system and the method of operation.

Some properties of saturated steam are listed in Table 8-1. Note the high value of latent heat, that is, the heat transferred as steam condenses. This makes steam an economical heat transfer medium, since relatively few pounds per hour of steam flow can carry a great deal of heat. For a given flow rate of dry, saturated steam, the pipe size required depends upon the initial pressure of the steam and the pressure drop, or velocity of flow. Charts similar to that in Figure 8-1 show how these factors relate to each other, allowing easy selection of pipe size for a given dry steam flow. The velocity of steam in heating systems is limited to prevent flow noise. Industrial, or "process," steam systems can tolerate higher velocities, and therefore can use smaller pipe sizes, because noise is not usually of great concern with these systems. Figure 8-1 is based on the assumption that condensate will not interfere with the flow of steam.

Steam pipes in some heating systems often carry a large proportion of condensate in addition to the steam. Tables for sizing these pipes, such as the ones provided, take this into account.

Special procedures may be required to size the condensate pipes in high-pressure systems since they can carry a mixture of flash steam and condensate.

SYSTEM CLASSIFICATIONS

Steam systems can be classified according to operating pressure range, piping arrangement, and the method used to return condensate to the boiler.

Classification by Operating Pressure Range

Steam systems may be classified by operating pressure as follows:

High pressure	100 psig (689 kPa) and above
Medium pressure	15 to 100 psig (103.4 to 689 kPa)
Low pressure	0 to 15 psig (0 to 103.4 kPa)
Vapor	Vacuum to 15 psig (103.4 kPa)
Vacuum	Vacuum to 15 psig (103.4 kPa)

Low-pressure steam is usually associated with space heating and other applications that do not require high-temperature heat transfer. Industrial applications that transfer heat at high temperatures must use higher-pressure steam, as is illustrated in the steam tables.

Vapor systems Vapor systems are one-pipe system designs that use the slow condensation of steam to lower pressure into the vacuum range overnight or at partial load so that the banked coal fire in large boilers can provide low-temperature steam to the system. These systems have been largely eliminated by the use of smaller

Table 8-1 Steam Table

Gauge Pressure (lb/in.²)	Temperature (°F)	Specific Volume, (ft³/lb)	Heat (Btu/lb)		
			Liquid	Latent	Total
0	212.00	26.800	180.07	970.3	1150.4
1	215.33	25.210	183.43	968.2	1151.6
2	218.50	23.800	186.61	966.2	1152.8
3	221.51	22.530	189.66	964.2	1153.9
4	224.39	21.400	192.56	962.3	1154.9
5	227.14	20.380	195.32	960.6	1155.9
6	229.80	19.460	198.01	958.9	1156.9
7	232.32	18.620	200.55	957.2	1157.8
8	234.76	17.853	203.04	955.6	1158.6
9	237.11	17.148	205.41	954.1	1159.5
10	230.39	16.496	207.72	952.6	1160.3
15	249.75	13.876	218.23	945.7	1163.9
20	258.76	11.999	227.38	939.6	1166.9
25	266.78	10.576	235.55	934.0	1169.6
30	274.02	9.438	242.95	929.0	1171.9
35	280.62	8.566	249.69	924.3	1174.0
40	286.71	7.826	257.99	918.4	1176.4
45	292.37	7.210	261.73	915.7	1177.4
50	297.66	6.685	267.18	911.9	1179.1
55	302.62	6.233	272.31	908.2	1180.5
60	307.32	5.829	277.14	904.6	1181.7
65	311.77	5.475	281.75	901.2	1183.0
70	316.00	5.185	286.13	898.0	1184.1
75	320.03	4.912	290.36	894.9	1185.3
80	323.90	4.665	294.34	891.9	1186.2
85	327.59	4.445	298.18	888.9	1187.1
90	331.15	4.244	301.88	886.1	1188.0
95	334.57	4.061	305.46	883.3	1188.8
100	337.88	3.892	308.91	880.7	1189.6
110	344.15	3.595	315.49	875.6	1191.1
120	350.04	3.339	321.67	870.7	1192.3
130	355.59	3.121	327.53	865.9	1193.4
140	360.84	2.927	333.07	861.5	1194.6
150	365.85	2.757	338.38	857.1	1195.6
160	370.62	2.607	343.44	853.0	1196.4
170	375.17	2.470	348.29	848.9	1197.2
180	379.54	2.348	352.95	845.0	1198.0
190	383.74	2.238	357.45	841.0	1198.5
200	387.78	2.137	361.78	837.5	1199.3
210	391.67	2.045	365.97	833.9	1199.9
220	395.43	1.9604	370.02	830.2	1200.2
230	398.99	1.8826	373.96	826.9	1200.9
240	402.60	1.8107	377.78	823.5	1201.3
250	406.01	1.7442	381.49	820.2	1201.7
236	409.33	1.6822	385.10	816.8	1201.9
270	412.55	1.6245	388.63	813.8	1202.4
280	415.70	1.5705	392.06	810.6	1202.7
290	418.73	1.5210	395.38	807.6	1203.0
300	421.71	1.4737	398.65	804.6	1203.2
320	427.46	1.3868	405.00	798.7	1203.7
340	432.96	1.3094	411.08	792.9	1204.0
360	438.22	1.2400	416.92	787.3	1204.2
380	443.26	1.1774	422.53	781.9	1204.4
400	448.12	1.1207	428.0	776.6	1204.6
420	452.79	1.0690	433.2	771.4	1204.6
440	457.32	1.0216	438.4	766.2	1204.6
460	461.68	0.9782	443.3	761.2	1204.5
480	465.90	0.9382	448.1	756.3	1204.4
500	469.99	0.9012	452.9	751.4	1204.3

Note: For more complete information and for superheated steam, refer to standard reference sources.

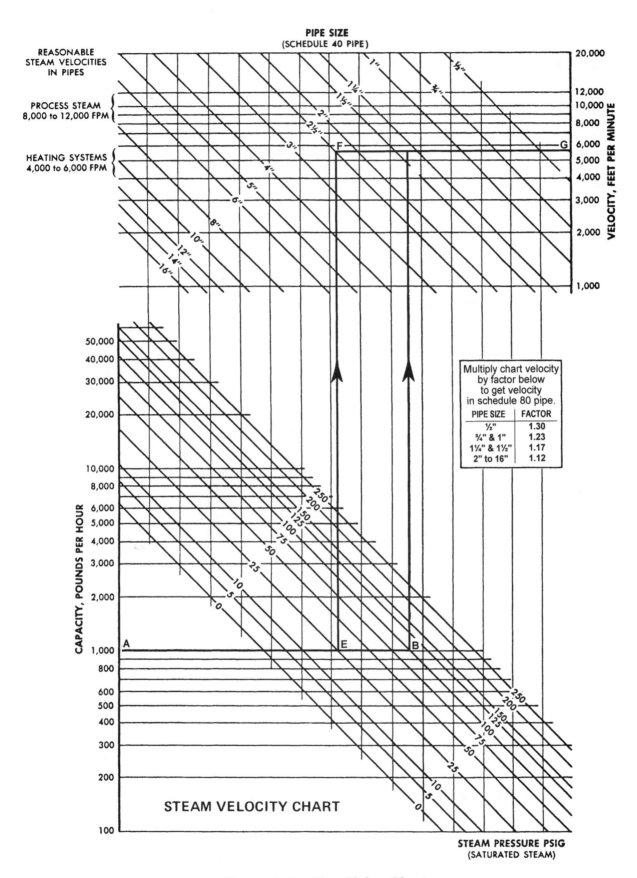

Figure 8-1 Pipe Sizing Chart

Source: Sarco *Hook-Up Manual.*

gas or oil-fired boilers, which do not allow the slow development of the system vacuum required for proper operation.

Vacuum systems Vacuum systems are two-pipe designs that use a mechanical vacuum pump to draw air out of the system, providing much more effective venting and faster and more even steam distribution. Condensate piping in a vacuum system is often undersized for a given flow rate compared to that for a nonvacuum system. The increased pressure differential caused by the vacuum pump allows the use of smaller pipes. (See the tables discussed below under "Two-Pipe Systems," for example.) This sometimes makes it difficult to convert a vacuum system to a conventional system.

Equipment rating—equivalent direct radiation
Steam heating equipment, like radiators, convectors, and unit heaters, is often rated in units of heat output called "square feet of equivalent direct radiation" (ft^2 EDR). One square foot EDR is defined as a heat output of 240 Btu/h (70.3 W) when the device is filled with steam at 215°F (102°C), (1psig) and surrounded by air at 70°F (21°C). Tables 8-2 through 8-4 show some typical EDR ratings for older equipment. The EDR rating for a given piece of steam radiation can also be obtained from the manufacturer or from Hydronics Institute Publication no. 200. Many pipe sizing tables for designing steam heating systems show pipe capacity in square feet of EDR; see Table 8-5, for example. If it is assumed that the latent heat of low-pressure steam is about 1000 Btu/lb, to convert square feet EDR to a weight flow rate:

Equation 8-1

$$EDR \times \frac{240 \text{ Btuh}}{EDR} \times \frac{1 \text{ lb}}{1000 \text{ Btu}} = \text{lb/h steam flow}$$

Since 240/1000 is approximately 0.25, the rule of thumb conversion is:

Equation 8-1a

$$\frac{EDR}{4} = \text{lb/h}$$

Classification by Piping Arrangement

One-pipe systems Residential steam heating systems sometimes use a single pipe to carry steam to the radiator and condensate back to the boiler. A "one-pipe" system similar to the one

in Figure 8-2 is full of air above the boiler water line at the beginning of the heating cycle. The boiler is filled to the recommended water line.

As boiler pressure rises, steam flows to the lower pressure in the rest of the system. Vents on each of the radiators and at the end of each steam main must remove the air in order to allow steam to fill the piping and radiators. If this venting isn't done, the system is said to be "air bound," meaning that steam flow is being blocked by unvented air. As steam flows through the piping, some of its pressure is lost due to friction. Steam enters the heating unit and condenses, transferring latent heat from the steam to the room.

The system shown in Figure 8-2 has "counterflow" steam mains, meaning that the pipe is pitched toward the boiler to return the condensate formed in the radiators. The amount of steam that can be carried in a given steam pipe depends on a number of factors, including the pitch of the pipe, as described in Table 8-5.

Counterflow piping designs have some shortcomings. They must be generously sized, since steam and water are moving opposite to one another at the same time. The cooler condensate is likely to surround small bubbles of steam, rapidly condensing the steam and causing noise that sounds like gravel rattling in the pipe. In addition to tending to produce this noise, highly pitched counterflow piping is difficult to install, and it must be large enough to: (1) allow for the increase in friction from the fluids traveling in opposite directions and (2) limit the velocity of steam flow to prevent water hammer. Tables for sizing counterflow piping take these limitations into account.

For all these reasons, steam system designers prefer to pitch the steam mains in the direction of steam flow, so that the steam and condensate will flow in the same direction, as is shown in Figure 8-3. These "parallel flow" mains are likely to be quieter and require less pitch and smaller pipe sizes for a given steam flow rate. Modern steam installations usually assume that parallel flow will be maintained to minimize interference between the steam and condensate.

All of these advantages are at least partly offset by the fact that the parallel flow system needs more pipes: "returns" must be installed at the end of the system to bring the condensate back to the boiler. A "dry return" is located above the water line of the boiler and therefore can

Table 8-2   Stock Assemblies of Small-Tube Cast-Iron Radiators

Number of Sections	RATING (ft²)							
	3-Tube	4-Tube		5-Tube		6-Tube		
	25 in.	25 in.	22 in.	25 in.	22 in.	32 in.	25 in.	19 in.
6	9.6	12.0	10.8	14.4	12.6	22.2	18.0	—
10	16.0	20.0	18.0	24.0	21.0	37.0	30.0	23.0
14	22.4	28.0	25.2	33.6	29.4	51.8	42.0	32.2
18	28.8	36.0	32.4	43.2	37.8	66.6	54.0	41.4
22	35.2	44.0	39.6	52.8	46.2	81.4	66.0	50.6
26	41.6	52.0	46.8	62.4	54.6	96.2	78.0	59.8
30	48.0	60.0	54.0	72.0	63.0	—	90.0	69.0
38	60.8	76.0	68.4	91.2	79.8	—	—	87.4

Number of Tubes per Section	Catalog Rating per Section (Ft²)	SECTION DIMENSIONS IN INCHES				
		A Height[a]	B Width		C Spacing	D Leg Height[a]
			Min.	Max.		
3	1.6	25	3¼	3½	1¾	2½
4	1.6	19	4⁷⁄₁₆	4¹³⁄₁₆	1¾	2½
4	1.8	22	4⁷⁄₁₆	4¹³⁄₁₆	1¾	2½
4	2.0	25	4⁷⁄₁₆	4¹³⁄₁₆	1¾	2½
5	2.1	22	5⅝	6⁵⁄₁₆	1¾	2½
5	2.4	25	5⅝	6⁵⁄₁₆	1¾	2½
6	2.3	19	6¹³⁄₁₆	8	1¾	2½
6	3.0	25	6¹³⁄₁₆	8	1¾	2½
6	3.7	32	6¹³⁄₁₆	8	1¾	2½

[a] Over-all height and leg height of radiator as made by some manufacturers is 1 in. greater than figures shown in Columns A and D. Radiators may be furnished without legs. Where greater than standard leg heights are required, this dimension is to be 4½ in.

NIPPLES
Sections are assembled with cast- or malleable-iron push nipples.

TAPPINGS
Tappings are standards iron-pipe size. Flow and return tappings are located horizontally opposite the top and bottom nipple ports. Air-vent tappings for water and steam radiators are provided on the end section opposite the supply section.

PIPE FITTINGS
Iron-pipe size plugs or bushings, or both, may be furnished with each radiator.

PAINTING
Each section or radiator assembled by the manufacturer is given one priming coat.

NUMBER OF SECTIONS
The stock assemblies are shown in the table. When assemblies of more sections than those listed are required, the maximum number should not exceed 56 to avoid damage in shipping and handling. Consult manufacturers' catalogs.

The square footage of equivalent direct steam radiation is defined as the ability to emit 240 Btu per hour, with steam at 215°F, in air at 70°F. These ratings apply only to radiators installed exposed in a normal manner—not to radiators installed behind enclosures, grilles, etc.

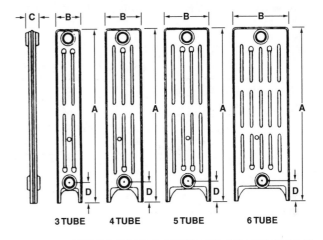

3 TUBE   4 TUBE   5 TUBE   6 TUBE

Source: U.S. Dept. of Commerce, Simplified Practice Recommendation R174-47.

carry steam and air in addition to condensate. A "wet return" is located below the boiler water line, is therefore flooded, and doesn't need to be pitched. It does require some hydrostatic head in the form of a column of water, however, to return condensate to the boiler.

Another characteristic of one-pipe systems is that, with such a system, difficulty is encountered controlling the heat output of an individual heating unit. Note that the steam supply valve must always act as both the steam supply and the condensate outlet from the unit. Partly closing the supply valve will reduce the area for steam flow, increase the steam's velocity, and "blow" the condensate back into the unit, preventing drainage. In one-pipe systems, the supply valve

must be either wide open or completely shut and part load control must be achieved through other means.

Vents Proper venting is important to prevent air binding and to allow steam to fill the system rapidly. Thermostatic vents similar to the one shown in Figure 8-4 are commonly found on each radiator and at the end of each main in one-pipe systems in order to:

- Vent air as boiler pressure rises, thus allowing the system to fill with steam,

- Prevent the loss of steam or condensate from the system, and

- Break the partial vacuum caused by condensing steam at the end of the heating cycle by having the vent reopen. This allows condensate to drain back to the boiler, thereby eliminating "water hammer" at the start of the next heating cycle.

The end-of-main vents play a particularly important role in one-pipe systems. If these vents are partly blocked, air venting will be slowed and the boiler will have to fire much longer to heat the building and satisfy the thermostat setting, resulting in higher fuel costs. Lack of vents on a steam main can also cause boiler "short cycling," wherein the air is rapidly compressed in the main, raising pressure to the point where the boiler pressure controls shut off the burner, though the thermostat has not been satisfied. Many system problems, such as uneven heating, failure to heat, noise, and water hammer, can be traced to malfunctioning or missing vents.

These vents should be installed as shown in Figure 8-5.

One-pipe steam heating systems were built to operate at very low pressures, well below the 15 psig defined as low-pressure steam. Therefore, the steam pipe must be large enough to carry the required steam load at the high specific volume for low-pressure steam shown in Table 8-1. The condensate load will be relatively heavy, since the steam piping also carries the condensate formed in the heating units, and proper air venting must occur throughout the heating cycle to prevent air binding.

Two-pipe systems Heating units in two-pipe systems, like the ones in Figures 8-6 and 8-7, have separate connections for the steam supply and the condensate return. Steam traps are installed at the condensate connection from each heating unit and at intervals along the steam

Table 8-3 Output of Direct Cast-Iron Radiators[a]

| Steam Pressure (approximate) | | Steam or Mean Water Temp. | Btu/Ft² E.D.R./ H | | | | | | |
| | | | Room Temperature (°F) | | | | | | |
Gage[b]	Absolute[c] (psi)	(°F)	80	75	70	65	60	55	50
Vacuum (in. Hg)									
22.4	3.7	150	93	102	111	120	129	139	148
20.3	4.7	160	111	120	129	139	148	158	167
17.7	6.0	170	129	139	148	158	167	178	188
14.6	7.5	180	148	158	167	178	188	198	209
10.9	9.3	190	167	178	188	198	209	218	229
6.5	11.5	200	188	198	209	218	229	240	250
3.9	12.8	205	198	209	218	229	240	250	261
Psi									
0.0	14.7	212	211	222	233	242	253	264	276
1.	15.6	215	218	229	240	250	261	273	282
2.	17.	220	229	240	250	261	273	282	296
6.	21.	230	250	261	273	282	296	308	316
10.	25.	240	273	282	296	308	316	329	343
15.	30.	250	296	308	316	329	343	353	364
27.	42.	270	343	353	364	375	387	400	414
52.	67.	300	414	421	436	453	462	471	490

Source: ITT Fluid Handling, Morton Grove, IL.

[a] These outputs also apply quite closely to the output of the "R" type cast-iron radiant baseboards. For exact outputs, the catalogs of the manufacturers of the baseboards involved should be consulted.

[b] At sea level only.

[c] At locations other than sea level, use temperature only or convert gage reading to absolute pressure. Add gage reading to atmospheric pressure in psi for given altitude. To convert vacuum (in. Hg) to absolute, multiply in. vacuum by 0.49 and deduct from atmospheric pressure (psi) for given altitude.

Table 8-4 Standard Column Radiation[a]

Single-Column Radiators

		HEATING SURFACE (FT^2)				
No. of Sections	Length 2½ in.-Sec	38 in. 3-ft^2 Sec.	32 in. 2½-ft^2 Sec.	26 in. 2-ft^2 Sec.	23 in. 1⅔-ft^2 Sec.	20 in. 1½-ft^2 Sec.
3	7½	9	7½	6	5	4½
4	10	12	10	8	6⅔	6
5	12½	15	12½	10	8⅓	7½
6	15	18	15	12	10	9
7	17½	21	17½	14	11⅔	10½
8	20	24	20	16	13⅓	12
9	22½	27	22½	18	15	13½
10	25	30	25	20	16⅔	15
11	27½	33	27½	22	18⅓	16½
12	30	36	30	24	20	18
13	32½	39	32½	26	21⅔	19½
14	35	42	35	28	23⅓	21
15	37½	45	37½	30	25	22½
16	40	48	40	32	26⅔	24
17	42½	51	42½	34	28⅓	25½
18	45	54	45	36	30	27
19	47½	57	47½	38	31⅔	28½
20	50	60	50	40	33⅓	30
21	52½	63	52½	42	35	31½
22	55	66	55	44	36⅔	33
23	57½	69	57½	46	38⅓	34½
24	60	72	60	48	40	36
25	62½	75	62½	50	41⅔	37½
26	65	78	65	52	43⅓	39
27	67½	81	67½	54	45	40½

Two-Column Radiators

		HEATING SURFACE (FT^2)					
No. of Sections	Length 2½-in-Sec	45 in. 5-ft^2 Sec.	38 in. 4-ft^2 Sec.	32 in. 3⅓-ft^2 Sec.	26 in. 2⅔-ft^2 Sec.	23 in. 2⅓-ft^2 Sec.	20 in. 2-ft^2 Sec.
3	7½	15	12	10	8	7	6
4	10	20	16	13⅓	10⅔	9⅓	8
5	12½	25	20	16⅔	13⅓	11⅔	10
6	15	30	24	20	16	14	12
7	17½	35	28	23⅓	18⅔	16⅓	14
8	20	40	32	26⅔	21⅓	18⅔	16
9	22½	45	36	30	24	21	18
10	25	50	40	33⅓	26⅔	23⅓	20
11	27½	55	44	36⅔	29⅓	25⅔	22
12	30	60	48	40	33	28	24
13	32½	65	52	43⅓	34⅔	30⅓	26
14	35	70	56	46⅔	37⅓	32⅔	28
15	37½	75	60	50	40	35	30
16	40	80	64	53⅓	42⅔	37⅓	32
17	42½	85	68	56⅔	45⅓	39⅔	34
18	45	90	72	60	48	42	36
19	47½	95	76	63⅓	50⅔	44⅓	38
20	50	100	80	66⅔	53⅓	46⅔	40
21	52½	105	84	70	56	49	42
22	55	110	88	73⅓	58⅔	51⅓	44
23	57½	115	92	76⅔	61⅓	53⅔	46
24	60	120	96	80	64	56	48
25	62½	125	100	83⅓	66⅔	58⅓	50

Three-Column Radiators

		HEATING SURFACE (FT^2)					
No. of Sections	Length 2½ in-Sec	45 in. 6-ft^2 Sec.	38 in. 5-ft^2 Sec.	32 in. 4½-ft^2 Sec.	26 in. 3¼-ft^2 Sec.	22 in. 3-ft^2 Sec.	18 in. 2¼-ft^2 Sec.
3	7½	18	15	13½	11¼	9	6¾
4	10	24	20	18	15	12	9
5	12½	30	25	22½	18¾	15	11¼
6	15	36	30	27	22½	18	13½
7	17½	42	35	31½	26¼	21	15¾
8	20	48	40	36	30	24	18
9	22½	54	45	40½	33¾	27	20¼
10	25	60	50	45	37½	30	22½
11	27½	66	55	49½	41¼	33	24¾
12	30	72	60	54	45	36	27
13	32½	78	65	58½	48¾	39	29¼
14	35	84	70	63	52½	42	31½
15	37½	90	75	67½	56¼	45	33¾
16	40	96	80	72	60	48	36
17	42½	102	85	76½	63¾	51	38¼
18	45	108	90	81	67½	54	40½
19	47½	114	95	85½	71¼	57	42¾
20	50	120	100	90	75	60	45
21	52½	126	105	94½	78¾	63	47¼
22	55	132	110	99	82½	66	49½
23	57½	138	115	103½	86¼	69	51¾
24	60	144	120	108	90	72	54
25	62½	150	125	112½	93¾	75	56¼
26	65	156	130	117	97½	78	58½
27	67½	162	135	121½	101¼	81	60¾

Four-Column Radiators

		HEATING SURFACE (FT^2)					
No. of Sections	Length 3 in.-Sec	45 in. 10-ft^2 Sec.	38 in. 8-ft^2 Sec.	32 in. 6½-ft^2 Sec.	26 in. 5-ft^2 Sec.	22 in. 4-ft^2 Sec.	18 in. 3-ft^2 Sec.
3	9	30	24	19½	15	12	9
4	12	40	32	26	20	16	12
5	15	50	40	32½	25	20	15
6	18	60	48	39	30	24	18
7	21	70	56	45½	35	28	21
8	24	80	64	52	40	32	24
9	27	90	72	58½	45	36	27
10	30	100	80	65	50	40	30
11	33	110	88	71½	55	44	33
12	36	120	96	78	60	48	36
13	39	130	104	84½	65	52	39
14	42	140	112	91	70	56	42
15	45	150	120	97½	75	60	45
16	48	160	128	104	80	64	48
17	51	170	136	110½	85	68	51
18	54	180	144	117	90	72	54
19	57	190	152	123½	95	76	57
20	60	200	160	130	100	80	60
21	63	210	168	136½	105	84	63
22	66	220	176	143	110	88	66
23	69	230	184	149½	115	92	69
24	72	240	192	156	120	96	72
25	75	250	200	162½	125	100	75

Source: ITT Fluid Handling, Morton Grove, IL.

[a] This table covers column radiation manufactured prior to 1926.

Table 8-5   Comparative Capacity of Steam Lines at Various Pitches for Steam and Condensate Flowing in Opposite Directions[a]

Pitch of Pipe	Pitch of Pipe in in. /10 ft./Velocity in ft/ s/Capacity in ft² EDR															
	¼ in.		½ in.		1 in.		1½ in.		2 in.		3 in.		4 in.		5 in.	
Pipe Size (in.)	Capacity	Max. Vel.	Capacity	Max. Vel.	Capacity	Max. Vel.	Capacity	Max. Vel.	Capacity	Max. Vel.	Capacity	Max Vel.	Capacity	Max. Vel.	Capacity	Max. Vel.
¾	12.8	8	16.4	11	22.8	13	25.6	14	28.4	16	33.2	17	38.6	22	42.0	22
1	27.2	9	36.0	12	46.8	15	51.2	17	59.2	19	69.2	22	76.8	24	82.0	25
1¼	47.2	11	63.6	14	79.6	17	98.4	20	108.0	22	125.2	25	133.6	26	152.4	31
1½	79.2	12	103.6	16	132.0	19	149.6	22	168.0	24	187.2	26	203.2	28	236.8	33
2	171.6	15	216.0	18	275.2	24	333.2	27	371.6	30	398.4	32	409.6	32	460.0	33

Source: ITT Fluid Handling, Morton Grove, IL.

[a] From research sponsored by ASHRAE.

main to eliminate any interference between the steam and liquid flow. This trap is the boundary between the steam and the condensate piping. Figures 8-6 and 8-7 also illustrate some common terminology used in pipe sizing tables. "Mains" are horizontal supply pipes. They must be pitched in order to ensure condensate drainage and parallel flow toward the trap. "Risers" are vertical pipes, and "runouts" are the short connections between the main and the heating unit.

Traps All steam traps must be able to:

- Vent air and other gases from the mains and heating units,

- Prevent the flow of steam into the condensate piping, and

- Allow condensate to drain into the condensate piping.

Many steam trap designs have been developed, but each of them falls into one of the following categories:

- *Thermostatic* The trap opens and closes by sensing the difference in temperature between steam and the condensate, which has been allowed to subcool to below steam temperature. Some examples of this type of trap include thermostatic bellows, solid expansion, and bimetallic traps. Figure 8-8 shows a typical solid expansion trap.

- *Mechanical* The trap operates by means of a float, which senses the density difference between steam and condensate. Examples of this type of trap include float and thermo-

static (F & T) or inverted bucket traps. Figure 8-9 shows a typical inverted bucket trap.

- *Thermodynamic* The trap senses differences in flow velocity or pressure caused by relatively high-velocity steam compared to lower-velocity condensate. Examples include thermodisc and impulse traps. A typical thermodisc trap is shown in Figure 8-10.

Each trap design gives the trap its own set of characteristics. Because there is such a variety of trap designs, one of the key decisions in condensate drainage design is the choice of the right type of trap. Often, this choice is easy, for example, low-pressure heating system radiators are almost always equipped with thermostatic traps because the characteristics of that type of trap match the condensate drainage and air venting requirements of low-pressure heating equipment. Sometimes, either of two different types of trap could be applied equally well to a given condensate drainage situation because either set of trap characteristics meets the drainage and venting requirements. There are some advantages and disadvantages to both, but either one could do the job. For example, a high-pressure steam main could be equipped with either a thermodynamic or an inverted bucket trap. The choice between them then becomes a nontechnical matter, for example, one of cost or personal preference. In some cases, a given kind of trap simply would not be able to do the job, for example, a thermodynamic trap requires a significant pressure drop between the steam condensing device and the condensate pipe. Such a trap installed in a low-pressure heating system would not have a great enough pressure differential to operate.

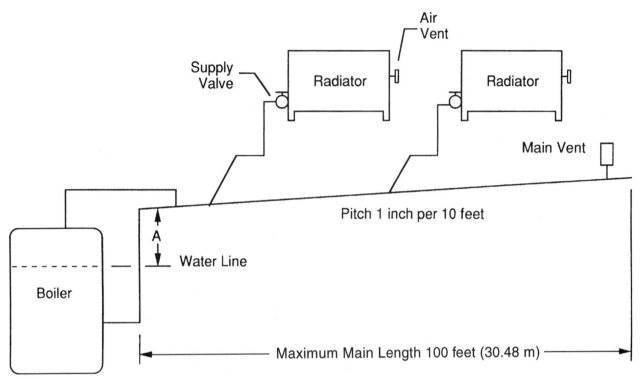

Figure 8-2   One-Pipe Counterflow System

Source: ITT Fluid Handling, Morton Grove, IL.

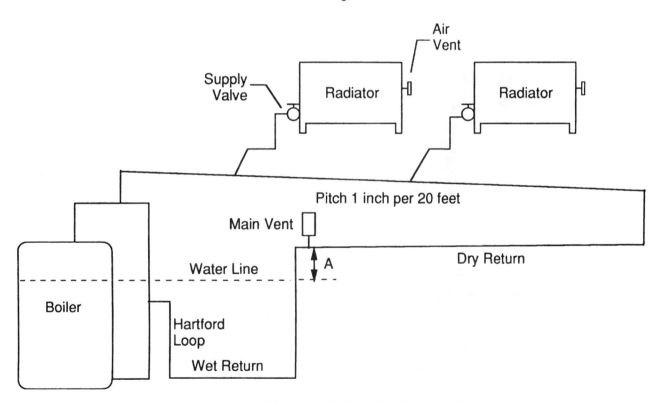

Figure 8-3   One-Pipe Parallel Flow System Dry Returns

Source: ITT Fluid Handling, Morton Grove, IL.

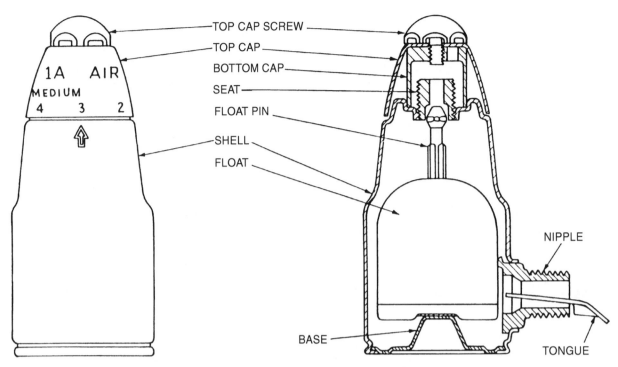

Figure 8-4   Radiator Vent Valve

Source: ITT Hoffman Steam Specialty.

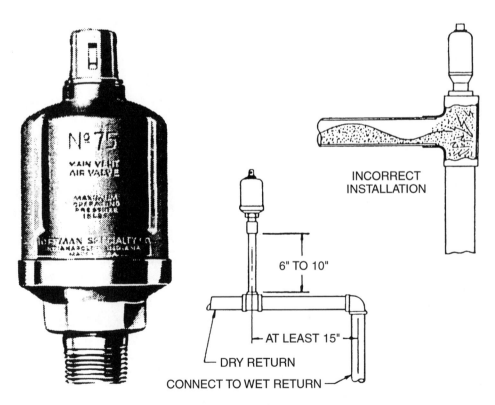

Figure 8-5   End of Main Vent

Source: ITT Fluid Handling, Morton Grove, IL.

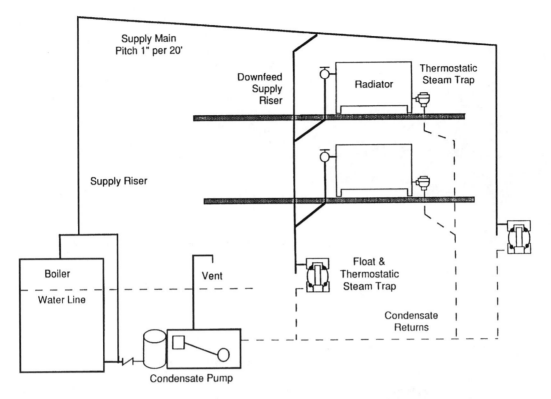

Figure 8-6   Two-Pipe System Downfeed Risers

Source: ITT Fluid Handling, Morton Grove, IL.

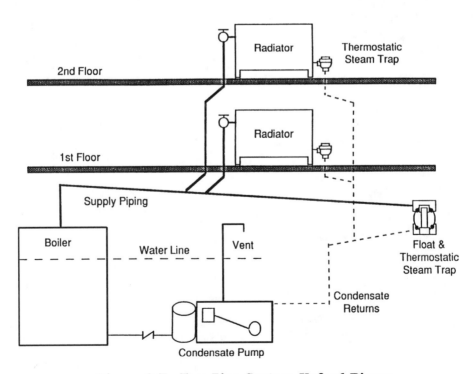

Figure 8-7   Two-Pipe System Upfeed Risers

Source: ITT Fluid Handling, Morton Grove, IL.

Figure 8-8   Thermostatic Steam Trap

Source: ITT Hoffman Steam Specialty.

Figure 8-9   Inverted Bucket Trap

Source: ITT Hoffman Steam Specialty.

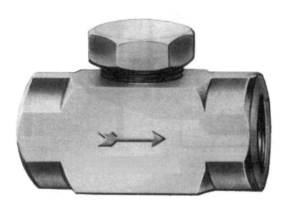

Figure 8-10   Thermodisc Trap

Source: ITT Hoffman Steam Specialty.

The two-pipe steam heating system requires more piping than does the one-pipe system, but it offers quieter operation, since the steam and condensate do not have as much opportunity to mix as they do in the one-pipe system, and better control over heat output, since the supply of steam can be throttled by the use of pressure or temperature regulators without interfering with condensate drainage. Use Tables 8-6 through 8-8 to design these systems.

Classification by Method of Condensate Return

Gravity return   Smaller heating systems use gravity acting on a vertical column of condensate to return water to the boiler. The "A" dimension shown in Figure 8-11 must be large enough to accommodate three factors:

Table 8-6   Steam Pipe Capacities for Low-Pressure Systems[a]

	CAPACITY (FT² EDR)				
	Two-Pipe Systems		One-Pipe Systems		
Nominal	Condensate Flowing Against Steam		Supply Risers Up-Feed	Radiator Valves & Vertical Connections	Radiator and Riser Horizontal Runouts
	Vertical	Horizontal			
A	B[b]	C[c]	D[d]	E	F[c]
¾	32	28	24	—	28
1	56	56	44	28	28
1¼	124	108	80	64	64
1½	192	168	152	92	64
2	388	362	288	168	92
2½	636	528	464	—	168
3	1,128	800	800	—	260
3½	1,548	1,152	1144	—	476
4	2,044	1,700	1520	—	744
5	4,200	3,152	—	—	1112
6	7,200	5,600	—	—	2180
8	15,000	12,000	—	—	—
10	28,000	22,800	—	—	—
12	46,000	38,000	—	—	—

Source: ITT Fluid Handling, Morton Grove, IL.

[a] For use on one-pipe or two-pipe systems in which condensate flows against the steam flow.

[b] Do not use Column B for pressure drops of less than 1 oz/100 ft of equivalent length of run.

[c] Pitch of horizontal runouts to risers and radiators should not be less than ½ in./ft. Where this pitch cannot be obtained, for runouts 8 ft in length or over, increase one pipe size larger than shown in this table.

[d] Do not use Column D for pressure drops less than ⅔ oz/100 ft of equivalent length of run except for pipe size 3 in. and over.

Table 8-7 Return Main and Riser Capacities for Low-Pressure Systems (Ft² EDR)

	Pipe Size (in.)	1/32 psi or 1/2 oz Drop per 100 ft			1/24 psi or 2/3 oz Drop per 100 ft			1/16 psi or 1 oz Drop per 100 ft			1/8 psi or 2 oz Drop per 100 ft			1/4 psi or 4 oz Drop per 100 ft			1/2 psi or 8 oz Drop per 100 ft		
		Wet	Dry	Vac.	Wet	Dry	Vac.	Wet	Dry	Vac.	Wet	Dry	Vac.	Wet	Dry	Vac.	Wet	Dry	Vac.
	G	H	I	J	K	L	M	N	O	P	Q	R	S	T	U	V	W	X	Y
MAINS	¾	—	—	—	—	—	168	—	—	400	—	—	568	—	—	800	—	—	1,132
	1	500	248	—	580	284	572	700	320	700	1,000	412	996	1,400	460	1,400	—	—	1,976
	1¼	852	520	—	992	596	976	1,200	672	1,200	1,700	868	1,707	2,400	964	2,400	—	—	3,392
	1½	1,352	824	—	1,572	944	1,552	1,900	1,060	1,900	2,700	1,360	2,696	3,800	1,512	3,800	—	—	5,260
	2	2,800	1,880	—	3,240	2,140	3,260	4,000	2,300	4,000	5,600	2,960	5,680	8,000	3,300	8,000	—	—	11,320
	2½	4,720	3,040	—	6,320	3,472	5,440	6,720	3,800	6,720	9,400	4,920	9,520	13,400	5,440	13,400	—	—	18,920
	3	7,520	5,840	—	8,520	6,240	8,720	10,720	7,000	10,720	15,000	9,000	15,200	21,400	10,000	21,400	—	—	30,240
	3½	11,000	7,880	—	13,200	8,800	13,000	16,000	10,000	16,000	22,000	12,920	22,720	32,000	14,320	32,000	—	—	45,200
	4	15,520	11,720	—	18,320	13,400	18,000	22,000	15,000	22,000	31,000	19,320	31,240	44,000	21,520	44,000	—	—	62,000
	5	—	—	—	—	—	31,520	—	—	38,720	—	—	54,800	—	—	77,600	—	—	109,200
	6	—	—	—	—	—	50,400	—	—	62,000	—	—	88,000	—	—	124,000	—	—	175,200
RISERS	¾	—	192	—	—	192	572	—	192	700	—	192	996	—	192	1,400	—	—	1,976
	1	—	452	—	—	452	976	—	452	1,200	—	452	1,704	—	452	2,400	—	—	3,392
	1¼	—	992	—	—	992	1,552	—	992	1,900	—	992	2,696	—	992	3,800	—	—	5,360
	1½	—	1,500	—	—	1,500	3,260	—	1,500	4,000	—	1,500	5,680	—	1,500	8,000	—	—	11,320
	2	—	3,000	—	—	3,000	5,440	—	3,000	6,720	—	3,000	9,520	—	3,000	13,400	—	—	18,920
	2½	—	—	—	—	—	8,720	—	—	10,720	—	—	15,200	—	—	21,400	—	—	30,240
	3	—	—	—	—	—	13,000	—	—	16,000	—	—	22,720	—	—	32,000	—	—	45,200
	3½	—	—	—	—	—	17,920	—	—	22,000	—	—	31,240	—	—	44,000	—	—	62,000
	4	—	—	—	—	—	31,520	—	—	38,720	—	—	54,800	—	—	77,600	—	—	109,200
	5	—	—	—	—	—	50,400	—	—	62,000	—	—	88,000	—	—	124,000	—	—	175,200

Source: ITT Fluid Handling, Morton Grove, IL.

- The rise in the column of water at the end of the system due to steam pressure differences between the boiler and the end of the main, the steam pressure drop due to friction,

- The additional head required to overcome friction losses in the return piping, and

- A safety factor to contain the "warm-up load," the additional heavy condensate load that forms whenever steam is introduced into a cool pipe. Warm-up load is determined by the mass of metal in the piping system and the total rise from ambient room temperature to the final steam temperature. Unless this heavy warm-up load can be contained in the A dimension, it will flood the steam piping or radiators, causing noise and uneven heating.

Most larger systems now use pumps to provide the head necessary to return water to the boiler, but gravity drainage principles continue to be important in removing condensate from the condensing unit.

Mechanical return As steam systems grew larger, it became increasingly difficult to get enough vertical distance between the water line of the boiler and the farthest steam carrying pipe, the "A

Table 8-8 Friction Allowance for Fittings for Steam (Ft of Pipe)[a]

Size of Pipe (in.)	LENGTH TO BE ADDED IN RUN (FT)				
	Standard Elbow	Side Outlet Tee	Gate Valve	Globe Valve	Angle Valve
½	1.3	3	0.3	14	7
¾	1.8	4	0.4	18	10
1	2.2	5	0.5	23	12
1¼	3.0	6	0.6	29	15
1½	3.5	7	0.8	34	18
2	4.3	8	1.0	46	22
2½	5.0	11	1.1	54	27
3	6.5	13	1.4	66	34
3½	8	15	1.6	80	40
4	9	18	1.9	92	45
5	11	22	2.2	112	56
6	13	27	2.8	136	67
8	17	35	3.7	180	92
10	21	45	4.6	230	112

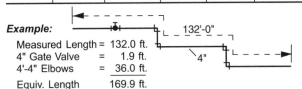

Example:
Measured Length = 132.0 ft.
4" Gate Valve   =   1.9 ft.
4-4" Elbows   = 36.0 ft.
Equiv. Length   169.9 ft.

Source: ITT Fluid Handling, Morton Grove, IL.

[a] To be added to actual length of run.

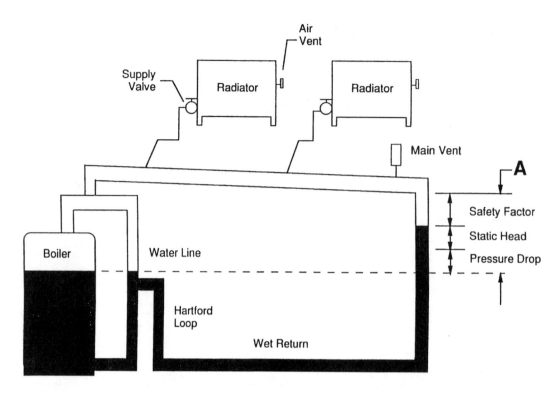

Figure 8-11   Gravity Return in a One-Pipe System

Source: ITT Fluid Handling, Morton Grove, IL

dimension." Eventually, pump head was introduced to return condensate to the boiler. The condensate transfer unit is shown in Figure 8-12.

Condensate transfer pumps   A typical condensate transfer pump consists of a vented receiver, a motor-driven centrifugal pump, and a float switch mounted in the receiver to turn the pump on and off depending on the level of condensate in the receiver. A typical low-temperature rated condensate transfer unit is shown in Figure 8-12. Instead of a single pump, this one has two pumps, their operation controlled by a mechanical alternator to alternate pump operation on each cycle. In higher-pressure steam systems, special pumping equipment might be used to handle higher-temperature condensate without cavitation or other damage. Pressure-powered pumps that use compressed air or steam to pump the condensate are also available.

In a two-pipe system the traps vent air and other noncondensable gases into the condensate piping. This piping must be able to carry the air to the receiver vent for it actually to be removed from the system.

Boiler feed pumps   Larger heating systems as well as commercial or industrial steam systems are likely to have boiler feed equipment in addition to condensate transfer units. Although the two units may look very much the same, they play different roles in the system. A condensate transfer unit has the job of collecting condensate and pumping it back to the boiler room as quickly as feasible, before it can cool off. Higher condensate temperatures relate directly to higher system efficiency, since the sensible heat of the condensate represents a reduction in the amount of fuel required. A boiler feed unit has the job of maintaining boiler water level within acceptable limits. A boiler feed unit differs from a condensate transfer unit in three major respects:

• The boiler feed pump is controlled by a level sensing control mounted on the boiler rather than a float switch mounted in the pump receiver.

• The boiler feed receiver must be large enough to act as a reservoir of feedwater that is immediately available in order to maintain the desired level in the boiler. The condensate unit receiver is relatively small to minimize heat loss as the receiver fills between pumping cycles.

- The boiler feed receiver is always equipped with some kind of device to make up for losses of water from the system. The condensate transfer unit receiver is never equipped with a makeup water supply.

Vacuum pumps Several types of vacuum pump have been developed for use in low-pressure steam heating systems. One of these is shown in Figure 8-13. It has a standard centrifugal pump that both draws a vacuum on the system and acts as a condensate transfer pump. Other kinds of vacuum equipment may use separate pumps for air and water removal. These are particularly useful in systems that have unusually large amounts of air to remove.

CONDENSATE DRAINAGE

Problems Resulting from Poor Condensate Drainage

- A loss of heat transfer performance will result unless condensate is drained from the steam heating unit. Since heat transfer in a

steam system is based upon the large amount of latent heat that becomes available as the steam condenses, it follows that, if the heating unit is flooded, only the sensible heat from the condensate will become available as it cools. Table 8-1 shows that the sensible heat is only a small fraction of the latent heat available in a pound of steam at any given pressure. The latent heat is transferred at constant steam temperature as the steam condenses, while the condensate would have to cool down to 32°F (0°C) in order for all the sensible heat to be available.

- Water hammer in an undrained or improperly drained steam main can be caused by the impact of a rapidly moving slug of water, as is shown in Figure 8-14. Unless the condensate is removed from low points in the steam mains, it gradually accumulates until the high-velocity steam forms ripples. As condensate builds up, it decreases the area available for steam flow, leading to even higher steam velocities. The slug of water accelerated by the steam can reach velocities in excess of 100 miles per hour (mi/h) before it hits some obstruction, such as an elbow or other fitting. The rapid change in speed can cause a loud noise or even severe damage to the system.

Figure 8-12   Condensate Transfer Unit

Source: ITT Domestic Pump, Morton Grove, IL.

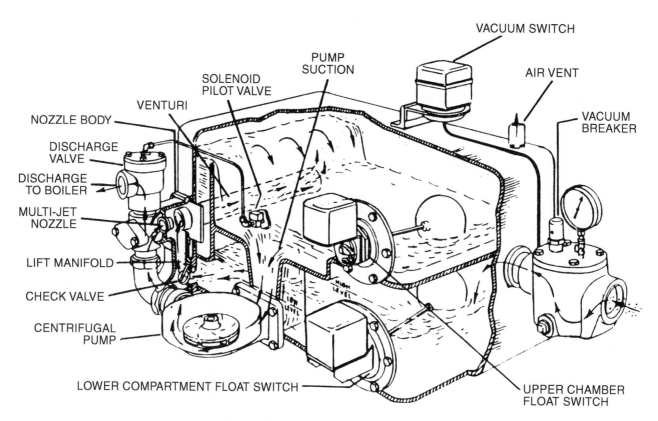

Figure 8-13   Vacuum Heating Unit

Source: ITT Domestic Pump, Morton Grove, IL.

- Corrosion occurs in units that are not properly drained. Several corrosion processes have been defined, including:

  A. Generalized corrosion, which removes metal more or less uniformly from the surface,

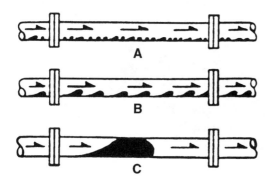

Figure 8-14   Water Hammer — Caused by Progressive Buildup of Condensate

  B. Oxygen pitting, which concentrates on small areas, rapidly creating holes, and

  C. Condensate grooving, which etches away the metal along the path followed by condensate, which has become acidic due to dissolved carbon dioxide.

Corrosion is accelerated by the presence of carbon dioxide, which can form in the boiler as chemical components like carbonates and bicarbonates decompose. Oxygen introduced by vacuum breakers or from makeup feedwater also increases the corrosion rate.

- Fouling or scaling on heat transfer surfaces is also increased by inadequate condensate drainage and venting.

Properly installed steam traps can minimize these problems by draining the condensate and venting noncondensable gases from steam piping and heat exchangers.

Proper Condensate Drainage from System Piping

Properly drained mains and care taken in starting up a cold system not only prevent water hammer damage but also improve the quality of the steam and reduce the maintenance required on pressure reducing valves, temperature controls, and other components. The heaviest condensate load in a steam main occurs during the warm-up period. Table 8-9 shows the amount of steam used to warm up a given length of variously sized mains. Once the steam main has been raised to the operating pressure, further condensation is the result of heat loss through the insulation and the separation of moisture from wet steam as described in Table 8-10.

A liberal steam trap load safety factor and oversized steam traps do not always provide an efficient and safe, steam main drain installation. The following points should also be considered by the designer:

• Method of heat up to be employed,

• Providing suitable reservoirs, or "collecting legs," for the condensate,

• Ensuring adequate pressure differential across the steam trap,

• Selecting and sizing the steam trap, and

• Proper trap installation.

Heat-up method The type and size of the steam trap used to drain steam mains depend on the method used to bring the system up to normal operating pressure and temperature. The two methods of system heat up commonly used are the supervised and the automatic heat up.

In the supervised heat-up method, manual drain valves are installed at all drainage points in the steam main system. The valves are fully opened to the condensate return or to drain before steam is admitted to the system. After most of the heat-up condensate has been discharged, the drain valves are closed, allowing the steam traps to drain the normal operating load. Therefore, the steam traps are sized to handle only the condensate formed due to radiation losses at the system's operating pressure. This heat-up method is generally used for large installations having steam mains of appreciable size and length and where the heat up generally occurs only once a year, such as in large systems where the system pressure is maintained

at a constant level after the start-up and is not shut down except in emergencies.

In the automatic heat-up method, the steam boiler brings the system up to full steam pressure and temperature without supervision or manual drainage. This method relies on the traps to drain the warm-up load of condensate automatically as soon as it forms. This heat-up method is generally used in small installations, which are shut down and started up at regular intervals, as occurs in heating systems or dry cleaning plants where the boiler is usually shut down at night and started up again the following morning.

Collection legs A reservoir, or "collecting leg," must be provided if the steam trap is to be effective, since a steam trap can discharge only the condensate that is brought into it. Collecting legs should be provided at all low points in the system and wherever the condensate can collect, such as at the ends of the mains; at the bottoms of risers; and ahead of expansion joints, separators, pressure-reducing valves and temperature regulators.

For long horizontal runs of steam mains and where there are no low drainage points, the collecting legs should be provided at intervals of 500 ft (152.4 m) for supervised heat up and 200 ft (61 m) for automatic heat up.

The diameter of the collecting leg should be the same as that of the steam main if possible, but not more than one pipe size smaller than the steam main. The collecting legs for systems using the automatic heat-up method should have a pipe diameter equal to that of the main. The collecting legs for supervised heat-up systems need not be as long as those for automatic heat-up systems, since the warm-up condensate is eliminated by manually operated drain valves. For either system, the length of a leg should be about 1.5 times the leg diameter and not less than 8 in. (203.2 mm).

Adequate pressure differential across the trap The trap cannot discharge condensate unless a pressure differential exists across it, that is, unless there is a higher pressure at the inlet than there is in the condensate line. The collecting leg should be of sufficient length to provide a hydrostatic head at the trap inlet so that the condensate can be discharged during warm-up, before a positive steam pressure develops in the steam main. For mechanical traps, not only the

Table 8-9   Warm-Up Load
(lb of steam/100 ft of steam main, ambient temperature 70°F)[a]

Steam Pressure (psig)	Main Size (in.)														32°F Correction Factor[b]
	2	2½	3	4	5	6	8	10	12	14	16	18	20	24	
0	6.2	9.7	12.8	18.2	24.6	31.9	48	68	90	107	140	176	207	208	1.50
5	6.9	11.0	14.4	20.4	27.7	35.9	48	77	101	120	157	198	233	324	1.44
10	7.5	11.8	15.5	22.0	29.9	38.8	58	83	109	130	169	213	251	350	1.41
20	8.4	13.4	17.5	24.9	33.8	43.9	66	93	124	146	191	241	284	396	1.37
40	9.9	15.8	20.6	29.3	39.7	51.6	78	110	145	174	225	284	334	465	1.32
60	11.0	17.5	22.9	32.6	44.2	57.3	86	122	162	192	250	316	372	518	1.29
80	12.0	19.0	24.9	35.3	47.9	62.1	93	132	175	208	271	342	403	561	1.27
100	12.8	20.3	26.6	37.8	51.2	66.5	100	142	188	222	290	366	431	600	1.26
125	13.7	21.7	28.4	40.4	54.8	71.1	107	152	200	238	310	391	461	642	1.25
150	14.5	23.0	30.0	42.8	58.0	75.2	113	160	212	251	328	414	487	679	1.24
175	15.3	24.2	31.7	45.1	61.2	79.4	119	169	224	265	347	437	514	716	1.23
200	16.0	25.3	33.1	47.1	63.8	82.8	125	177	234	277	362	456	537	748	1.22
250	17.2	27.3	35.8	50.8	68.9	89.4	134	191	252	299	390	492	579	807	1.21
300	25.0	38.3	51.3	74.8	104.0	142.7	217	322	443	531	682	854	1045	1182	1.20
400	27.8	42.6	57.1	83.2	115.7	158.7	241	358	492	590	759	971	1163	1650	1.18
500	30.2	46.3	62.1	90.5	125.7	172.6	262	389	535	642	825	1033	1263	1793	1.17
600	32.7	50.1	67.1	97.9	136.0	186.6	284	421	579	694	893	1118	1367	1939	1.16

[a] Loads based on Schedule 40 pipe for pressures up to and including 250 psig and on Schedule 80 pipe for pressures above 250 psig.
[b] For outdoor temperaturee of 32°F, multiply load value in table for each main size by correction factor corresponding to steam pressure.

Table 8-9(M)   Warm-Up Load
(kg of steam/100 m of steam main, ambient temperature 21.1°C)[a]

Steam Pressure (kPa)	Main Size (in.)														0°C Correction Factor[b]
	2	2½	3	4	5	6	8	10	12	14	16	18	20	24	
0	9.2	14.5	19.1	27.1	36.6	47.5	71.5	101.3	134.1	159.4	208.5	262.2	308.3	309.8	1.50
34.5	10.3	16.4	21.5	30.4	41.3	53.4	71.5	114.7	150.4	178.7	233.9	294.9	347.1	482.6	1.44
69.0	11.2	17.6	23.1	32.8	44.5	57.8	86.4	123.6	162.4	193.6	251.7	317.3	373.9	521.3	1.41
137.9	12.5	20.0	26.1	37.1	50.4	65.4	98.3	138.5	184.7	217.5	284.5	359.0	423.0	589.8	1.37
275.8	14.8	23.5	30.7	43.6	59.1	76.9	116.2	163.9	216.0	256.2	335.1	423.0	497.5	692.6	1.32
413.7	16.4	26.1	34.1	48.6	65.8	85.4	128.1	181.7	241.3	286.0	372.4	470.7	554.1	771.6	1.29
551.6	17.9	28.3	37.1	52.6	71.4	92.5	138.5	196.6	260.7	309.8	403.7	509.4	600.3	835.6	1.27
689.5	19.1	30.2	39.6	56.3	76.3	99.1	149.0	211.5	280.0	330.7	432.0	545.2	642.0	893.7	1.26
861.9	20.4	32.3	42.3	60.2	81.6	105.9	159.4	226.4	297.9	354.5	461.8	582.4	686.7	956.3	1.25
1034.2	21.6	34.3	44.7	63.8	86.4	112.0	168.3	238.3	315.8	373.9	488.6	616.7	725.4	1011.4	1.24
1206.6	22.8	36.1	47.2	67.2	91.2	118.3	177.3	251.7	333.7	394.7	516.9	650.9	765.6	1066.5	1.23
1379.0	23.8	37.7	49.3	70.2	95.0	123.3	186.2	263.6	348.5	412.6	539.2	679.2	799.9	1114.2	1.22
1727.7	25.6	40.7	53.3	75.7	102.6	133.2	199.6	284.5	375.4	445.4	580.9	732.8	862.4	1202.0	1.21
2068.4	37.2	57.1	76.4	111.4	154.9	212.6	323.2	479.6	660.0	790.9	1015.8	1272.0	1556.5	1760.6	1.20
2757.9	41.4	63.5	85.1	123.9	172.3	236.4	359.0	533.2	734.3	878.8	1130.5	1446.3	1732.3	2457.7	1.18
3447.4	45.0	69.0	92.5	134.8	187.2	257.1	390.3	579.4	796.9	956.3	1228.9	1538.7	1881.2	2670.7	1.17
4136.9	48.7	74.6	100.0	145.8	202.6	277.9	423.0	627.1	862.4	1033.7	1330.1	1665.3	2036.2	2888.1	1.16

[a] Loads based on Schedule 40 pipe for pressures up to and including 1723.7 kPa and on Schedule 80 pipe for pressures above 1723.7 kPa.
[b] For outdoor temperature of 0°C, multiply load value in table for each main size by correction factor corresponding to steam pressure.

minimum differential but also the maximum allowable differential, the trap "seat pressure rating," must be considered. In draining devices, like heat exchangers, that are controlled by temperature-regulating valves that could possibly operate in a vacuum at part load, install a vacuum breaker to ensure that pressure upstream of the trap cannot fall below atmospheric pressure and ensure that adequate hydrostatic head is available.

Selecting and sizing the trap In general, traps should be selected by:

- Determining the condensate load and the differential pressure available to force it through the trap.

- Selecting the trap type on the basis of the system's most important drainage and venting requirements.

Table 8-10 Condensation Load (lb/h/100 ft of insulated steam main, ambient temperature 70°F, insulation 80% efficient)[a]

Steam Pressure (psig)	Main Size (in.)														32°F Correction Factor[b]
	2	2½	3	4	5	6	8	10	12	14	16	18	20	24	
10	6	7	9	11	13	16	20	24	29	32	36	39	44	53	1.58
30	8	9	11	14	17	20	26	32	38	42	48	51	57	68	1.50
60	10	12	14	18	24	27	33	41	49	54	62	67	74	89	1.45
100	12	15	18	22	28	33	41	51	61	67	77	83	93	111	1.41
125	13	16	20	24	30	36	45	56	66	73	84	90	101	121	1.39
175	16	19	23	26	33	38	53	66	78	86	98	107	119	142	1.38
250	18	22	27	34	42	50	62	77	92	101	116	126	140	168	1.36
300	20	25	30	37	46	54	68	85	101	111	126	138	154	184	1.35
400	23	28	34	43	53	63	80	99	118	130	148	162	180	216	1.33
500	27	33	39	49	61	73	91	114	135	148	170	185	206	246	1.32
600	30	37	44	55	68	82	103	128	152	167	191	208	232	277	1.31

a Chart loads represent losses due to radiation and convection for saturated steam.

b For outdoor temperature of 32°F, multiply load value in table for each main size by correction factor corresponding to steam pressure.

Table 8-10(M) Condensation Load (kg/h/100 m of insulated steam main, ambient temperature 21.1°C, insulation 80% efficient)[a]

Steam Pressure (kPa)	Main Size (in.)														0°C Correction Factor[b]
	2	2½	3	4	5	6	8	10	12	14	16	18	20	24	
69.0	8.9	10.4	13.4	16.4	19.4	23.8	29.8	35.8	43.2	47.7	53.6	58.1	65.5	78.9	1.58
206.8	11.9	13.4	16.4	20.9	25.3	29.8	38.7	47.7	56.6	62.6	71.5	76.0	84.9	101.3	1.50
413.7	14.9	17.9	20.9	26.8	35.8	40.2	49.2	61.1	73.0	80.4	92.4	99.8	110.2	132.6	1.45
689.5	17.9	22.3	26.8	32.8	41.7	49.2	61.1	76.0	90.9`	99.8	114.7	123.6	138.5	165.3	1.41
861.9	19.4	23.8	29.8	35.5	44.7	53.6	67.0	83.4	98.3	108.7	125.1	134.1	150.4	180.2	1.39
1206.6	23.8	28.3	34.3	38.7	49.2	56.6	78.9	98.3	116.2	128.1	146.0	159.4	177.3	211.5	1.38
1723.7	26.8	32.8	40.2	50.6	62.6	74.5	92.3	114.7	137.0	150.4	172.8	187.7	208.5	250.2	1.36
2068.4	29.8	37.2	44.7	55.1	68.5	80.4	101.3	126.6	150.4	165.3	187.7	205.6	229.4	274.1	1.35
2757.9	34.3	41.7	50.6	64.1	78.9	93.8	119.2	147.5	175.8	193.6	220.5	241.3	268.1	321.7	1.33
3447.4	40.2	49.2	58.1	73.0	90.9	108.7	135.6	169.8	201.1	220.5	253.2	275.6	306.8	366.4	1.32
4136.9	44.7	55.1	65.5	81.9	101.3	122.1	153.4	190.7	226.4	248.8	284.5	309.8	345.6	412.6	1.31

a Chart loads represent losses due to radiation and convection for saturated steam.

b For outdoor temperature of 0°C, multiply load value in table for each main size by correction factor corresponding to steam pressure.

- Applying a safety factor to the condensate load to provide enough discharge capacity to cover variations in flow, pressure, or other possible operating conditions. Table 8-11 shows typical safety factors for different trap types.

- Choosing the trap size from the manufacturer's capacity tables or computer software. Never size a trap on pipe size alone.

Table 8-11 Recommended Safety Factors for Steam Trap Condensate Loads

Type of Trap	Safety Factor
Thermostatic	2 to 4
Float & thermostatic	1.5 to 2.5
Inverted bucket	2 to 4
Thermodynamic	1.0 to 1.2

Source: ITT Fluid Handling, Morton Grove, IL.

Note: The safety factor to be applied depends upon the accuracy of the estimates of condensate load and differential pressure as well as on the possibility of any unusual conditions.

Example 8-1 Determine the trap requirements for 1000 ft (304.8 m) of 10 in. (254 mm) horizontal main with a maximum operating pressure of 250 psig (1723.7 kPa). Assume the supervised heat-up method will be used.

Step 1

Using Table 8-10 find the condensate load due to heat loss for a 10 in. (254 mm) pipe at 250 psig (1723.7 kPa) to be 77 lb/h per 100 ft (114.7 kg/h/100 m) of pipe length.

Step 2

For 1000 ft (304.8 m), the condensate load is:

$$\frac{77 \times 1000}{100} = 770 \text{ lb/h}$$

$$\left(\frac{114.7 \cdot 304.8}{100} = 349.6 \text{ kg/h} \right)$$

Step 3

To drain 1000 ft (304.8 m) of horizontal main, a minimum of 2 traps should be used at approximately 500 ft (152.4 m) intervals. The capacity required for each trap at 250 psig (1723.7 kPa) steam pressure is:

$$\frac{770}{2} = 385 \text{ lb/h}$$

$$\left(\frac{349.6}{2} = 174.8 \text{ kg/h} \right)$$

Step 4

The type and size of the trap might be:

A. Thermodynamic.

B. The safety factor recommended from Table 8-11 is 1.2.

C. Selection: A thermodynamic trap with a capacity of 385 × 1.2 = 450 lb/h at 250 psig (204.3 kg/h at 1723.7 kPa).

Step 5

The size of the collecting leg would be:

A. Diameter 10 in. (254 mm)

B. Length: 1.5 × 10 = 15 in. (381 mm)

See Figure 8-15 for installation details.

The same general procedure should be followed to determine the size of the trap and the collecting leg for a system using the automatic heat-up method.

Example 8-2 Determine the trap requirements for 75 ft (22.9 m) of 4 in. (101.6 mm) main, maximum steam pressure 15 psig (103.4 kPa) and heat-up time of 15 min. In determining the heat-up time, safety is the main consideration. Liberal time for heat up should be allowed to limit the stresses in the piping system caused by thermal expansion, allow drainage in order to minimize the possibility of water hammer, and reduce the size of the trap required. Small bypass valves installed around the large main valves are often used to warm up the main slowly.

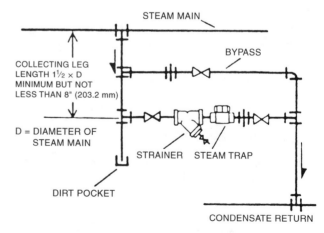

Figure 8-15 Trap Installation for Supervised Heat Up of Steam Mains

Step 1

From Table 8-9, the warm-up load for 100 ft (100 m) of 4 in. main from 70°F, 0 psig (21°C, 0 kPa) to 15 psig (103.4 kPa) is found to be 23.5 lb (35 kg).

Step 2

The condensation load for a 75 ft (22.9 m) main is:

$$\frac{75 \times 23.5}{100} = 17.6 \text{ lb}$$

$$\left(\frac{22.9 \cdot 35}{100} = 8 \text{ kg} \right)$$

Step 3

Calculate the average condensate formation rate during the heat-up period.

$$\frac{17.6 \times 60}{15} = 70.4 \text{ lb/h}$$

$$\left(\frac{8 \cdot 60}{15} = 32 \text{ kg/h} \right)$$

Step 4

The collecting leg size would be:

A. Diameter: 4 in. (101.6 mm)

B. Length: Minimum 28 in. (711.2 mm) to provide a minimum 1 psig (6.9 kPa) hydrostatic head at the inlet of the trap during warm-up.

Step 5

The type and size of the trap might be:

A. Float and thermostatic.

B. Capacity: 70.4 lb/h at 1 psig pressure differential (32 kg/h at 6.9 kPa)

C. Maximum operating pressure: The trap must be able to open against differential pressures of at least 15 psig (103.4 kPa).

D. Maximum safety factor recommended: 1.5.

E. Trap capacity

70.4 × 1.5 = 105.6 lb/h

(32 · 1.5 = 48 kg/h)

See Figure 8-16 for installation details.

Trap installation The following recommendations should be observed.

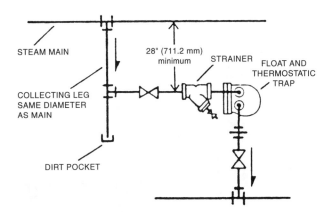

Figure 8-16 Trap Installation for Automatic Heat Up of Steam Mains

1. The steam trap should be installed as close as is possible to the collecting leg.

2. Lifting the condensate or piping condensate directly to a return line under pressure should be avoided. If the condensate must be lifted or discharged into a return system under pressure, the condensate should be collected in a vented flash tank and pumped to the elevated return or return system under pressure. If the trap must discharge to a return line that may be under pressure, then the differential pressure across the trap and the trap capacity will be reduced. A check valve on the discharge side of the trap is always required if the trap discharges into an elevated or pressurized return. See Figure 8-17.

3. Pipe connections to and from the steam trap should be at least equal to the pipe size of the trap connection, and full-size isolation valves should be installed on each side of the trap to allow service.

4. A strainer equipped with a blowdown valve should be installed before the steam trap.

5. A test and pressure relief fitting is recommended downstream of the trap to ensure that the service valves are holding before the trap is serviced. It can also provide for quick testing of the trap.

6. All low points of the steam main and wherever condensate can collect, such as ahead of pressure reducing valves and temperature regulators, should be drained.

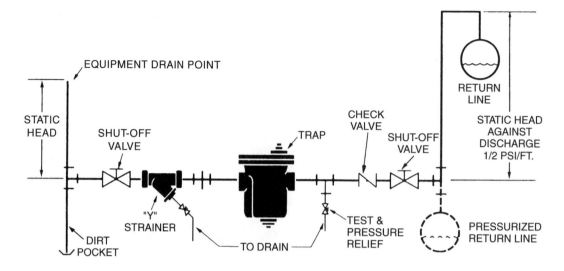

**Figure 8-17   Trap Installation: Trap Draining to Overhead Return Line
or Pressurized Return Line**

Source: ITT Hoffman Steam Specialty.

Parallel trapping   For the automatic heat-up method, the largest load that the steam trap must deal with is the warm-up load. Consequently, the steam trap must be sized on the warm-up load. Depending on the size of the installation, this situation can result in a steam trap that is considerably oversized in terms of the system operating under normal operating pressure. Oversized steam traps can create problems, particularly in high-pressure installations. For example, inverted bucket traps can lose their prime and pass live steam. All steam traps wear more rapidly on light loads than they do on heavy loads. The frequent release of small quantities of condensate at the full discharge rate of the steam trap can create undesirable pressures in the condensate return piping system.

These problems can be reduced by installing smaller steam traps with the same aggregate capacity in parallel. Figure 8-18 shows a typical such installation. It is recommended that parallel trapping be considered in any situation where a single large steam trap would otherwise be required. In addition to the economies inherent in a parallel piping hookup, it provides emergency protection in the event that one steam trap becomes clogged or fails closed.

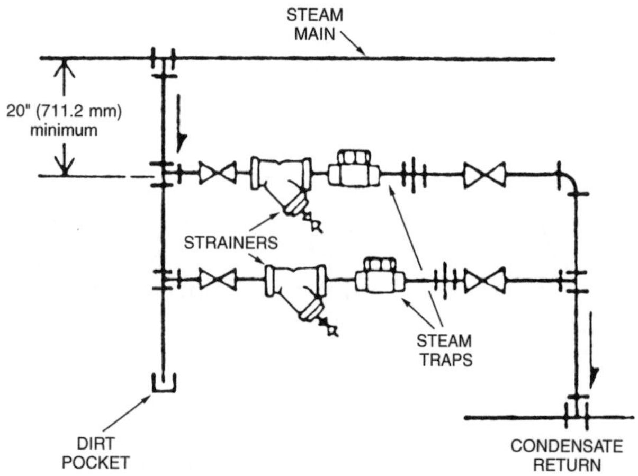

Flashing Flow and High-Pressure Condensate Piping

Flash tanks play an important role in condensate drainage. They get their name from the sudden evaporation, or "flashing," that occurs when condensate at higher pressure is suddenly released to lower pressure. The production of flash steam is also influenced by other components in the system. For example, thermostatic steam traps open only after the condensate has subcooled to below saturation temperature for the given pressure. This subcooled condensate contains less energy than does condensate at saturation temperature, so the amount of flash steam for a given drop in pressure will be re-

Figure 8-18   Parallel Trapping

duced. Figure 8-19 shows the amount of reevaporation, or the percentage of flash steam, that will occur for different conditions of initial pressure and pressure drop. In sizing condensate returns for high-pressure systems, this flash steam must be considered, since it will provide a great deal more friction loss than would be the case if the flashing did not occur and the pipe was carrying only liquid.

To size condensate pipes to carry flashing condensate:

• Determine the percentage of flash steam using Figure 8-19.

• Multiply the total high-pressure condensate flow by the flash steam percentage to determine the flash steam flow rate.

• Size the condensate pipe as if it was a steam pipe carrying nothing but the flash steam flow.

This procedure will oversize the condensate pipe to accommodate the flash steam without generating excess return line pressures.

REFERENCES

1. American Society of Heating, Refrigerating and Air Conditioning Engineers (ASHRAE). *Fundamentals handbook*. Atlanta, GA: ASHRAE.

2. Hydronics Institute. Publication no. 200.

3. ITT, Fluid Handling Division. *Hoffman steam heating systems design manual and engineering data*, Training manual TES 181. Morton Grove, IL: ITT.

4. ITT, Fluid Handling Division. *High temperature condensate return*, Training manual TES 582. Morton Grove, IL: ITT.

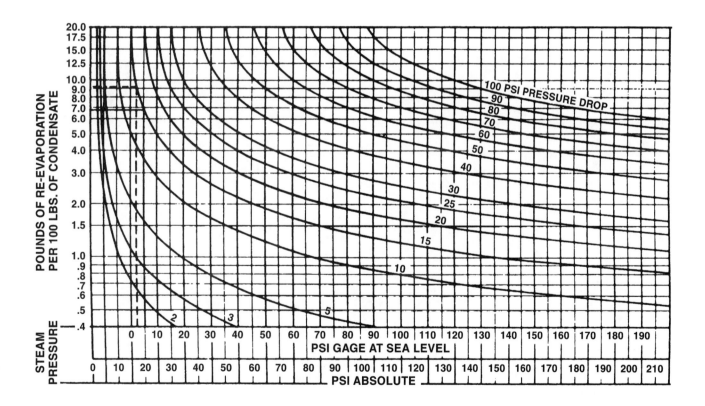

Figure 8-19 Reevaporation Chart for Traps, etc., Discharging into Lower Pressures

Source: ITT Fluid Handling, Morton Grove, IL.

Compressed Air Systems

INTRODUCTION

Compressed air is used to produce linear motion, as is required in hand tools, air hammers, paving breakers, rock drills, paint chippers, and vibrators. It also is employed to actuate linear movement through a piston and cylinder or a diaphragm for air-actuated valves, doors, dampers, brakes, etc. Atomizing, spraying, and moving hard-to-pump fluids are other applications. Compressed air can be bubbled up to measure fluid levels, agitate liquids, and inhibit ice formation in bodies of water. Another use of compressed air is for instrumentation. Air circuits solve the most complex problems in automatic control, starting/stopping, and modulation of valves, machines, and processes.

This chapter discusses compressed air for light industrial and commercial applications. For a discussion of compressed (medical) air used in health care facilities, refer to the *Data Book* chapter "Plumbing Design for Health-Care Facilities."

GENERAL INFORMATION

Air is a fluid. The two types of fluids are liquids and gases. Gases have a weaker cohesive force holding their molecules together than liquids do. Ambient air is a mixture of gases whose main components are oxygen and nitrogen; it has many other gases in minor concentrations.

The actual volume of an atom of gas in relation to the total volume of a gas molecule is quite small, and so, gases are mostly empty space.

This is why gases can be compressed. Pressure is produced when the molecules of a gas in an enclosed space rapidly strike the enclosing surfaces. If the gas is confined to smaller and smaller spaces, the molecules strike the container walls more and more frequently, producing greater pressure.

Because free air is less dense at higher elevations, a correction factor must be used to determine the equivalent volume of air at low and high elevations. Temperature is also a consideration. Because a volume of free air at a high temperature will exert a higher pressure than the same volume of air at a lower temperature, a correction factor must be used to determine the equivalent volume of air at different temperatures.

DEFINITIONS AND UNITS OF MEASURE

Definitions

A *compressed gas* is any gas stored or distributed at a pressure greater than atmospheric pressure (14.7 psia, 101.4 kPa).

The following are basic compressed air processes:

- An *isobaric process* takes place under constant pressure.
- An *isochoric process* takes place under constant volume.
- An *isothermal process* takes place under constant temperature.

- *Polytropic process* is a generalized expression for all three of the above-named processes when variations in pressure, temperature, or volume occur during the compression cycle.

- An *adiabatic process* of compression allows a gas to gain temperature. This is the most commonly used process in facility compressed air production.

Standard air conditions are different for various disciplines. For the American National Standards Institute (ANSI) and the Compressed Gas Association, standard air is considered to be dry, with a relative humidity of 0.0%, a temperature of 60°F (15.6°C), and a pressure of 14.7 psig (101.4 kPa). For the chemical industry, standard air is 68°F (20°C), at a relative humidity of 0.0% and a pressure of 14.7 psig (101.4 kPa). Some manufacturers use a relative humidity of 36%, a temperature of 68°F (20°C) and a pressure of 14.2 psig (100.0 kPa) for performance test ratings. It is imperative that the conditions under which a compressor rating is calculated are obtained from the owner and manufacturer.

Free air is air at ambient conditions at a specific location. Temperature, barometric pressure, and moisture content may be different from those of standard air. The term "free air" is not to be used unless the ambient temperature, humidity, and barometric pressure conditions at the compressor location are stated.

Standard cubic feet per minute (scfm) (normal liters per minute [nL/min]) is a volume measurement of air at standard conditions. Outside the United States, "standard" is commonly referred to as "normal," hence "nL/min" and "nL/s."

Actual cubic feet per minute (acfm) (actual liters per minute [aL/min]) is a volume measurement of standard air after it has been compressed. The term "acfm (aL/min)" is not to be used unless the pressure is stated.

Units of Measure

Pressure Pressure measurements are made using force acting upon an area. In the United States, pressure is commonly measured using inch-pound (IP) units of measurement, and expressed as pounds per square inch (psi). Another common unit of measurement for low-pressure systems is inches of water column (in. wc). In International System (SI) units, pressure is commonly measured in kilopascals (kPa).

Standard reference points The two basic reference points for measuring pressure are standard atmospheric pressure and a perfect vacuum. When pressure is measured using standard atmospheric pressure as the point of reference, the measurement is called "gauge pressure," expressed as pounds per square inch, gauge (psig). If the reference pressure level is a perfect vacuum, the term used is "absolute pressure," expressed as pounds per square inch, absolute (psia). Local barometric pressure, which is the prevailing pressure at any specific location, is variable and should not be confused with standard atmosphere, which is mean theoretical barometric pressure at sea level. Theoretical standard atmospheric pressure at sea level is equal to 14.696 (generally shortened to 14.7) psia or 0 psig and 29.92 in. Hg (101.4 kPa and 760 mm Hg). A perfect vacuum has a value of 0 psia (0 kPa) and 0 in. Hg. Theoretical standard atmospheric temperature is 60°F (15.6°C).

Flow rate The most common IP unit of measure for flow rate is cubic feet per minute (cfm). If the flow rate is low, it is commonly expressed in cubic feet per hour (cfh). The SI units used for flow rate are cubic meters per minute (m³/min), liters per minute (L/min), and liters per second (L/s). Flow rate must reference scfm or acfm (nL/min or aL/min). Some manufacturers use "nm³/min," which means normal cubic meters per minute, or "nL/min," which means normal liters per minute. It is mandatory that all equipment selection flow rate criteria be in the same units.

WATER VAPOR IN AIR

Air contains varying amounts of water vapor, depending on its temperature and pressure. When a given volume of free air is compressed under conditions used in facilities, an increase in temperature occurs. An increase in temperature results in an increased ability of the air to retain moisture. An increase in pressure results in a decrease in its ability to hold water. With each 20°F (5.6°C) increase in temperature, the ability of air to accept water vapor doubles. Because of the high temperature of the air during the compression cycle, water is not precipitated during compression inside the compressor; rather, it is precipitated after the cycle has been completed. There are various methods of expressing the water vapor present.

Relative Humidity

"Relative humidity" is the amount of water vapor actually present in the air expressed as a percent of the amount present when the air is saturated. Relative humidity is dependent on both pressure and temperature.

Dew Point

The "dew point" is the temperature at which water in the air will start to condense on a surface; it is the preferred method to express the dryness of compressed air. The lower the dew point, the dryer the air. Since the dew point of air varies with the air pressure, it must be referred to as the pressure dew point. The dew point of compressed air is not affected by the temperature of compressed air.

CONTAMINANTS

There are four general classes of contamination:

1. Liquids (oil and water).
2. Vapor (oil, water, and hydrocarbons).
3. Gas.
4. Particulates.

A knowledge of the various pollutants in the air is helpful when an engineer has to decide what equipment is required to effectively reduce or remove them. The required level of protection from the various contaminants depends upon the purpose for the air. The performance criteria for each system, along with the identity and quantity of pollutants, must be determined prior to the selection of equipment.

COMPRESSOR TYPES

The purpose of an air compressor is to concentrate free air, decreasing its volume and thereby increasing its pressure. There are two general categories of air compressors: positive displacement and dynamic.

The positive displacement compressor is essentially a constant volume, variable pressure machine capable of operating over a wide range of discharge pressures at a relatively constant capacity. Positive displacement compressors can be separated into reciprocating and rotary machines. Typical reciprocating compressors include piston and diaphragm types. Rotary compressors include such types as sliding vane, liquid ring (or liquid piston), and screw. The most widely used types of dynamic compressors include the centrifugal and the axial flow.

Dynamic compressor characteristics are opposite those of the positive displacement compressor. This machine operates over a relatively wide range of capacity at a relatively constant discharge pressure.

Reciprocating Compressor

A reciprocating compressor uses positive displacement, which is accomplished by a piston moving in a cylinder. When compression occurs on only one stroke it is called a "single-acting cylinder," and when compression occurs on both strokes it is called a "double-acting compressor." The cylinders can be horizontal, vertical, or angled. The cylinders can be sealed and lubricated with oil when traces of oil in the discharge air will cause no problems. Oil-free machines are also available, but at a higher cost than those requiring oil.

Cooling is accomplished by air or water. Water cooling is generally more effective than air cooling and consumes less power, but the initial and operating costs are higher. A two-stage compressor consumes less power than a single-stage unit for the equivalent output.

Sliding Vane Compressor

Sliding vane compressors work by utilizing vanes that are mounted eccentrically in a cylindrical rotor and are free to slide in and out of slots. As the rotor turns, the space between the compressor casing and the vanes decreases and the air is compressed.

These are compact units, well suited for direct connection to a relatively high-speed motor. Their efficiency is usually less than that of an equivalent piston unit. Their best application is for situations where small, low-capacity compressors, generally in the range of 100 cfm to 75 psi (2832 L/min to 517.1 kPa), are required.

Liquid Ring Compressor

Liquid ring compressors, sometimes referred to as "liquid pistons," are rotary positive displacement units that use a fixed-blade rotor in an elliptical casing. The casing is partially filled with liquid. As the rotor turns, the blades set the liquid in motion. As they rotate, the blades extend deeper into the liquid ring, compressing the trapped air.

The resulting air is completely oil free. This type of compressor can also handle wet, corrosive, or explosive gases. Various liquids, which are compatible with specific gases to be compressed, can be used. This unit is very well suited for hospital and laboratory use. A practical limitation of 100 psi (689.5 kPa) exists, and there is higher power consumption than with piston units of a similar rating.

Straight Lobe Compressor

Straight lobe (often referred to as "rotary lobe") compressors function in a manner similar to that of gear pumps. A pair of identical rotors, each with lobes shaped like the figure "8" in cross section, are mounted inside a casing. As they rotate, air is trapped between the impeller lobes and pump casing and carried around without compression. This air is then discharged, using the existing pressure in the system to increase pressure. These units are available oil free and are generally recommended for pressures up to 200 psig (1379 kPa) and 150 scfm (4285 nL/min).

Rotary Screw Compressor

Rotary screw compressors use a pair of close-clearance, helical lobe rotors turning in unison. As air enters the inlet, the rotation of the rotors causes the cavity in which air is trapped to become smaller and smaller, increasing pressure. The air reaches the end of the screw at high pressure and flows out smoothly at the discharge port. The majority of rotary screw compressors in use today are of the oil-flooded type. Designs that produce oil-free air are available. These compressors produce pulse-free air and are generally available for pressures from 150 to 300 psi (1034 to 2068 kPa) and 300 scfm (8496 nL/min).

Centrifugal Compressor

Centrifugal compressors are dynamic machines that utilize impellers to add kinetic energy to the air stream by centrifugal action. The velocity of the air is increased as it passes through each impeller. A diffuser section decelerates the high-velocity air, converting the kinetic energy into potential energy. The volute further increases the pressure and directs the air into the discharge piping.

Centrifugal compressors typically produce large volumes of air at relatively low pressures. Higher pressures can be attained by adding stages with intercooling between the stages. The centrifugal compressor takes up less floor space but requires more power than a reciprocating unit of equal output. Its inherently oil-free air delivery is a major advantage in many applications.

COMPRESSOR ACCESSORIES

Silencers

With today's emphasis on noise control, the installation of an intake silencer is probably necessary for most projects. There are two types of silencer: reactive and absorptive. The reactive type is used to attenuate (reduce) low-frequency sound in the order of 500 hertz (Hz), and is most often found on reciprocating compressors. The absorptive type is often used on centrifugal and screw type compressors, where frequencies are above 500 Hz. There is no practical limit in cfm (L/min) for either type.

Silencers may be combined with inlet filters for more economical installations. They can also be mounted directly on compressors, outside the building walls, or at the roof level as separate units.

Aftercoolers

An aftercooler is a device used to lower the temperature of compressed air immediately after the compression process. Air leaving the compressor is very hot. It is desirable to reduce the temperature of discharged air to a range of between 70 and 110°F (21.1 and 43°C). A primary reason the temperature is lowered is to remove moisture that would otherwise condense elsewhere in the system as the air cools to ambient conditions. Therefore, it is considered good practice to install the cooling unit as close to the compressor discharge as practical. An aftercooler is also useful to precondition air where additional conditioning is necessary. There are three general types of aftercooler:

1. Water-cooled.

2. Air-cooled.

3. Refrigerant.

Air-cooled is the most often used type of aftercooler. Since large amounts of water are usually removed from the air in an aftercooler, a moisture separator is usually provided. The separator could be either an integral part of the aftercooler or a separate unit.

Additional factors to be considered when selecting an aftercooler are pressure drop through the unit, space and clearance requirements, operation costs, and maintenance.

Filters

The purpose of any filter is to remove or reduce impurities or contaminants in the airstream to an acceptable or predetermined level. Filter nomenclature has been developed based on the type of filter medium used and generally on where it is placed in a compressed air system. Inlet filters, prefilters, after-filters and point-of-use filters are some examples. Generally speaking, nothing prevents any kind of filter from being used for any application, provided that the required reduction of contaminants is achieved and the filter is suitable for the purpose intended. Following is a brief, general discussion of various types of filter:

Inlet filters of some type are required for every installation to protect the compressor from damage. They remove large amounts of contaminants, including particulates, at the inlet to the air compressor. These filters are integral to compressors that draw air from the room they are installed in or from the building exterior.

Prefilters are generally used before air enters a dryer to remove various contaminants that might foul the unit. These filters are usually of the coalescing type so they remove particulates and vapors, such as oil, hydrocarbons, and water. When combined with separators at this point, these filters may be called "separator/filters."

After-filters are generally used after the drying process to remove particulates smaller than those removed by a prefilter. Some dryers produce a very small-diameter dust (fines) that must be removed from the airstream. These filters remove particulates only.

Point-of-use filters are generally used immediately prior to any tool or individual piece of equipment that requires removal of particulates, oil, or moisture to a greater extent than is done with an after-filter.

Oil-removal filters are special filters used only for the removal of unwanted oil aerosols that are too small to be removed by coalescing. Activated carbon filters are used to remove gaseous oil and other hydrocarbons as well as small particulates that are too small to be removed by coalescing.

Separators

A separator is a type of filter used to remove large quantities of liquid water or oil, individually or in combination with each other, from the air stream. Often, oil and water form an emulsion inside the compressor and are discharged together.

Since suspended liquids are present after air leaves the aftercooler or compressor, this is the most common location for a separator. The general design of these units should allow for the removal of between 90 and 99%, by weight, of liquids.

COMPRESSED AIR DRYERS

Air dryers are devices used to remove water vapor from the airstream. Large volumes of water consisting of large droplets are removed by a moisture separator. If additional reduction of water vapor content is desired, it must be accomplished by the use of an air dryer. There are five general categories of dryer, defined by the method of drying (see the discussion below):

1. High pressurization of the compressed air.

2. Condensation.

3. Absorption.

4. Adsorption.

5. Heat of compression.

High Pressurization

High pressurization reduces the quantity of water vapor by compressing air to pressures greater than those required for actual use. An increase in pressure decreases the ability of air to hold moisture. Since pressurization requires large amounts of energy, this process is rarely used.

Condensation

Condensation utilizes the principle of lowering the temperature of the airstream through a heat exchanger to produce a lower dew point. Lowering the dew point reduces the capacity of air to retain moisture. Moisture then condenses out of the air onto the coils of the dryer. A moisture separator removes the condensate. The cooling medium in the coil could be water, brine, or a refrigerant. The most common type of dryer uses a refrigerant and is called a "refrigerated dryer." A refrigerated dryer requires operation within a small range of pressure and air flow rate to be effective. In general, a minumum of 20% of rated air flow is required to achieve specified moisture removal.

The greatest limitation of these dryers is that they cannot practically produce a pressure dew point lower than 35°F (1.7°C). Otherwise, the condensed moisture would freeze on the coils. Advantages are that they have a low operating cost and they do not introduce impurities into the airstream.

Absorption

Absorption dryers use either a solid or a liquid medium and operate on the principle that when the airstream containing water vapor passes through or over a deliquescent material the water causes the medium to change state (or dissolve). The solvent is then drained away, thus the water is removed and the amount of material available for absorption is reduced. Solid absorbers are much more common than liquid ones. The advantage of this type of dryer is that it requires no outside source of power or connection to any other system. A disadvantage is that impurities may be introduced to the airstream.

Adsorption

Adsorption dryers use a porous, non-consumable material that causes water vapor to condense as a very thin film on the material's surface. This material is called a "desiccant." There is no chemical interaction, and the adsorption process is reversible. Desiccant dryers are capable of producing pressure dew points as low as –100°F (–73.3°C). The method of regeneration is the primary way of distinguishing between types of desiccant dryer.

The two general regeneration methods, and the two types of desiccant dryer, are: duplex bed pressure swing (heatless) dryers, which use approximately 15% of the compressor capacity to dry one bed while the other is operating, and heat activated dryers (which use internal or external type heaters). Additional compressor capacity is necessary to provide this extra air.

Desiccant materials include silica gel, activated alumina, and aluminosilicate (molecular sieve). Each material also has applications for the removal of specific impurities other than water. Desiccant materials age when in use over a period of years, which may affect their capacity. In addition, care must be taken to avoid contamination of the materials, particularly by oils.

Heat of Compression

This type of dryer also uses a desiccant to adsorb the moisture in the compressed airstream. The dessicant material is continuously regenerated using a portion of the hot air directly discharged from the compressor before it goes into the aftercooler. The difference between this and the pressure swing type dryer is that for continuous duty the pressure swing regenerates one whole bed at a time, requiring a second bed to dry the airstream. The heat of compression dryer has only one bed that rotates and regenerates a portion of the dessicant material on a continuous basis, leaving the remainder of the bed to dry the air. The air used to regenerate the desiccant is then returned into the main airstream. There are no regeneration air losses or electric heaters used. This dryer could be cooled by a fan (air cooled) or water cooled. Units that are cooled with air at 95°F (35°C) often give a pressure dew point of –15°F (–26.1°C).

Dryer Selection

The single most important requirement in the selection process is to determine the lowest required pressure dew point for the intended application. This may eliminate some types of dryer. An excessive flow rate may eliminate other dryer types. The economics of initial and operating costs, which vary from one unit to another, is another determining factor. Space conditions and maintenance availability should also be considered.

COMPRESSOR REGULATION

If the total system demand for both air pressure and volume exactly matched the compressor output for as long as the compressor operated, no regulation would be required. Since this does not usually happen, whenever system demand varies, some method must be found to regulate output to match the variable pressure and flow rate demands of the system.

Compressor capacity can be regulated by either continuous or discontinuous methods. One continuous means would require regulation of the compressor either by using an adjustable speed coupling or by controlling the drive motor speed. Another continuous method would be to bleed compressed air from the discharge either to the atmosphere or back into the inlet. This is called "unloading" or "blow-off" and is wasteful of energy. A final continuous method is alteration of the internals of a compressor, by adjusting valves, clearances, etc., to make it less efficient. The last method is the least desirable of all, because the correct speed of the compressor can only be determined and the internal adjustment accomplished by the manufacturer. This makes it almost impossible for maintenance personnel to repair in the field.

Discontinuous regulation is the most common method of controlling compressor capacity. This is accomplished by using a mechanical or electro-mechanical pressure-regulating device that is arranged to stop the compressor at a preset high pressure and start it again at a preset low pressure. A receiver (tank) is used to store air. The tank gives a reserve capacity to keep the compressor from starting too often.

Also, pressure may be regulated at the point of use. Combination point-of-use units allow moisture removal, filtering, and regulation of pressure from a single unit. This type of regulator should be adjustable to allow flexibility for the intended purpose of the outlet.

STARTING UNLOADER

The starting unloader is used only when starting a compressor. After the first time pressure has been established in the system and the compressor has stopped, the system remains pressurized. When the compressor must start again, it has to overcome the force exerted by the air still under pressure in the casing. There is not enough power in the drive motor to overcome this pressure. Therefore, a means must be provided to vent only the air under pressure in the compressor casing to atmosphere, and allow the compressor to start under no load. This is done with a starting unloader.

COMPRESSED AIR RECEIVERS

The primary purpose of a receiver is to store air. A secondary purpose is to even out pulsations from a compressor. Determination of the need for a receiver is always based on the type of regulation the system uses. If the compressor runs 100% of the time and has constant blow-off, an air receiver is not required.

For most applications, an air compressor is regulated by starting and stopping, with a receiver used to store air and prevent the compressor from cycling too often. Generally accepted practice for reciprocating compressors is to limit starts to about 10 per hour and running time to 70% of the time. Centrifugal, screw, and sliding vane compressors are best run 100% of the time.

An air receiver serves the following purposes:

1. Storage of air.

2. Equalizing of pressure variations (pulsations).

3. Collection of residual condensate.

Piping connections should be made in such a way that the incoming air is forced to circulate and mix with the air already inside the tank before being discharged. Receivers should be American Society of Mechanical Engineers (ASME) stamped for unfired pressure vessels. An automatic drain valve is required for the receiver to discharge to an adjacent floor drain through an air gap. Manufacturers have standard receiver sizes measured in gallons (liters) of water capacity.

Receivers should be sized on the basis of system demand and compressor size, using the starts per hour and running time best suited for the project. The design engineer must keep in mind 1) that a compressor operates to satisfy the pressure switch rather than the use of air and 2) the receiver is an integral part of the system that must function with respect to load conditions, amount of storage, and pressure differential. Often, the manufacturer has a standard size receiver for specific compressor models. A commonly used formula to find the receiver size is:

$$T = \frac{V \times (P_1 - P_2)}{C \times P_a}$$

where:

T = Time receiver takes to go from the upper to lower pressure limits, min

V = Volume of tank, ft³ (m³)

P_1 = Maximum tank pressure, psia (kPa)

C = Free air needed, scfm (nL/min)

P_a = Atmospheric pressure, psia (kPa)

P_2 = Minimum tank absolute pressure, psia (nL/min)

While it is common practice to locate a receiver near the compressor equipment for air storage, the designer should consider the locations of the largest air consumers. Installation of a receiver at a remote point on the piping system would allow the system to handle surges and possibly eliminate the need for an additional compressor.

A common piping scheme used in large manufacturing facilities is to provide a loop header around the plant. This scheme provides flexibility for future connections and reduced pressure drops to remote locations. Oversizing the header one pipe size also provides storage capacity and may eliminate the need for a remote receiver.

PIPING SYSTEM DESIGN

The compressed air system must be controlled, regulated, and sized to ensure that an adequate volume of air, at a pressure and purity that will satisfy user requirements, is delivered at any outlet, particularly the most hydraulically remote, during the period of heaviest use.

The design process is an iterative one because the performance of one or several components may have an effect on the performance of other equipment. Therefore, various adjustments are usually necessary as the design progresses.

Design Sequence

1. Locate and identify each process, work station, or piece of equipment using compressed air. They should be located on a plan, and a complete list should be made to simplify record keeping.

2. Determine the volume of air used at each location.

3. Determine the pressure range required at each location.

4. Determine the conditioning requirements for each piece of equipment, such as allowable moisture content, particulate size, and oil content.

5. Establish how much time the individual tool or process will be in actual use for a one-minute period of time. This is referred to as the "duty cycle."

6. Establish the maximum number of locations that may be used simultaneously on each branch, on each main, and for the project as a whole. This is known as the "use factor."

7. Establish the extent of allowable leakage.

8. Establish any allowance for future expansion.

9. Select the piping material.

10. Make a preliminary piping layout and assign a preliminary pressure drop.

11. Select the air compressor type, conditioning equipment, equipment location, and air inlet, making sure that scfm (nL/min) or acfm (aL/min) is used consistently for both the system and compressor capacity rating.

12. Produce a final piping layout and size the piping network.

The following paragraphs explain the items in the design sequence:

Project air-consuming devices location (item no. 1 above) This speaks for itself. To accomplish this task, mark on a plan the location and requirements of all air-consuming devices. This facilitates the branch piping layout. Prepare a list, for future reference, of all the devices marked on the plan, noting their location and actual required flow rate.

Pressure and flow rate requirement (item nos. 2 and 3) All tools use air, either through an orifice or to drive a piston, to do work. Information about pressure and flow rate parameters for individual equipment and tools is usually obtained from the manufacturer, end user, facility planner, or owner. Often this information is incomplete and additional investigation is required to find the specific values needed. Very often, it is useful to assign preliminary pressure and flow rate requirements of the system, in order to arrange equipment space and give preliminary mechanical data to other disciplines. Table 9-1 lists general air requirements for various tools.

The best approach is to obtain actual equipment cuts from the manufacturer of the proposed equipment due to the wide variation in the requirements of similar air-consuming devices from different manufacturers.

Compressed air conditioning (item no. 4) The selection of conditioning equipment depends upon end-use requirements, usually obtained in the process of doing above-listed steps 2, 3, and 4. Conditioning equipment includes dryers, filters, lubricators, and pressure regulators.

Dryer selection is based on the most demanding user requirement, except where special, dedicated equipment may be required. If a very low dew point is required, the only selection possible is a desiccant type dryer. If, however, a high dew point is acceptable, several different types of dryer can be considered.

Deliquescent dryer The deliquescent dryer is the least efficient type, but it requires no power to operate and has the lowest initial cost of all the dryers. It has a moderate operating cost, since only the drying medium must be replenished at regular intervals. This type of dryer loses efficiency if the inlet air temperature is over 100 °F (37.8 °C), and so an efficient aftercooler is mandatory. The type of deliquescent material used affects the quality of air. Salt normally reduces the dew point about 12 to 20 °F (−11.1 to −6.7 °C), while potassium carbonate lowers the dew point about 30 °F (−1.1 °C). A filter is necessary after the dryer to remove any chemical carryover (fines) in the airstream.

Refrigerated dryer Refrigerated dryers produce pressure dew points as low as 36 °F (2.2 °C), but for practical purposes, a figure in the range of 38 to 40 °F (3.3 to 4.4 °C) is generally used. Both initial and general operating costs are moderate. External requirements are floor drains and

electric power.

This type of dryer operates at rated effectiveness only when the unit is run at or near its rated capacity and pressure. Consult the manufacturer for actual operating parameters.

Desiccant dryer The twin tower (pressure swing) desiccant dryer produces the lowest dew points. These dryers have the highest initial and operating costs. The pressure swing purge is the fastest, but it uses about 15% of the system air for purging. If the incoming air temperature is too high, this can be detrimental to the desiccant material. An aftercooler is usually recommended for most dryer installations because it is an economical way to reduce the moisture content of air. The aftercooler should be selected in conjunction with the dryer. The aftercooler does add cost to the project, however, and it is not always used.

The heat of compression dryer uses the heated air directly discharged from the compressor to continuously dry a desiccant material. The heated air is piped back into the main airstream. This type of dryer does not require additional compressor capacity.

Filters There are two factors used to select a filter: effectiveness and pressure drop. Do not specify a filter that produces air that is cleaner than necessary. If one station or process requires a much higher purity than others, use a point-of-use filter for that area and a less restricted filter for the main supply. It is possible for a filter to have the largest pressure drop of all the equipment in the system. In general, a filter produces a 3 to 10 psig (20.7 to 68.9 kPa) pressure drop when dirty. If the actual figure proves to be too much, it is a good idea to oversize the filter to cut down the pressure drop. In most cases, it is more economical to pay the added initial cost of a larger filter than to increase energy requirements to compress air to a higher pressure for the life of the system.

Duty cycle (item no. 5) The duty cycle is how long a tool or device is available for use during a shift. To determine the duty cycle, consult the users, for in most cases they are the only authorities capable of discussing actual operations for their facility. In most industrial applications, tasks of a similar nature are grouped together. This allows sections or branches to be calculated independently.

Table 9-1   Compressed Air Requirements for Tools and Equipment[a]

Type of Tool	Air Usage, scfm (nL/s)
Hoist	1 (0.5)
Car lift	6 (3.1)
Grease gun	4 (2.3)
Grinders, 6 and 8-in. (152.4 and 203.2-mm) wheels	50 (23.6)
Grinders, 2 and 2 ½-in. (50.8 and 63.5-mm) wheels	14–20 (6.6–9.4)
File and burr machines	18 (8.5)
Rotary sanders, 9-in. (228.6-mm) pads	53 (25.0)
Rotary sanders, 7-in. (177.8-mm) pads	30 (14.2)
Sand rammers and tampers	
1 x 4 in. (25.4 x 101.6 mm) cylinder	25 (11.8)
1 ¼ x 5 in.(31.8 x 127 mm) cylinder	28 (13.2)
1 ½ x 6 in.(38.1 x 152.4 mm) cylinder	39 (18.4)
Chipping hammers, weighing 2–4 lb (0.9–1.8 kg)	12 (5.7)
weighing 10–13 lb (4.5–5.9 kg)	28–30 (13.2–14.2)
weighing more than 13 lb (5.9 kg)	39 (18.4)
Nut setters to ¼ in. (7.9 mm) weighing 8 lb (3.6 kg)	20 (9.4)
Nut setters ½–¾ in. (12.7–19.1 mm)	20–30 (9.4–14)
Sump pumps, 145 gal (548.8 L) at 50 ft (15.2 m) head	70 (33.0)
Paint sprayers, average	7 (3.3)
range	2–20 (0.9–9.4)
Bushing tools (monument)	15–25(7.1–11.8)
Carving tools (monument)	10–15(4.7–7.1)
Plug drills	40–50(18.9–23.6)
Riveters, ½ –1 in.(12.7–25.4 mm) rivets	12 (5.7)
5 in. (127 mm)	35 (16.5)
Rivet busters	35–39 (16.5–18.4)
Wood borers to 1 in. (25.4 mm) rivets	12 (5.7)
2 in. (50.8 mm) diameter	35 (16.5)
Steel drills, rotary motors	
Capacity up to ¼ in. (6.4 mm)	18–20 (8.5–9.4)
Capacity ¼ – ⅜ in. (6.4–9.5 mm)	20–40 (9.4–18.9)
Capacity ½ – ¾ in.(12.7–19.1 mm)	70 (33.0)
Capacity ⅞ – 1 in. (22.2–25.4 mm)	80 (37.8)
Capacity 1 ¼ in. (31.8 mm)	95 (44.8)
Steel drills, piston type	
Capacity ½ – ¾ in. (12.7–19.1 mm)	45 (21.2)
Capacity ⅞ – 1 ¼ in. (22.2–31.8 mm)	75–80 (35.4–37.8)
Capacity 1 ¼ – 2 in.(31.8–50.8 mm)	80–90 (37.8–42.5)
Capacity 2–3 in.(50.8–76.2 mm)	100–110(47.2–51.9)

[a] Free air, cfm at 90 psig (L/s at 620.5 kPa).

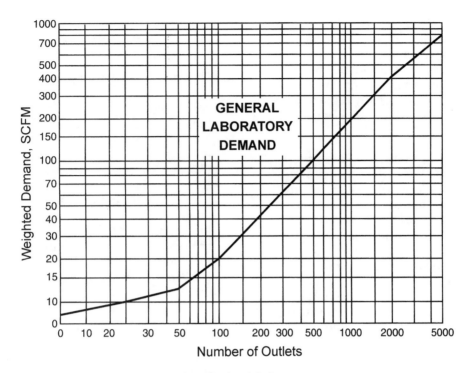

Note: To convert to metric, multiply scfm by 28.32 to obtain nL/min.

Figure 9-1   Laboratory Use Factors

Source: Frankel, M. 1996.

Use factor (item no. 6) The use factor is how many of the tools connected to the system will be in use at once. Experience indicates that it is almost impossible to accurately determine a use factor. Therefore, sufficient receiver capacity or larger compressor capacity to allow for possible variances must be provided. In laboratories, air is used less often than it is in industrial applications, mostly for chemical reactions. Refer to Figure 9-1 for laboratory use factors. The exceptions are classrooms and some research facilities, where the use factor may be quite high. Although extremely general in nature, Table 9-2 gives some guidance in the selection of use factors for light manufacturing facilities. These should be verified with the owners.

Allowable leakage (item no. 7) There is no method to accurately determine a reasonable figure for leakage. Leakage is a function of the number and type of connections, the number of repeated connects/disconnects, the age of the system, and quality of the pipe assembly. Many smaller tools and operations generally have a greater leakage of air than a few larger use points.

A well-maintained system will have a leakage of about 2 to 5%. Average conditions will result in a 10% leakage. Poorly maintained systems have been known to have a 25% leakage factor. The facility's maintenance department should be consulted when selecting a leakage value. The leakage should be considered when the selected compressor capacity barely meets system requirements.

Table 9-2   General Use Factors

Number of Outlets	Use Factor
1	1.0
11	0.80
31	0.60
78	0.50
148	0.40
320	0.35
575	0.30

Future expansion (item no. 8) The owner must give guidance as to the possibility and extent of any future expansion. In anticipation of expansion, consideration should be given to oversizing some components, such as filters, dryers, and main pipes, to avoid costly replacement in the future and to save down time while expansion is underway.

Compressed air piping materials (item no. 9) Consult with the owner regarding which piping materials are compatible with the facility environment. Piping materials that could be used include copper, carbon steel, stainless steel, aluminum, and plastic. Temperature, pressure, total installation cost, and location also affect material selection. Care should be taken not to use piping materials that are not acceptable for high temperatures near the compressor discharge (often 70°F [21°C] above ambient temperature). Valves include ball and gate types and are selected using water, oil, and gas (WOG) pressure ratings.

Piping sizing (item nos. 10 and 12) Produce a preliminary piping layout on the plans. Check for space, clearances, interferences, and securely anchored drops to equipment. Then make a final piping layout incorporating all the above items.

It should now be possible to start sizing the piping network using the following procedure:

1. In order to use pressure drop tables, it is necessary to find the equivalent length of run from the compressor to the farthest point in the piping system. The reason is that the various pipe sizing tables are based on a pressure drop developed using friction loss for a given length of pipe. Measuring the actual length is the first step. In addition to the actual measured pipe length, the effect of fittings must be considered. This is because fittings and valves create an obstruction to the flow of air. This degree of obstruction has been converted to an equivalent length of pipe in order to make calculations easy. Table 9-3 indicates the equivalent pipe length for fittings and valves, which should be added to the actual measured run to establish a total equivalent run. Instead of actually counting the number of valves and fittings, it is sometimes considered accepted practice to add 50% of the actual measured run to give an approximation of the total equivalent run, and therefore the means to select a pipe size.

This "rule-of-thumb" method for fittings should not be used in systems where pressure becomes a critical factor.

2. Determine the actual pressure drop that will occur only in the piping system. Generally accepted practice is to allow 10% of the proposed system pressure for pipe friction loss. For a 125 psi (861.9 kPa) system, allow a 12 to 15 psi (103.4 to 129.3 kPa) loss. Since the air compressor has not been selected yet, this figure is variable. A smaller pipe size may lead to higher compressor horsepower. It is considered good practice to oversize distribution mains to allow for future growth and the addition of conditioning equipment that may add a pressure drop not anticipated at the time of original design. However, this practice results in a higher initial cost for the piping system.

3. Size the piping using the appropriate charts, having first calculated the scfm (nL/min) and the allowable friction loss in each section of the piping being sized. Since all pipe sizing charts are calculated using loss of pressure per some length of piping (usually 100 ft [30.5 m]), it is necessary to arrive at the required value for the chart you are using. Figure 9-2 presents friction loss of air in psi (kPa) for a 100-ft (30.5-m) length of pipe from 15 to 100 psi (103.4 to 689.5 kPa) line pressure. Use the lowest system working pressure to determine pipe size.

The following general design parameters can be used as a guide when calculating piping systems' total pressure drop:

1. Equipment drop leg: 2 psi (13.8 kPa) loss (1 psi [6.9 kPa] if possible)

2. Hose allowance: 2 to 5 psi (13.8 to 34.5 kPa) loss

3. Quick disconnect coupling: 4 psi (27.6 kPa) loss

4. Lubricator: 1 to 4 psi (6.9 to 27.6 kPa) loss

5. Point-of-use filter: ½ to 2 psi (3.4 to 13.8 kPa) loss

Selecting the air compressor assembly (item no. 11) There is now enough information to size the compressor assembly, which includes the intake system, compressor, compressor installation requirements, and receiver. To start, the following information must be available:

Table 9-3   Fitting Equivalent Length of Run (ft)

Pipe Size (in.)	90° Elbow	Tee (branch)	Tee (run)	Gate Valve (full open)	Globe Valve (full open)
½	1 ¾	3 ¼	1	¾	18
¾	2 ¼	4 ½	1 ½	1	24
1	2 ¾	5 ½	1 ¾	1 ¼	30
1 ¼	3 ¼	7 ½	2 ¼	1 ½	35
1 ½	4 ½	8 ½	2 ¾	2	46
2	5 ¼	10 ½	3 ½	2 ¼	59
2 ½	6 ¼	12 ½	4 ¼	2 ¾	70
3	7 ¾	15 ½	5 ¼	3 ½	87
4	10 ¼	20 ¼	6 ¾	4 ½	114

Table 9-3(M)   Fitting Equivalent Length of Run (m)

Pipe Size (mm)	90° Elbow	Tee (branch)	Tee (run)	Gate Valve (full open)	Globe Valve (full open)
15	0.53	0.99	0.31	0.23	5.5
20	0.69	1.4	0.46	0.31	7.3
25	0.84	1.7	0.53	0.38	9.1
32	0.90	2.1	0.69	0.46	10.7
40	1.4	2.6	0.84	0.60	14.0
50	1.6	3.2	1.1	0.69	18.0
65	1.9	3.8	1.3	0.84	21.3
80	2.4	4.7	1.6	1.1	26.5
100	3.1	6.2	2.1	1.4	34.7

1. Total connected cfm (L/min) of all air-using devices, including flow to the air dryer system if applicable.

2. Maximum pressure all air-using devices require.

3. Duty cycle and use factors for these devices giving maximum expected use of air.

4. Leakage and future expansion allowance, cfm (L/min).

5. Allowable pressure drops for the entire system, including piping and conditioning equipment.

6. Altitude, temperature, and contaminant removal corrections.

7. Location where adequate space is available for air compressor and all ancillary equipment.

Having this information, first design the inlet piping system. Since air compressor performance depends on inlet conditions, this system deserves special care. The air intake should provide a supply of air to the compressor that is as clean, cool, and dry as possible. The proposed location should be studied for the presence of any type of airborne contamination; inlets should be positioned to avoid the probability of contaminated intake. Whenever possible, use outside air.

For an external installation, the inlet should have a rain cap and a screen. An inlet filter should always be provided inside the building. If the manufacturer of the selected compressor

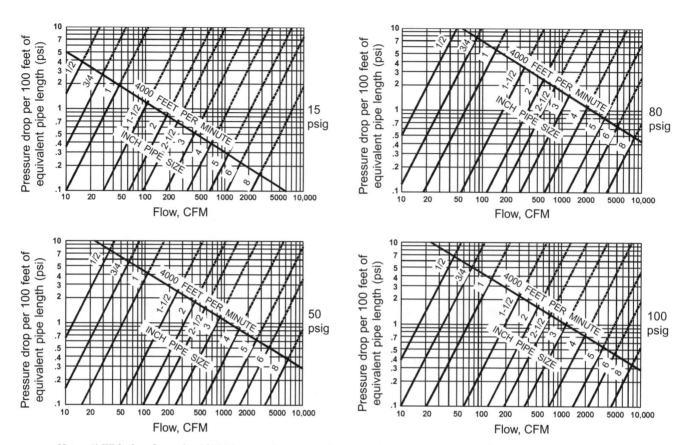

Notes: 1) With the cfm and psi/100 known, the appropriate psig chart can be used to determine the correct pipe sizes. The velocity must always be maintained below 4000 fpm. 2) For metric conversion, use the following: cfm × 28.32 = L/min; Pressure drop (psi) × 6.89 = kPa; Velocity (fpm) × 5.08 = mm/s.

Figure 9-2 Flow Charts

indicates that noise may be a problem, a silencer must be installed. If a duplex, triplex, etc., each compressor should have an independent air intake.

Uncontrolled piping pulsations can harm inlet piping, damage the building structure, and affect compressor performance. Air flow into a reciprocating compressor pulsates because of the cyclic intake of air into the compressor cylinder. The variable pressure causes the air column in the pipe to vibrate, which creates a traveling wave in the pipe moving at the speed of sound. The inlet pipe itself vibrates at some natural frequency, depending on its length. If the air column vibrates at or near the same frequency as the length of pipe does, the system is said to be "resonant." Large pressures could result when this occurs. Resonant pipe lengths can be calculated by the

compressor manufacturers and the critical length given to the engineer. For example, with a 600 rpm compressor, avoid pipe lengths of 3.2 to 12.5 ft (1.0 to 3.8 m), 16.8 to 26.2 ft (5.1 to 8.0 m), and 32.3 to 41.5 ft (9.8 to 12.6 m). Also a surge chamber can be used to eliminate this problem.

The pressure loss of air through the intake piping should be held to a minimum. The velocity of intake air should be limited to about 1000 ft/min (5080 mm/s) to avoid noise problems, and friction loss should be limited to about 4 in. of water column (995.2 Pa). Inlet louver velocity should also be low enough to avoid drawing in rainwater. Depending on louver construction, this may be as low as 500 ft/min (2540 mm/s). Standard round duct charts can also be used for sizing. In general, if air requirements are less than 500 scfm (14 160 nL/min), the intake can be indoors.

It should be noted that the architect needs to be consulted concerning the aesthetic impact of exterior intakes. Provide an automatic drain on the line leading to the compressor, and pitch the intake piping to the drain point. If indoor air temperature is usually higher than 100°F (37.8°C), the intake should be outdoors.

Many different factors are involved in the selection of a compressor type:

1. Space limitations.

2. Noise limitations.

3. Compressor pressure capability.

4. Capacity.

5. Availability, cost, and quality of cooling water.

6. Need for oil-free air.

7. Electrical power limitations.

8. Costs—both initial and long-term.

The following reasons should be considered when in doubt about selecting a duplex or triplex, rather than a simplex, unit:

1. The cost of down time. The owner may request two or three 100%-capacity machines to eliminate the possibility of a shutdown.

2. Where a facility has a steady requirement (called a base load) and, in addition, there are substantial variations due to periodic or intermittent use, this may necessitate using two units sized at 75% of load or three units sized at 67% of load.

3. When electrical starting requirements would overload the system, two or three units starting at different times would eliminate the problem.

4. Where floor space for one large compressor and ancillary equipment is unavailable, using two or three units would allow more flexibility in arranging the units.

5. Where widely separated concentrations of heavy use exist, using two or three compressors, or possibly two sets of compressors, is a good idea.

Experience has shown that a properly sized, constantly working compressor usually requires less maintenance than one that runs intermittently. If multiple compressors are utilized, an alternator is required to alternate the load evenly among the units to properly balance the wear on the equipment.

Most of the heat produced by a compressor is rejected through the various cooling systems into the space where the compressor is located. This information must be relayed to the HVAC systems engineer so space conditioning can be considered. Good ventilation is mandatory in the area where the compressor is installed.

Selection of the proper type of compressor foundation and mounting is based on the lowest frequency and magnitude of pump vibration and load bearing requirement of the slab on which the compressor rests. Metal, rubber, coils, and spring type materials are available for use as isolators. The isolators' manufacturers should be consulted to confirm the proper type for the purpose and conditions expected.

Vibration isolation is achieved by locating properly selected resilient devices between the pump base and the building structure. This is accomplished by placing isolators between the pump and the floor, flexible connections on all piping from the compressor, and spring type hangers on the piping around the compressor for a distance of about 20 ft (6.1 m).

If the compressor is to be installed in a highly active seismic zone, restraints will be required to prevent equipment movement or damage to the piping system. Also, proper restraints will be required on the hangers supporting the piping system. Refer to the *Data Book* chapter, "Seismic Protection of Plumbing Equipment."

REMOVAL OF CONDENSATE

Moisture will be removed from the system at the compressor, dryer, and receiver. Drain valves should also be provided at low points throughout the piping system for blow-down and condensate removal after startup. Condensate should be discharged to a local hub or floor drain with an air gap provided between the discharge and the drain. This condensate may contain oil from the compressor, which should be discharged to the appropriate waste disposal system. Alternate lubricants that are biodegradable can be used in the compressor. Coordinate with the owner the proper disposal location and obtain permits where required.

REFERENCES

1. Compressed air data. *Compressed Air Magazine.*

2. *Compressed air handbook.* McGraw-Hill.

3. Compressed Gas Association. *Compressed air and gas handbook.* 4th ed.

4. Frankel, M. 1986. Compressed air design for industrial plants. *Plumbing Engineer* Sept.-Oct.

5. Frankel, M. 1996. *Facility piping systems handbook.* New York: McGraw-Hill.

6. Ingersoll-Rand. *Compressed air fundamentals.*

10 Site Utility Systems

INTRODUCTION

This chapter discusses the components and design of building services for all plumbing systems and their installation from the building wall to their connection to a source. Such connections could be to a public water supply or main, or with regard to drainage, to any ultimate point of disposal, which could include a public sewer, retention basin, or other method, as appropriate. Systems discussed include:

1. Potable water supply.

2. Fire protection water supply.

3. Sanitary sewer.

4. Storm water sewer.

5. Natural gas service.

Other methods of supply, such as wells and surface water, are outside the scope of this chapter.

PRELIMINARY INFORMATION FOR ALL SYSTEMS

The following general information shall be obtained for all systems on each project. Information for specific items are discussed under the individual systems.

1. Obtain an architectural site plan showing the location of the building on the site. Part of the site plan should be a location plan of the surrounding area. Also included should be the block and lot number, building address, building classification, and building height. There is a big difference between the actual height and the legal height. Both dimensions are necessary to determine fire protection requirements. Other information includes the location of existing buildings and any natural interferences, such as boulders and trees not being removed.

2. Obtain an existing utility site plan from the various purveyors or suppliers if the utilities are not shown on the architectural site plan. An investigation should be conducted to ensure availability of all of the services that are required.

3. For your reference create a contact sheet showing all of the building and plumbing subcode officials, fire marshal, fire subcode officials, and every other person or department necessary for development, design, and approval of plumbing systems. One of the most important items for the record is the utility information, such as water pressure, gas information, sanitary sewer disposal information, and storm water sewer and disposal information.

4. Make certain that north is clearly and consistently indicated on all drawings.

5. If the project is an alteration, obtain all available existing plans.

6. Conduct a through code search to find all codes applicable to the project, including the requirements for grease traps and storm water management systems.

7. Obtain from the plumbing and other subcode officials all of the submittal and approval requirements for plans and other contract documents prepared for the project.

8. Obtain requirements for fire protection systems from the fire department, fire marshal, and insurance carrier.

9. Obtain existing and finished grades on a topographical plan, as well as temporary or intermediate used grades for any purpose.

10. Obtain soil boring information, including ground water level.

Typical general site notes apply only to the site. They are intended to be a general series of notes and some may not apply to a specific project. Typical general site notes are given in Appendix 10-A.

DOMESTIC WATER SERVICE

Introduction

The domestic water system provides water suitable for human consumption to all fixtures and equipment throughout a facility. The domestic water building service conveys water from a public utility or other source into a facility for further distribution.

Codes and Standards

There are various codes applicable to domestic water services. It is recommended that you check with your local or state authorities to determine which codes apply in your area. Water purveyors may also have regulations that must be complied with.

General

The single most important piece of information concerning the water service connecting to a public water supply is the calculation of the water pressure available at the entrance into the building. It is based on this that a decision regarding the necessity for a pressure boosting system is made.

The purpose of the following discussion is to define the various components of the service and all the relevant criteria necessary to calculate the available pressure.

We start with the public water main. The water pressure in this main is called the "static," or "actual," pressure. From this actual pressure, the pressure losses through all the installed components are deducted. In addition, the difference in height between the water main and the building entrance (or point of connection to the interior distribution system) is either added or deducted. After all the service losses due to connected equipment or devices have been subtracted, the result is the available pressure.

General System Requirements

The first step in determining general system requirements is to find the water purveyor or utility company providing water to the site.

Next, calculate the preliminary (or final, if possible) maximum instantaneous water service requirements, in gallons per minute (gpm) (L/min). This is done from a preliminary (or final, if available) fixture count; an additional 10% is added as an allowance for cooling tower fill, boiler fill, and other miscellaneous uses of water in addition to the domestic use. For specialized facilities, add a flow rate obtained from the owner for additional processes and equipment that may use potable water. In order to calculate the maximum probable gpm, proceed as follows:

1. Count all the fixtures to be installed in the facility by fixture type.

2. Based on each type of fixture, find the water fixture unit value (wfu) for each. Refer to Table 10-1 for wfu values for each type of fixture.

3. Add all facility wfus together to calculate the total water load in wfus.

4. Refer to Figure 10-1 to convert wfu to the maximum probable gpm.

Once this is accomplished, a formal letter to the utility should be written to obtain the following information for your files. The importance of this cannot be overemphasized. The following should be requested:

1. A site plan from the utility company showing all water mains adjacent to the site.

2. Other information appearing in a typical water utility letter. Such a letter is provided in Appendix 10-B.

Once the utility company has answered the utility letter and provided most of the information requested and a site plan showing the location and size of the main and the location of the building on the site has been provided, the information obtained can be used to determine the following major design items:

1. Based on a preliminary assessment of available pressure inside the building wall, a decision regarding the method to use to increase water pressure in the facility, if required, can be made. The general space requirements for the necessary pumps and tanks inside the building or water tanks outside on the site shall be determined.

2. Using a complete fixture count, the maximum water supply flow rate can be calculated.

3. The run into the building should be determined and the meter assembly should be selected and located.

4. A typical domestic water service and all generally installed devices can now be discussed in detail. Included will be a description of the various required information, installed components, and necessary design criteria.

Typical Domestic Water Building Service

Service components and design considerations

Static and residual water pressure A hydrant flow test is the most often used method to determine static and residual water pressure. This test consists of choosing the two adjacent fire hydrants closest to the site where the project is located and taking three separate pressure readings, two with water flowing through a hydrant. For a typical test arrangement and nomenclature, refer to Figure 10-2.

The first pressure reading is obtained from a pressure gauge connected to one hydrant (hydrant A) with no water flowing out of either hydrant. This is called the "static pressure" because there is no flow through the test hydrant. The second reading then involves both hydrants. The hydrant with the pressure gauge attached (hydrant A) remains unchanged. The second hydrant (hydrant B) is now opened and a velocity pressure reading is taken using a pitot tube held directly in the water stream. A pitot tube is illustrated in Figure 10-3, and the method of taking the reading is illustrated in Figure 10-4. At the same time, another reading is taken from the first hydrant (hydrant A) while the second hydrant (hydrant B) is flowing water. The actual flow rate must be known for this test to be meaningful. This is calculated by converting the velocity pressure read from the pitot gauge into

Table 10-1 Water Fixture Unit Values Assigned to Fixtures

Fixture	Occupancy	Type of Supply Control	Water Fixture Units
Bathroom group	Private	Flush tank	3.6
Bathroom group	Private	Flush valve	8.0
Bathtub	Private	Faucet	1.4
Bathtub	Public	Faucet	4.0
Bidet	Private	Faucet	2.0
Combination fixture	Private	Faucet	3.0
Dishwashing machine	Private	Automatic	1.4
Drinking fountain	Offices, etc.	3/8-in. valve	0.25
Kitchen sink	Private	Faucet	1.4
Kitchen sink	Hotel, restaurant	Faucet	4.0
Laundry trays (1–3)	Private	Faucet	1.4
Lavatory	Private	Faucet	1.0
Lavatory	Public	Faucet	2.0
Service sink	Offices, etc.	Faucet	3.0
Shower head	Public	Mixing valve	4.0
Shower head	Private	Mixing valve	1.4
Urinal	Public	1-in. flush valve	10.0
Urinal	Public	¾-in. flush valve	5.0
Urinal	Public	Flush tank	3.0
Washing machine (8 lb)	Private	Automatic	1.4
Washing machine (8 lb)	Public	Automatic	3.0
Washing machine (15 lb)	Public	Automatic	4.0
Water closet	Private	Flush valve	6.0
Water closet	Private	Flush tank	2.2
Water closet	Public	Flush valve	10.0
Water closet	Public	Flush valve	5.0
Water closet	Public or private	Flushometer tank	2.0

Notes:

1. For fixtures not listed, loads should be assumed by comparing to listed fixtures that use water in similar quantities and at similar rates.

2. For SI conversion, 1 in. = 25.4 mm.

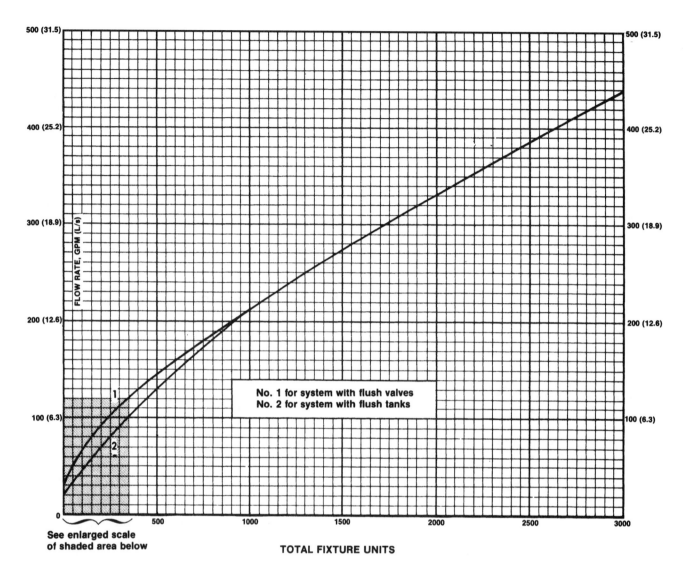

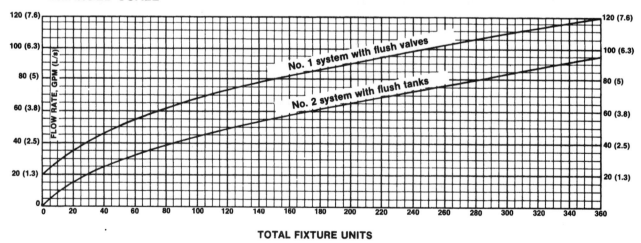

Figure 10-1 Conversion of Fixture Units to GPM

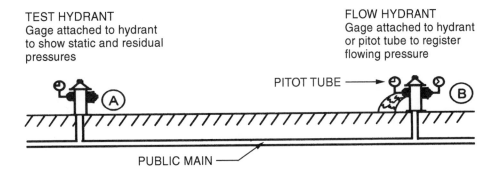

Figure 10-2   Hydrant Flow Test Arrangement

Source: Reprinted with permission from NFPA 13. This reprinted material is not the complete and official position of the NFPA on the subject, which is represented only by the standard in its entirety.

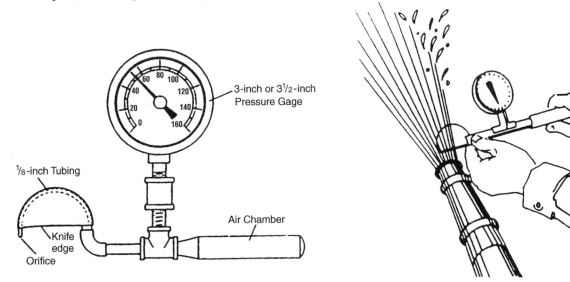

Figure 10-3   Pitot Tube with Gage and Air Chamber

Figure 10-4   Obtaining Nozzle Pressure with a Pitot Tube

gpm by referring to a typical relative discharge curve, such as that illustrated in Figure 10-5. For fire hydrants use the curve labeled "A" for "2½ open hydrant butt."

The time of the year and time of day the test is taken are conditions that affect the flow test data. There are seasonal variations, such as occurs in the summer, when the flow is generally regarded as being greater than it is at other times of the year in generally residential areas. The time of day also often accounts for large differences of flow, leading to lower residual pressures. Consult with the water utility company to decide if these items are important in determining the actual pressure available to the project.

The static and residual pressure and the flow rate represent only two pieces of information. With these two points known, it is now possible to determine the pressure available at any flow rate. This is important since the flow rate for the project under design will almost certainly be less than the flow rate at which the hydrant flow test was conducted. The method used is to plot these two points on hydraulic graph paper. The vertical axis has the pressure, in psi, and the horizontal axis has the flow rate, any one scale of which can be selected for the flow rate established. By connecting the two points on the graph and using care to use the proper gpm scale, any other point on the line will give the residual pres-

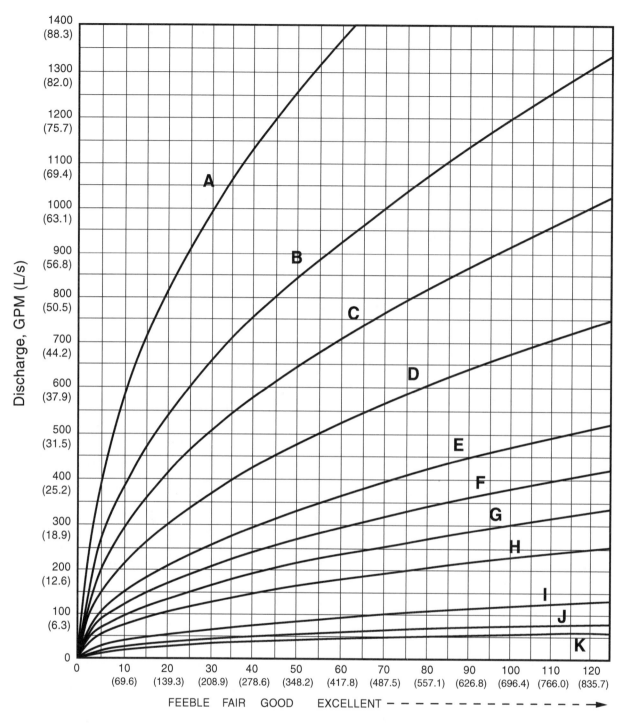

A – 2½" open hydrant butt   E – 1¼" smooth nozzle   I – ¾" smooth nozzle
B – 2" smooth nozzle   F – 2½" hose with 1⅛" smooth nozzle   J – ½" smooth nozzle
C – 1¾" smooth nozzle   G – 1" smooth nozzle   K – ½" sprinkler head
D – 1½" smooth nozzle   H – ⅞" smooth nozzle

Figure 10-5   Relative Discharge Curves

Source: *Chemical Engineers' Handbook*. McGraw-Hill.

sure if the flow rate desired is plotted on the line drawn.

Pressure loss and installation of taps A "tap" is the connection into a water main. The connection for a private residence or other building that does not require a "major" service is illustrated in Figure 10-6. This type of service should be limited to approximately 2 in. size and smaller. Typical large main wet tap (a connection under pressure) excavation dimensions are given in Figure 10-7. There are other methods of wet tapping into a main and the dimensions are approximately the same.

The pressure lost through taps shall be obtained from the specific manufacturer.

Pressure lost through valves and fittings This information is available from standard engineering texts. Because the size of the service could be large, it is recommended that all valves and fittings be individually counted and calculated rather than adding a set amount common for the distribution network inside a building. The final calculation will result in an equivalent number of feet run of pipe.

Total pressure loss in the piping run The measured distance is from the main to the point of connection with the water distribution network inside the building. To the measured distance, add the equivalent number of feet run of pipe from pressure lost through all valves, fittings, and devices installed in the building service. Using the maximum probable gpm flow and equivalent number of feet run of pipe, the velocity and friction loss for the entire service is obtained from standard engineering texts such as *Cameron's Hydraulic Data*.

Backflow preventers (BFP) The water utility company is responsible for protecting the public water supply from any possibility of contamination by backflow resulting from pollutants and contaminants. The most common reason for the utility company to require a BFP is the potential backflow from a facility that uses or produces any pollutant and contaminant. These facilities are separated into three general categories: low, moderate, and severe hazard. The facility category designated by the local authorities will mandate the type of BFP that shall be used. Another consideration is the presence of a

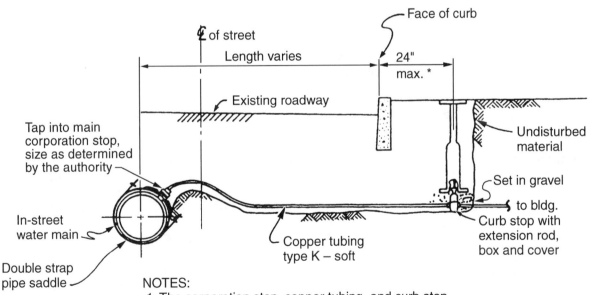

Figure 10-6 Service Connection Schematic

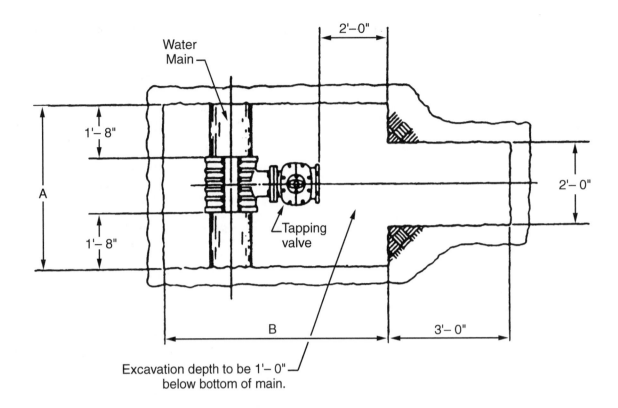

MINIMUM EXCAVATION DIMENSIONS

Header Size	A	B
3" thru 8"	5'– 0"	5'– 6"
10" thru 12"	5'– 6"	6'– 0"
14" thru 24"	6'– 0"	7'– 0"

Figure 10-7   Large Wet Tap Excavation Dimensions

close supply of unpure water (such as a stream) that could be used by a fire department to supply water that will be pumped into a building to fight a fire. This creates a potential source of contaminated water that could find its way back into a public main due to the pressure of the fire apparatus pumper.

The facility rating or classification should be made only after consulting with the proper authorities. The categories mentioned cannot list every circumstance or facility type. Judgment must be used in the final selection. The following are often used categories based on the use, toxicity, nature, and availability of contaminants:

1. *Low (minor) hazard.* Private homes, commercial establishments without complex plumbing or fire protection systems.

2. *Moderate (medium) hazard.* Commercial buildings and establishments, fire protection storage tanks and mains with no additives and facilities that discharge water at higher than normal temperature. The fire protection system will have only stagnant water present in the pipe.

3. *Severe (high) hazard.* Any facility that uses chemicals considered toxic or has the potential for discharge of toxic waste. Typical facilities are hospitals; laboratories; water or sewage treatment plants; and facilities involving chemical processing or manufacturing, pharmaceutical processing and manufacturing, food processing or manufacturing, or industrial manufacturing or processing.

For hazardous locations, a reduced pressure zone (RPZ) BFP will be required near the property line at the connection to the public main or immediately inside a building. Figure 10-8 illustrates an RPZ BFP installed in an exterior aboveground enclosure. For lesser hazards, a double-check valve (DCV) is often acceptable. A double-check valve in a below ground pit is illustrated in Figure 10-9. It is important to allow for adequate drainage from the RPZ discharge. The flow rate of discharge from an RPZ BFP is given in Table 10-2. There is no discharge from a DCV.

Table 10-2   Discharge from a Typical RPZ BFP

BFP Size (in.)	Drainage Required (gpm)
¾ – 1	200
1¼ – 2	300
2½ – 3	450
4 – 6	750
8 – 10	1100

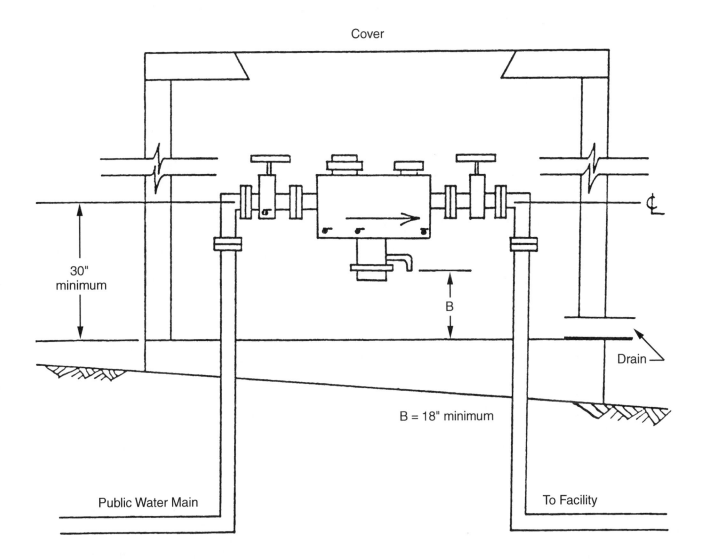

Figure 10-8   Aboveground Reduced Pressure Zone Backflow Preventer

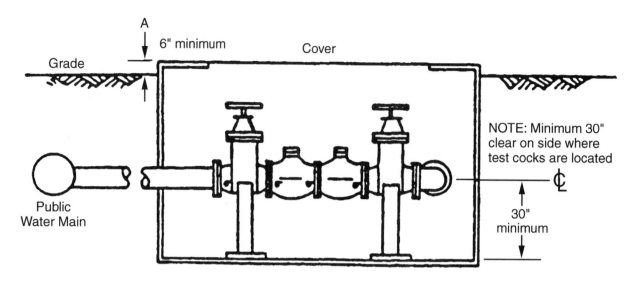

Figure 10-9   Double-Check Valve Installed in a Pit

A typical pressure loss through an RPZ BFP is 10 psi. A typical pressure loss through a DCV BFP is 5 psi. Since there are many types of BFP, check with the manufacturer regarding the exact amount of discharge and pressure loss. They vary with size. Tests at the independent Foundation for Cross-Connection Control and Hydraulic Research at the University of Southern California have established that various manufacturers do not represent the pressure losses of their BFPs correctly. It would be appropriate to request the flow curves produced at the foundation for the most accurate method of comparing various devices.

Strainer losses Strainers are commonly used, especially for water with known particulate problems. Losses through different strainer types should be obtained from the manufacturer for greatest accuracy.

Meter losses Water meters are usually selected by the water utility company, which very often will also provide the installation. Pressure losses through typical meters conforming to AWWA standards are given in ASPE *Data Book*, Volume 2, Chapter 5, "Cold Water Systems." Consult manufacturers for exact losses.

Difference in elevation The difference in elevation from the centerline of the public water main to the centerline of the service inside the building where it connects to the distribution network is an important item to consider. This distance shall be added or subtracted from the actual pressure (depending on whether it is higher or lower than the point of connection) along with all of the above items.

A calculation sheet showing all the data used to calculate the final water service pressure should be prepared to provide a permanent record for your files.

FIRE PROTECTION WATER SUPPLY

Introduction

The fire protection building service provides the water necessary for fire suppression purposes inside a building, such as sprinkler and fire standpipe systems. This service could be combined with the domestic water supply.

The fire protection building service continues from a connection with a source of water to a point inside a building where there is a connection to the fire suppression piping network. The source is usually a public water main, but could also include other sources. The building service includes water storage tanks, backflow preventers, meters, valves, hydrants, and other devices that may be required based on the nature of the water service, insurance carrier requirements, and local regulations. This section is not intended to cover a complete private fire service main, which is outside the scope of this chapter.

Codes and Standards

The most often used standard for the design of private fire protection water mains is NFPA-24, *Installation of Private Service Mains.* If Factory Mutual is the fire insurance carrier, Factory Mutual Loss Prevention Data Sheet 3-10, *Installation of Private Fire Mains,* generally must be conformed with.

Building Water Supply

If the water supply to a building is a combined service, that is both domestic and fire service, the main shall be considered a fire service until the domestic water connection is made. Typical connections to a public water main are illustrated in Figure 10-10. If the source is a well, an aquifer performance analysis and investigation of the history of adjacent wells should be made. For many facilities where loss of water would be an extreme hardship, such as hospitals, multiple water supplies from two separate public mains is a very desirable feature. This allows water to be supplied to the facility from either of two directions. If multiple connections are made to a single main, a sectionalizing valve installed in the source main somewhere between the two connections may be required.

Contamination of the public water supply is a prime concern of the water company that supplies water to the project. Determination of the

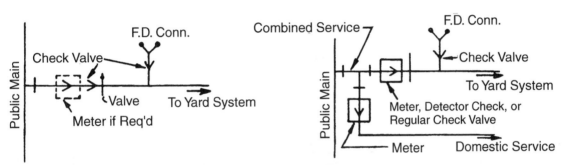

PUBLIC WATER CONNECTIONS

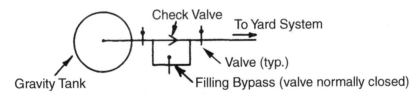

GRAVITY TANK CONNECTION

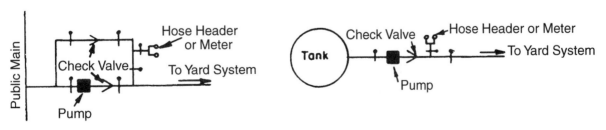

BOOSTER PUMP CONNECTION **FIRE PUMP AND TANK**

Figure 10-10 Connections to a Public Water Main

acceptable device for preventing contamination of the fire protection water supply will be made by either the health department, the water purveyor, or the plumbing subcode official. The two most often used are the double-check valve (DCV) assembly and a reduced pressure zone back flow preventer (RPZ BFP). These devices were discussed in the domestic water supply section. See Figures 10-8 and 10-9.

The mains shall be buried below the frost line. A generalized map of the United States is given in Figure 10-11 to aid in the determination of that depth. Local authorities shall be contacted for conditions at the project site.

In many cases, it is not possible to supply the required flow rate or volume of water for firefighting purposes from the public supply. For these situations, the use of a water storage tank is called for. Such tanks can be either elevated or installed on the ground. The design of these tanks

is outside the scope of this chapter. Connections from the water supply to a storage tank shall terminate 1 ft. 0 in. over the overflow level. The overflow shall be two pipe sizes larger than the water supply pipe size. Various connections from the storage tanks are shown in Figure 10-12.

Ancillary Devices

Fire hydrants Fire hydrants are directly connected to the site main or the building service. They shall be installed adjacent to roadways to allow easy connection of fire department apparatus to them. If reasonable, they shall be located on all sides of the building being protected. A desired separation from the building wall is 50 ft 0 in. to provide some protection from building wall collapses. Recommended separation between hydrants is 300 ft 0 in. at a building location. Hydrants located near a road shall be protected by guard posts. It is good practice to provide a

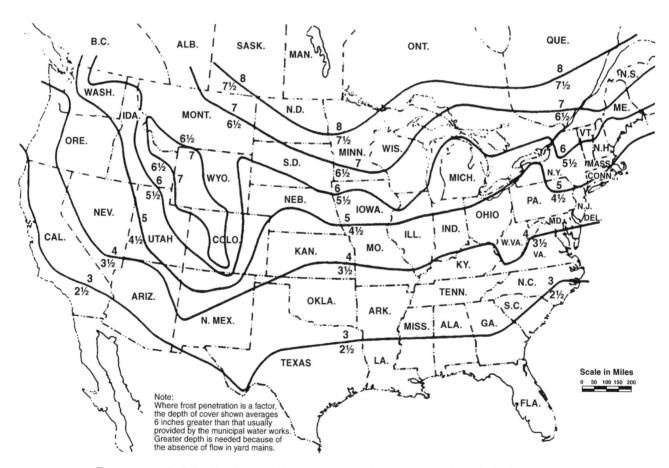

Recommended depth of cover (feet) above underground mains. (1 ft. = 0.3 m)

Figure 10-11   Frost Depth Map of the Continental United States

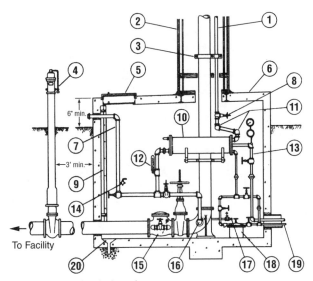

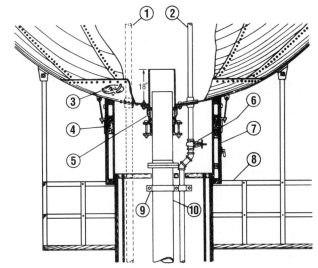

1. Hot water circulating pipe
2. Frostproof casing
3. Pipe clamps. Locate at about 25 ft (7.6 m) intervals. Loose fit around hot water circulating pipe.
4. Indicator-post valve. May be replaced with indicating-type valve in pit on yard side of check valve if space is not available for indicator post.
5. Hatch cover
6. Valve pit
7. Drain pipe
8. OS&Y gate valve
9. Ladder
10. Tank heater with relief valve set at 120 psi (825 kPa)
11. Four-elbow swing joint
12. Thermometer
13. Steam supply pipe
14. Drain cock, 1/2 in. (13 mm)
15. Approved check valve with bypass
16. Cold water circulating pipe
17. Pipe to mercury gauge
18. Steam trap
19. Condensate return
20. Valve-pit drain

Valve pit and pipe connections at base of tank on independent tower. Tank has a pipe riser and steam-heated gravity circulating heating system.

1. Inside brass overflow pipe, if used
2. Hot water circulating pipe
3. Handhole for removing sludge
4. Frostproof casing when required
5. Expansion joint
6. Approved OS&Y gate valve
7. Door in frostproof casing
8. Walkway
9. Brace for hot water circulating pipe
10. Pipe riser

Details of pipe connections to bottom of steel gravity tank with pipe riser.

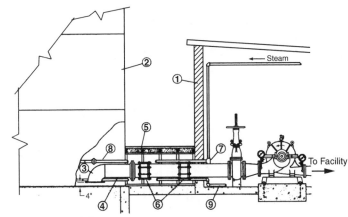

1. Pump room
2. Approved aboveground suction tank
3. Entrance elbow with vortex plate or flange 4 in. (102 mm) above bottom of tank
4. Suction pipe
5. Frostproof casing, about 4 ft (1.2 m) high and 4 ft (1.2 m) wide
6. Flexible couplings
7. Steam trap on steam supply
8. Heating coil inside tank
9. Condensate return line to steam trap

Discharge pipe connected to side of suction tank.

Figure 10-12   Typical Connections to Water Storage Tanks

shut-off valve on the branch line to a hydrant to allow easy repair without having to shut down the main or the service. A detail of a typical hydrant is given in Figure 10-13.

Guard posts Guard posts may be necessary to protect any device that is installed above grade near roads. A typical guard post is illustrated in Figure 10-14.

Post indicator valve (PIV) A post indicator valve is used only to shut off the supply of water, never to control the flow. It is used as a section valve on water mains and also on building services. Since it is critical for emergency personnel to be certain that any control valve is open or closed, an indicator is positioned above grade with a window or some other method of allowing easy observation of the valve position. A typical post indicator valve is illustrated in Figure 10-15.

Joint restrainers When run in a straight line, properly specified joints will provide a leakproof installation. When there is any change in direction of the pipe, pressure is exerted by the flowing water on the fitting. The joints may not provide sufficient resistance to the force exerted by the pressure of the water against the fitting. In order to prevent joint failure due to the pressure exerted, most pipe joints must be restrained in some manner.

Mechanical and push-on joints are sealed by a rubber type gasket compressed in a space be-

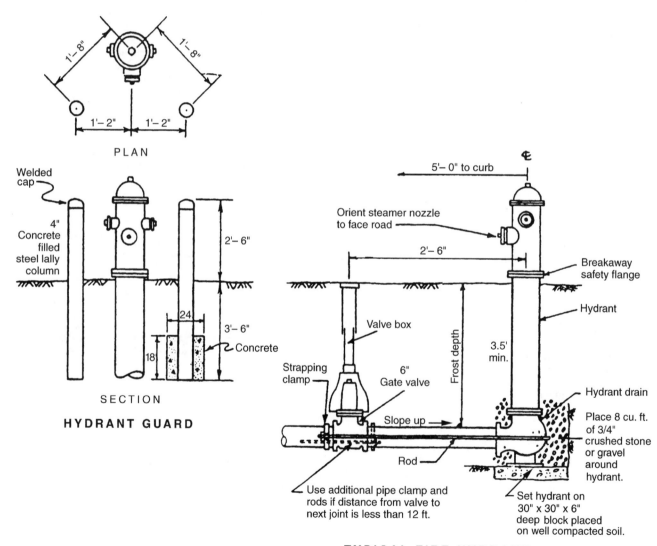

Figure 10-13   Typical Fire Hydrant

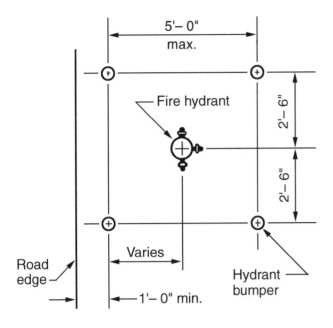

**BUMPER ARRANGEMENT
FOR HYDRANTS AND P.I.V.**

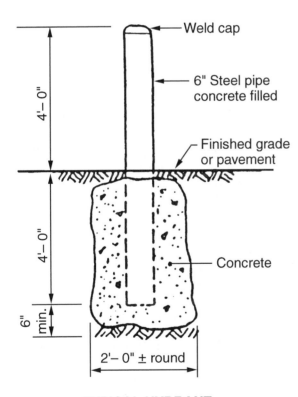

**TYPICAL HYDRANT
BUMPER DETAIL**

Figure 10-14   Typical Guard Post

tween the spigot end of the pipe and the bell. These joints will not resist the pressure of the water on the joint. The method of restraint used is external clamps and rods. Friction clamps are bolted around the pipe on both sides of the joint or joints. These clamps engage steel tension rods, sometimes called "tie rods," across the joint, preventing it from separating. This will combine the resistance of these joints to prevent separation. Calculations are necessary to determine the actual number of joints to be restrained.

Another method of restraint used is integrally cast glands for mechanical joint pipe with internally locked, grooved and keyed, push-on joints. This type of restraint is usually recommended only for the repair of existing systems.

The most common method of restraint is to use a block of concrete contacting the fitting and poured against undisturbed soil. The size of the block varies with the water pressure (the higher the pressure, the larger the block), the pipe size (the larger the pipe, the larger the block), and the bearing pressure of the soil (the less the soil bearing pressure, the larger the block). A typical detail of thrust block dimensions is given in Figure 10-16. Table 10-3 gives values for soil bearing loads. The main problems with this method are that (1) on many project sites there is often no undisturbed soil against which to base the thrust block and (2) the size of the concrete block prevents piping from being placed adjacent to the run of pipe being protected.

Table 10-3   Soil Bearing Loads

Soil	Bearing Load (lb/ft^2)
Muck	0
Soft clay	1000
Silt	1500
Sandy silt	3000
Sand	4000
Sandy clay	6000
Hard clay	9000

Sizing the Fire Protection Water Service

General When all of the information required for design has been obtained for the domestic water system, the fire marshal, the fire protec-

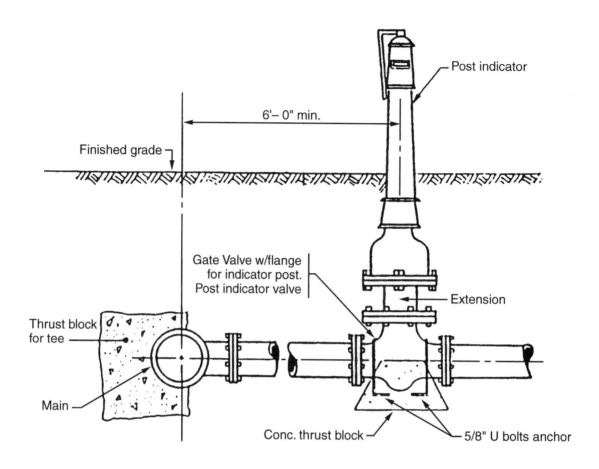

Figure 10-15 Typical Post Indicator Valve

tion subcode official, and the insurance company shall be contacted for their installation requirements.

What constitutes an adequate water supply has generated much discussion over time. There are many factors that, when all are considered, will result in an adequate water supply. The water supply should be capable of supplying the largest demand, which is usually the sprinkler or standpipe system, and expected hose flow under reasonably adverse conditions. If other factors, such as building occupancy, yard storage, external structures that must be protected, exposure protection, and a catastrophic hose demand, are considered, they will all add to the flow rate.

Demand flow rate The demand flow rate used to size the building service for the facility under design usually is based on several factors. The first is the gpm based on the calculated flow rate for the sprinkler system, which is based on hy-

draulic calculations. The second is the flow of water for additional hose streams used by the fire department to fight the fire.

The following figures are presented for preliminary discussion purposes only. They are not to be used for actual design, which should only be made on a specific project basis after consulting with the fire marshal, insurance carrier representative and fire code official.

The fire department hose streams depend on the occupancy hazard, which can be:

1. Light and ordinary hazard—500 gpm (1900 L/min).

2. Extra hazard, Group 1—750 gpm (2900 L/min).

3. Extra hazard, Group 2—1000 gpm (3800 L/min).

4. High-piled storage—as required by insurance company.

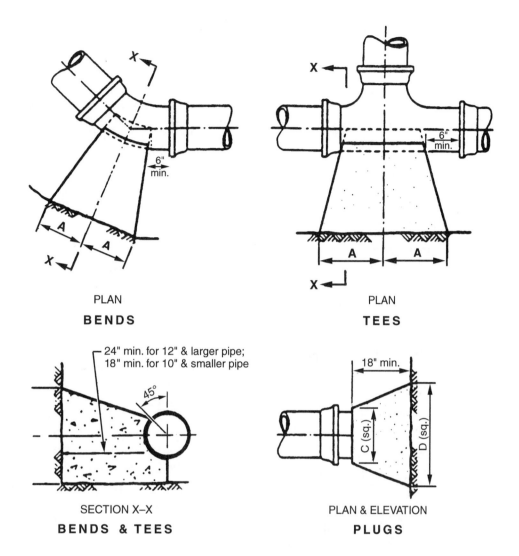

PLAN
BENDS

PLAN
TEES

SECTION X–X
BENDS & TEES

PLAN & ELEVATION
PLUGS

Thrust Block Dimensions

Type	Size (in.)	1/4 Bends		1/8 Bends		1/16 Bends		Tees		Plugs	
		A (in.)	B (in.)	A (in.)	B (in.)	A (in.)	B (in.)	A (in.)	B (in.)	C (in.)	D (in.)
Type I 4000 PSF Soil	6	8	10	6	8	3	8	8	8	10	15
	8	12	12	8	10	5	9	9	12	12	20
	10	16	14	10	12	6	10	11	14	14	25
	12	19	16	12	14	8	11	14	16	16	30
	14	23	18	14	16	10	12	16	18	18	34
	16	26	20	16	18	11	13	18	20	20	38
Type II 2000 PSF Soil	6	16	10	9	10	6	8	10	12	10	21
	8	22	13	12	13	8	10	13	16	12	29
	10	26	17	14	17	10	13	16	20	14	36
	12	29	21	16	21	11	16	18	24	16	41
	14	35	24	19	24	12	20	22	27	18	48
	16	38	27	21	27	12	24	24	30	20	54

Note: Based on 100 psi static pressure plus AWWA water hammer. All bearing surfaces to be carried to undisturbed ground.

Figure 10-16   Thrust Block Installation

5. The hose demand shall be increased by 25% for the following conditions:

   A. Combustible construction.

   B. Possible delay in response by public fire department.

   C. Minimum protection less than recommended by insurance company requirements.

   D. Limited access to remote interior sections.

6. Additional requirements for monitors. Allow 500 gpm for each monitor.

For the design of a larger site consisting of multiple buildings, typical fire protection flow rate requirements are given in Table 10-4.

Table 10-4 Typical Fire Protection Flow Rate Requirements

Land Use	GPM range	Average GPM
Single-family residential	500 – 2000	750
Multifamily residential	1500 – 3000	2000
Commercial	2500 – 5000	3000
Industrial	3500 – 10,000	
Central building district	2500 – 15,000	3000

Tank capacity If the gravity tank is the sole source of water, the tank should be capable of being filled in 8 hours. In evaluation of the total capacity consideration should be given to the following storage capacities, based on the categories appearing in NFPA 13, *Design of Sprinkler Systems*:

1. Light and ordinary hazard occupancies, Group 1—2 hours.

2. Ordinary hazard occupancies, Groups 2 and 3—3 hours.

3. Extra hazard occupancies—4 hours.

SANITARY SEWER

Introduction

The purpose of the sanitary house sewer is to convey all sanitary waste from a facility to a point of disposal, which is usually a public sewer.

General

The first step is to find the department or jurisdiction responsible for the approval, design, and installation of sanitary and storm water sewers. Once this is established, a formal letter should be written to obtain the following information for your files. A typical sewer letter is given in Appendix 10-B. In addition, the following information shall be obtained and the following questions asked:

1. The size, location and invert of all available sewers fronting the property.

2. Are the sewers sanitary, storm, or combined?

3. What is the material of these sewers?

4. If there are no available sewers, who is the authority having jurisdiction (AHJ) for a private disposal system (septic tank and field)? What codes and standards regulate the design and installation of the septic system?

5. Are street sewer connections preferred at spurs between manholes or shall a manhole be used for the connection? Are there standard details? Will these manholes be constructed by the plumbing contractor or the AHJ?

When the utility company has answered your letter and provided most of the information requested, the following work can be accomplished:

1. The run from the building to the sewer can be selected. If the invert elevations are not suitable, determine if a force main will be necessary.

2. The house sewer can be sized based on the fixture count and the slope of the sewer.

Sizing the Sanitary Sewer

The size of the sewer from the building to the property line is based on the applicable plumbing code requirements. If the house sewer extends beyond the property line in order to connect to a pubic sewer, the plumbing code may not apply. However, there may be other applicable codes in your area. A self-scouring velocity must be maintained in order to avoid the settling out of solids and the stopping of the pipe. Table 10-5 is provided to allow sizing at a minimum slope to maintain 2 to 2½ fps velocity. Figure 10-17 can be used to convert the sanitary drainage fixture units to gpm.

Table 10-5 Sewer Size Based on Velocity and Slope

Slopes of cast-iron, soil-pipe sanitary sewers required to obtain self-cleansing velocities of 2.0 and 2.5 fps (based on Manning's Formula with n = 0.012)

PIPE SIZE (in.)	VELOCITY (fps)	1/4 Full		1/2 Full		3/4 Full		Full	
		SLOPE (ft/ft)	FLOW (gpm)	SLOPE (ft/ft)	FLOW (gpm)	SLOPE (ft/ft)	FLOW (gpm)	SLOPE (ft/ft)	FLOW (gpm)
2.0	2.0	0.0313	4.67	0.0186	9.34	0.0148	14.09	0.0186	18.76
	2.5	0.0489	5.84	0.0291	11.67	0.0231	17.62	0.0291	23.45
3.0	2.0	0.0178	10.77	0.0107	21.46	0.0085	32.23	0.0107	42.91
	2.5	0.0278	13.47	0.0167	26.82	0.0133	40.29	0.0167	53.64
4.0	2.0	0.0122	19.03	0.0073	38.06	0.0058	57.01	0.0073	76.04
	2.5	0.0191	23.79	0.0114	47.58	0.0091	71.26	0.0114	95.05
5.0	2.0	0.0090	29.89	0.0054	59.79	0.0043	89.59	0.0054	119.49
	2.5	0.0141	37.37	0.0085	74.74	0.0067	111.99	0.0085	149.36
6.0	2.0	0.0071	43.18	0.0042	86.36	0.0034	129.54	0.0042	172.72
	2.5	0.0111	53.98	0.0066	107.95	0.0053	161.93	0.0066	215.90
8.0	2.0	0.0048	77.20	0.0029	154.32	0.0023	231.52	0.0029	308.64
	2.5	0.0075	96.50	0.0045	192.90	0.0036	289.40	0.0045	385.79
10.0	2.0	0.0036	120.92	0.0021	241.85	0.0017	362.77	0.0021	483.69
	2.5	0.0056	151.15	0.0033	302.31	0.0026	453.46	0.0033	604.61
12.0	2.0	0.0028	174.52	0.0017	349.03	0.0013	523.55	0.0017	698.07
	2.5	0.0044	218.15	0.0026	436.29	0.0021	654.44	0.0026	872.58
15.0	2.0	0.0021	275.42	0.0012	550.84	0.0010	826.26	0.0012	1101.68
	2.5	0.0032	344.28	0.0019	688.55	0.0015	1032.83	0.0019	1377.10

Table 10-5(M) Sewer Size Based on Velocity and Slope

Slopes of cast-iron, soil-pipe sanitary sewers required to obtain self-cleansing velocities of 0.6096 and 0.762 m/s (based on Manning's Formula with n = 0.012)

PIPE SIZE (mm)	VELOCITY (m/s)	1/4 Full		1/2 Full		3/4 Full		Full	
		SLOPE (m/m)	FLOW (L/s)	SLOPE (m/m)	FLOW (L/s)	SLOPE (m/m)	FLOW (L/s)	SLOPE (m/m)	FLOW (L/s)
50	0.6096	0.0313	0.295	0.0186	0.59	0.0148	0.89	0.0186	1.18
	0.762	0.0489	0.369	0.0291	0.74	0.0231	1.11	0.0291	1.48
75	0.6096	0.0178	0.68	0.0107	1.35	0.0085	2.03	0.0107	2.71
	0.762	0.0278	0.85	0.0167	1.69	0.0133	2.54	0.0167	3.38
100	0.6096	0.0122	1.2	0.0073	2.4	0.0058	3.6	0.0073	4.8
	0.762	0.0191	1.5	0.0114	3.0	0.0091	4.5	0.0114	6.0
125	0.6096	0.0090	1.89	0.0054	3.77	0.0043	5.65	0.0054	7.54
	0.762	0.0141	2.36	0.0085	4.72	0.0067	7.07	0.0085	9.42
150	0.6096	0.0071	2.72	0.0042	5.45	0.0034	8.17	0.0042	10.9
	0.762	0.0111	3.41	0.0066	6.81	0.0053	10.22	0.0066	13.62
200	0.6096	0.0048	4.87	0.0029	9.74	0.0023	14.61	0.0029	19.48
	0.762	0.0075	6.09	0.0045	12.17	0.0036	18.26	0.0045	24.34
250	0.6096	0.0036	7.63	0.0021	15.26	0.0017	22.89	0.0021	30.52
	0.762	0.0056	9.54	0.0033	19.08	0.0026	28.61	0.0033	38.15
300	0.6096	0.0026	11.01	0.0017	22.02	0.0013	33.04	0.0017	44.05
	0.762	0.0044	13.77	0.0026	27.53	0.0021	41.3	0.0026	55.06
380	0.6096	0.0021	17.38	0.0012	34.76	0.0010	52.14	0.0012	69.52
	0.762	0.0032	21.72	0.0019	43.45	0.0015	65.17	0.0019	86.9

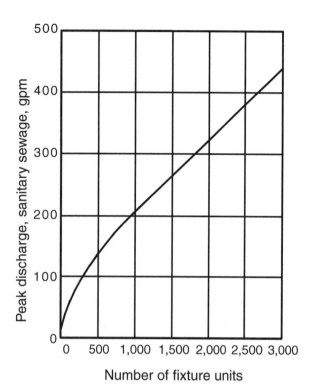

Figure 10-17 Fixture Unit Conversion to GPM

Sewer Components and Design Criteria

Public sewer availability The question of availability is a concern. It is up to the AHJ to determine whether the project shall connect to any particular sewer. This is a potential problem in rural areas, where considerable distances are necessary to connect to a sewer. A run by gravity is the preferred method, but this is costly for a long run and a larger size. A force main may be desirable, which is discussed later.

Trenching and bedding Bedding is the point of contact between the pipe and the earth. The type of bedding has an important influence on the load the pipe can support.

There is a difference between bedding for metallic pipe and that for plastic pipe because the trench walls help support the plastic pipe. A typical trench for plastic pipe is shown in Figure 10-18, and one for metallic pipe in Figure 10-19. The methods shown are for class "B" bedding,

as is suitable for the majority of piping buried underground. If there is a concern about the weight placed upon the buried pipe, other bedding methods that will increase the resistance of the pipe to be crushed can be used.

Typical sewer house connection A typical small house or building will connect to the sewer in a manner similar to that illustrated in Figure 10-20, where a spur is provided. A "spur" is a preinstalled fitting located at fixed distances along the length of a sewer line.

Drainage structures A drainage structure is any appurtenance built into a sewer run, including manholes, storm water inlets, and catch basins.

Manholes (MH) Manholes can be made of poured concrete, bricks, blocks, or precast sections. Precast manholes are the most widely used type. Manholes are installed for the following reasons:

1. At changes of direction of the sewer.

2. For inspection and cleaning purposes.

3. At substantial changes of grade.

4. At changes of pipe size.

5. To make a connection to a public sewer for larger sewers.

The primary purpose of a manhole is to provide a smooth invert to allow pipes that join the main sewer to have an unimpeded entry to that sewer and to provide a smooth invert when pipes change size and pitch. In order to accomplish this, the bottom of the manhole is channeled smooth from the invert of all of the pipes entering the manhole. It is accepted practice to have the tops of the joining sewer pipes even, with the invert of the larger pipe lower than the smaller pipe. A detail of a typical precast manhole is given in Figure 10-21. Manhole construction requirements should be verified with the authority having jurisdiction.

If the depth from finished grade to the invert of the sewer is 3 ft 0 in. or less, a shallow manhole should be used. A shallow manhole is illustrated in Figure 10-22.

When there is a difference of more than approximately 2 in. to 2 ft 0 in., the falling water will cause the lower pipe to erode. When this is the case, a chute shall be created at the manhole bottom. If the difference in the inverts of the pipes is greater than 2 ft 0 in., a drop manhole should be installed, as shown in Figure 10-23.

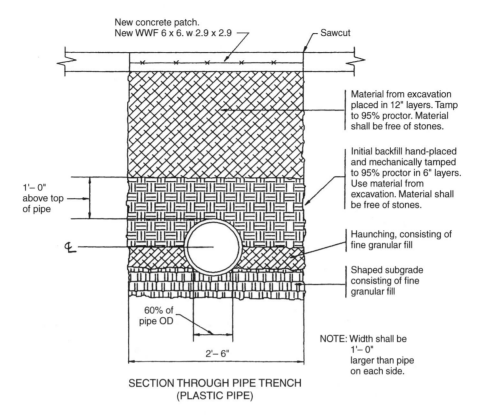

New concrete patch.
New WWF 6 x 6. w 2.9 x 2.9 — Sawcut

Material from excavation placed in 12" layers. Tamp to 95% proctor. Material shall be free of stones.

Initial backfill hand-placed and mechanically tamped to 95% proctor in 6" layers. Use material from excavation. Material shall be free of stones.

Haunching, consisting of fine granular fill

Shaped subgrade consisting of fine granular fill

1'– 0" above top of pipe

℄

60% of pipe OD

2'– 6"

NOTE: Width shall be 1'– 0" larger than pipe on each side.

SECTION THROUGH PIPE TRENCH
(PLASTIC PIPE)

Figure 10-18   Bedding for Plastic Pipe

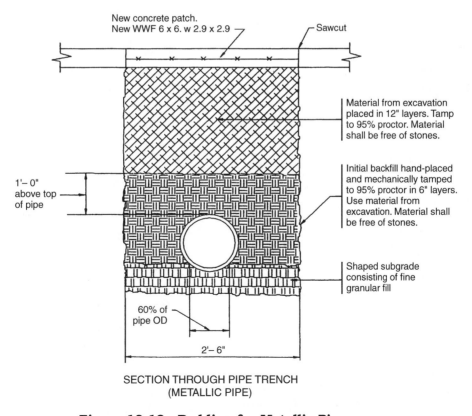

New concrete patch.
New WWF 6 x 6. w 2.9 x 2.9 — Sawcut

Material from excavation placed in 12" layers. Tamp to 95% proctor. Material shall be free of stones.

Initial backfill hand-placed and mechanically tamped to 95% proctor in 6" layers. Use material from excavation. Material shall be free of stones.

Shaped subgrade consisting of fine granular fill

1'– 0" above top of pipe

60% of pipe OD

2'– 6"

SECTION THROUGH PIPE TRENCH
(METALLIC PIPE)

Figure 10-19   Bedding for Metallic Pipe

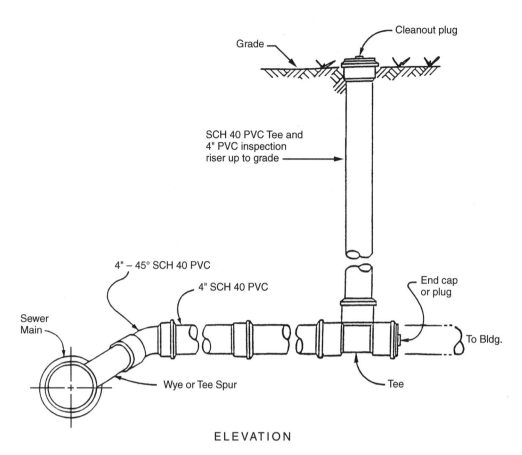

Figure 10-20   Typical House Sewer Connection

Other manhole accessories are manhole steps and standard manhole and watertight frames and covers. In some cases where the watertight manhole cover is required, there may not be an outlet for the air that accumulates in the manhole. Where this is a concern, a vent should be installed. Such an installation is illustrated in Figure 10-24.

For short runs of sewers into the main, cleanouts shall be provided on the site every 75 ft 0 in. or as dictated by code to allow for the rodding out of the line in the event of a stoppage. General manhole spacing and locations are given in Table 10-6.

Force Mains

There are situations where the difference in elevation between a sewer from a facility and the public sewer will not allow a gravity connection. In such a case, a pumped system is required. The discharge of the ejector pumps into the public sewer is called a "force main."

Sizing pumps and pits   The actual design of the ejector pumps and pits is outside the scope of this chapter. The design should conform to the standards of the authority having jurisdiction.

Force main sizing   With the pump gpm selected, the discharge head shall be calculated as follows:

1. Determine the difference in elevation from the bottom of the pit to the invert of the public main into which you will be discharging.

2. Calculate the friction loss through the discharge pipe (with two pumps running) and the friction loss through the valves and fittings.

3. Select the pipe size that minimizes the horsepower of the ejector pump.

Force main design considerations   The most commonly used method of connecting a force main into a gravity public sewer is illustrated in Figure 10-25. This method allows accumulated air to be discharged through the top of the connection.

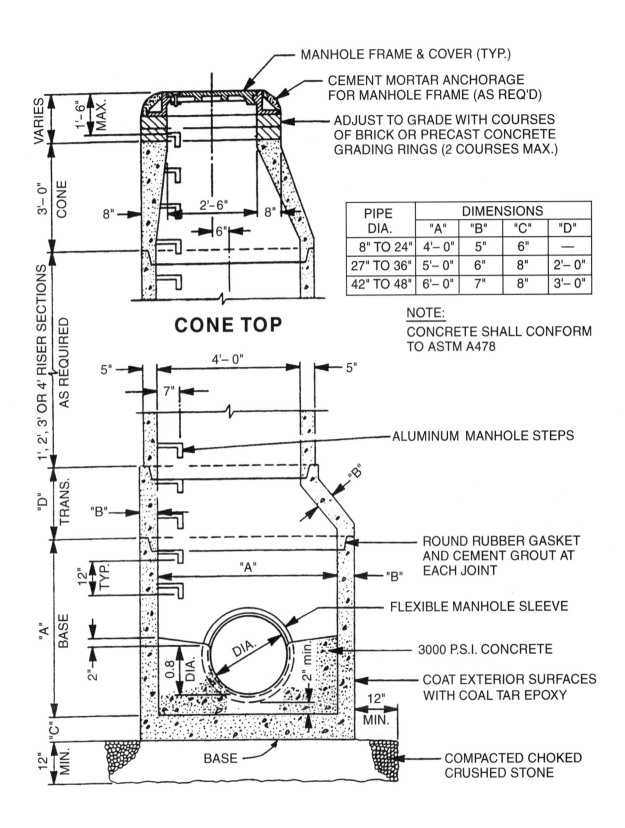

PIPE	DIMENSIONS			
DIA.	"A"	"B"	"C"	"D"
8" TO 24"	4'– 0"	5"	6"	—
27" TO 36"	5'– 0"	6"	8"	2'– 0"
42" TO 48"	6'– 0"	7"	8"	3'– 0"

NOTE:
CONCRETE SHALL CONFORM
TO ASTM A478

CONE TOP

MANHOLE FRAME & COVER (TYP.)

CEMENT MORTAR ANCHORAGE
FOR MANHOLE FRAME (AS REQ'D)

ADJUST TO GRADE WITH COURSES
OF BRICK OR PRECAST CONCRETE
GRADING RINGS (2 COURSES MAX.)

ALUMINUM MANHOLE STEPS

ROUND RUBBER GASKET
AND CEMENT GROUT AT
EACH JOINT

FLEXIBLE MANHOLE SLEEVE

3000 P.S.I. CONCRETE

COAT EXTERIOR SURFACES
WITH COAL TAR EPOXY

COMPACTED CHOKED
CRUSHED STONE

BASE

Figure 10-21   Typical Precast Manhole

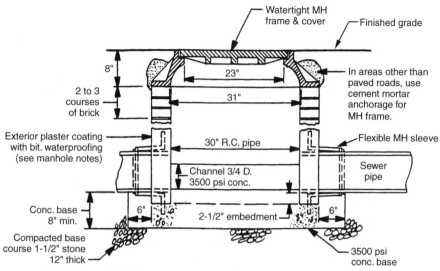

NOTES:
1. Shallow MH (circular) to be used at locations where distance from finished grade to pipe invert is 3'– 0" or less.
2. For depths of 3'– 0" and less, measured from the top of the pipe, contractor shall install ductile iron pipe, Class 52, under traffic areas.

Figure 10-22 Shallow Manhole

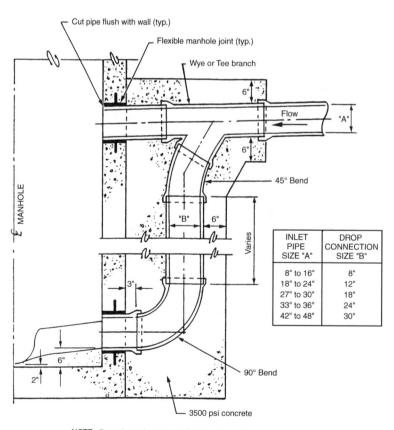

INLET PIPE SIZE "A"	DROP CONNECTION SIZE "B"
8" to 16"	8"
18" to 24"	12"
27" to 30"	18"
33" to 36"	24"
42" to 48"	30"

NOTE: Drop pipe to be used in all cases where difference between inlet invert and lowest outlet invert is 2 feet or greater.

Figure 10-23 Drop Manhole

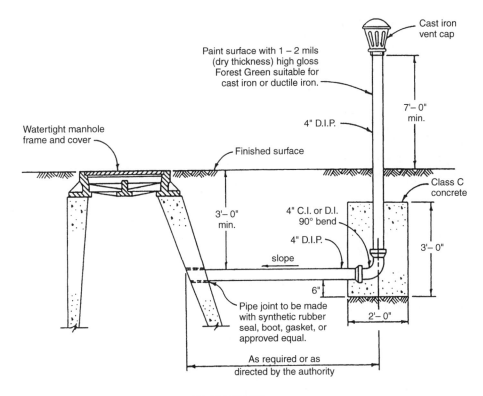

ELEVATION

Figure 10-24   Detail of Waterproof Manhole

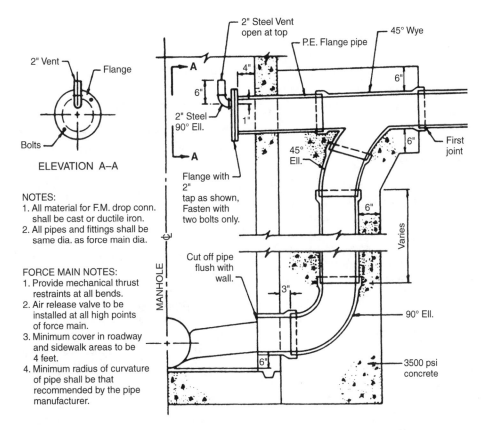

Figure 10-25   Detail of Force Main Connection to Public Sewer

Table 10-6   Manhole Spacing and Location of Pipe Sewers

A. Maximum Spacing of Manhole on Pipe Sewers

Pipe Sizes, in. (mm)	Recommended Max. Spacing, ft (m)	Absolute Max. Spacing, ft (m)
10 Dia. to 24 Dia. (254 to 610) Circular 14 H × 23 W (356 × 584) Horiz. Elliptical Pipe 23 H × 14 W (584 × 356) Vert. Elliptical Pipe	150 (45.7)	200 (61)
27 Dia. to 48 Dia. (686 to 1219) Circular 19 H × 30 W to 48 H × 76 W (483 × 762 to 1219 × 1930) Horiz. Elliptical Pipe 30 H × 19 W to 49 H × 32 W (962 × 483 to 1245 × 813) Vert. Elliptical Pipe	300 (91.4)	400 (121.9)
54 Dia. to 66 Dia. (1372 to 1676) Circular 53 H × 83 W to 68 H × 106 W (1346 × 2108 to 1727 × 2692) Horiz. Elliptical Pipe 53 H × 34 W to 68 H × 43 W (1346 × 864 to 1727 × 1092) Vert. Elliptical Pipe	400 (121.9)	500 (152.4)
72 Dia. (1829) and larger Circular 72 H × 113 W (1829 × 2870) and larger Horiz. Elliptical Pipe 76 H × 48 W (1930 × 1219) and larger Vert. Elliptical Pipe	500 (152.4)	600 (182.8)

B. Manhole Location on Pipe Sewers

1. Change in grade or elevation
   (a) At all changes in grade or elevation for all sizes of sewers.

2. Change in alignment
   (a) At all changes in alignment for circular sewers up to and including 42 in. (1067 mm) diameter.
   (b) At all changes in alignment for elliptical pipe sewers up to and including 43 in. H × 68 in. W (1092 mm × 1727 mm) and 42 in. H × 27 in. W (1067 mm × 686 mm) sizes.

Cleanouts are generally required along the pipe run. A cleanout in a manhole is illustrated in Figure 10-26.

Air and vacuum relief valves shall be installed at all high points. A typical detail of valves in a manhole is given in Figure 10-27.

Alternative Methods of Disposal

Problems are compounded by not having available public sewers at the project site. Alternative methods of disposal include a private sewage disposal system, generally consisting of a septic tank and disposal field; and a sewage treatment plant discharging into seepage trenches, the designs of which are outside the scope of this chapter.

STORM WATER SEWER

Introduction

The storm water sewer removes rainwater from roofs and other areas exposed to the weather. It is not permitted to receive any other waste, including clear waste, without the permission and approval of the code official.

Codes and Standards

The applicable plumbing code is used to size the storm water sewer from the building wall to the property line. If additional drainage from the site connects to this line, code requirements should be verified with the authority having jurisdiction.

General

The first step is to find the department or jurisdiction responsible for the design and installation of sewers. It may be the same plumbing code official responsible for sanitary sewers. In some jurisdictions where there is a storm water management requirement, there may be a separate department responsible for storm water sewers. The information needed should be part of the utility letter outlined in Appendix 10-B.

It shall be determined whether there is a storm water management program in place. Such

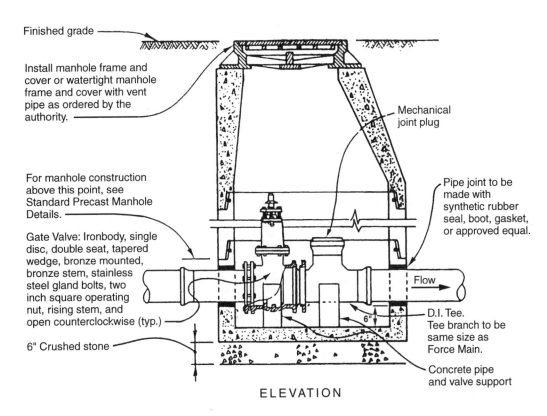

Finished grade

Install manhole frame and cover or watertight manhole frame and cover with vent pipe as ordered by the authority.

For manhole construction above this point, see Standard Precast Manhole Details.

Gate Valve: Ironbody, single disc, double seat, tapered wedge, bronze mounted, bronze stem, stainless steel gland bolts, two inch square operating nut, rising stem, and open counterclockwise (typ.)

6" Crushed stone

Mechanical joint plug

Pipe joint to be made with synthetic rubber seal, boot, gasket, or approved equal.

Flow

6"

D.I. Tee. Tee branch to be same size as Force Main.

Concrete pipe and valve support

ELEVATION

Figure 10-26   Force Main Cleanout in Manhole

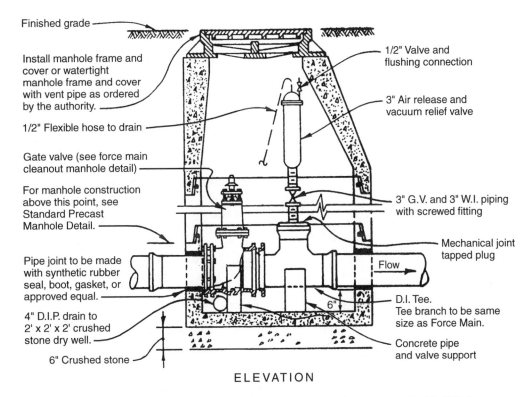

Finished grade

Install manhole frame and cover or watertight manhole frame and cover with vent pipe as ordered by the authority.

1/2" Flexible hose to drain

Gate valve (see force main cleanout manhole detail)

For manhole construction above this point, see Standard Precast Manhole Detail.

Pipe joint to be made with synthetic rubber seal, boot, gasket, or approved equal.

4" D.I.P. drain to 2' x 2' x 2' crushed stone dry well.

6" Crushed stone

1/2" Valve and flushing connection

3" Air release and vacuum relief valve

3" G.V. and 3" W.I. piping with screwed fitting

Mechanical joint tapped plug

Flow

6"

D.I. Tee. Tee branch to be same size as Force Main.

Concrete pipe and valve support

ELEVATION

Figure 10-27   Force Main Air Release and Vacuum Relief Valves

a program is established where the AHJ wishes to limit the storm water discharge from the developed site to the same flow rate that existed before the site was developed.

The next step is to determine the point of disposal. This could be either a public sewer; a local waterway or body of water; or a developed drainage pattern on the site, that is, an existing flow path the storm water follows on the undeveloped site. Every effort should be used to follow this pattern. Drywells can be used if the soil structure will permit this method. A retention basin can be used if there is a method of disposal for the rainwater, but it can not accept the full flow rate during a design storm. A detention basin can be used where the water on the site is routed to be evaporated and absorbed into the ground.

The Rational Method of Determining Design Flow

The "rational method" will be used to determine the theoretical water inflow into the storm sewer system. Since its introduction slightly before the turn of the century, it has been widely used. It is an empirical formula suited for the design of small watersheds, less than 10 square miles (mi^2). The formula is

Equation 10-1

$$Q = A\,I\,R$$

where

Q = Quantity of storm water runoff [cubic feet per second (cfs)] (**Note**: 450 gpm =1 cfs)

A = Area to be drained (acres) (**Note**: 43,560 ft^2 = 1 acre)

I = Imperviousness factor of surface comprising drainage area

R = Rate of rainfall (in./h)

The following discussion provides an understanding of the basic values used in the rational formula.

Design storm The rational method reduces an inexact set of conditions to an exact formula. Such variables as rainfall rate, overland water flow, and the amount of storm water that actually reaches the drainage system can never be exactly determined. Because of this unpredictability, it is important to realize that some judgment is required in applying the calculated and

obtained information in the design of a storm water system.

The storm water drainage system is generally designed to remove the maximum expected runoff as quickly as it falls to avoid ponding or flooding. The ability to calculate the flow rate is complicated by one's inability to predict accurately many of the factors affecting the actual amount of runoff resulting from any given storm. For the purpose of calculating the estimated maximum runoff, an artificial "design storm" is created. This storm serves as a simulation for the purpose of predicting runoff volume accurately enough to provide a basis for the design of the piping network.

Design storms are based on actual rainfall records and have been presented in a convenient form by the National Oceanic and Atmospheric Administration/National Weather Service (NOAA). Design storms are available as either intensity-duration-frequency curves or as charts and formulas appearing in several technical memoranda covering different areas of the United States. The intensity-duration-frequency charts are in a very convenient, easy-to-use form and are considered accurate for the watersheds that are the subject of this data book. A typical chart is illustrated in Figure 10-28. Charts for various cities throughout the US are available in Technical Paper no. 40. However, it has been superseded by technical memorandum NWS Hydro 35, because of the longer period of data collection for the memorandum, which must be considered the latest information available. However, the intensity-duration-frequency charts obtained from Technical Paper no. 40 are more often used because of their simplicity of use. Use of this information is discussed later in the chapter.

Imperviousness factor The imperviousness factor allows for the loss of rainwater as it flows over the ground from a remote point of the tributary area until it enters the drainage inlet. Such losses are caused by factors including infiltration of water into the soil, ponding, and water remaining on vegetation. The average figures for imperviousness of various surfaces are found in Table 10-7.

Inspection, if possible, is the best way to determine the nature of an existing surface. In places where the exact nature of future development is uncertain, the figure selected should represent the least loss that might be expected, to allow the largest quantity of storm water to

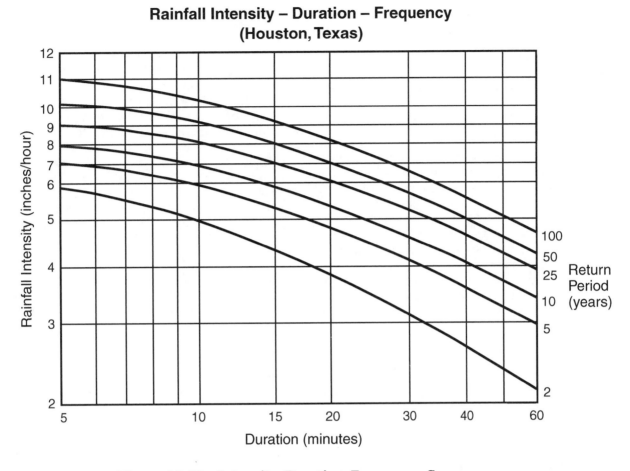

Figure 10-28   Intensity–Duration–Frequency Curves

Table 10-7   Imperviousness Factors

Surface	Flat Slope, < 2%	Average Slope, 2.0–7.0%	Steep slope, > 7.0%
Roofs & pavement (all types)[a]	0.95	0.95	0.95
Clay – sparse vegetation	0.40	0.55	0.70
Clay – lawn	0.15	0.20	0.30
Clay – dense vegetation	0.10	0.15	0.20
Clay – dense woods	0.07	0.12	0.17
Sand – sparse vegetation	0.20	0.30	0.40
Sand – lawn	0.07	0.12	0.17
Sand – dense vegetation	0.05	0.10	0.15
Sand – dense woods	0.03	0.08	0.13

Source: Baltimore County Design Standards.

[a] For ease of calculation, the factor for roofs and pavement could become 1.0 if excessive runoff will not result in a significant overdesign.

reach a drainage inlet. Where any area consists of different types of surfaces and/or soil combinations, a weighted overall value may be assigned for ease of calculations.

Rate of rainfall (rainfall intensity) The rate, or intensity, of rainfall is determined from the rainfall intensity-duration-frequency curves, obtained from NOAA/NBS Hydro 35 or Technical Paper no. 40 for durations up to 60 min. For longer durations, Technical Paper no. 40 alone should be used. The intensity is measured in inches per hour (in./h).

Return period (frequency) The design storm return period, or frequency, is the statistical period of years that must elapse to produce the most severe design storm once in that period of time. The theory is that the worst storm that would be expected to occur once in 100 years is much more severe than the worst storm that would be expected to occur once in 2 years.

The curve for a given frequency is actually a plot of different storms of varying lengths, each with a different duration, not a single storm plotted against time. Therefore, a storm of 10 min duration is one that lasts for exactly 10 min and then stops. It is not an extension of any other plot. Any storm with a longer duration would have a lower instantaneous peak flow.

Flooding will result if the design storm is exceeded. Special consideration should be given to the degree of protection provided for the building and its contents by the rapid removal of rainfall by the storm water drainage system. This depends on the importance of the facility, how flooding may affect access, the importance of uninterrupted service, and the value of the equipment or material installed or stored. Since a severe thunderstorm or hurricane could produce rainfall rates greater than those anticipated, the property value may necessitate the selection of a frequency longer than the minimum determined.

The return period should be based on code requirements or the degree of safety desired.

Rainstorm duration (time of concentration) The duration, or time of concentration, is measured in minutes. It is found by calculating the overland flow time and the time in pipe of a theoretical drop of water as it moves from the most remote point on the site to any design point on a branch or main drainage line.

This is important because the shorter the time, the more intense the rate of rainfall. This heavy rainfall, multiplied out to 1 h, would be much greater than the rainfall expected for a 1 h period. As an example, for New York City, the heaviest total amount of rain on record for a 5 min period is 0.75 in. Multiplying the 5 min reading out to determine the 1 h rate gives an hourly figure of 9 in./h of rain. Yet the largest amount of rainfall every recorded over a 1 h period is 5.01 in. It can thus be seen that the rate of rainfall measured during a short period is much more intense than the rate measured over a longer period of time.

The underlying theory is that the rainfall will stop at the exact moment the entire design area is contributing to the flow in this particular section of the sewer. Therefore, calculations must establish the shortest amount of time a drop of water takes to run from the farthest point of the site to any design point of our sewer. This is necessary so that the shortest time of concen-tration is obtained and the largest hourly rainfall rate is used for design purposes.

Overland flow time (inlet time) The overland flow time, often called the "inlet time," is the number of minutes it takes a drop of water to travel on the surface of the ground from the farthest point of the area contributing flow to a drainage inlet until it spills into the inlet. The impedance to overland flow of water by a grass surface is greater than that by an asphalt surface. For equal distances and slope, it takes longer for a drop of water to enter a drainage inlet from the farthest point of a lawn than it does from a paved parking lot. The slope of the land is also a factor since for any given surface the steeper the slope, the faster water flow.

Figure 10-29 offers a way to determine overland flow time when the slope of grade and type of surface are known. During a rainstorm, the flow of water from surfaces covered with pavement is in the form of a very shallow sheet of water covering the surface of the ground. This phenomenon is known as "sheet flow."

Finding the velocity in feet per second and multiplying that figure by the actual distance in feet gives the time in seconds, which is used to calculate the overland flow time. Convert this to minutes.

Time in pipe The time in pipe is the number of minutes the theoretical drop of water takes to flow from the drainage inlet to the design point. Determining this requires that the pipe be sized and the velocity of the storm water be known.

Finding the velocity, in feet per second, and multiplying that figure by the actual pipe length, in feet, gives the time in pipe, in seconds. Convert this to minutes.

Final Calculations

When the inflow into the piping network (total flow rate) from all sources has been calculated for each design point using the intensity-frequency-duration curve, the run of storm water piping on the site shall be made in order to determine the slope of the pipe.

Pipe sizing criteria The pipe size is calculated using the Manning formula. This formula requires that a value be selected to account for the roughness of the pipe being sized. This is called the "n" value, given in Table 10-8. Pipe

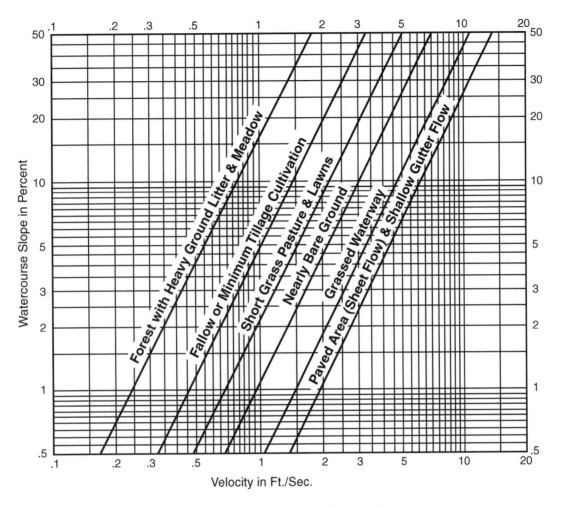

Figure 10-29   Overland Flow Time

sizing is based on the pipe flowing full during design flow.

Table 10-8   *"n"* Value for Pipe Used in the Manning Formula

Pipe Material	Range of n Values	Generally Accepted Value[a]
Asbestos-cement	0.011–0.015	0.013
Corrugated metal pipe	0.022–0.026	0.024
Cast iron	0.011–0.015	0.013
Concrete pipe	0.011–0.015	0.013
Ductile iron (cement lined)	0.011–0.015	0.013
Plastic pipe, all kinds	0.009–0.015	0.010
Steel pipe	0.012–0.020	0.015
Vitrified clay	0.011–0.015	0.013

[a] Values will vary based on condition of pipe.

To size pipes, use Figure 10-30 using the flow rate and the slope of the pipe. An adjustment is provided to the flow and velocity figures to allow for values of "n" that are different from the 0.013 used as the basis of the chart.

Storm Water Disposal Methods

Disposal into a public sewer This is the simplest method, requiring only a sewer that is properly sized using the applicable code from the building wall into the sewer. The connection should be made to a manhole. Codes call for the sewer to be sized from the building wall to the property line if only receiving runoff from the roof. A problem exists if the building roof and surrounding areas are larger than the areas appearing in the charts provided in the applicable code. If this is the case, the rational method of

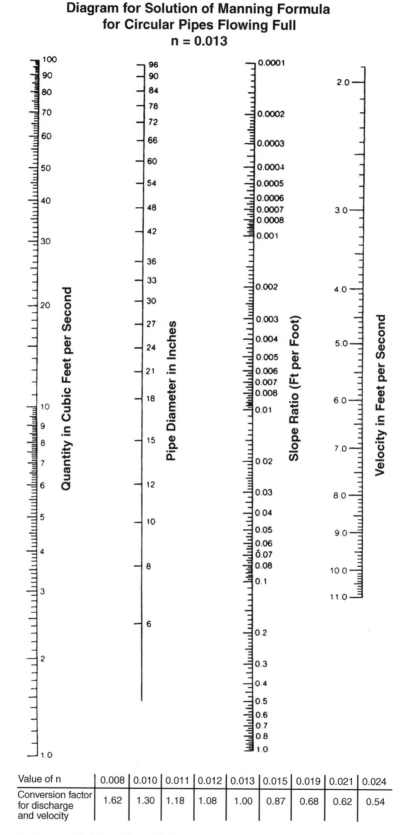

**Diagram for Solution of Manning Formula
for Circular Pipes Flowing Full
n = 0.013**

Value of n	0.008	0.010	0.011	0.012	0.013	0.015	0.019	0.021	0.024
Conversion factor for discharge and velocity	1.62	1.30	1.18	1.08	1.00	0.87	0.68	0.62	0.54

Figure 10-30   Pipe Sizing Using the Manning Formula

calculating the volume of storm water runoff shall be used. Sizing is discussed at the end of this section.

The storm water sewer shall be a separate line leaving the building, even if there is a combined public sewer. A combined sewer is one that receives both sanitary and storm water drainage. The reason for separate lines is that if separate public sewers are constructed in the future a new connection can easily be accomplished. The final connection to the public sewer shall be into a hooded manhole or catch basin to prevent sewer gas from entering the storm water sewer.

Disposal into drywells A "drywell" is an underground structure with openings or porous walls that allow the storm water entering the drywell to escape out the sides and be absorbed into the surrounding soil. This disposal method is only used in very limited areas where there is AHJ approval and where there is sandy soil, permitting its effective use. Local codes specify the number and size of drywell sections or depth of bury and the distance between structures.

Disposal into recharge basins "Recharge basins" are depressed areas on a site that is normally dry with no outlet. These basins are sized to collect runoff from the surrounding area due to a storm of a given duration, usually a 100 year, 24 hour storm, with a 10% safety factor and additional height above the top to account for wave action when full. When in such a basin, the water is mostly absorbed into the surrounding soil and some evaporates into the air. A headwall should be constructed to avoid erosion of the outflow.

Disposal into retention basins A "retention basin" is intended to collect rainwater and allow discharge at a rate that is slower than the rate of inflow into the basin because a storm water management program is in effect. The design engineer should first determine the discharge from the undeveloped site and then calculate the discharge from the developed site. The volume of water in the retention basin to be stored is based on the allowable discharge flow rate volume compared to inflow flow rate over a period of time while not exceeding the allowable discharge flow rate.

Limited-discharge roof drains Another possible storage method is a limited-flow roof drainage system. Special roof drains are available with limited discharge characteristics that store water on the roof and discharge the rainwater at a rate that is slower than the rate at which it accumulates. This is rarely used and its use must be coordinated with the architect and structural engineer to ensure provision of a watertight roof and elevated sections at entrances to roof stairways.

Discharge into an existing flow path A project may be constructed on a site where there is no other method of removing storm water from the site except by discharging it into swales or ditches that exist on the site. These flow paths eventually find their way into a remote watercourse.

Sizing a Ditch

The following criteria shall be used to size a ditch:

1. The discharge into the ditch shall be from a headwall. A headwall is necessary because the outflow from the pipe will eventually wear away the invert over a period of time.

2. The slope sides should be no steeper than 1 on 3 to allow mowing.

3. A 4 ft 0 in. high fence may be required for larger channels.

4. The suggested cross section is given in Table 10-9.

5. The roughness coefficient, or "n" value, shall be as listed in Table 10-10.

6. The maximum recommended velocity is listed in Table 10-11.

The ditch is sized using the Manning formula. This formula requires that a value be selected to account for the roughness of the area being sized. When sizing, it is a reasonable assumption for the ditches to flow full during design flow.

Using the design flow and calculating the wetted length of the ditch sides and bottom, converted to the diameter of a pipe, use Figure 10-30 to size ditches.

Table 10-9 Typical Cross Sections for Ditches—Depths of 10 Ft and Less

Asphalt or concrete lined	1.5 horizontal to 1 vertical
Grass lined	3 horizontal to 1 vertical
Gravel lined	2 horizontal to 1 vertical
Clay	2 horizontal to 1 vertical

Table 10-10   "n" Values for Ditches Used in the Manning Formula

Description	n
Paved invert corrugated metal steel pipe	0.020
Cast iron, ductile iron, concrete, and steel pipe	0.013
Unpaved corrugated metal steel pipe	0.024
Small plant ditches (no vegetation, fair condition)	0.025
Main plant ditch (grass, some weeds, fair condition)	0.030
Natural ditches (dense weeds, high as flow depth, poor condition)	0.120

Note: "n" = coefficient of roughness.

Table 10-11   Design Velocity of Water in Ditches

Ditch Material	Max. Velocity (fps)
Unlined:	
Fine sand	1.5
Silt loam or silt	1.5
Fine gravel	2.5
Sandy clay or clay	3.0
Sod	3.0
Still clay or coarse gravel	4.0
Shale and hardpan	6.0
Lined:	
Asphalt, concrete, and granite	8.0

Design depth and slope Ditches should be sized to run full at the design discharge rate with a minimum freeboard of 6 in. The preferred minimum freeboard on larger ditches is 12 in. For ditches running parallel to plant roads, the maximum design water surface elevation should not be higher than the bottom of the road base. Low-capacity ditches should have a minimum slope of 0.002 ft/ft. Larger ditches should be hydraulically designed to set the ditch slope.

NATURAL GAS SERVICE

Introduction

This chapter discusses natural gas sizing and distribution on a site from the property line to the building.

General

Natural gas is obtained from either of two sources. The first, restricted to very large users of gas, is a transportation gas company whereby the gas is directly purchased by the facility from the point where gas is originated. The second is a franchised public utility. As part of this service, the utility company usually supplies and installs the service line from the utility main in addition to providing a regulator/meter assembly in or adjacent to the building.

An installation fee may be charged if the utility company regulations concerning the time of payback from expected revenue does not justify the cost of installing the service. The same might be true if the volume of gas intended for a commercial or industrial facility is considered too little. In such a case, it would be the responsibility of the owner to pay for the design and installation of the complete site service in conformity with utility company regulations.

Codes and Standards

The standard most often used for the design of natural gas systems is ANSI/NFPA 54, *National Fuel Gas Code*, along with applicable provisions of the local plumbing code. Some insurance carriers, such as Factory Mutual and Industrial Risk Insurers, have standards that may be more stringent than those listed.

General Procedures

The first step is to find the utility company who supplies gas in the area. If the project is existing, the owner can tell you the utility company name. In general, the engineering department of the utility company will be the first contact for information necessary for design. The next step is for the design engineer to calculate the total connected load in cubic feet per hour (cfh). This is done based on information about the boilers obtained from the HVAC department, water heating requirements, cooking requirements, and process requirements, if any. This total connected load shall be given to the utility company, which has its own method of calculating the actual load.

Before discussing the information the utility requires, we should discuss the various types of service that a utility company may provide, each with a different cost (or rate). (Specific types of service may be unavailable or known by different names in various localities.) The types of service are

1. *Firm or uninterruptible service.* This type of service provides a constant supply of gas under all conditions without exception. This service has the highest rate.

2. *Interruptible service.* This type of service allows the utility company to stop the gas supply to the facility, under predetermined conditions, and start it again when these conditions no longer exist. The rate is lower than that for firm gas, and the service will require a backup source of fuel, such as fuel oil or liquid propane.

3. *Light or heavy process service.* This type of service is provided for industrial or process use and is reserved for quantities of gas that the utility company defines for this class of service.

4. *Commercial/industrial service.* This type of service is provided for heating and cooling system loads for this class of building usage.

5. *Transportation gas service purchased directly from a company other than the public utility, with the gas actually carried to the site by the utility company mains.* In addition to the cost of the gas, the utility company will charge a fee for this service.

The following criteria and information should be obtained in writing from the public utility company:

1. BTU content of the gas provided.

2. Minimum pressure of the gas at the outlet of the meter.

3. Extent of the installation work done by the utility company and the point of connection by the contractor.

4. The location of the utility supply main and the proposed run of pipe on the site by the utility company.

5. Acceptable location of the meter and/or regulator assembly and any work required by the owner to allow the assembly to be installed (such as a meter pit or slab on grade).

6. Types of service available and the cost of each.

In order for the utility company to provide this data, the following information must be given to it:

1. The total connected load. The utility will use its own diversity factor to calculate the size of the service line. If the design engineer is responsible for the installation, this is not required since the diversity factor calculated by the design engineer for the facility shall be used.

2. Minimum pressure requirements for the most demanding device.

3. Site plan indicating the location of the proposed building on the site and the specific area of the building where the proposed NG service will enter the building.

4. Preferred location of the meter/regulator assembly.

5. Expected date of the start of construction.

The gas utility letter

A typical gas utility letter is given in Appendix 10-B. The following explains the information in this letter.

Btu content of the gas There is a variation in the Btu content of natural gas in various parts of the country. Generally, a figure of 1050 Btu/ ft^3 of gas (reduced to 1000 Btu for ease of calculations) has been used for design purposes. It is recommended that the design engineer request that the supplier provide the Btu content supplying each specific project for your records.

System operating pressures The pressure in a site main is dependent on that existing in the mains of the utility company, since pressure is not reduced until the point where the facility meter is installed. This pressure is generally in the range of 15 to 50 psig.

The maximum allowable system operating pressure of fuel gas when installed inside a building is governed by NFPA 54, unless local codes or insurance carriers have more stringent requirements. Natural gas systems are not permitted to exceed 5 psig unless all of the following conditions are met:

1. Local authorities permit a higher pressure.

2. All piping is welded.

3. The pipe is run inside buildings or areas used only for industrial processes, research, warehouse, or boiler and/or mechanical equipment rooms.

Placement of the meter assembly The requirements of various utility companies differ regarding the placement of the meter assembly. It could be installed either in an underground, exterior meter pit, at an above ground exterior location exposed to the weather, or inside the building in a well-ventilated area or mechanical equipment room. The utility company often has installation requirements for the gas service pipe into the facility that shall be conformed with.

Major System Components

Gas line filters Filters for natural gas are installed on the site service to protect the regulator and meter from injury due to particulate clogging, which may damage the equipment inside the building. They should be considered when:

1. Line scale, dirt, or rust is known to be present.

2. Dirty gas is obtained from a transmission company.

3. "Wet" gas (sometimes referred to as "sour gas") is known to be present, such as occurs after large utility company pressure reducing valves.

The filter consists of a housing and a cartridge filter element. Selection of the housing is based on the highest flow rate and pressure expected and the size of the proposed building service. The housing should be capable of having interchangeable elements to allow replacing of the original filter if desired. Having a filter oversized is considered good practice if the cost of the larger size is not excessive, since this allows a longer service life.

The filter element is usually cellulose or synthetic fiber. Generally, the cellulose type is used for sizes 3 in. and less and fiber for 4 in. and larger. Fiber is stronger and should be considered where the pressure differential may be excessive and when recommended by the manufacturer. A filter rating of 10 microns is suggested as a starting point with actual operating experience being the final criterion.

The size of the filter is based on actual cubic feet per minute (acfm) and velocity across the filter. The pressure drop across the filter when it is dirty shall be considered in the actual pressure loss allowed for the service assembly. Since the filter should be changed when the pressure difference approaches 10% of the operating pressure, it is good practice to provide pressure

gauges on both sides of the filter. If no filter is installed on the service, a spool piece should be provided if there is a possibility that one may be required. Most filters are mounted horizontally.

Gas meters Gas meters are part of a service assembly that may consist of filters, valves, regulators, and relief valves. The complete assembly is usually supplied and installed by the utility company. For the rare instances where this is not the case, gas meters are selected using the local utility company standards, with the size and arrangement of the entire meter assembly based on flow rate and pressure. Because steady pressure is necessary for accurate metering, the regulator is installed before the meter. The utility company will provide sketches and details, with space requirements, of typical meter assemblies for various capacities and pressures. This permits accurate determination of the dimensional and space requirements for the area where the complete assembly will be installed. Obtain from the utility company all requirements for the specific installation being designed.

The plumbing contractor is usually responsible for providing a pit for the assembly or a concrete slab under the complete meter assembly when it is installed outside the building. This includes determining meter slab size for outdoor meter installations and pit sizes and access openings for meters installed in pits. For facilities with large demands for boilers and other equipment, a meter assembly with dimensions of 6 ft 0 in. (2 m) wide by 25 ft 0 in. (8 m) long may not be uncommon.

Generally, if the contractor is installing the site service, the utility company will either supply the meter or install the entire assembly. This must be confirmed in the utility letter.

Pressure regulators "Gas pressure regulators" are pressure-reducing devices used to reduce a variable high inlet pressure to a constant lower outlet pressure. Two types of regulator are available—direct acting and pilot operated. The direct-acting type uses the difference in pressure between the high and regulated sides of the regulator to directly move a closure (adjusting) member inside the regulator to adjust the pressure. The pilot-operated type uses a primary regulator to sense and magnify differences in pressure between the high and low pressure sides and a second, main valve with the closure member to achieve the desired pressure.

There are several categories of regulator, with the end use determining the nomenclature. The first is the line regulator, which is used to reduce high pressure, often in a range of between 25 and 50 psig (170 and 345 kPa), from the gas service provided by the utility company to a lower pressure used for the building service. An intermediate regulator is used to reduce the lower pressure, often in the range of 3 to 5 psig (21 to 35 kPa), to a pressure required to supply terminal equipment such as a boiler gas train. The third type is an appliance regulator used at the individual piece of equipment for final pressure.

The line regulator can be pilot operated and provided with an internal or external relief valve. The regulator is pressure rated to withstand the highest pressure expected. The relief valve is installed downstream from the regulator and is set to trip at a pressure that is about 10% higher than the highest set pressure. The line regulator is placed upstream from the meter in order to provide the meter with a constant pressure, allowing accurate measurement. This line pressure regulator is most often selected and installed by the utility company as part of the gas meter assembly.

An intermediate regulator is used within a facility where high pressure used for distribution purposes must be reduced to a lower pressure, which is required by the terminal appliances. This is the most often used regulator. There are two types of intermediate regulator, and the choice is determined by the accuracy desired and the ability to install a relief valve and associated gas vent discharge. One type of regulator has an internal relief valve set to discharge when the pressure rises above the set point. This has the lowest initial cost and the least degree of accuracy. Another type of intermediate regulation, called a monitor type, consists of two pilot-operated regulators. They can be installed in two configurations, both of which use regulators in series. The first uses the upstream regulator to reduce the inlet pressure initially to some intermediate value and the downstream regulator to further reduce the pressure to the final set point. This arrangement puts less stress on each of the regulators. The second configuration uses the upstream regulator wide open and lets the downstream regulator do all of the pressure reducing. If the gas pressure goes above the set point, the upstream regulator closes to partially lower the pressure. This installation has a high initial cost.

The appliance regulator is used to control the pressure of gas directly connected to the terminal appliance or equipment. This is most often provided by the manufacturer as part of the equipment gas train. The gas train is an assembly of piping, valves, regulators, relief vents, etc., used to connect the gas supply directly to the terminal equipment. For larger pieces of equipment, such as boilers, the gas train arrangement is dictated by insurance carrier requirements. An additional requirement of most gas trains is small relief vents from various devices. These vents must be piped outside the building to a point where they can be diluted by the outside air and pose no threat to the public or create a fire hazard. This is usually above a roof or the highest point of the structure.

Another type of appliance regulator is called an "atmospheric regulator" or a "zero governor." This is a very sensitive type of regulator that works with a very low gas pressure and extremely small differentials.

A differential regulator is a multiple port type regulator used to produce a single, uniform outlet pressure when supplied with multiple inlets of different pressures.

A back-pressure regulator is a regulator arranged to provide accurate inlet pressure control. It is used as a relief valve where the application requires a higher degree of regulation and sensitivity than is possible with a standard poppet type relief valve. When operating as a relief valve, it limits inlet pressure to a set point. At pressures below this point, it remains closed. If the pressure rises above the set point, it begins to open and will bleed off enough pressure to maintain the system set point.

A piped gas vent must be provided from regulators to a point several feet above the roof of any adjacent structure and must be properly sized to carry the amount of gas that will be discharged. This is necessary to protect the system from overpressure in the event of malfunction or failure to lock up fully.

Regulator selection considerations It is common practice to oversize the capacity of a regulator by about 15% to provide a margin for accurate regulation. However, care should be taken when sizing a gas pressure regulator not to provide a large regulator when small loads are connected. It may be advisable to provide a separate regulator to handle the small loads, such as a kitchen. For large loads, regulators in parallel are often used to keep the pressure drop to a minimum.

The adjustment range of a regulator should be approximately from 50% over the desired regulated pressure to 50% under that pressure.

The utility company may require that regulators be of the "lock out" type. The lock out feature will stop regulator operation when the pressure falls below a predetermined set point when the downstream portion of the piping is normally under pressure.

Drip pots Drip pots are necessary to prevent water that is in the utility company mains from reaching the building. Modern technology has reduced, but not eliminated, the presence of moisture in the utility company mains.

Site Distribution

The site distribution portion of the system starts at the property line of the customer and usually ends above grade (or the concrete pad) at the valve after the meter. The connection to the utility company mains and the installation of the meter assembly is generally done by the utility company.

The most often used piping material for underground installations is high density polyethylene (HDPE). The rating for pipe 4 in. and smaller should be SDR 11, and that for pipe 5 in. and larger SDR 13.5. The pipe shall be buried a minimum of 3 ft 0 in. below ground and a 14 AWG corrosion-resistant tracer wire placed in the pipe trench 6 in. over the pipe. Another detection method is to put a warning tape containing metallic material with the words "natural gas" on it. This will allow location by a metal detector and warn of the gas line immediately below the tape if digging takes place without the pipe being located beforehand.

The pipe aboveground shall be metal; therefore, a transition fitting is required if HDPE is used for the supply service. The transition fitting shall comply with ASTM D-2513. Refer to Figure 10-31.

Testing and Purging

After installation of the pipe is complete, the site system shall be tested, purged of air, and then filled with natural gas. The testing phase shall

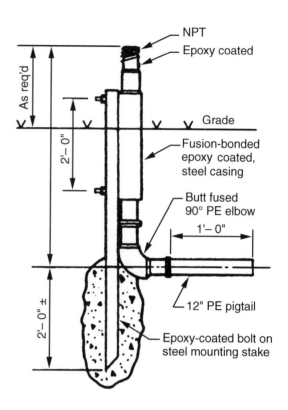

Figure 10-31 Transition Fitting from Plastic to Steel

be done with compressed air at a gauge pressure 50% higher than the highest pressure expected in the main. The larger the total volume of the pipe, the longer the test shall last. No loss of pressure shall be allowed. The test period is based on the size of the line and the length of run. Table 10-12 gives the recommended test periods.

After successful testing, the line shall be purged of air with dry nitrogen. The reason for this is to prevent a flammable mixture of gas and air when the pipe is filled with natural gas for the first time. This is accomplished by calculating the volume of the piping and introducing an equal volume of nitrogen into the pipe. After the nitrogen purge, natural gas is then introduced until the nitrogen is displaced and left under pressure.

Methods of Sizing

Site service sizing procedure

Pressure required The pressure in the main provided by the utility company and the flow rate are the basis for design, which is done by the utility using proprietary charts for the specific pressure in the gas main. If these charts are not available, compressed-air friction-loss tables can be used, based on the pressure in the gas service main with adjustments made to compensate for the difference in specific gravity of the gas. This will provide sizing within a range that is acceptable for this system. The pressure drop selected is at the discretion of the design professional but is generally kept to approximately 10% of the available pressure in psig. To use the pressure loss tables, calculate the pressure drop per 100 ft of pipe.

If the design engineer is responsible for sizing the meter and regulator, the following information must be calculated or established:

1. The adjusted maximum flow rate, in acfm, for all connected equipment in the facility.

2. The highest pressure required for the most demanding equipment inside the building.

3. The pressure in the building service main immediately downstream of the regulator. If a pressure loss through a filter is expected, this will reduce the pressure.

4. The allowable pressure loss for the piping system inside the facility.

5. The pressure differential between the service main pressure and the pressure required inside the building. This is the sum of items 2 and 4 above subtracted from item 3.

6. The regulator and meter can now be sized using literature and catalog information from the manufacturers.

Maximum probable demand For some types of buildings, such as multiple dwellings and laboratories, the total connected load is not used to size the piping system since not all of the connected devices will be used at the same time. For design purposes, it is necessary to apply a diversity factor to reduce the total connected load when calculating the maximum probable demand. The demand and diversity factors are given in ASPE *Data Book*, Volume 2, Chapter 7, "Fuel-Gas Piping Systems."

This calculation first requires the listing of every device using gas in the building and the demand, in Btu/h, for each. The manufacturer of each device should be consulted to find its actual input gas consumption.

For industrial or process installations and for major gas using equipment, such as boilers and water heaters, in all building types, the connected load with no diversity factor is used

Table 10-12 Test Duration for Plastic Gas Mains

Main Size (in.)	Maximum Length of Pipe Being Tested (ft)[a]												
	Test Duration (h)												
	2	3	4	6	8	10	12	14	16	18	20	22	24
1 or less	6590	11,000	15,400	24,200									
2	1700	2,830	3,960	6,220	8490								
3	743	1,240	1,730	2,730	3720	4710	5700						
4	439	732	1,030	1,610	2200	2780	3370	3960	4540	5130			
6	189	315	442	694	947	1200	1450	1710	1960	2210	2460	2730	2970
8	108	180	252	396	541	685	829	973	1120	1260	1410	1550	1700
12	48	80	112	177	241	306	370	435	499	563	628	692	757
14	41	68	96	151	206	261	316	371	426	482	537	592	647
16	30	50	70	110	150	191	231	271	311	352	392	432	472
20	19	31	44	69	95	120	146	171	197	222	247	273	298
24	13	21	30	48	65	83	100	118	135	153	170	188	205

[a]Mains to operate at less than 125 psig.

because it is possible for all connected equipment of these types to be used at the same time.

NG pipe sizing methods The most conservative method for sizing piping systems is by the use of tables, such as those prepared by the American Gas Association and included in Appendix C of the *National Fuel Gas Code,* NFPA 54. Other methods using tables appear in ASPE *Data Book,* Volume 2, Chapter 7, and calculators are available. Calculators are considered more accurate than prepared tables.

Pipe and System Materials

All of the piping materials must be listed in NFPA 54 and other applicable codes. In addition to the codes, the recommendation of the utility company, which has experience in the area of the project, should be considered. The most often used material for underground lines is high density polyethylene (PE). The material for larger lines and piping for high pressure (over 100 psig) is steel pipe protected against corrosion by wrapping with a plastic coating.

Codes do not permit plastic pipe to be run aboveground. For aboveground lines, the piping and jointing methods depend on pipe size and system pressure. For piping up to 3 psig (21 kPa), black steel, ASTM A53, or A106 pipe is used with cast or malleable iron screwed fittings in sizes 3 in. (75 mm) and smaller and butt welded joints in sizes 4 in. (100 mm) and larger. Where natural gas is considered "dry gas," type "L" copper pipe is widely used. All piping for pressures over 3 psig (21 kPa) should be steel with welded joints. Welded fittings shall conform to ANSI 16.9. Screwed fittings shall be black malleable iron, 150 lb class conforming to ANSI A-197. Check valves shall be cast iron, 316 SS trim, disk type, with a soft seat. In sizes 3 in. and smaller use screwed joints. Larger sizes shall be flanged.

Joints for PE should be butt type, heat fused joints. Socket type joints have been found to introduce a stiffness in the joint area that is undesirable. Joints for steel pipe shall be screwed for pipe sizes 4 in. (100 mm) and smaller. Sizes 5 in. (125 mm) and larger should be welded. Where flanged connections are necessary to connect some devices, flanges are heat welded to the HDPE pipe ends.

In order to make the transition from underground plastic pipe to aboveground steel pipe, an adapter fitting is required. Such a fitting is illustrated in Figure 10-31.

APPENDIX 10-A

TYPICAL GENERAL NOTES—
SITE UTILITIES ONLY

1. ALL ELEVATIONS ARE IN FEET (METERS).

2. ALL CONTOUR LINES ARE IN _____ FOOT (METER) INTERVALS.

3. CONNECTIONS TO ALL PUBLIC UTILITIES SHALL BE IN STRICT CONFORMANCE WITH RULES AND REGULATIONS OF THE _____ (AHJ).

4. STREET DRAINAGE AND TRAFFIC SHALL BE MAINTAINED AT ALL TIMES.

5. TOP ELEVATIONS OF EXISTING MANHOLE FRAMES AND GRATES SHALL BE ADJUSTED TO CONFORM TO NEW GRADES WHERE REQUIRED.

6. THIS CONTRACTOR SHALL COMPLY WITH ALL RULES AND REGULATIONS OF GOVERNING BODIES AND AHJ REGARDING REMOVAL, REPLACEMENT, AND DISPOSAL OF ANY PUBLICLY OWNED PROPERTY WITHIN THE (_____ PROPERTY). ALL MATERIAL SHALL BE TAKEN TO A LOCATION WITHIN _____(CITY) AS DIRECTED BY AHJ. IF NO DIRECTIVE IS GIVEN, ALL SUCH PROPERTY SHALL BE DISPOSED OF BY THIS CONTRACTOR AT HIS/HER OWN EXPENSE.

7. SURVEY INFORMATION FROM SURVEY _____TITLE, BY_____, DATED_____.

8. ALL ELEVATIONS REFER TO _____ DATUM.

9. ALL WORK SHOWN ON THIS DRAWING WHICH IS BEYOND THE SCOPE OF THE CONTRACT AND CONTRACT DRAWINGS IS SHOWN ONLY FOR THE PURPOSE OF EXPEDITING THE PROGRESS OF THE JOB AND DOES NOT IN ANY WAY CONSTITUTE ADDITIONAL WORK.

Figure 10-A1 Typical General Notes—Site Utilities Only.

APPENDIX 10-B LETTERS

Date:

To: Water Utility Company

Re: Project name
         Lot and block number
         Address

Dear sir or madam:

We are the engineers responsible for the design of the mechanical [and electrical] work for this proposed new [addition to an existing] project. We are enclosing three site plans which give a detailed location of the proposed structure and also our desired location for the point of entry into the building. At this time our preliminary estimate for this project is a maximum instantaneous demand of _____ gpm.

Based on the above data, we request the following information:

A.   What are the size and location(s) of any existing water mains adjacent to the project site that can be utilized for both domestic and fire protection water service? If at present no such service exists, what is the expected date of completion for such services? Would you please mark up one copy of the enclosed site plan with this information?

B.   What is the depth of bury of the water mains based on the datum taken from the enclosed site plans?

C.   What is the static and residual pressure in these mains? If there is any cost involved for obtaining this information, or if you do not normally conduct such tests, please advise us. If weather conditions do not permit such tests at this time, please advise us when such tests would be conducted.

D.   Please advise us about the requirements of, and any specific required locations for, both domestic and fire protection meter assembly installations. Is a separate meter required for both domestic and fire water service? Please include dimensions for all such meter assembly installations.

E.   Are there any requirements or preferred piping materials and jointing methods for this service?

F.   Please provide us with a breakdown of the work provided by you, the utility company, and all work required to be performed by the plumbing contractor relating to the domestic and fire protection service from the main into the building and the installation of the water meter assembly. Who is responsible for connecting to the public water main? If it is our contractor, please provide us with any rules and regulations regarding the installation.

G.   Please provide us with any rules and regulations regarding the requirements for and installation of backflow preventing devices. If you are not responsible for such installations, please provide us with the name and address of the agency or department having jurisdiction in this matter. If there are none, please so state.

H.   Based on your experience, would you please advise us of the minimum depth of bury acceptable for water mains in your jurisdiction.

I.   At the present time, we expect construction to start on or about _____.

If I can be of further assistance in this matter, please call.

Sincerely,

_____

Figure 10-B1 Typical Water Service Letter.

Date:

To:

Re:

Gentlemen:

We are the engineers responsible for the design of the mechanical [and electrical] work for this proposed new [addition to an existing] project. The address of the project is:

_____

We are enclosing three site plans which give a detailed location of the proposed structure and also our desired location for the point of entry into the building. At this time we estimate that this project will produce the following maximum sewage and storm water flow:

	PRESENT	FUTURE	ULTIMATE
SEWAGE			
STORM WATER			

Based on the above data, we request the following information:

A. Are there sanitary, storm water, or combined sewers adjacent to the site? Could you please provide us with their location and elevation based on the datum of the enclosed site plan? Would you please mark up one copy of the enclosed site plan with this information? If at present no such sewers exist, what is the expected date of completion for such services?

B. Do your regulations permit disposing of storm water into the sanitary sewer system?

C. What are your regulations regarding specific limits of pollutants of concern for disposal of industrial or chemical waste into the sanitary sewer system? If you are not responsible for such installations, please provide us with the name and address of any agency or department having jurisdiction in this matter.

D. What are your regulations for the installation of grease traps in your jurisdiction? If you are not responsible for such installations, please provide us with the name and address of any agency or department having jurisdiction in this matter. If there are none, please so state.

E. Are there any storm water management programs in effect for your jurisdiction? If you are not responsible for such installations, please provide us with the name and address of any agency or department having jurisdiction in this matter. If there are none, please so state.

F. If there are no sewers available to the site, please provide us with the rules and regulations for private sewage and storm water disposal. If you are not responsible for such installations, please provide us with the name and address of any agency or department having jurisdiction in this matter. If there are none, please so state.

G. Please provide us with a breakdown of all work required to be performed by the plumbing contractor relating to the installation of the sanitary and storm water house sewer from the building into the public sewer. Who is responsible for connecting to the public sewer? If it is our contractor, please provide us with any rules and regulations regarding the installation.

H. Are there any unique requirements for the use of any piping material and jointing methods required for installation of the normal sanitary and storm water piping in your jurisdiction other than those listed in the applicable code?

If I can be of further assistance in this matter, please call.

Sincerely,

_____

Figure 10-B2 Typical Sewer Letter.

Date:

To:

Attn:

Re:

Gentlemen:

We are the engineers responsible for the mechanical [and electrical] design for this proposed new [addition to the existing] project. This building will be constructed at _____. We anticipate that construction will start on or about _____.

We are enclosing a copy of the site plan which gives the location of the proposed structure and our desired location for the point of entry into the building and our preferred location of the gas meter assembly. At this time we estimate that this project will have a maximum instantaneous gas demand of _____CFH (BTUH).

The total gas input in CFH of all connected devices is as follows:

      A. Device. Range of pressure is _____ to _____ in. wc. [in. Hg] [psi].

      B. _____

1.   There will be [no] dual fuel requirements. We intend to use fuel oil [propane] as the second source of fuel.

2.   No [The following] equipment will be equipped with a pilot light. [The consumption will be _____ CFH and a required pressure of _____ in. wc.]

3.   We request that the supply be firm [interruptible]. Please inform us of the conditions that will require you to interrupt the supply of gas.

4.   All of the equipment will be operating 24 hours a day. [The hours of operation for equipment other than boilers will be _____.]

5.   There will be no requirements for future equipment. [We estimate that the following future equipment may be installed:]

      A. Device. Range of pressure is _____ to _____ in. wc. [in. Hg] [psi].

6.   Is there any other type of gas service available for this area that may reduce the overall cost of gas for our client?

7.   Because of design considerations based on the location of the Mechanical Equipment Room, we request that the meter be located on the _____ side of the building. Do you anticipate any problem with this location?

Figure 10-B3 Typical Gas Utility Letter.

(continued)

(continued)

We request the following information:

A. The size and location of any existing gas main adjacent to our property that we can utilize to supply our project. If at present no such service exists, what is the scheduled completion date?

B. What is the BTU content, specific gravity, and pressure of the gas in the main from which you intend to supply our project?

C. Will your regulations permit [or require] a meter to be located inside the building, in a pit outside the building, or exposed, adjacent to the building? Could you also provide a dimensioned drawing, both plan and section, of the proposed complete meter assembly?

D. Please provide us with a breakdown of the work provided by you and by the utility company and the work to be performed by the plumbing contractor in conjunction with the service extension from the main into the building and any ancillary work to be performed by the owner, such as concrete pad, telephone connections, electrical connections, etc., and the exact point of connection of the building piping with your service and meter asssembly. Who will make the final connection?

If you have any questions or we could be of any further assistance, please do not hesitate to call.

Sincerely,

_____

Figure 10-B3 Typical Gas Utility Letter (continued).

Index

F

mound soil-absorption systems, 1999 V2: 220, 1999 V2: 226

mounting fire extinguishers, 2000 V3: 27, 2000 V3: 28

MPC (medium-pressure condensate), 1998 V1: 11

mph, MPH (miles per hour), 1998 V1: 20

MPS (medium-pressure steam supply), 1998 V1: 11

mps, MPS (medium-pressure steam), 1998 V1: 20

mrem (millerems), 1999 V2: 339

MSDS (material safety data sheets), 2000 V3: 90

MSS (Manufacturers Standardization Society of the Valve and Fittings Industry, Inc.), 1998 V1: 34, 1998 V1: 60

MTD (mean temperature difference), 1998 V1: 20

mthw, MTHW (medium-temperature hot water), 1998 V1: 20

MU (viscosity), 1998 V1: 2, 1998 V1: 23, 1998 V1: 41

mudballing in filters, 2000 V3: 132, 2000 V3: 150

muds in feed water, 1999 V2: 289

mufflers on vacuum systems, 2000 V3: 70

multi-effect distillation, 1999 V2: 298, 1999 V2: 299

multi-graded sand filtration, 1999 V2: 298

multifamily building firefighting demand flow rates, 2000 V3: 232

multilevel pools, 2000 V3: 108, 2000 V3: 109

multimedia filtration, 1999 V2: 298, 1999 V2: 300, 1999 V2: 322–323

multiple. *See also entries beginning with* double-, multiple-, *or* two-

multiple-compartment septic tanks, 1999 V2: 229

multiple-degree-of-freedom systems, 1998 V1: 161

multiple-gang-service outlets, 2000 V3: 56

multiple gas-train vents, 1999 V2: 177

multiple pools, 2000 V3: 108

multiple pressure-regulated valve installation, 1999 V2: 153

multiple-tray waterfall aerators, 1999 V2: 293

multiplication in SI units, 1998 V1: 42

multipurpose dry chemicals, 2000 V3: 19, 2000 V3: 27

multistage pressure breakdown systems for pump plants, 1998 V1: 202

multistory buildings. *See* large buildings

municipal sewers. *See* public sewers

municipal water supply
   fire protection connections, 2000 V3: 225
   irrigation usage, 2000 V3: 105
   sprinkler systems, 2000 V3: 3
   types of, 2000 V3: 8
   water mains and pressure, 2000 V3: 216

muriatic acid, 1999 V2: 305, 1999 V2: 333, 2000 V3: 148, 2000 V3: 149, 2000 V3: 150

mussels, 1999 V2: 282

MV (medical vacuum), 1998 V1: 11

N

n (nano) prefix, 1998 V1: 42

N (newtons), 1998 V1: 41

N (nitrogen). *See* nitrogen

N (numbers), 1998 V1: 20

n c, N C (normally closed), 1998 V1: 20

n i c, N I C (not in contract), 1998 V1: 20

N m (newton-meters), 1998 V1: 41

n o, N O (normally open), 1998 V1: 20

$N^{1.85}$ graph paper, 2000 V3: 5

N_2O (nitrous oxide), 1998 V1: 11

na, N/A (not applicable), 1998 V1: 20

NACE Basic Corrosion Course, 1998 V1: 152

NACE (National Association of Corrosion Engineers), 1998 V1: 148, 1998 V1: 152

NACE Standard RP-01, 1998 V1: 148

NaCI (ionized salts), 2000 V3: 46

nails, protecting against, 1999 V2: 19

Nalco Chemical Co., 1999 V2: 325

Nalco Water Handbook, 1999 V2: 325

"nano" prefix, 1998 V1: 42

nanofilter membranes, 1999 V2: 284, 1999 V2: 300, 1999 V2: 308–311, 1999 V2: 310

NAPHCC (National Association of Plumbing-Heating-Cooling Contractors), 1998 V1: 81, 1999 V2: 65

naphtha, 1999 V2: 13

National Association of Corrosion Engineers (NACE), 1998 V1: 148, 1998 V1: 152

National Association of Home Builders Research Foundation, 1999 V2: 65

National Association of Plumbing-Heating-Cooling Contractors (NAPHCC), 1998 V1: 81, 1999 V2: 65

National Board of Boiler and Pressure Vessel Inspectors (NBBPVI), 1999 V2: 166

National Bureau of Standards
   electromotive force series, 1998 V1: 151
   publications, 1999 V2: 19, 1999 V2: 65, 1999 V2: 155
   reduced-size venting, 1999 V2: 49
   stack capacities study, 1999 V2: 4

National Coarse of US Thread, 1998 V1: 24

National Collegiate Athletic Association (NCAA), 2000 V3: 151

National Committee for Clinical Laboratory Standards, Inc. (NCCLS), 1999 V2: 279, 1999 V2: 317, 1999 V2: 319

National Easter Seal Society, 1998 V1: 99

National Electrical Code (NEC), 1999 V2: 170, 2000 V3: 115, 2000 V3: 121

National Fire Alarm Code (NFPA 72), 2000 V3: 24, 2000 V3: 29

National Fire Protection Association, Inc., 1998 V1: 34
   address, 1998 V1: 60, 2000 V3: 86, 2000 V3: 97

pseudo-dynamic elastic analysis, 1998 V1: 161–162

psf, PSF (pounds per square foot)

psf absolute (psfa, PSFA), 1998 V1: 21, 1999 V2: 254

psf gage (psfg, PSFG), 1998 V1: 21, 1999 V2: 254

symbols for, 1998 V1: 21

psfa, PSFA (psf absolute), 1998 V1: 21, 1999 V2: 254

psfg, PSFG (psf gage), 1998 V1: 21, 1999 V2: 254

psi, PSI (pounds per square inch)

cast iron radiators, 2000 V3: 180

converting to metric units, 2000 V3: 29

measurements, 2000 V3: 200

psi absolute (psia, PSIA), 1998 V1: 21, 1999 V2: 254, 2000 V3: 85, 2000 V3: 200

psi gage (psig, PSIG), 1998 V1: 21, 1999 V2: 254, 2000 V3: 68, 2000 V3: 85, 2000 V3: 200

symbols for, 1998 V1: 21

psia, PSIA (psi absolute), 1998 V1: 21, 1999 V2: 254, 2000 V3: 85, 2000 V3: 200

psig, PSIG (psi gage), 1998 V1: 21, 1999 V2: 254, 2000 V3: 68, 2000 V3: 85, 2000 V3: 200

public, educating on gray-water systems, 1999 V2: 33

public areas

estimating sewage quantities, 1999 V2: 236

fixtures for, 2000 V3: 33–34

heel-proof grates, 1999 V2: 10

sediment buckets, 1999 V2: 12

Public Building Service, 1998 V1: 204

public hydrants, 1998 V1: 15

Public Law 90-480, 1998 V1: 100

Public Law 93-112, 1998 V1: 100

Public Law 98, 2000 V3: 154

Public Law 616, 2000 V3: 154

public sewers, 2000 V3: 234, 2000 V3: 245–247

defined, 1998 V1: 35

discharging into, 1999 V2: 328

neutralizing acid wastes for, 1999 V2: 334–337

public storm sewer systems, 1999 V2: 67, 1999 V2: 98, 1999 V2: 105

radioactive waste systems and, 1999 V2: 342

public swimming pools. *See* swimming pools

public use, defined, 1998 V1: 35

Publicly Owned Treatment Works (POTW), 2000 V3: 89

puddle flanges, 2000 V3: 116

pulsation

air compressors, 2000 V3: 212

electric fans, 1998 V1: 201

magnetic field pulsation, 1998 V1: 201

pump discharge lines (PD), 1998 V1: 9

pump heads, 1999 V2: 105

pumped sewage-disposal systems, 1999 V2: 226

pumper connections, 1998 V1: 15

pumping head, 1999 V2: 245

pumping septic tanks, 1999 V2: 227, 1999 V2: 230

pumping wells, 1999 V2: 241–243

pumps

acoustics, 1998 V1: 201, 1998 V1: 202, 1998 V1: 203, 1998 V1: 206

automatic shutdown, 2000 V3: 90

bases, 1999 V2: 243, 1999 V2: 245

bearings, 1998 V1: 202

boiler feed pumps, 2000 V3: 188–189

cavitation, 2000 V3: 112

condensate transfer pumps, 2000 V3: 188

design of, 1998 V1: 205

earthquake protection, 1998 V1: 165

efficiency, 1998 V1: 8

ejector pumps, 2000 V3: 236

fire pumps, 2000 V3: 25–26

fountains, 2000 V3: 108, 2000 V3: 112, 2000 V3: 120, 2000 V3: 125

geothermal energy systems, 1998 V1: 132

gravity tank systems, 1999 V2: 150–152

hydropneumatic-tank systems, 1999 V2: 150

impellers, 1998 V1: 201

liquid fuel systems, 2000 V3:170

liquid-waste decontamination systems, 1999 V2: 344

matching water storage to pump flow, 1999 V2: 248

plant noise, 1998 V1: 202

pulsation in, 1998 V1: 201

pump affinity laws, 1998 V1: 7–8

pump journals, 1998 V1: 201

pump speeds, 1998 V1: 206

pump suction, 1999 V2: 249

secondary containment areas, 2000 V3: 90

starter controls, 2000 V3: 120

static deflection for vibration, 1998 V1: 211

strainers and suction screens, 2000 V3: 116

submersible, 1999 V2: 243, 2000 V3:170, 2000 V3: 170

sulfuric acid and, 1999 V2: 332

sump pumps in sanitary drainage systems, 1999 V2: 9

swimming pools, 2000 V3: 129, 2000 V3: 139, 2000 V3: 140–142, 2000 V3: 145–146

systems for water supplies, 1999 V2: 245–247

vacuum pumps, 2000 V3: 189

vibration isolation, 1998 V1: 212, 1998 V1: 214

well pumps, 1999 V2: 245–247

Pumps and Pump Systems Handbook, 1998 V1: 49, 1999 V2: 152

pure tones, 1998 V1: 216

pure-water systems, 1999 V2: 279. *See also* water purification

health-care facilities, 2000 V3: 43, 2000 V3: 46–48

piping materials, 2000 V3: 47–48

types of pure water, 2000 V3: 46

purging

medical gas zones, 2000 V3: 72, 2000 V3: 80, 2000 V3: 81–82

X

x-ray areas, 2000 V3: 39, 2000 V3: 51
x-rays, 1999 V2: 337
X#A (compressed air). *See* compressed air (A, X#, X#A)
XP explosion-proof construction, 1999 V2: 179
XP junction boxes, 1999 V2: 179
XPAN (expansion. *See* expansion

Y

y (years), 1998 V1: 23, 1998 V1: 42
y-type strainers, 2000 V3: 116
yards (yd, YD)
    converting to SI units, 1998 V1: 48
    symbols for, 1998 V1: 23
yards and lawns
    lawn imperviousness factors, 2000 V3: 243
    lawn sprinkler supply (LS), 1998 V1: 10
    sprinkler systems (irrigation)
      lawn sprinklers, 1999 V2: 121
    storm-drainage systems and, 1999 V2: 67
    yard cleanouts (CO), 1998 V1: 14
YB (valves in yard boxes), 1998 V1: 12
yd, YD (yards), 1998 V1: 23, 1998 V1: 48
year-round pools, 2000 V3: 129
years (yr, YR), 1998 V1: 23, 1998 V1: 42
Yeh, K.L., 1999 V2: 325
yellow brass, 1998 V1: 141
yoke vents, 1998 V1: 39
Young, Virgil E., 2000 V3: 105
yr, YR (years), 1998 V1: 23, 1998 V1: 42
Yrjanainen, Glen, 1999 V2: 114

Z

z, Z (zones), 1998 V1: 23, 1998 V1: 185
Zelmanovich, Y., 1999 V2: 325
zeolite process, 1999 V2: 244
zeolites, 1999 V2: 302
zero-flow potential, 1998 V1: 152
zero governors, 2000 V3: 251
zeta potential, 1999 V2: 294
zinc
    anodes, 1998 V1: 147
    corrosion, 1998 V1: 137
    electromotive force series, 1998 V1: 141
    galvanic series, 1998 V1: 140
zirconium, 2000 V3: 20
ZN (zones), 1998 V1: 23, 1998 V1: 185
zone valves, 2000 V3: 49, 2000 V3: 71
zones (z, Z, ZN)
in seismic force calculations, 1998 V1: 185
symbols for, 1998 V1: 23